Prosecuting Superior Responsibility in International Criminal Law

Humoud Y. Al-Fadhli

Prosecuting Superior Responsibility in International Criminal Law

From Tokyo and Nuremberg to The Hague and Beyond

ASSER PRESS

Springer

Humoud Y. Al-Fadhli
Department of International Law
Kuwait University College of Law
Sabah Al-Salem University City, Kuwait

ISBN 978-94-6265-734-2 ISBN 978-94-6265-735-9 (eBook)
https://doi.org/10.1007/978-94-6265-735-9

Published by T.M.C. ASSER PRESS, The Hague, The Netherlands www.asserpress.nl
Produced and distributed for T.M.C. ASSER PRESS by Springer-Verlag Berlin Heidelberg

This T.M.C. ASSER PRESS imprint is published by the registered company Springer-Verlag GmbH, DE, part of Springer Nature.
The registered company address is: Heidelberger Platz 3, 14197 Berlin, Germany

Foreword

In International Humanitarian Law and International Criminal Law, superiors are not just culpable for the acts they order, they are also liable for the foreseeable atrocities that their subordinates commit. The doctrine of superior responsibility—an enduring and enigmatic feature of international criminal law—has perplexed scholars, jurists, and practitioners for decades. It has survived and evolved through wars, legislation, juridical decisions, and fluctuating jurisprudential views. And yet, it remains one of the most important and at the same time conceptually unsettled modes of liability in the international legal regime. What does it mean to hold a commander criminally responsible not for what they did, but for what they failed to prevent? Can omission rise to the level of culpability equal to direct perpetration? Can responsibility be justified structurally, rather than individually?

In this profoundly insightful and impressively rigorous work, Humoud Al-Fadhli confronts these questions not merely by retracing old debates, but by offering a fresh theoretical lens—"consequential culpability"—that challenges and enriches how we understand superior responsibility as a *sui generis* mode of liability. The book is neither a doctrinal summary nor a theoretical abstraction. It is a powerful synthesis of history, legal reasoning, philosophical inquiry, and normative argument—one that repositions superior responsibility not as an uncomfortable aberration in international criminal law, but as a necessary evolution in a field grappling with hierarchy, authority, and atrocity.

From its foundation in the Lieber Code, and even earlier in antiquity in the Art of War by Sun Tzu, and its early judicial application by the Military Tribunal in the Yamashita trial, to the interpretive drift seen in the *Bemba case* at the International Criminal Court, this book analyzes how jurisprudential inconsistencies and conceptual ambiguities have weakened the coherence of this doctrine. And more importantly, it offers a path forward.

What makes this book truly unique is its ability to balance historical depth with normative clarity. The author resists the temptation to simply analogize international criminal responsibility to domestic criminal law. Instead, this work insists on the autonomy of international criminal law's logic, architecture, and goals. It refuses to shoehorn international crimes into frameworks that were never built to account for the horrors of genocide, systemic torture, or command/authority-driven atrocities. In doing so, this book makes three distinct contributions. First, it reframes superior responsibility as a foundational principle of international law, grounded in structural authority and legal obligation, rather than in traditional notions of moral blame. Second, it offers a compelling normative theory—consequential culpability—that bridges the divide between deontological justice and humanitarian necessity. Third, and most importantly, it provides a practical roadmap for courts, scholars, and legal practitioners by distilling clear conceptual elements from decades of fragmented jurisprudence.

Above all, this is a courageous book. It challenges orthodoxy, speaks with moral clarity, and urges us to rethink what it means to be accountable at the highest levels of power. It is both an academic contribution and a clarion call—to recognize that responsibility in international criminal law must evolve to match the complexities of modern warfare, political superiority, and human suffering.

August 2025

Michael P. Scharf
Joseph C. Hostetler-BakerHostetler
Professor of Law
Case Western Reserve University
School of Law
Cleveland, OH, USA

Michael P. Scharf is the Joseph C. Hostetler-BakerHostetler Professor of Law at Case Western Reserve University where he served as Dean from 2013-2024. He is also currently President of the American Branch of the International Law Association and Managing Director of the Public International Law & Policy Group, a Nobel Prize-nominated NGO. He previously served as Attorney-Advisor for U.N. Affairs and Attorney Advisor for Law Enforcement and Intelligence at the U.S. Department of State.

Preface

This book, originally written as a doctoral dissertation, was conceived in response to enduring philosophical, theoretical, and practical tensions surrounding the doctrine of superior responsibility in International Criminal Law (ICL). Although the doctrine has served as a critical tool for attributing liability to individuals in positions of military and political authority, its legal character remains conceptually unsettled, its application inconsistent, and its interpretation the subject of ongoing—perhaps eternal—debate.

My aims in writing this book are manifold. I aim to clarify the legal and normative basis of superior responsibility, challenge prevailing assumption—sespecially those drawn from domestic liberal criminal law account—and propose a principled yet functional framework for its future application. The book is driven by the conviction that ICL must be viewed with complexities of modern command and authority structures and the gravity of mass atrocity crimes in mind.

The chapters are organized both thematically and chronologically. The book begins by tracing the doctrine's historical origins, then critically examines its conceptual components, interpretative evolution, and application in international case law. It concludes by proposing a syllogistic model to guide future applicationi—ncluding the potential extension of superior responsibility to serious human rights violations and treaty-based crimes. While the subject matter may appear narrowly focused, this book is written with a broader audience in mind: scholars, legal practitioners, judges, prosecutors, and advanced students interested in the evolution of liability in ICL. Though grounded in rigorous legal analysis, it aims at making complex theoretical insights both accessible and practically relevant. Drawing on historical sources, jurisprudence, statutory developments, and normative theory, the book strives to offer clarity and coherence where the existing doctrine has often fallen short.

I would like to express my gratitude to those who made this book possible. In particular, I thank my late supervisor and dear friend, Professor Johan D. van der Vyver (may he rest in peace), whose wisdom, kindness, and unwavering guidance shaped me, personally, and this work, professionally, in profound ways. I am also grateful to Professors John Witte, Michael Scharf, Leila Sadat, Beth Van Schaack, Michael Newton, Elies van Sliedregt, Kevin Jon Heller, the late Robert Cryer (may he too rest in peace), Darryl Robinson, Douglas Guilfoyle, Kai Ambos, Gerhard Werle, Andrew Clapham, William Schabas, Carsten Stahn, Mark Klamberg, Ahmed Al-Dawoody, Michael Broyde, and Abdulaziz Hashem—each of whom contributed to my intellectual development in meaningful ways. I further extend my sincere appreciation to Frank Bakker of T.M.C. Asser Press for seeing potential in this study and to Kiki van Gurp for taking good care of the production process. My heartfelt thanks go to Kirsten Schaetzel and Taylor Frank for their insightful support with language and structure. I offer my apologies to those whose names could not be listed here. I additionally extend my gratitude to the Lauterpacht Centre for International Law at the University of Cambridge for its academic hospitality and exceptional scholarly resources during my stay as an academic visitor (2024–2025), and to my home institution, Kuwait University, for its continued support. Above all, I thank my family for their patience, love, and unwavering belief in this endeavor.

Sabah Al-Salem University City,
Kuwait
September 2025

Prof. Dr. Humoud Y. Al-Fadhli

About This Book

This book offers a comprehensive and critical analysis of the doctrine of superior responsibility within International Criminal Law. Tracing its historical roots from early military codes to its codification in the Rome Statute, this book answers how this mode of liability has evolved from a disciplinary measure *for omission* into a *sui generis* (autonomous) mode of liability for holding military and political superiors accountable *for crimes* committed by their subordinates.

Combining rigorous doctrinal analysis, meticulous jurisprudential review, and novel normative argumentation, this book challenges conventional interpretations—especially those influenced by most liberal criminal law accounts—and proposes a reconceptualization of superior responsibility as a *sui generis* mode of liability grounded in consequentialism and structural culpability. Importantly, it places an emphasis on a more pressing concern: the need to clarify and recalibrate the doctrine's conceptual foundations before addressing questions of application or expansion. In doing so, it tackles longstanding ambiguities surrounding the doctrine's conceptual components, its uneven application across international and hybrid tribunals, and, through syllogistic reasoning, its potential for broader application to serious human rights violations and treaty-based crimes.

Written with scholars, legal practitioners, and students in mind, this book serves both as a theoretical inquiry and a practical guide for navigating one of International Criminal Law's most complex and contested doctrines.

Contents

About the Author

Dr. Humoud Y. Al-Fadhli is an Assistant Professor of International Criminal Law at Kuwait University, College of Law, International Law Department (2022–present). He has previously served as a Visiting Academic at the Lauterpacht Centre for International Law, University of Cambridge, Faculty of Law (2024–2025); as a Teaching Assistant at Kuwait University (2017–2022); and as a State Attorney in the Legal Advice and Legislation Department of the Kuwaiti Council of Ministers (2011–2017). His research interests lie in international criminal law, international humanitarian law, and international human rights law. Dr. Al-Fadhli is the author of or has contributed to several scholarly works, including:

- *From Nuremberg to The Hague and Beyond: Reincorporating "Taking a Consenting Part" into International Criminal Modes of Liability, Netherlands International Law Review*, Vol. 72, Issue 2, *(forthcoming, 2025)*
- *Corruption in the MENA: Between State Crime and International Criminal Law, in The Palgrave Handbook of Criminology and the Global South (forthcoming, 2025)*
- *Prosecuting the Russian Crime of Aggression Against Ukraine: Hopes and Challenges A Study Within the West's Standards, Kuwait University Law Journal*, April 2025
- *The International Right to Peaceful Assembly: A Potential Lacuna in National Legislations and Kuwaiti Law, Qatar University International Journal of Law*, February 2025
- *Gulf War I: The Legality of Prosecuting Existing Iraqi Ba'ath Party in Response to Kuwait's Deceased Captives, Kuwait University Law Journal*, March 2021
- *Police Force Organ to Support the ICC's Judgments and Arrest Warrants: A Proposition to Amend Article 86 of the Rome Statute, Courts & Justice Law Journal*, April 2019

About the Author

[illegible]

Abbreviations

AC	Appeals Chamber of the International Criminal Court
API/II	Additional Protocols to the Geneva Conventions of 12 August 1949
CAR	Central African Republic
DRC	Democratic Republic of Congo
ECCC	Extraordinary Chambers in the Courts of Cambodia
ECHR	European Convention on Human Rights
ICC	International Criminal Court
ICCPR	International Covenant on Civil and Political Rights
ICJ	International Court of Justice
ICL	International Criminal Law
ICPPED	International Convention for the Protection of All Persons from Enforced Disappearance
ICTR	International Criminal Tribunal for Rwanda
ICTY	International Criminal Tribunal for the former Yugoslavia
IHL	International Humanitarian Law
ILoW	Islamic Law of War
IMTs	International Military Tribunals
LoAC	Law of Armed Conflict
MLC	Movement for the Liberation of Congo
NMT	Nuremberg Military Tribunal
OTP	Office of the Prosecutor of the International Criminal Court
POWs	Prisoners of War
SCSL	Special Court for Sierra Leone
SNTs	Subsequent Nuremberg Trials
SPET	Special Panels in East Timor
STL	Special Tribunal for Lebanon
TC	Trial Chambers of the International Criminal Court
TMI	Tokyo Military Tribunal
UDHR	Universal Declaration of Human Rights
UN	United Nations
VCLT	Vienna Convention on the Law of Treaties

WWI	World War I
WWII	World War II

Chapter 1
Charting the Course of the Book: Themes and Components

Contents

Abstract Since its formulation in the jurisprudence of the International Military Tribunals (IMTs) and the Subsequent Nuremberg Trials (SNTs), and even earlier in antiquity, the doctrine of superior responsibility has been widely debated by scholars, particularly in efforts to justify its nature by drawing parallels with principles of domestic criminal law. As noted by a judge in the NMTs, this doctrine remains, in many respects, a "strange" legal construct. Its conceptual ambiguities contribute to persistent challenges in its (in)consistent application to superiors at the international level. Debate continues along two primary lines: first, regarding its legal characterization; and second, though less frequently addressed, the inconsistent jurisprudence concerning its constitutive elements. This book provides an accessible and comprehensive examination of the doctrine, with a focus on clarifying its conceptual components. It undertakes two main tasks: (1) a pragmatic and critical analysis of how the doctrine's components have been—or ought to be—interpreted in international jurisprudence; and (2) a normative proposal to reconceptualize superior responsibility not as personal culpability, but as consequential culpability. This approach is justified through the doctrine's historical roots, the structural gravity of hierarchical authority, the normative force of entrusted obligations, and its evolving interpretation in international law. While prior scholarship has sought to analogize superior responsibility with domestic criminal law, this book contends that it should instead be understood as an autonomous and foundational principle of international criminal law (ICL). This chapter, however, outlines the key parameters of the book and provides a roadmap of its structure.

H. Y. Al-Fadhli, *Prosecuting Superior Responsibility in International Criminal Law*,
https://doi.org/10.1007/978-94-6265-735-9_1

Keywords Superior responsibility · Command responsibility · Personal culpability · Consequential culpability · International criminal law · International modes of liability

1.1 Introductory Remarks

Crimes against international law are committed by men, not by abstract entities, and only by punishing individuals who commit such crimes can the provisions of international law be enforced.[1]

As the title suggests, this book deals with the very essence of the international modes of liability in the field of international criminal law (ICL), *to wit*, the doctrine of superior responsibility.[2] Though to lay the groundwork for this inquiry, it is first important to note that this chapter sets out the book's overarching theme. It sketches the foundational parts that collectively frame the book's central purpose: developing a holistic yet accessible manual for the prosecution of superior responsibility in ICL. To this end, it approaches this exclusive concept through a doctrinal and critical analytical lens, which I believe is integral to fully assimilating this doctrine in light of its jurisprudential origins and its subsequent (a)symmetrical evolution.

Before delving into the curious history of the doctrine's inception, the (in)consistent jurisprudential evolution that structurally (mis)shaped its conceptual components, and its later murky application—as explored in the following chapters—it is, first and foremost, necessary to provide a generic overview of ICL's inception. This includes the evolution of international law in gradually accommodating ICL's central focus: individual accountability—particularly that of superiors, as examined within the specific context of this book. What follows then briefly traces a pivotal shift in international law: the movement from regulating abstract entities, such as states, to recognizing individuals as subjects of criminal responsibility. This transition, especially as it pertains to superior responsibility, has been inspired by, yet often remains at odds with, the foundational principles of domestic criminal law.[3] Resultantly, according to Robinson, this doctrine has posed significant challenges to the "deontological constraints" underpinning national criminal justice systems, which are largely grounded in "non-consequentialist" reasoning.[4]

The International Military Tribunals (IMTs), established in the aftermath of World War II (WWII), marked a transformational moment when international law ceased to concern only abstract entities. Previously, international law was initially founded and

---

[1] International Military Tribunal (Nuremburg) 1947, pp. 172, 221.

[2] I have purposefully chosen the term *superior responsibility* rather than *command responsibility*, as the former serves as a retronym that broadens the concept to encompass not only military commanders but also political superiors, while also capturing certain nuances related to the requirements of responsibility.

[3] See generally Steer 2014.

[4] See generally Robinson 2020.

structured with a benevolent determination as to regulate states' interactions.[5] The emergence of this field is depicted in the principles and rules of demarcations, international agreements between states beyond demarcations, and the responsibility and sovereignty mandates of states.[6] Until the international community began to argue for individual responsibility in response to the emergence of violations committed in the context of an armed conflict—at which point states signed treaties to govern individual responsibility at the international level[7]—this governance continued to be applied to states, although it remained in the form of state responsibility.[8] For instance, alongside state responsibility and practice, *the Geneva Conventions of 12 August 1949* and their *Additional Protocols* set out the parameters regulating individual responsibility during wartime, which form the modern rules of the Law of Armed Conflict (LoAC).[9] As a side but related note, the need for these agreements stemmed both from the atrocious, widespread, and systematic nature of the violations of humanity during armed conflicts,[10] and from domestic regimes' "inability" or "unwillingness" to hold such violators responsible, in an attempt to end the impunity of certain high-ranking officials.[11]

Despite commendable efforts to hold those high-ranking individuals accountable at the international level, a new problem emerged: how to establish criminal labels (modes of liability) that accurately reflect the nature of international crimes while still adhering to the domestic rationality of criminal principles. To this end, an emerging sense of "discomfort"[12] and even an "identity crisis"[13] has been noted in legal scholarship, essentially driven by the uneasy interplay between pragmatism and dogmatism.[14] This tension is further complicated by the shifting and sometimes conflicting roles of criminal law theory (liberal accounts) and humanitarian and human rights' victim-centered approaches to ICL in the ongoing effort to refine and

---

[5] See Murphy 2012, pp. 3–10. See also *S.S.* Lotus *(France v. Turkey)*, Judgment, 1927 P.C.I.J. (ser. A) No. 10, p. 18.

[6] Ibid. See also Triffterer 2002, p. 180.

[7] Ibid.

[8] Ibid., pp. 453–459.

[9] Under modern international law practice, LoAC, Laws of War (LOWs), and International Humanitarian Law (IHL) are all synonyms; however, in this study, I shall use LoAC as it is the most comprehensive legal term to describe *jus in bello* and all regulations relating to warfare and hostilities. Additionally, IHL is controversial in the academic literature as it has never been used in the subject-matter of any armed conflict treaty. See Wilson 2017, pp. 563–570. The International Committee of the Red Cross (ICRC) affirmed that IHL applies to "those rules of the law of armed conflict which are clearly *humanitarian* in nature". ICRC 1971, Introduction, pp. 25–26 [emphasis added].

[10] For the purposes of this book, international crimes refer to the core international crimes stated in the legal instruments of international(ized) criminal tribunals, such as war crimes, crimes against humanity, genocide, and the crime of aggression.

[11] See Triffterer 2002, p. 186.

[12] Guilfoyle 2011, p. 256.

[13] See Robinson 2020, pp. 5–7.

[14] See generally Minkova 2023.

evolve accountability mechanisms.[15] In terms of drawing parallels between ICL and national criminal law, some scholars relentlessly pushed forward a normative and, to some degree, convincing argument that ICL norms must be viewed as *sui generis*, which is in contrast to national criminal law.[16]

In light of this transformative shift that later engendered normative troubles, ICL was established to hold individuals—specifically those most responsible, who are often in superior positions vertically and horizontally—criminally accountable, rather than relying solely on the responsibility of states.[17] In its narrowest sense, ICL emerged as a response to the growing globalization of criminal conduct constituting the Crime of Aggression, Genocide, Crimes Against Humanity, and War Crimes, which increasingly exceeded the prosecutorial capacities of national legal systems.[18] This rationale featured prominently in the subject-matter jurisdiction of the IMTs, which were established with a focus on prosecuting "the most responsible" rather than "the little people", as articulated in Justice Jackson's oratory statement at Nuremberg.[19] As noted earlier, the central issue, however, was not merely identifying whether international perpetrators were blameworthy in terms of deciding *ratione materiae*. Rather, the more complex task was identifying the means (*i.e.*, modes of liability) under which conducts constituting *ratione materiae* were executed.

Nevertheless, the IMTs laid the cornerstone in the founding of ICL, including the articulation of contextual elements and definitions of international crimes, as well as the modes of liability, particularly as applied to individuals in positions of superiority.[20] However, owing to its absence from the IMTs' enabling instruments, and the *carte blanche* granted to judges in constructing a "normative architecture",[21] one of the most controversial departures from conventional legal reasoning in the practice of the IMTs was the prosecution of a particular individual under the doctrine of superior responsibility.[22] In its generic sense, this *sui generis* mode of liability permits the assigning of criminal responsibility to superiors *for* crimes committed by their subordinates, not on the basis of (in)direct involvement, but due to a failure to discharge entrusted duties.[23] This automation of identically switching the criminal responsibility from the subordinates to their superior curiously, and sometimes exotically, challenges foundational principles such as personal culpability, raising

---

[15] Ibid.

[16] See van Sliedregt 2012, pp. 1172–1188.

[17] See Wise et al. 2009, pp. 1–5.

[18] See Ambos 2009, pp. 127–157. (In its broadest sense, ICL covers all crimes with an international character, *e.g.*, treaty crimes.) See also Stewart 2014, pp. 3–6.

[19] Nuremberg Trial Proceedings 1945, p. 98.

[20] Namely conspiracy and superior responsibility theories. See Stewart 2014, pp. 31–34.

[21] Falk (2005) Remembering the Holocaust and the Geopolitical Persistence of Indifference. Keynote speech presented at the Conference on Law and the Humanities: Representation of the Holocaust, Genocide, and Other Human Rights Violations, Thomas Jefferson School of Law, 17 January 2005.

[22] Heller 2011, pp. 262–271.

[23] Van der Vyver 2021, p. 567.

serious morality and legality concerns.[24] As voiced by Phillip Ruddock during the Yamashita trial, "it is a bad law".[25]

Some critical examples may be useful here to illustrate the challenges. Critics argue that this blurs the line between personal guilt and responsibility for crimes committed in a pluralistic fashion, straining the core tenets of fairness, legality, and agency in criminal law.[26] Nevertheless, as I contend in this book, the justification for the doctrine is grounded not only in humanitarian and human rights approaches to ICL's principles, but also in historical pedigree, particularly within military and command structures, which invites an evolving understanding of, and open-mindedness to, the concept of accountability in complex hierarchical systems such as those underlying ICL. This, in turn, demands a thorough reassessment of the doctrine's deeper history—one that could change the way we conceptually think about it. As Douglas aptly observes, "[w]hat we need are not new tools, but different ways of understanding existing concepts".[27]

To briefly outline the 19th century historical background and military context of this doctrine, the concept of holding superiors responsible can be traced back to the United States' *1863 Lieber Code*.[28] However, this military code refers to superior responsibility in its *latu sensu* view, that is, as direct superior responsibility.[29] According to this code, the death penalty can be imposed on military commanders for "ordering and encouraging" soldiers under their supervision to commit war crimes.[30] The said code was then adopted by the LoAC, particularly in the Hague and Geneva Conventions.[31] Rather than adopting it merely as a form of disciplinary responsibility, ICL was inspired by such conceptual developments to incorporate superior responsibility as a distinct mode of criminal responsibility—one that does not initially comply with the principle of personal culpability, unlike other modes of liability that somehow require a strict link between the individual's conduct and their blameworthiness state of affairs.[32]

Of note here is the uneven transition of the doctrine of superior responsibility; from the Lieber Code through the development of the LAC and into the first application in ICL (the Yamashita trial) as a criminal theory, albeit absurdly lacking a fundamental culpability requirement, *i.e.*, the mental requirement. This uneven transition has predictably contributed to persistent misunderstandings nowadays. Since its

---

[24] Stewart 2012, p. 3.

[25] Reel 1949, p. 8.

[26] Robinson 2020, p. 61.

[27] Guilfoyle 2011, p. 255.

[28] See Bassiouni 2011, p. 531. See also Triffterer 2002, pp. 181–186 (note that this book in fact traces the roots of this concept much further than the nineteenth century).

[29] Direct superior responsibility refers to the criminal responsibility of a superior for ordering and for being an accomplice to the crimes, as exemplified under Article 25 of the Rome Statute.

[30] Ibid., p. 180.

[31] Van der Vyver 2021.

[32] Ibid. (casting aside *sui generis* modes of liability like Joint Criminal Enterprise and their developed versions that deviate from personal culpability).

inception in the Yamashita trial, through the jurisprudence of the UN *ad hoc* tribunals, and up to the present-day practice of the ICC, the doctrine of superior responsibility has been marked by inconsistent judicial reasoning—either concerning its legality or, more critically, its conceptual components. These inconsistencies have, at times, resulted in unwarranted convictions or acquittals. More recently, international cases adjudicating superior responsibility have demonstrated a degree of jurisprudential overlap. Nonetheless, the resulting outcomes have often diverged from a coherent and accurate application of the doctrine. This is exemplified by the controversial case of Mr. Jean-Pierre Bemba Gombo before the ICC.[33]

On 8 June 2018, the ICC Appeals Chambers delivered a decision regarding the war crimes and crimes against humanity committed by Mr. Bemba's troops.[34] The judgment reversed that of the Trial Chamber, wherein Mr. Bemba, commander of the Movement for the Liberation of Congo (MLC) army wing situated in the Central African Republic (CAR), was convicted of being criminally responsible for crimes committed by his troops.[35] This judgment backfired, triggering a heated debate between scholars and international lawyers. Due to the legal repercussions of this decision, the international community has expressed concerns about the future of international criminal justice and the credibility of the ICC.

For example, I argue that the Appeals Chamber of the ICC reshaped the doctrine of superior responsibility, both in terms of nature and conceptual components, contrary to international customs, the Rome Statute, and the jurisprudence of UN *ad hoc* tribunals.[36] In my view, the Chamber's interpretation of Article 28 of its enabling statute has somewhat haphazardly exceeded its discretionary bounds, incorporating questionable elements—such as the assertion that a superior need only take "some measures" to discharge their duties.[37] This diluted standard may eventually present potential loopholes that could enable superiors to evade accountability, undermining the doctrine's intended purpose of ensuring superiors' responsibility for international crimes. This is particularly apparent when we compare the understanding of the doctrine set out in the Rome Statute with the understanding set out in the statutes

---

[33] See van der Vyver 2021, p. 567.

[34] Appeals Chamber, *Prosecutor v. Jean-Pierre Bemba Gombo* (8 June 2018), Case No. ICC-01/05-01/08 A.

[35] Jean-Pierre Bemba was a former political leader of the MLC. Bemba commanded the MLC troops in operations from 2002 to 2003 in Democratic Republic of Congo, which involved international crimes such as sexual violence, rape, and pillaging. MLC is a political and military movement in support of President Ange-Felix Patasse in the Democratic Republic of Congo (DRC). See BBC News 2018.

[36] For example, this has been exposed to many events that made it evolutionary-orientated, starting with the minimal obligations imposed on a commander by international agreements. This is still evolving owing to international criminal case laws that have either interpreted this doctrine differently or applied new elements through judicial interpretations. On this matter, Kosfålt said that: "…the approach taken to individual criminal responsibility differed greatly from that of previous international tribunals…[a]s well the elements of each mode of liability have evolved through case law…interpreting the diverse elements differently". See Klamberg 2017, p. 264.

[37] *Prosecutor v. Jean-Pierre Bemba Gombo*, Judgment, 8 June 2018, Case No. ICC-01/05-01/08 A, paras 168–170.

of the international(ized) criminal tribunals.[38] Moreover, in its judgment, the ICC addressed Mr. Bemba as both a commander and a superior.[39] According to the Rome Statute, conflating these distinct categories under the doctrine of superior responsibility may amount to a critical misnomer—particularly given the mental requirement differences between command responsibility and political superior responsibility within the specific context of Article 28. Such imprecision, in my view, cannot then be overlooked in the assessment of criminal responsibility.[40]

Considering the foregoing remarks on the evolution of ICL, the principled concerns it raises—particularly in relation to superior responsibility—and the inconsistencies surrounding the doctrine's conceptual development, this book thus adopts an epistemologically holistic approach to superior responsibility. Its aim also includes opening the door for further scholarly debate on the doctrine's nature, based on my proposal, to assign what I normatively term consequential culpability[41] and, more importantly, to address inconsistencies in case law, particularly regarding its triggering components. Beyond courtroom application and publicists' debates, this book also wishes to serve as a resource for students and professionals working in the ICL field. For the purposes of this chapter, however, I shall limit myself to highlighting the book's structure, leaving room in the subsequent chapters to cover topics pertinent to this doctrine.

Excluding introductory remarks, this chapter comprises five key sections: Sect. 1.2 sets out the research statement and core questions underpinning the book; Sect. 1.3 describes the research methodology and methods employed; Sect. 1.4 presents a succinct review of the literature in this area, particularly the academic literature relating to the components of this doctrine; and, finally, Sect. 1.5 outlines the structure of the remainder of this book.

---

[38] For instance, in the *Bemba* case, regarding the *mens rea*, the Pre-Trial Chamber of the ICC did not endorse the structure of superior responsibility in the ICTY and ICTR, respectively. Rather, it endorsed only the criteria or *indicia* applied by the *ad hoc* tribunals for meeting the standard of "had reason to know", applying it to the "should have known" standard set out in the Rome Statute. *Prosecutor v. Jean-Pierre Bemba Gombo*, PTC II, Decision on the Confirmation of Charges, 15 June 2009, Case No. ICC-01/05-01/08-424, para 434.

[39] *Prosecutor v. Jean-Pierre Bemba Gombo*, Judgment, 8 June 2018, Case No. ICC-01/05-01/08 A, paras 29–30.

[40] *Rome Statute of the International Criminal Court*, 2187 UNTS 90, 1 July 2002, Article 28 (a) and (b).

[41] More discussion on this term will be dealt with in Chap. 3, noting that both terms are used interchangeably throughout this book.

1.2 Book Statement, Novelty, and Challenges

ICL has always functioned within a sphere of exceptionalism, shaped by legal constructs that are not easily transposed from domestic legal systems.[42] One such construct is the doctrine of superior responsibility—a principle that has perplexed even the most experienced jurists. Judge Powers, in his dissenting opinion in the *Ministries* case at the NMTs, famously struggled to articulate its legal nature, particularly as a *sui generis* mode of liability.[43] He remarked: "[t]he government of the Third Reich committed many crimes; the defendants held prominent positions in that government, and knew of some of these crimes; therefore, they are guilty."[44] He concluded that such reasoning "smacks more of something else than a proceeding to fix the legal responsibility for crime."[45] Powers ultimately characterized this rationality as a "strange" doctrine—and an even stranger line of reasoning—to "be advanced by lawyers representing American justice and the American concept of crime".[46]

That confusion is emblematic of the broader conceptual and doctrinal challenges at play. In fact, the exclusivity of ICL norms was present from the outset of the law's development, where norms emerged not from settled consensus, but from necessity, experimentation, legal imagination, and "progressive law-making"[47] privileges. The *sui generis* character of superior responsibility is not only inherent but integral to understanding how international accountability operates at the highest levels of command and/or authority. This book then seeks to clarify the doctrine's conceptual, theoretical, and jurisprudential architecture in ways that render it more intelligible, accessible, and consistent.

To that end, the book's analysis is framed around three central pillars. First, the theoretical framework which explores the historical ontology of superior responsibility and its evolving legal characterization, grounding it in the broader trajectory of ICL. Second, the critical examination of the conceptual elements of this doctrine, focusing on its codification and identifying how inconsistent judicial reasoning has, to varying degrees, undermined legal coherence. Third, the doctrine's practical application is critically assessed through its adjudication in international criminal tribunals, especially the ICC, where haphazard or selective interpretation has resulted in a controversial acquittal. Rather than dwelling on justifying the nature of the doctrine, this book places greater emphasis on a more pressing concern, *i.e.*, the jurisprudential inconsistencies surrounding its core elements, particularly those that have proven

[42] See Robinson 2020, p. 61, n. 8.

[43] *Cf.* U.S. Military Tribunals 1952, 1127, para 874 (noting that he was specifically referring to a nuanced—though reasonably contested—mode of liability now often may be identified as command responsibility). See generally Al-Fadhli 2025.

[44] U.S. Military Tribunals 1952, 1127, para 874.

[45] Ibid.

[46] Ibid.

[47] Cassese 2004, p. 585.

determinative in either conviction or acquittal. Nonetheless, I shall engage with this important and ongoing debate on the doctrine's nature, albeit peripherally, as follows:

Throughout this book, in terms of legal characterization, I advance the view that the superior responsibility doctrine should be reconceptualized and not merely seen as a form of liability that requires adherence to personal culpability. Alternatively, I invite scholarship to consider consequential (or structural) culpability[48]—a historically grounded form of responsibility based on permissive consequentialist reasoning, which justifies the imposition of principal-level punishment beyond the limits of personal or collective culpability—as a complementary norm to personal culpability, which, as Robinson argues, is typically rooted in non-consequentialist, deontological constraints. Importantly, this reconceptualization is proposed solely as a normative basis for superior responsibility, while preserving the strict adherence to personal culpability for contributory modes of liability. It must be noted that international criminal law does not discard deontological constraints such as due process, the principle of legality, and defendants' rights. However, it can accommodate consequentialist reasoning—at least in the context of superior responsibility—allowing both frameworks to operate synergistically.[49]

Alongside its current debatable nature in the literature, this justifying approach is particularly attractive in further supporting scholarly efforts to consider alternative approaches to the doctrine's nature. Simply, from a consequentialist perspective to vicarious punishment—favoring permissive reasoning over the deontological emphasis on moral constraints—the above refers to situations in which a superior possesses both authority and foresight yet fails to act within a "climate of moral degeneracy"[50] where international crimes are sufficiently foreseeable to warrant intervention in the ordinary course of events. This failure in such a specific context *ipso facto* gives rise to a distinct form of culpability: consequential culpability.

As previously noted, in contexts characterized by an Orwellian morality—where individuals operate within environments notoriously associated with international crimes, and where practices such as torture are rebranded as *enhanced interrogation*—any failure to act or intervene assumes a qualitatively different and more severe significance.[51] It amounts not just to omission, but to some degree, a tacit non-contributory approval, effectively "sending a signal that such offenses may be committed with impunity",[52] with amnesty being guaranteed. While this approach may appear radical from a liberal interpretation of criminal law, it aligns harmoniously with humanitarian and human rights–oriented, victim-centered objectives. In any case, to overcome the knee-jerk rejection of humanitarian advocacy in criminal accountability, which diverges from liberal principles while maintaining humanistic features, I will reconcile such concerns with the concept of consequential culpability as a legitimate basis for assigning vicarious liability.

---

[48] Both terms are used interchangeably throughout this book.

[49] Cryer et al. 2019, p. 23.

[50] Fletcher 2002, p. 1541.

[51] See generally Al-Rashidi and Al-Fadhli 2025.

[52] Morris and Scharf 1995, pp. 100–101.

In addition to the gravity test[53] and the historical evidence to its *sui generis* nature, I argue that consequential culpability represents a form of liability which extends beyond the personal commission of a crime, justifying vicarious responsibility when an individual holds a position that foreseeably entails accountability for the crimes of their subordinates. This is particularly applicable when the individual has failed to fulfil their duties to prevent, repress, or, as exemplified in the Rome Statute, report the criminal conduct to competent authorities.[54] The following equation succinctly illustrates this argument: personal culpability is excluded when it is proven that the accused did not personally commit the criminal act; consequential culpability, by contrast, is negated when it is established that the superior, having met the other conceptual requirements, took all necessary and reasonable measures to discharge his/her duties.

If one then accepted the concept of consequential culpability, it may invite a range of nuanced considerations. For example,—though not without reasonable controversy—it may shed light on the rationale behind the Rome Statute's deliberate distinction between military commanders and political superiors within a single principle. Moreover, it may justify the doctrine's high evidentiary threshold, requiring proof that a superior failed to take all reasonable measures within their command/authority to prevent, punish, or report the crimes. Last but not least, it may justify both the statutory—and, to a lesser extent, judicial—tendency to prosecute superiors for the underlying crimes themselves, rather than for omission as a standalone offense.

The above argumentative attempt to establish this form of responsibility is grounded not in the superior's personal connection to the direct perpetrator, but in the foreseeable consequences of that superior's failure to discharge a duty of supervision. This logic then holds only when superior responsibility is viewed as a principle in its own right, establishing a *sui generis* mode of liability as, for example, exemplified exclusively in Article 28 of the Rome Statute. Additionally, and as established in historical developments, this notion may syllogistically find its roots in the aphorism expressed by Hugo Grotius: "We must accept the principle that he who knows of a crime and is able and bound to prevent it but fails to do so, himself commits a crime".[55] Therefore, one might turn to history as a means of re-evaluating the philosophical foundations of consequential culpability. For that matter, though not intended to undermine such efforts, it becomes increasingly evident that the attempted—albeit commendable from a legalistic perspective—reconciliation of personal culpability with the autonomous logic of superior responsibility may ultimately lead to an impasse.

The proposal to consequential culpability reflects the first part of the book's purpose. The second and more central purpose is to highlight the less-compelling pragmatic and principled approaches to the conceptual components of the doctrine—concerns that, in my view, warrant greater attention in scholarly discourse. Rather than argumentatively situating the doctrine's nature within the context of national

[53] See generally Urs 2024.

[54] Rome Statute 1998, Article 28.

[55] Grotius 1964, p. 171.

criminal justice systems or even within the framework of ICL, this book offers an analytical critique of the asymmetrical patterns evident in the doctrine's application by international courts—patterns that largely stem from divergent and, at times, inconsistent judicial interpretations.

While the current book aims to develop a holistic manual for the assimilation of this *sui generis* mode of liability, such endeavor requires a comprehensive examination of the various factors that have shaped this doctrine—whether in practice, jurisprudence, historical evolution, or normative character. Simply, assimilating the doctrine of superior responsibility demands engaging beyond the confines of socio-legal debates or evaluating the doctrine's legal characterization through deontological constraints.[56] It requires a deeper historical assessment of how this doctrine acquired its *sui generis* status (a foundational principle in ICL, in its own right), particularly within the context of international crimes—crimes that often had to be jurisprudentially defined *ex nihilo* to justify their exceptional legal analysis.[57] According to some analysts, within this specified context, a superior's failure to discharge legally and customarily rooted responsibilities cannot be viewed merely as omission liability.[58]

On a related but important note, this book, as noted earlier, addresses another significant ambiguity: the distinction between military commanders and political superiors.[59] While often conflated in practice, these categories differ in the scope, authority, and nature of their responsibilities, especially when addressing the mental element of this doctrine, as distinctively penned in the Rome Statute. The confusion is evident in case law, including the Bemba judgment, and is tolerated by scholars to a certain degree.[60] This book contends that such distinctions matter and deserve clearer articulation in both the academic literature and judicial reasoning.

This book's originality lies in its examination of how international(ized) criminal tribunals—particularly the ICC—often rely on precedential interpretations developed in academic literature. A key contribution of this work is its effort to distill coherent conceptual components from otherwise inconsistent jurisprudence. This analysis is grounded in statutory interpretation, historical pedigree, legal characterization, and the most reasoned and persuasive judicial decisions to date. When courts are called upon to interpret ambiguous components, they may do so through *proprio motu* reasoning, reliance on precedent (*stare decisis*), or by citing academic commentary as a subsidiary source of law. Notably, in the *Bemba* case, the Prosecutor requested the Appeals Chamber to consider an academic article as supplemental authority on unresolved points of law:

> After filing these additional submissions, a respected academic journal on international criminal law published a paper on superior responsibility under Article 28 of the Rome

[56] Robinson 2020, pp. 20–56.

[57] Ibid., p. 48.

[58] Meloni 2007, pp. 619–637.

[59] The terms *political superior* and *civilian superior* are used interchangeably in this book, as both are commonly employed in the literature to refer to non-military superiors in contrast to military commanders.

[60] Murphy 2019.

> Statute. This paper is directly relevant to one of the issues arising from Mr [sic] Bemba's appeal against the Trial Chamber's Judgment under article 74 and may therefore assist the Appeals Chamber in deciding on that aspect of the appeal. This paper was not previously available to the Parties since it was only placed online in 'April 2018'.[61]

In terms of the above matter, this book could serve as a reference to future requests.

In conclusion, the novelty of this book stems from its attempt to address key issues of debate concerning the doctrine of superior responsibility. First, it addresses doctrinal disputes over the legal characterization of superior responsibility, seeking to determine whether it refers to a mode of liability or a separate prosecutable omission offence. Second, it critically examines scholarship, commentaries, and court decisions regarding the definition and key elements of this doctrine, with a view to providing clear guidance on these elements and how courts can prosecute superiors in accordance with the provision. Third, it discusses the latest judgment from the Appeals Chambers of the ICC in the *Bemba* case, the reasoning of which the literature has struggled to conceptualize in a dedicated chapter. Finally, although this may appear to diverge from the overarching theme of the book, it contributes to a different yet related field by seeking to confirm the legality of invoking superior responsibility in cases of human rights violations and treaty-based crimes.[62] It also proposes a syllogistic prototype for extending the jurisdiction of ICL to encompass such offences.[63]

Ultimately, given the concept's extreme complexity, there are far too many challenges to mention, with two of the key examples set out below:

1. Overcoming the fact that most of the academic literature on the *international* concept of superior responsibility has been analyzed through the lens of *national* criminal law; and
2. Compensating for the scarcity of scholarship on the controversial decision in the *Bemba* case and on issues such as the legality of prosecuting superiors for human rights violations as well as treaty-crimes under this doctrine.

In addressing the first challenge, I shall examine the need for scholars and decision-makers to carefully scrutinize the interpretations and analyses of the rules governing the conceptual components of superior responsibility, rooted both in international law and in criminal law theory, while maintaining an "open mind" particularly toward the latter.[64] In light of this challenge, scholarship needs to move toward analysis based on the history, customs, and specific contexts of international crimes.[65] This need to redirect the scholarship stems from a logical understanding of the widespread, systematic

[61] *Prosecutor v. Jean-Pierre Bemba Gombo*, 13 April 2013, Request No. ICC-01/05-01/08, p. 3.

[62] See SáCouto and Sellers 2019, p. 599.

[63] Mr Pompeo, U.S. Secretary of State, officially stated that the commander-in-chief of Myanmar and some personnel and their first-degree families are banned from entering the U.S. in regard to gross human rights violations towards the Rohingyas, although these personnel are not the *de facto* superiors of the military who committed the crimes. See U.S. Department of State 2019.

[64] de Hemptinne et al. 2019, p. 438.

[65] See van Sliedregt 2012.

nature of international crimes, which sets a different standard for the culpability of the perpetrators of such crimes, who are mostly organized in accordance with a chain of authority.[66] As Cryer argues, even though the superior's culpability is somewhat low (involving an omission *per se*), the harm caused is immense (international crimes).[67]

1.3 Book Methodology and Methods

As previously noted, this book aims at providing a holistic examination of the doctrine of superior responsibility alongside a critical analysis of the relevant academic literature and judicial decisions. To achieve this, a combination of doctrinal and empirical legal research approaches is adopted.

The doctrinal component focuses on addressing the inconsistencies surrounding the interpretation and application of the doctrine of superior responsibility in international(ized) criminal tribunals. This involves a detailed analysis of the relevant treaties and statutes to examine how the doctrine is codified and regulated across various enabling instruments. The book then describes and analyzes the content of such treaties and statutes, offers commentary where applicable, identifies underlying legal themes and conceptual connections, clarifies the legal requirements defining the doctrine, and explores both literal and teleological interpretations of the said doctrine's conceptual components. It also assesses whether judicial decisions reflect a coherent understanding of the doctrine as a systemic legal concept, highlights ambiguities and criticisms in current scholarship, and proposes potential resolutions. The primary sources for this doctrinal analysis include treaties and statutes of international(ized) criminal tribunals, judicial decisions applying the doctrine, *travaux préparatoires* (where available), and relevant legal commentaries and academic literature.

Complementing this approach is the empirical component, which employs a qualitative approach grounded in critical analysis and conceptual description. Drawing on both primary sources, such as treaties, tribunal statutes, and case law, and secondary sources, including academic commentaries, books, and journal articles, the qualitative analysis in turn seeks to trace how courts and scholars have/had (mis)interpreted the doctrine. It evaluates the influence of these (mis)interpretations on the development and application of ICL and reflects on their broader implications for victims and those in positions of command/authority.

With that being said, this book involves no human participants, personal data, or procedures requiring ethical approval. Nonetheless, ethical standards were observed throughout, and all sources have been properly cited and acknowledged.

---

[66] Guilfoyle 2011, p. 256.

[67] Cryer 2015, p. 324.

1.4 Literature Review

There exist countless studies concerning the concept of superior responsibility in which scholars mostly address the topic through either critical or descriptive analysis methodologies.[68] Although these studies do not provide a comprehensive examination of the topic, they do address it as part of their broader analysis—whether in a book chapter, a section of an article, or a blog post.[69] A review of the above scholarship also indicates that the leading scholars disagree when it comes to the definition, legal nature, and requirements of this doctrine. Therefore, in the present section, I shall annotatively review the current academic literature that deals with these aspects, leaving more room in the book's remaining chapters for other topics pertinent to this doctrine, such as characterization, rudimentary elements, history, and different contexts of human rights violations and treaty-crimes. The present section provides a descriptive review of the literature; however, my critical analysis and reflections on both this literature and additional literature, as well as the related research problems, will be presented in the subsequent chapters.

1.4.1 Definitions of Superior Responsibility in the Literature

Leading scholars have defined superior responsibility in a dual sense, covering both the *latu* and *strictu* senses.[70] As regards *latu sensu*, Triffterer,[71] Ambos,[72] Meloni,[73] Vetter,[74] and Damaška[75] all share the same view of superior responsibility in its broad sense. Damaška argues that "command responsibility is an umbrella term used in military and international law to cover a variety of ways in which individuals in positions of leadership may be held accountable".[76] Van Sliedregt further contends that: "[superior responsibility is] an important tool in punishing those in superior positions for lack of supervision over persons under their command or authority".[77]

---

[68] See van Sliedregt 2012, n. 1. See also Jackson 2022, pp. 437–458.

[69] Ibid.

[70] The *latu sensu* definition of superior responsibility refers to a superior's criminal liability for their actions and omissions, whereas the *strictu sensu* of superior responsibility refers to the superior's vicarious liability for the crimes committed by their subordinates because of a failure of supervision.

[71] See Triffterer and Arnold 2016. (Noting that a newer edition of this commentary was published in 2022, in which Triffterer was replaced by Miles Jackson as an author to Article 28 along with Roberta Arnold. However, as the updates were minimal, I have chosen to cite the earlier edition instead of the newer one.)

[72] See Ambos 2002, p. 824.

[73] See Meloni 2007, p. 632.

[74] See Vetter 2000, p. 92.

[75] See Damaška 2001, p. 455.

[76] Ibid.

[77] Van Sliedregt 2012, pp. 183–184.

Arnold and Triffterer both define this doctrine from a *strictu sensu* perspective, asserting that "the definition of command and superior responsibility has been acknowledged as the longest definition of a single modality concerning individual criminal responsibility under international law",[78] proceeding to define it as "a legal institution to hold superiors responsible for crimes committed by their subordinates".[79] Triffterer appears to employ this definition not within the confines of the doctrine itself, but rather as a starting point to trace its historical origins.[80] By contrast, van der Vyver explicitly deals with both the *latu* and *strictu sensu* views of superior responsibility. Regarding its *latu sensu*, he explains:

A person in authority can face prosecution:

- For not complying with one's duty to exercise proper control over subordinates;
- For giving orders to his or her subordinates to commit a crime;
- For participating in the commission of a crime that he or she ordered the subordinates to commit.

In each of these circumstances, the superior can be held accountable as the principal or co-principal perpetrator.[81]

In its *strictu sensu* definition, van der Vyver defines this mode of liability as: "the liability of the person in authority for a crime committed by his or her subordinates because of the failure of the person in authority to exercise the measure of control required by law over the subordinates who actually committed the *actus reus* constituting the crime (indirect liability)".[82] Consequently, he proposes a detailed definition of the doctrine that covers all of its conceptual components and that is applicable to all superiors.

1.4.2 The Legal Characterization of Superior Responsibility in the Literature

In terms of legality, the legal characterization of superior responsibility is disputed (perhaps will continue as such eternally). As discussed in Chap. 3, one challenge revolves around whether courts should consider it an omission offense and charge the superior accordingly, or as a mode of liability, where the charge applies to the crimes of the superior's subordinates, as a form of derivative liability (otherwise known as vicarious liability). As noted earlier, disputes in scholarship have arisen as a result of scholars approaching the doctrine from the perspectives of their respective national

---

[78] Triffterer and Arnold 2016, p. 1059.

[79] Triffterer 2002, p. 179.

[80] Ibid., p. 180.

[81] Van der Vyver 2021, pp. 568–569.

[82] Ibid., p. 570.

criminal systems. For instance, while Canadian legislation considers this doctrine a crime of omission, British legislation views it as a form of complicity.[83]

At the scholarly level, principled concerns arise, at least in part, from national tensions between pragmatic and dogmatic legal systems and, more broadly, from within the regime itself,[84] where testing the doctrine against the foundational norms of criminal law often leads to a conceptual impasse. Within the confines of criminal law norms, it remains irrational to hold a superior criminally responsible for crimes committed by others solely due to a failure to control those others.

Within the confines of this doctrine at the international level, equating civilian and military superiors under the same liability standard also raises principled concerns, given the differences in proximity and authority. The doctrine is further complicated by the application of a negligence standard to military commanders—who are typically more directly present—whereas political superiors are often held to a lesser recklessness standard or a greater willful blindness standard, frequently excused by arguments of remoteness and evidentiary distance. Additionally, expecting superiors to take all reasonable measures may conflict with legal precedents that require only some action. Notably, implementing this doctrine in domestic systems also raises difficulties, especially given the contrast between international pragmatism and domestic dogmatism, where, in the later, omission offenses exist but stem from different legal foundations.[85]

Under the Rome Statute, ambiguity persists around whether superior responsibility should align with Article 31's general *mens rea* or its own *sui generis* standard—"knew", "should have known", or "consciously disregarded information".[86] The doctrine's emergence also sparked scholarly debate: should judges be bound by strict deontic principles such as personal culpability and legality, or should they adopt a more pluralistic, tolerant approach to manage the doctrine identity crisis?[87] This book later revisits these longstanding debates to establish, in turn, a coherent framework for superior responsibility.

For the purposes of this subsection, the syllogistic approach to defining the legal nature of superior responsibility in the academic literature comprises three perspectives on the doctrine, according to which it is viewed: (i) as a mode of liability, (ii) according to complicity theory, and (iii) as a separate offense of omission. Robinson, for example, advocates that complicity theory forms the basis of the doctrine's legal nature,[88] suggesting that the superior's "omission" is based on an active role on their part, and that the superior contributes to the crime(s). In his view, the superior is an accessory to the crimes committed by their subordinates, and this accessorial role is based on the superior's failure to act.[89] The aforementioned view is explained by

[83] See Cryer 2015, p. 325.

[84] Minkova 2023, p. 76.

[85] Ibid.

[86] Rome Statute 1998, Articles 31 and 28.

[87] Robinson 2020, pp. 20–58.

[88] See Robinson 2012, p. 3.

[89] Ibid.

the International Criminal Tribunal for the former Yugoslavia (ICTY) in the case of *Prosecutor v. Hadžihasanović*:

> [A] superior who exercises effective control over his subordinates and has reason to know that they are about to commit crimes, but fails to take the necessary and reasonable measures to prevent those crimes, incurs responsibility, both because his omission created or heightened a real and reasonably foreseeable risk that those crimes would be committed, a risk he accepted willingly, and because that risk materialized in the commission of those crimes. In that sense, the superior has substantially played a *part* in the commission of those crimes.[90] (emphasis added)

Meloni holds the above view only "if a superior knew, in this case, they would be an accessory to crimes committed by his or her subordinates".[91] Meloni,[92] Schabas,[93] and van Sliedregt[94] (in line with the majority of academic literature) understand this mode of liability as a *sui generis* liability for an omission only when the superior should have known about the commission of the crimes. Conversely, Damaška,[95] Cryer,[96] and Cassese[97] conceptualize this doctrine as "a distinct crime, consisting of the failure to discharge supervisory duties".[98] According to this paradigm, Damaška conceives of superior responsibility as "a separate offense of reckless or negligent supervision of one's subordinates…[this] stigma and framework of punishment are determined by his culpable omission, rather than the wrongdoing of his underlings".[99] This view is explained in the case of *Prosecutor v. Krnojelać*, where the Appeals Chamber of the ICTY held that: "It cannot be overemphasized that, where superior responsibility is concerned, an accused is not charged with the crimes of his subordinates but with his failure to carry out his duty as a superior to exercise control".[100]

Finally, van der Vyver and Guilfoyle underscore the distinct nature of the mode of liability associated with the superior responsibility doctrine proposed in this book (a *sui generis* mode of liability). Van der Vyver notes that: "[T]he truth is, though, that a neglect of duty is an offense in its own right, but one dealt with domestically within the disciplinary structures of the armed forces and which as such ought not to be of concern in international criminal law",[101] and that "a military commander

[90] *Prosecutor v. Enver Hadžihasanović et al.*, Decision on Interlocutory Appeal Challenging Jurisdiction in Relation to Command Responsibility, Case No. IT-01-47-AR72, para 193, 16 July 2003.

[91] Meloni 2007, p. 637.

[92] Ibid.

[93] See Schabas 2004, pp. 241, 249–250.

[94] See van Sliedregt 2003.

[95] See Damaška 2001, p. 483.

[96] See Cryer 2015, p. 394.

[97] Cassese et al. 2013, p. 192.

[98] Ibid.

[99] See Damaška 2001, pp. 466, 480, 483.

[100] Appeals Chamber, *Prosecutor v. Milorad Krnojelać*, Case No. IT-97-25-A, para 171, 17 September 2003.

[101] Van der Vyver 2021, p. 597.

who has been prosecuted for neglect of duty cannot raise the defense of *ne bis in idem* if subsequently they were to be charged to stand in trial… for the war crime".[102] Guilfoyle supports this view, arguing that: "A peculiar form of liability in international criminal law is superior responsibility, which makes a civilian or military superior responsible for the crimes of subordinates which they have failed to prevent or punish".[103]

This understanding of a distinct mode of liability may, as previously noted, echo, in part, Grotius's conclusion that an individual who knows a crime is being committed, possesses both the ability and duty to prevent it, yet chooses not to act, is themselves responsible for that crime.[104] The ICTY Appeals Chamber also supported this view in the case of *Prosecutor v. Zejnil Delalic et al.*, holding that:

> As a practical matter, the seriousness of a superior's conduct in failing to prevent or punish crimes must be measured to some degree by the nature of the crimes to which this failure relates. A failure to prevent or punish murder or torture committed by a subordinate must be regarded as being of greater gravity than a failure to prevent or punish an act of plunder, for example.[105]

1.4.3 The Elements of Superior Responsibility as Described in the Literature

Within the ICL regime, the conceptual components and practical application of superior responsibility are arguably the most critical aspects of the doctrine addressed in this book, as they are essential to determining whether a conviction or acquittal is warranted. Since its inception, the doctrine of superior responsibility has been examined by both scholars and courts. Although often addressed partially, it has consistently been challenged by key issues—namely, the superior–subordinate relationship, the element of fault attributable to the superior, and the failure to act. This subsection revisits these controversial aspects, offering an annotated review of the contentious issues surrounding each element.

Regarding the first requirement (the existence of a superior–subordinate relationship), Arnold notes that, as long as the superior has only material ability over a group of subordinates, superior responsibility can be triggered on the superior's part even if they are rank-less.[106] Guénaël has begged to differ, however,[107] arguing that "[t]he first requirement of superior responsibility relationship between the accused and the

[102] Ibid., p. 8.

[103] See Guilfoyle 2011, p. 266.

[104] Grotius 1964, p. 171.

[105] Appeals Chamber, *Prosecutor v. Zejnil Delalic et al.*, Case No. IT-96-21-A, para 732, 20 February 2001.

[106] See Triffterer and Arnold, 2016 p. 1091.

[107] See Mettraux 2009, pp. 139–140.

perpetrator, *demands* a hierarchical relationship".[108] In the *Čelebići* case, the ICTY Appeals Chamber combined these two views in its decision, holding that:

> The ability to exercise effective control in the sense of a material power to prevent or punish, which the Appeals Chamber considers to be a minimum requirement for the recognition of the superior-subordinate relationship, will almost invariably not be satisfied unless such a relationship of subordination exists. However, it is possible to imagine scenarios in which one of [sic] two persons of equal status or rank – such as two soldiers or two civilian prison guards – could in fact exercise "effective control" over the other at least in the sense of a purely practical ability to prevent the conduct of the other by, for example, force of personality or physical strength. The Appeals Chamber does not consider the doctrine of command responsibility – which developed with an emphasis on persons who, by virtue of the position which they occupy, have authority over others – as having been intended to impose criminal liability on persons for the acts of other persons of completely equal status.[109]

Regarding the position of the superior within the confines of this doctrine, Fenrick noted that the superior may impose a business influence on subordinates, where their material ability over them may be delineated through a financial effect, such as salaries or monetary awards.[110] This note was adopted in the *Pohl* case heard by the NMT.[111] It was also supported by the ICTY in the *Čelebići* case, where the Court held that: "A superior's ability to exert 'substantial influence' over someone who was neither a *de jure* nor a *de facto* subordinate was sufficient to establish command responsibility."[112]

Concerning the superior's failure to act (*i.e.* their failure to fulfill their duty to prevent or punish), Kortfält notes that the wording of the *ad hoc* tribunals' statutes on this matter suggests that the superior is required either to prevent the commission of a crime or to punish the perpetrators.[113] He states that "the superior failed to take the necessary and reasonable measures to prevent such acts or to punish...[t]he duties placed on the superior in these statutes are thus two-fold".[114] However, van der Vyver and van Sliedregt hold opposite views.[115] Van der Vyver notes that the "failure of the superior to prevent the commission of a crime in cases where it was within his or her power to do so cannot be remedied by subsequently fulfilling the duty to repress, or by referring the matter to the competent authorities for investigation and punishment".[116] In the *Blaškić* case, the ICTY supported this view in the Trial Chamber, where the Court held that:

---

[108] Ibid.

[109] Appeals Chamber, *Prosecutor v. Zejnil Delalic et al.*, Case No. IT-96-21-A, para 303, 20 February 2001.

[110] Fenrick 1999, p. 520.

[111] U.S. Military Tribunals 1950, para 1052.

[112] *Prosecutor v. Zejnil Delalic et al.*, Judgment, Case No. IT-96-21-T, para 647, 16 November 1998.

[113] Kortfält 2017, p. 292.

[114] Ibid.

[115] See van Sliedregt 2003, p. 190.

[116] Van der Vyver 2021, p. 593.

> The Trial Chamber stresses that the obligation to "prevent or punish" does not provide the accused with two alternative and equally satisfying options. Where the accused knew or had reason to know that subordinates were about to commit crimes and failed to prevent them, he cannot make up for the failure to act by punishing the subordinates afterwards.[117]

Lastly, regarding the fault element of superior responsibility, this doctrine requires that the superior have either knowledge (intent) or reason to know (negligence/recklessness/willful blindness) about the crime. With respect to the knowledge element on the part of the superior, Ambos explains the *mens rea* requirement of the doctrine, according to which the knowledge held by the superior is twofold. He states that according to this requirement, the superior must know that they are negligent when it comes to executing their duties and must also know the nature of the crimes committed by their subordinates.[118] However, he does not endorse the idea that a superior should be charged—at all—with the crimes of their her subordinates, restricting the conviction to omission only.[119] Cassese supports this view, noting that "knowledge of the occurrence of a crime is insufficient; the superior must also know that his subordinates are involved."[120] Nerlich and Arnold disagree with Cassese's opinion. Nerlich asserts that "the jurisprudence of the ICTY does not require that the superior share the genocidal intent [of the subordinates]".[121] In the *Radoslav* case, the ICTY supported Nerlich's and Arnold's opinions, deciding that "superior responsibility ... does not require proof of intent to commit a crime on the part of the superior...It is, therefore, necessary to distinguish between the *mens rea* required for the crimes perpetrated by the subordinates and that required for the superior".[122]

Regarding the reason-to-know requirement, the academic literature either equates "had reason to know" with the "should have known" standard (negligence),[123] sets a higher standard for "should have known", or describes it as willful blindness (as a form of intent).[124] Ambos and Weigend have suggested that "had reason to know" and "should have known" standards denote the same state of mind, namely, negligence.[125] Van Sliedregt suggests that "had reason to know" constitutes intent but often comes close to "should have known" (negligence).[126] Sadat goes further, contending that "knew" and "should have known" or, in the case of a civilian superior, "consciously disregarded information", all denote criminal negligence.[127] In her view, the superior responsibility doctrine is based on culpable negligence, and should be interpreted

117 *Prosecutor v. Tihomir Blaškić*, Judgment, Case No. IT-95-14-T, para 336, 3 March 2000.

118 See Ambos 2002, pp. 851–853.

119 Ibid.

120 Cassese 2004, p. 190.

121 Nerlich 2007, p. 672; Arnold 2016, p. 1084.

122 *Prosecutor v. Radoslav Brdjanin*, Judgment, Case No. IT-99-36-T, paras 720–721, 1 September 2004.

123 Ambos 2002, p. 864. See also Landrum 1995, p. 300; Vetter 2000, pp. 122–123.

124 Van Sliedregt 2003, p. 188.

125 See Ambos 2002, p. 864.

126 Van Sliedregt 2012.

127 Sadat 2002, p. 207.

accordingly.[128] In the book, I address these different views concerning the fault element of superior responsibility, as will be showcased in the subsequent chapters.

1.5 Structure

In addition to this introductory chapter, the book comprises five chapters.

Chapter 2 presents major historical insights directly or indirectly connected to the current conceptual components of superior responsibility. As Lael argues: "Only by reexamining the past can one sensibly determine the current legal validity of that concept of command responsibility which led to Yamashita's execution in February 1946 and prompted the subsequent lengthy debate".[129] To this end, to arrive at rational conclusions on the nature of superior responsibility in current law, an examination of the doctrine's history is necessary.

The first section of Chap. 2 provides a brief description of the historical trajectory of superior responsibility. Chap. 2, Sect. 2.2 traces the history of the doctrine in its *latu sensu* from a religious and cultural perspective, for instance, in relation to the history of Islamic and Christian rules during wartime regarding the army and its commander. Given the paramount importance of the history on justifying the characterization as well as the conceptual components, I shall also discuss the role of this concept in ancient military codes, such as "the Code of Hammurabi (*circa* 1750 BC); the Hindu Mahabharata (200 BC); the Chinese Wei Liaozi (403–221 BC); the orders of Islam's first caliph, Abu Bakr (*circa* 632AD); and codes of chivalry (1170–1220)".[130]

Similarly, in Chap. 2, Sect. 2.3, I shall trace the origins of the superior responsibility doctrine, from the medieval age in Europe and the U.S. Liber Code, to the Hague Convention and the early 1863 Geneva Convention. I will also consider the interplay of the LoAC, ICL, and international human rights law roles, which often overlap on specific subjects. Finally, in Chap. 2, Sect. 2.4, I introduce the contemporary norm on the doctrine of superior responsibility and how International Humanitarian Law (IHL) incorporated it into ICL (from the IMTs to the Geneva Conventions and their Additional Protocols until the Rome Statute). This discussion shall be based on the *travaux préparatoires* of international treaties and reports, as well as the statutes of the international(ized) criminal courts. It also provides auxiliary historical background for Chap. 4, which examines the unpromising application of superior responsibility at the ICC. In terms of responding to the research questions, Chaps. 3 and 4 constitute the core of this study.

Chapter 3 consists of five sections: Chap. 3, Sect. 3.1 sets out an introduction to the rudiments of the superior responsibility doctrine; Chap. 3, Sect. 3.2 presents certain definitions of the doctrine and other similar criminal responsibilities; Chap. 3,

[128] Ibid.

[129] Lael 1982, p. 7.

[130] Green 2008.

Sect. 3.3 explores whether superior responsibility is a mode of liability, a hybrid mode of liability and omission, or a separate prosecutable offense through an analysis of its legal characterization; Chap. 3, Sect. 3.4 identifies the requirements of this doctrine and how courts interpreted and applied them; and Chap. 3, Sect. 3.5 concludes by proposing general remarks and propositions based on the overall discussion set out in this chapter.

Chapter 4 discusses the doctrine of superior responsibility within the ICC's subject-matter jurisdiction—the Rome Statute and the late controversial judgment of the Appeals Chamber in the *Bemba* case. This chapter is divided into three sections: Chap. 4, Sect. 4.1 introduces the structure of the ICC and the Rome Statute, for contextual and methodology-related purposes. Section 4.2 of Chap. 4, also for contextual and methodology-related purposes, explores the (a)symmetry between the UN *ad hoc* tribunals and the ICC. Although it might appear to diverge from the chapter's primary focus, it is nonetheless useful to draw interpretative parallels between the ICC and the UN *ad hoc* tribunals. This approach is grounded in Article 21(1)(b) of the Rome Statute—*Applicable Law to the Court*—which provides that the ICC shall, as a secondary source, apply "the principles and rules of international law, including the established principles of the international law of armed conflict".[131] In light of this provision and its parallels with the jurisprudence of other international(ized) courts, reference to Articles 31 and 32 of the *Vienna Convention on the Law of Treaties*—as interpretative tools—will help frame the doctrine's components and characterization as reflected in those tribunals' enabling statutes. A more detailed examination of this approach will be undertaken in Chap. 5. Chapter 4, Sect. 4.3 discusses the superior responsibility structure of the Rome Statute, particularly in comparison with the parallel statutes of the international(ized) criminal tribunals, while also analyzing the *Bemba* case in detail. As noted earlier, this case is reasonably new and has received little attention in scholarly writing or analysis.

In **Chap. 5**, I shall argue for the applicability of this doctrine outside war crimes and wartime contexts, before presenting the concluding remarks in the second section. Chapter 5, Sect. 5.2 attempts to test the legality of applying this doctrine to superiors of international human rights violators and the principals of treaty-crimes.[132] As such, I shall consider, by way of example, whether it is applicable to try the superiors of human rights violators before criminal or human rights courts, and, if so, whether this should be conducted under the doctrine of superior responsibility or under a different set of rules. This example is empirically inspired by the origins of the doctrine phenomenon, which began as a military disciplinary measure, and gradually evolved into a criminal mode of liability applied to military commanders and political superiors. Accordingly, in this section, I shall examine the capacity of the UN, the ICC, and national systems (which I present as trio-regimes) to hold superiors criminally accountable, as these regimes—I argue—constitute the original sources and primary enforcers of the doctrine of superior responsibility.[133]

---

[131] Rome Statute 1998, Article 21(1)(b).

[132] Universal Declaration of Human Rights 1948, Article 3.

[133] ICRC 2017.

In Sect. 5.3 of Chap. 5, I present the multiple findings of this study and my observations from the preceding chapters. In this section, I compile all the results of the questions addressed, particularly in relation to the *Bemba* case and, notably, my examination of the applicability of the doctrine of superior responsibility in human rights law.

1.6 The Concluding Remarks of the Book

To recap in a nutshell, the following points summarize the purpose of this book:

First, it begins with the foundational premise that superior responsibility is an international construct and must not be analogous to national criminal law principles. Unlike traditional criminal liability, it assigns the conduct of subordinates to the superior vicariously, justified not by any means of involvement but by the violation of inherently entrusted obligations by virtue of the superior's role. The superior's culpability for the crimes does not arise from personally committing or assisting in them, but rather derives from the foreseeable consequences of their failure—whether intentional, negligent, or reckless—to prevent or punish their commission. As Scharf aptly observed, the failure to prevent and punish the subordinates sends a dangerous signal of tolerance toward such crimes with amnesty being guaranteed.

Second, this book challenges the misconception that superior responsibility is a standalone omission offense akin to that found in domestic criminal law. Instead, it is a *sui generis* mode of liability that must be understood within its international context. Domestic interpretations that reduce it to omission-based offenses, especially in national codes such as Germany's *Völkerstrafgesetzbuch* or Commonwealth models, create legal inconsistencies, particularly regarding *mens rea*. These variations, as discussed herein, may, for example, complicate the Rome Statute's harmonization efforts with domestic systems, especially with respect to the negligence threshold and the concept of constructive knowledge.

Third, it critiques the inappropriate treatment of superior responsibility as an *alternative* mode of liability in judicial practice. While courts sometimes consider this an alternative to other liability modes, the current book argues that such an approach risks conceptual confusion and undermines legal precision. Superior responsibility should be treated as an autonomous mode of liability and a principle, in its own right, that applies only when its full set of elements (including their internal parameters) is met. Importantly, it must be noted that most convictions against superiors can be based on both the direct mode(s) of liability and superior responsibility, as a superior's duties to prevent and punish remain at play even when they are accused of committing the principal crimes as either principals or accessories, though courts apply one aggravated sentence to avoid double-sentencing.

Fourth, a detailed examination of the requirements of the doctrine is provided. Each element must be fully satisfied, and partial compliance cannot establish liability. This book emphasizes that international justice demands both clarity and fairness—not only for victims, but also for accused superiors—within the framework of satisfying the elements of superior responsibility.

Fifth, the mental element (*mens rea*) attached to superiors must be distinguished from that attached to their subordinates. Proving a superior's *mens rea* for liability does not require establishing the mental state of the subordinates who committed the crimes, nor intent specifically tied to the omission; rather, it suffices to demonstrate that the superior had actual knowledge, was negligent, reckless, or willfully blind in failing to fulfill their duty to prevent or punish the crimes. This conceptual separation is essential for the proper understanding and application of the doctrine. I intend to discuss the nuances in the subsequent chapters.

Sixth, this book rejects the necessity of a causal link, as defined in many national systems, for the application of superior responsibility. Rather than demanding a causal connection between the superior's omission and the crimes committed, ICL holds that a superior's failure to fulfill their duties is sufficient to incur responsibility—so long as that failure enabled or failed to prevent the crimes. As such, the causal link requirement may be considered superfluous within this framework.

Seventh, the distinction between superior responsibility and the civil law concept of *respondeat superior* is clarified. Whereas the latter addresses civil compensation, the former is a mode of criminal liability for the most serious international crimes, such as War Crimes, Crimes Against Humanity, and Genocide.

Eighth, it is hoped that this book will bridge the accountability gap in prosecuting superiors for human rights violations under the doctrine of superior responsibility, particularly during the ongoing evolution of international criminal justice.

Ninth, this book presents improvement appraisals and offers targeted recommendations for refining the doctrine's implementation. These include, for example, clarifying the status of subordinates (civilian *vs.* military), standardizing the *mens rea* element, and articulating a more concrete understanding of what constitutes "all necessary and reasonable measures".

References

Al-Fadhli H (2025) From Nuremberg to the Hague and beyond: Reincorporating "taking a consenting part" into international criminal modes of liability. Netherlands International Law Review, 72(2)

Al-Rashidi K, Al-Fadhli H (2025) Corruption in the MENA: Between State Crime and International Criminal Law. In: Carrington K, Dixon R, Zajdow A, Marotta S (eds) The Palgrave Handbook of Criminology and the Global South, 2nd edn. Palgrave Macmillan

Ambos K (2002) Superior Responsibility. In: Cassese A, Gaeta P, Jones J (eds) The Rome Statute of the International Criminal Court: A Commentary. Oxford University Press, pp. 823–872

Ambos K (2009) Command Responsibility and Organisationsherrschaft: Ways of Attributing International Crimes to the "Most Responsible". In Nollkaemper A and van der Wilt H (eds) System Criminality in International Law. Cambridge University Press, pp. 127–157

Bassiouni MC (2011) Crimes against Humanity: Historical Evolution and Contemporary Application. Cambridge University Press, Cambridge

BBC News (2018) Profile: Jean-Pierre Bemba, DR Congo's ex-rebel and vice-president. BBC News, 8 June 2018. Available at: https://www.bbc.com/news/world-africa-35845556/. Accessed 1 December 2019

Cassese A (2004) The ICTY: A living and vital reality. Journal of International Criminal Justice 2: pp. 585–597

Cassese A et al. (2013) Cassese's International Criminal Law, 3rd edn. Oxford University Press, Oxford

Cryer R (2015) International Criminal Law: General Principles of Liability in International Criminal Law, vol. II. Routledge, London

Cryer R, Friman H, Robinson D, Wilmshurst E (2019) An Introduction to International Criminal Law and Procedure, 4th edn. Cambridge University Press, Cambridge

Damaška M (2001) The shadow side of command responsibility. American Journal of Comparative Law 49, pp. 455–496

de Hemptinne J, Roth R, van Sliedregt E (2019) Concluding Observations. In: de Hemptinne J, Roth R, van Sliedregt E (eds) Modes of Liability in International Criminal Law. Cambridge University Press, Cambridge, pp 433–438

Fenrick W (1999) Commentary on the Rome Statute of the International Criminal Court: Article by article. In: Triffterer O (ed) Commentary on the Rome Statute of the International Criminal Court. C.H. Beck, Munich, 108–180

Fletcher GP (2002) Romantics at War: Glory and Guilt in the Age of Terrorism. Princeton University Press, Princeton

Green L (2008) The Contemporary Law of Armed Conflict, 3rd edn. Manchester University Press, Manchester

Grotius H (1964) De Jure Belli ac Pacis Libri Tres (Kelsey FW (transl.)). Oceana, New York, Bk. II, Ch. 1(ii)

Guilfoyle D (2011) Responsibility for collective atrocities: Fair labelling and approaches to commission in international criminal law. Current Legal Problems 64, pp. 255–286

Heller KJ (2011) The Nuremberg Military Tribunals and the Origins of International Criminal Law. Oxford University Press, Oxford

ICRC (1971) Introduction. Report submitted to the Conference of Government Experts on the Reaffirmation and Development of International Humanitarian Law Applicable in Armed Conflicts, Geneva

ICRC (2017) Ad hoc tribunals. Available at: https://www.icrc.org/en/document/ad-hoc-tribunals/. Accessed 1 December 2019

International Military Tribunal (Nuremberg) (1947) Judgment and Sentences. American Journal of International Law 41, pp. 172–221

Jackson M (2022) Causation and the legal character of command responsibility after Bemba at the International Criminal Court. J Int Crim Justice 20(2):437–458

Klamberg M (ed) (2017) Commentary on the Law of the International Criminal Court. TOAEP, Brussels

Kortfält L (2017) Individual criminal responsibility. In: Klamberg M (ed) Commentary on the Law of the International Criminal Court. TOAEP, Brussels, pp. 781–844

Lael R (1982) The Yamashita Precedent: War Crimes and Command Responsibility. Rowman & Littlefield, Lanham

Landrum BD (1995) The Yamashita war crimes trial: Command responsibility then and now. Military Law Review 149, pp. 293–301

Meloni C (2007) Command responsibility: Mode of liability for the crimes of subordinates or separate offence of the superior? Journal of International Criminal Justice 5(3), pp. 619–637

Mettraux G (2009) The Law of Command Responsibility. Oxford University Press, Oxford
Minkova L (2023) Responsibility on Trial: Liability Standards in International Criminal Law. Cambridge University Press, Cambridge
Morris V, Scharf M (1995) An Insider's Guide to the International Criminal Tribunal for the Former Yugoslavia. Transnational Publishers, New York
Murphy R (2019) Command responsibility after Bemba. Yearbook of New Zealand Jurisprudence, Brill, Leiden, The Netherlands, pp. 94–118
Murphy S (2012) Principles of International Law, 2nd edn. Reuters, London
Nerlich V (2007) Superior responsibility under Article 28 ICC Statute: For what exactly is the superior held responsible? Journal of International Criminal Justice 5(3), pp. 665–682
Nuremberg Trial Proceedings (1945) Trial of the Major War Criminals before the International Military Tribunal, vol. 2, 23 Nov 1945
Reel FA (1949) The Case of General Yamashita. University of Chicago Press, Chicago
Robinson D (2012) How command responsibility got so complicated: A culpability contradiction, its obfuscation, and a simple solution. Melbourne Journal of International Law 13, pp.1–58
Robinson D (2020) Justice in Extreme Cases: Criminal Law Theory Meets International Criminal Law. Cambridge University Press, Cambridge
SáCouto S, Sellers PV (2019) The Bemba Appeals Chamber judgment: Impunity for sexual and gender-based crimes? William & Mary Bill of Rights Journal 27, pp. 599–622
Sadat LN (2002) The International Criminal Court and the Transformation of International Law: Justice for the New Millennium. Transnational Publishers, New York
Schabas WA (2004) The right to a fair trial. In: Lattanzi F, Schabas WA (eds) Essays on the Rome Statute of the International Criminal Court, vol. 2. Il Sirente, Rome
Steer C (2014) The Prosecutor v. Delic: What Are the Limits of Command Responsibility? In: Klip A, Sluiter G (eds) Annotated Leading Cases of International Criminal Tribunals, Vol 37. Intersentia, The Hague
Stewart D (2014) International Criminal Law in a Nutshell, 2nd edn. West Academic, St. Paul
Stewart JG (2012) The End of "Modes of Liability" for International Crimes. Leiden Journal of International Law, 25(1), 165–219
Triffterer O (2002) Causality: A separate element of the doctrine of superior responsibility as expressed in Article 28 of the Rome Statute? Leiden Journal of International Law 15, pp. 179 - 205
Triffterer O, Arnold R (2016) Article 28 Responsibility of commanders and other superiors. In: Triffterer O, Ambos K (eds) The Rome Statute of the International Criminal Court: A Commentary, 3rd edn. C.H. Beck, Munich, pp. 1056–1106
Urs P (2024) Gravity at the International Criminal Court: Admissibility and Prosecutorial Discretion. Oxford University Press, Oxford
U.S. Department of State (2019) Public Designation Due to Gross Violations of Human Rights of Burmese Military Officials. Available at: https://www.state.gov/on-public-designation-due-to-gross-violations-of-human-rights-of-burmese-military-officials/
U.S. Military Tribunals (1950) Trials of War Criminals before the Nuremberg Military Tribunals under Control Council Law No. 10, vol V. U.S. Government Printing Office, Washington, DC, (Pohl et al.)
U.S. Military Tribunals (1952) United States v. von Weizsäcker et al. (The Ministries Case), Trials of War Criminals before the Nuremberg Military Tribunals under Control Council Law No. 10, vol XII. U.S. Government Printing Office, Washington, DC, p 1127, (Powers, dissenting)
Van der Vyver JD (2021) International criminal law: Crimes within the jurisdiction of the International Criminal Court. LAP Lambert Academic Publishing, Saarbrücken
Van Sliedregt E (2003) The Criminal Responsibility of Individuals for Violations of International Humanitarian Law. T.M.C. Asser Press, The Hague
Van Sliedregt E (2012) Individual Criminal Responsibility in International Law. Oxford University Press, Oxford

Vetter G (2000) Command responsibility of non-military superiors in the International Criminal Court (ICC). Yale Journal of International Law 25, pp. 92–123
Wilson P (2017) The Myth of International Humanitarian Law. 93 International Affairs 563, pp 563–579
Wise EM, Podgor ES, Clark RS (2009) International Criminal Law: Cases and Materials, 3rd edn. LexisNexis, Newark

Case Law

Prosecutor v. Enver Hadžihasanović et al., Decision on Interlocutory Appeal Challenging Jurisdiction in Relation to Command Responsibility, Case No. IT-01-47-AR72, 16 July 2003
Prosecutor v. Jean-Pierre Bemba Gombo, Appeals Chamber, Case No. ICC-01/05-01/08 A, 8 June 2018
Prosecutor v. Jean-Pierre Bemba Gombo, Judgment, Case No. ICC-01/05-01/08 A, 8 June 2018
Prosecutor v. Jean-Pierre Bemba Gombo, PTC II, Decision on the Confirmation of Charges, Case No. ICC-01/05-01/08–424, 15 June 2009
Prosecutor v. Jean-Pierre Bemba Gombo, Request for Leave to Appeal, Case No. ICC-01/05-01/08, 13 April 2018
Prosecutor v. Milorad Krnojelac, Appeals Chamber, Case No. IT-97-25-A, 17 September 2003
Prosecutor v. Radoslav Brdjanin, Judgment, Case No. IT-99-36-T, 1 September 2004
Prosecutor v. Tihomir Blaškić, Judgment, Case No. IT-95-14-T, 3 March 2000
Prosecutor v. Zejnil Delalić et al., Appeals Chamber, Case No. IT-96-21-A, 20 February 2001
Prosecutor v. Zejnil Delalić et al., Judgment, Case No. IT-96-21-T, 16 November 1998
S.S. Lotus (France v. Turkey), Judgment, 1927, Permanent Court of International Justice (PCIJ), Series A No. 10

Other Documents

Rome Statute of the International Criminal Court (1998) 2187 UNTS 90
Universal Declaration of Human Rights (1948) G.A. Res. 217A, U.N. GAOR, 3d Sess., 1st plen. mtg., U.N. Doc. A/810

Chapter 2
From Antiquity to Status Quo: The Genesis of Superior Responsibility

Contents

Abstract This chapter offers a historical analysis of the doctrine of superior responsibility, tracing its conceptual origins and practical applications from antiquity to its modern form under international criminal law. It examines how military, cultural, and religious traditions—particularly within ancient Asian and Islamic contexts—shaped early notions of command accountability. The chapter critically evaluates

H. Y. Al-Fadhli, *Prosecuting Superior Responsibility in International Criminal Law*,
https://doi.org/10.1007/978-94-6265-735-9_2

the transition of superior responsibility from a state-based disciplinary mechanism to a sui generis mode of liability in international criminal adjudication. Emphasis is placed on how misinterpretations of the doctrine by international judges—often a result of a lack of historical grounding—have led to inconsistent applications in case law. Through a descriptive and hierarchical approach, this chapter highlights the doctrinal evolution across three key historical phases: ancient civilizational customs, Medieval European developments, and modern international law. This analysis in turn aims at providing a foundational understanding necessary for the normative, philosophical, and prosecutorial proposals developed in subsequent chapters.

Keywords History of international criminal law · Islamic law of war · Law and religion · Command responsibility · Superior responsibility · Customary international law

2.1 Prologue

> *Only by reexamining the past can one sensibly determine the current legal validity of that concept of command responsibility.*[1]

Because one of the primary objectives of this book is to offer a doctrine guideline regarding superior responsibility for practitioners and decision-makers, it is essential to conduct a historical analysis of this legal phenomenon to understand how international law incorporated a military-based accountability concept into a broader international criminal mode of liability. The insights that emerge from this historical overview may also help to explain why publicists and international judges find the parameters underpinning this doctrine particularly paradoxical and inapplicable, based on their respective domestic critical frameworks.[2] This is particularly important as it further supports the philosophical account of consequential culpability developed in the subsequent chapter. That said, superior responsibility is not only a standard mode of liability but also an unusual "proxy" to prosecute superiors for the crimes of others—that is, vicarious liability.[3] A historical analysis of this mode of liability supports both its novelty and the prerequisite interpretations by scholars and international judges within the scope of unified international standards. In this context, Julius Stone once argued that:

> If international judges could be found with supreme skill [*sic*] as historians, and supreme objectivity as judges, they might still reconstruct an approximation to the full truth by gathering together, cross-checking, correcting, and re-integrating [international legal concepts].[4]

---

[1] Lael 1982, p. 7.

[2] See Chap. 3, Sect. 3.2. See also Bassiouni 2011, p. 473. Bassiouni emphasizes that international judges rely heavily on their domestic law systems, particularly common law ones.

[3] Damaška 2001, p. 455.

[4] Stone 2011, p. 144.

This statement could be used as a benchmark for the misinterpretations presented by judges, as will be discussed in the following chapters. These misinterpretations, to varying degrees, have led international judges to both exonerate and incriminate superiors owing to a failure to engage in a historical analysis of the conceptual components and practical applications of this doctrine.[5] Arguably, such omissions could continue to produce less compelling analyses that may affect future superior responsibility adjudications.[6] To rectify these fragmentations and progress toward a more objective approach to international criminal justice, this chapter will focus on evaluating the historical chain of developments related to this doctrine.

While the willingness to prosecute individuals at the international level properly emerged in the twentieth century,[7] the applicability of this concept can be traced back to antiquity, particularly the BC era.[8] Moreover, although this concept was chronicled historically on many occasions, it was initially applied only within the context of state practice.[9] Only later did it transform into an internationally recognized yet complex criminal mode of liability.[10] In its *latu sensu*,[11] the doctrine of superior responsibility has been applied either as a military disciplinary tool for superior orders, or as a cultural and religious principle stemming from cultural customs and divine scriptures.[12] In these contexts, one of the most cited ancient accounts of superior responsibility in academic literature is Sun Tzu's draft manual *The Art of War*, which refers to the doctrine as a culturally oriented principle.[13]

However, the literature cited above overlooks other important historical contexts of superior responsibility—at least in its latu sensu form—such as Islamic law, which articulates the doctrine within a military framework. To this end, I intend to explore this historical context in order to draw out its nuances in relation to modern interpretations. Though, rather than engaging with the legality of waging war—a subject extensively explored in *jus ad bellum* literature—my discussion will be limited to Islam and its approach to armed conflict, following the same approach taken with other cultural and religious insights referenced throughout this chapter. This decision regarding the inclusion of Islam is based on two reasons: (i) the considerable unfamiliarity with its essence and the irreconcilable views presented in Western scholarship in relation to its resorting-to-war character; and (ii) the role this doctrine plays, given its celestial military structure, in emphasizing the responsibility of superiors.

---

[5] See, for instance, van der Vyver 2021, pp. 601–602.

[6] In this regard, for adjudicating superior responsibility cases, many UN criminal tribunals rely heavily on the *Čelebići* case, for instance. Moreover, in the *Ongwen* case at the ICC, the Court explicitly indicated that it relied on precedents from the ad hoc tribunals owing to the lack of jurisprudence at the ICC, with only one case—*Bemba*—having been decided. ICC, *The Prosecutor v. Dominic Ongwen*, 6 May 2021, Case No. ICC-02/04-01/15, para 103.

[7] The *Yamashita* case in the aftermath of WWII. See Bellot 1922, p. 63.

[8] Parks 1973, pp. 3–4.

[9] Meloni 2010, p. 74.

[10] Ibid.

[11] See Sect. 2.1.

[12] McCormack 1997, p. 242.

[13] Ibid.

Other studies have sought to trace the roots of the doctrine of superior responsibility in customary law. Of particular interest is the analysis by William J. Fenrick, who traces the doctrine back to the provisions "annexed to the 1907 Hague Convention No. IV", which is now considered one of the customary principles of the law of armed conflict.[14] The literature also underscores the role that the modern history of international prosecutions, particularly in the aftermath of WWII (1939–45), played in the development of the components of this doctrine,[15] which can in fact be traced back to before the emergence of international law.

The analysis in this chapter is grounded in a historically descriptive approach. I shall engage in a hierarchical narration of the history of superior responsibility—from antiquity to modern times—that resulted in the formation of this phenomenon in its *latu* and *strictu* senses. Moreover, as part of the methodological approach adopted here, I have chosen to focus exclusively on historical events that support the perennial status of superior responsibility as a distinct criminal mode of liability, rather than the commonly debated approach that inaccurately characterizes it as a crime of omission *per se*. This is particularly important given that punishment for omission liability typically carries a mitigated sentence, and not for the principal crime committed by subordinates—as is institutionally and historically observed in the concept itself and in the application that ensues under this doctrine. Ultimately, this chapter is intended to provide a historical background to the rudiments of superior responsibility described in the following chapter, and as a context for understanding this doctrine under the ICC's subject matter jurisdiction, as addressed in Chap. 4.

This chapter consists of three main sections. Section 2.3 explores the intersectionality between cultural customs and religion and their impact on superiors' duties in relation to subordinates' responsibilities. Section 2.4 discusses the question of holding superiors responsible in the Middle Ages, particularly within European history. Finally, Sect. 2.5 analyzes the modern history of international law, focusing on how a military-based doctrine developed into an international criminal mode of liability.

2.2 Antiquity: The Role of Cultural Customs and Religious Commandments in Constructing Superior Responsibility

In antiquity, crimes against humanity essentially resulted from a commanding officer's order to resort to war. As van der Vyver and Ben Ferencz argue, the concept of warfare constitutes a predestined yet regrettable reality that has accompanied human interactions since the beginning of humanity.[16] Cain and Abel's conflict resembled

[14] Fenrick 1999, p. 516.

[15] Parks 1973.

[16] Van der Vyver 2015, p. 1, quoting Ferencz 2010, https://benferencz.org/articles/2010-present/illegal-armed-force-as-a-crime-against-humanity/.

a war-like act driven by jealousy over divine favor.[17] Warfare and the responsibilities of military soldiers and their commanders are also described in the ancient Hindu texts of India, such as the *Mahabharata* (the Laws of Manu) and the *Code of Bushido*.[18] The latter, for instance, outlines the responsibilities of a superior *vis-à-vis* their subordinates as follows: "[E]very soldier must report to the commander about prisoners of war…He shall be guilty of manslaughter if he kills them with his own hands. Prisoners of war (POW) shall not be executed wantonly regardless of whether they laid down their arms and fought to the last arrow."[19] In this regard, British military historian and theorist Captain Liddell Hart asserts: "The profoundest truth of war is that the issue of battle is usually decided in the minds of the opposing commanders, not in the bodies of their men."[20] Because waging war has thus never been the responsibility of an individual soldier, the concept of superior responsibility has always been a decisive principle in disciplining military commanders.

In antiquity, the doctrine of superior responsibility was also applied within the context of armed conflict.[21] However, at the time, armed conflict was associated only with religious and culturally based wars, in contrast with the Middle Ages and modern eras, when wars became associated with colonialism and imperialism.[22] One of the culturally based codifications of superior responsibility is the above-mentioned manual by Sun Tzu, which had a significant impact on the history of the doctrine.[23] Given the significance of this manual, which had a profound effect on the modern structure of superior responsibility, I shall dedicate this section to describing how it outlines the role of superiors and their responsibilities. Through such an account, my aim is to provide evidence of how, in the ancient era, superiors were held responsible for the actions of their subordinates owing to their failure to execute supervisory duties.

2.2.1 *Superior Responsibility Before Christ*

In the sixth century B.C., General Sun Tzu began writing his thirteen-chapter military manual, *The Art of War*, with the assertion that "Command is…severity".[24] As a legal adviser, Sun Tzu was asked by King He Lu, the ruler of China at the time,

[17] In this sense, Professor Theodor Meron argues that: "To genuinely humanize humanitarian law, it would be necessary to put an end to all kinds of armed conflicts. But wars have been a part of the human condition since the struggle between Cain and Abel, and regrettably they are likely to remain so." Meron 2000, p. 240.

[18] Armour 1922, pp. 71, 74, 81; Bühler 1886, p. 90.

[19] Adachi 1988, pp. 13, 17.

[20] Roberts 2019, p. 184.

[21] McCormack 1997. See also Meloni 2010.

[22] Meloni 2010, p. 242.

[23] Ibid.

[24] Tzu and Minford 2002, vol. 23, no. 3, p. 5.

to establish a military code for disciplinary purposes, to be used by the Chinese military between 556 and 479 B.C.[25] Throughout history, this military code has had a profound influence on global leaders and has shaped modern military institutional structures. It is worth noting, for instance, that *Napoleon* owned a copy in the French translation,[26] and even leaders in modern times, such as Mao Zedong, Chairman of the Communist Party in China, relied on this manual as a reference for military training in guerilla warfare.[27] The manual's most predominant excerpts underscore the clear responsibilities of military commanders, which are commensurate with their disciplinary duties.

Sun Tzu's manual was not limited to war and military instruction, however; it also addresses business transactions.[28] On the question of waging a war, Sun Tzu nonetheless focuses on five factors that an army (or a state) cannot bypass: "(1) Moral Law; (2) Heaven; (3) Earth; (4) The Commander; (5) Method and discipline".[29] In *The Art of War*, Sun Tzu conceptualizes the act of waging war as "a matter of life and death…[h]ence it is a subject of inquiry that can on no account be *neglected.*"[30] At that point in ancient history, one can assume that states were held responsible for negligence during war. However, as noted earlier, given the limited powers of the state sovereignty principle in the Law of Nations, no consideration was given to prosecuting individual responsibility internationally. International law, however, was ultimately formed to regulate how states deal with limits of legal powers. Even in antiquity, warfare regulations were confined to cultural and religious standards and were not merely the practice of individual states.

Perhaps the most significant rule of modern superior responsibility described in *The Art of War* manual is that: "When troops flee, are insubordinate, distressed, collapse in disorder, or are routed, it is the fault of the general. None of these disorders can be attributed to natural causes."[31] This rule explains many conceptual components of superior responsibility, such as the causal link, which is a putative requirement of superior responsibility in the Rome Statute.[32] According to commentators, there is a direct causal link between the troops' insubordination, distress, collapse, and disorder and the superior's authority, with the former being considered the fault of the superior, for which he or she is held vicariously liable.[33] This rule also encapsulates the superior's order defense, meaning that a subordinate's commission of a crime based on a superior's order cannot be used as an exculpatory defense on his or her part

[25] Ibid., p. 25. See also Parks 1973.

[26] See, generally, Bonaparte 2001.

[27] Mao 1965, vol. 1.

[28] Tzu and Minford 2002, p. 6.

[29] Ibid.

[30] Ibid.

[31] Tzu 1963, p. 125 (arguing that several thousand years ago, commanders were held responsible for the actions of their men).

[32] See Chap. 4.

[33] Tzu 1963.

and therefore relieve him or her criminal liability.[34] Within this context, a subordinate's commission of a crime resulting from insubordination, distress, collapse, and disorder cannot be used as a superior order defense in its own right. Finally, this rule can also be seen as an ancient basis for the current superior–subordinate relationship requirement—that is, a superior's fundamental duty to instruct their subordinates.[35] Rule Thirteen of the manual also emphasizes the effective command and control test for the superior responsibility doctrine, as reflected in its modern structure—*i.e.*, both the *de facto* and *de jure* positions. According to Sun Tzu, a state must consider: "Which of the two generals has most ability".[36] At that time, for the purposes of practical application, a nation needed to take into account the effective command and control test, which remains a key component of the doctrine in its current form for holding commanders liable.

Despite the harsh, unmerited critiques directed at it, the theories outlined in Sun Tzu's manual, including those related to superior responsibility, prompted the king to put them to the test.[37] Thus, when Sun Tzu completed the manual, the king requested that these theories be validated by applying them to 180 women.[38] These women, who played the role of soldiers, were divided into two groups, with each group assigned an officer.[39] The king ordered the groups of women to hold up their spears and delivered the following instructions: "When I say, 'Eyes front,' you must look straight ahead. When I say, 'Left turn,' you must face towards your left hand. When I say, 'Right turn,' you must face towards your right hand. When I say, 'About turn', you must face right round towards your back."[40]

Both groups complied and were therefore deemed ready to comply with their commander's orders. However, once the order was given and the drums were drumming, both groups stood still and began "laughing" for no reason.[41] In response, Sun Tzu asserted: "If words of command are not clear and distinct, if orders are not thoroughly understood, then the general is to blame."[42] Sun Tzu repeatedly ordered them to "turn left" to ensure that his orders were directed at the groups. Defiantly, the groups of women simply laughed again and did not execute the order. Sun Tzu then ordered that their assigned officers be beheaded, based on the rule set out in *The Art of War*, which states: "But if [the commander's] orders are clear, and the soldiers nevertheless disobey, then it is the fault of their officers."[43]

---

[34] See, generally, Chap. 4.

[35] See the superiors' duty requirement, as discussed in Sect. 2.4.1. See also Solf and Cummings 1977, p. 206, https://scholarlycommons.law.case.edu/jil/vol9/iss2/2 (accessed 23 April 2021), citing Draper 1972, pp. 54–58.

[36] Giles 1910, para 58.

[37] Parks 1973, p. 4.

[38] Ibid., pp. 3–4.

[39] Ibid.

[40] Ibid.

[41] Ibid.

[42] Ibid.

[43] Ibid.

In line with the deterrence effect implied here, the group of women, later, complied with the final order, which was executed by a *de facto* commander. This ancient narrative therefore aligns with the requirements of the superior–subordinate relationship in accordance with superior responsibility in the *strictu sensu*, and with the superior's orders in accordance with superior responsibility in the *latu sensu*.[44] As the assigned offers held *de jure* status, while he was a *de facto* superior, Sun Tzu's initial order was not made on a *de jure* basis. However, Sun Tzu's repeated order somehow transferred *de facto* authority to the assigned officers, consequently establishing a duty on the part of the latter to ensure that the orders were carried out. Eventually, they were sentenced to death if the groups failed to comply for a third time.

Although the ancient Chinese concept of superior responsibility was applied in a cultural context, ancient Greece, which dates about a century after Sun Tzu's manual, had a criminal tribunal resembling the modern prosecutions of superiors. During this era. a war crimes tribunal emerged that bears similarities to modern prosecutions of such offenses.[45] Lysander, the military commander of the Spartans, promulgated some rules in the form of superior orders (*latu sensu* superior responsibility) that were to be followed before, during, and after the armed conflict between the Athenians and the Spartans in Greece.[46] In 405 B.C., an armed conflict broke out between the Athenians and the Spartans over two lands, Lampascus and Aegospotami,[47] which led to Lysander occupying Lampascus through naval combat. The naval combat resulted in the capture of unlawful combatants, and Lysander decided to establish a criminal tribunal to prosecute them.[48] The Spartans' deliberations in the tribunal used language strikingly similar to modern texts on superior responsibility (the forces were committing or about to commit such crimes).[49] Consequently, the unlawful Athenian combatants were accused of "reproaching for illegal acts already committed and for those acts which they had been determined to commit, contrary to law, when victors at sea."[50] The tribunal ultimately decided to slice off their hands, including those of their military commander, Philocles, for issuing unlawful orders and betraying the Greeks.[51]

A similar concept of superior responsibility is also narrated in the battle mentioned above. When the Spartan military commander, Lysander, killed the Persian ambassadors, he offered two of his soldiers to the King of Persia as a reciprocal gesture, acknowledging that he had violated the law of men.[52] However, the King of Persia

44 See Sect. 2.4.1.

45 Bassiouni 2011, p. 530. See also Philipson 1911, p. 60; McCormack 1997, p. 241.

46 Maridakis 1952, p. 1.

47 Ibid., pp. 3–7.

48 Ibid.

49 Rome Statute of the International Criminal Court, 17 July 1998, 2187 U.N.T.S. 3 (entered into force 1 July 2002), http://untreaty.un.org/cod/icc/statute/romefra.htm [hereinafter Rome Statute], Article 28.

50 Maridakis 1952.

51 Ibid.

52 Lanni 2008, pp. 469–489.

responded: “[I] would not behave like the Spartans, who, by murdering the ambassadors of a foreign power, had broken the law of all men, and that he would not be guilty himself of the same crime they had commit.”[53] Conversely, and by analogy, this implied that, notwithstanding the immunity offered by the law of men, a military commander could be prosecuted for the crimes of others, somehow aligning with the vicarious liability of modern superior responsibility. In conclusion, the doctrine of superior responsibility in antiquity has been the subject of considerable attention and can be considered a key reference for modern understandings of the doctrine. Among legal historians, the general consensus is that the responsibilities of superiors and their potential liability trace back to these early periods.

Before proceeding to discuss Islamic law, it is important to note that the concept of superior responsibility can also be witnessed in the history of the Holy Roman Empire, which precedes the emergence of Islam. Under the auspices of the Roman Empire, two promulgations regulated soldiers’ conduct during warfare: the *Strategica* and *Ex Ruffo Leges Militares*.[54] While the former refers to the Articles of War, the latter is a disciplinary code designed by Ruffus.[55] The *Ex Ruffo Leges Militares* (the Ruffus Code) explicitly refers to the orders of superiors and strict subordination.[56] It states: “If any person, in war, commits an act that is forbidden by his commander, or fails to execute a command, he shall be punished with death, even if his mission is successfully accomplished.”[57] This Article was drafted following an execution carried out by Manilius Torquatus, who sentenced his son—also his subordinate—to death for violating the order of his superior, his father. Ultimately, unlike religious commands, under the rules of contemporary ICL, superior orders do not constitute a valid defense for subordinates when the orders in question are unlawful.[58]

[53] Ibid.

[54] Brand 1968, pp. 195–196.

[55] Ibid. Some historians have suggested that Ruffus may have been a fictional character rather than a real person in Ancient Greece.

[56] Ibid., pp. 163–165.

[57] Ibid., p. 159.

[58] I shall discuss superior orders further in the following chapter.

2.3 Islamic Superior Responsibility: The Intersectionality Between International Law and Religion

2.3.1 *Prolegomenon to Islam*

Islamic law has often—erroneously—been criticized for being puritanical, both in general and specifically in relation to its rules of war and their justifications.[59] To date, within the context of modern acts of aggression and/or terrorism, most orientalists have depicted the Islamic Law of War (ILoW) as an act of aggression.[60] As Firestone asserts, this characterization is empirically imprecise: "Islam is perhaps the most misunderstood religion to the West."[61] This misconception is largely connected with the actions of extremist and radicalized religious groups and militias,[62] where political agendas are carried out through terrorism,[63] rather than to the peaceful forms of proselytization promoted through the Prophet's revelations and ordered by Allah.[64] This misunderstanding is, to some extent, justified given the perplexing theological exegesis of ILoW and the mischaracterization of its hermeneutic corollary to the *Qur'an* (such as the Prophet's sayings), which were not always meticulously scrutinized and handled.[65]

While the vast majority of orientalists have conceptualized ILoW as atrocious in the context of armed conflict, the direct sources for the rules of war—the *Qur'an*, the *Sunnah* (Prophet's teachings and practices), *Ijma* (consensus), and *Qiyas* (analogical reasoning)—suggest otherwise.[66] The following *Qur'anic* verse summarizes the justifications for defensive war and the prohibition of aggression, which are often misunderstood in the above-mentioned conceptualization. The verse instructs Muslims to "not fight them until you invite them to Islam; and do not commence combat until they initiate it; and if they initiate, do not respond violently until they have killed one of our soldiers; and when this happens to confront them and ask them, 'Is there not a better recourse than this?'"[67]

In another pertinent example from the *Qur'an*, Allah orders the Prophet, as the Muslim military commander, not to initiate aggression: "Fight in the way of Allah

---

[59] McCormack 1997, p. 242.

[60] See, generally, Nafziger and Walton 2003.

[61] Firestone 1999, p. 13.

[62] E.g., ISIS, Houthis, and sectarian armed conflicts.

[63] Van Aarde 2018, pp. 3–4. See also, generally, Al-Badr 1425 AH, pp. 51–62; Bassiouni 2013; Weeramantry 1988; Boisard 1987.

[64] Nafziger and Walton 2003.

[65] Abou El Fadl 2017, pp. 1–2.

[66] For instance, ibid., p. 9: "[F]ailing to appreciate the role of context and contingency in the Islamic jurisprudential tradition has led to persistent misunderstandings of Islamic law in the contemporary age and especially, the Islamic classical tradition on war." See also, generally, Donner 1991.

[67] The *Qur'an*, at 2:190, https://quran.com/search?query=not+fight+them+invite+them&language=0&translation=0. All subsequent references are to this edition.

against those who fight against you but begin not hostilities. Allah loveth not aggressors."[68] Moreover, Allah said: "And one who makes aggression upon you, attack him in like manner as he attacked you."[69] The *Qur'anic* text thus emphasizes the rules governing the conduct of military commanders, who must abide by humanitarian rules. This includes the responsibility to prevent, repress, or punish violations committed by their subordinates.

2.3.2 The Resurgence of Islam and the Islamic Law of War

In brief, Islam emerged during the mid-life of Muhammed[70] (the Prophet) in the year A.D. 610, in Mecca.[71] Home to the *Ka'ba* (the holy house), Mecca was primarily populated by idolaters—a clan called the *Quraysh*. When the *Qur'an* was first conveyed to the Prophet through the archangel Gabriel (*Jibril*) in a secluded cave that the Prophet often visited to reflect, he was appointed as the superior of the Muslims, in addition to his prophetic obligations.[72] However, the *Qur'an* was not revealed all at once. Rather, individual chapters (*Surahs*) were recited to the Prophet before, during, or after incidents that occurred during his prophecy. As the Prophet's role grew, the Quraysh began to feel concerned about his increasing influence in Mecca, which began to clash with the idolaters' concerns about their own status in the city.[73] Fears emerged that members of the Quraysh might become seditionists; it was feared that if they followed the Prophet, the Quraysh idolaters would face economic ruin, with Islam taking over their wealth.[74] Concurrently with Muhammed's prophecy, the moral and physical persecution of the Prophet and his followers began.

This peaceful expression of delivering Allah's message, alongside the polarization of idolaters in response to this message, had significant repercussions. On one occasion, the Prophet found himself 'encircled' by a group of non-believers, who attempted to attack and kill him. When the Prophet's friend, Abu Bakr, approached to save him, he asked: "Would you kill a man for saying Allah is my Lord?"[75]

The Prophet's relentless persecution by the idolators (including Quraysh) led to his forced emigration to Medina, 280 miles from Mecca. The Quraysh nonetheless found ways to continue persecuting the Prophet even in Medina, prompting the Jewish inhabitants of the city to attempt to persecute him.[76] As their superior, the Prophet

[68] Ibid.

[69] Ibid., 2:191.

[70] The Prophet Muhammed received the Divine afflatus at the age of forty.

[71] See Al-Dawoody 2017. See also, generally, Watt 2018, pp. 52–60.

[72] This assignment (as a superior) is comparable to the modern norm of superior responsibility, where the term encompasses both military commanders and civilian leaders.

[73] Nafziger and Walton 2003, pp. 2–3.

[74] Ibid.

[75] Al-Dawoody 2011, pp. 267–269.

[76] Nafziger and Walton 2003, pp. 4–5.

had an obligation to protect the Muslims who had emigrated with him, as did the latter toward him, deriving this obligation from the *Qur'an*.[77] In sum, like any prophet in the Abrahamic religions, the Prophet's life was marked by numerous persecutions, the full extent of which cannot be covered here. I shall therefore continue to examine Allah's orders and the Prophet's revelations, which are reminiscent of the modern understanding of superior responsibilities and orders.

Tangentially, it is important to note that, as part of the Abrahamic tradition, Islamic law presents an unparalleled system of punishment, distinct from positive law, owing to its celestial origin (legality vs morality). With that in mind, *religious* Muslims must demonstrate allegiance not only to potential terrestrial judgment, such as *lex talionis* (retribution or "an eye for an eye"),[78] but also to divine judgment in the promised land. Unlike crimes under positive law, if an individual sins he or she will be held accountable on Judgment Day. However, this moral fear of judgment does not automatically imply that Islamic law lacks criminal prosecutions for sinful behavior. Instead, this fear increases the burden of proof for moral behavior, including military personnel. If they were not held accountable by the state (or their superior in the case of armed conflict), they would be held responsible on Judgment Day.[79]

In light of this unique mechanism of holding perpetrators accountable through moral accountability, at the outset, ILoW did not typically involve *mundane* criminal prosecutions of either superiors or subordinates, except in certain cases where military commanders were isolated on account of their violation of Islamic law.[80] Rather, ILoW is primarily concerned with divine commands and the Prophet's revelations, to which Muslims, including military personnel, are bound. Disobeying these commands could therefore result in moral violations (iniquities) for which individuals would be held accountable on Judgment Day, which is considered more serious than mundane prosecutions by religious Muslims.[81]

---

[77] *Qur'an*, 3:144.

[78] Retribution is the Islamic law of punishment, which can be compared to the principle of "an eye for an eye." In this sense, the Prophet once asserted: "If Fatimah [my daughter] stole, I would cut off her hand." Sunan Ibn Majah, The Chapters on Legal Punishments, Hadith, p. 2546, https://sunnah.com/ibnmajah:2547.

[79] *Qur'an*, 22:69.

[80] Abou El Fadl 2017, pp. 8–9.

[81] Cf. ibid., p. 7. According to Abou El Fadl, he uses the role of an executioner as an example to demonstrate the outcome of disobeying orders. He states that: "[M]ost jurists agreed that the state has the right to fire or otherwise punish…for failing to perform [moral job], but at the same time, most jurists agreed that obeying orders against his/her conscience means that the executioner has committed a sin for which he/she will be held accountable in the Hereafter."

2.3.3 *Jihad as a Form of a Superior's Order to Self-Defense (Islamic War)*

In addition to mundane Islamic values and the normative obligations governing individuals' interactions, the *Qur'anic* text also contains several rules of war (*jus in bello*) and justifications for resorting to war (*jus ad bellum*) against non-believers, which has, unfortunately, been referred to as Jihad in modern times.[82] Given the resurgence of extremist groups acting aggressively in the name of Allah, the concept of Jihad has become one of the most controversial religious concept in the modern world, even within scholarship on ILoW.[83] Accordingly, the term Jihad has been frequently conceptualized as a bloody, heinous act of aggression, now often associated with acts of terrorism committed by individuals referred to as Jihadists.[84] By definition, however, Jihad is a multifaceted concept aimed at fostering the good and praiseworthy state of mind that a Muslim (or non-Muslim) may seek to attain.[85] In Islamic law and practice, both literally and tautologically, the term Jihad can refer to a variety of actions, including seeking education; defending one's neighbors from trespassers; caring for the destitute and orphans; practicing religion; and lastly, fighting in a war for self-defense.[86] However, the misconception of this concept has led to its confusion with the latter example—unlawful aggression carried out by radicalized groups. Moreover, the misinterpretations in Western [Islamic] scholarship have led some scholars to conclude that Jihad automatically means resorting to war.[87]

According to scholars of classical Islamic theology, within the context of armed conflict, Jihad refers to self-defense, along with the other characteristics noted above. To this end, Muslims are strictly prohibited from taking up arms except in self-defense.[88] On this point, Professor Khalid Abou El Fadl argues that: "Jihad cannot be a struggle pursued unrighteous or for ungodly reasons, and a struggle that is

---

[82] See Naqvi 1974, pp. 25–26. See also Firuzabadi 1933, p. 286. (For the *Qur'anic* use of Jihad in the sense of exertion, see the *Qur'an*, VI: 108 and XXI: 7.) See Kadduri 1984, pp. 164–173.

[83] Al-Dawoody 2015, pp. 30–32.

[84] Van Aarde 2018, p. 2.

[85] Abou El Fadl 2017.

[86] Ibid., p. 9.

[87] Abou El Fadl 2017. *Contra* Blank *The Use of Force to Prevent Recurrence of Conflict: Where Are the Limits of Self-Defense?*, 86 Brook. 2021, pp. 32–33. https://brooklynworks.brooklaw.edu/blr/vol86/iss1/1, citing Weiss and Hassan, Here's What the Trump Administration is Really Plotting in Syria, *Daily Beast* (4 April 2018), https://www.thedailybeast.com/is-trump-serious-about-syria-do-we-stay-do-we-go-and-who-pays https://perma.cc/K26A-ETKK; Mona Yacoubian, A New U.S. Strategy Will Keep American Troops in Syria, U.S. INST. OF PEACE (2018), https://www.usip.org/publications/2018/01/new-usstrategy-will-keep-american-troops-syria [https://perma.cc/6NSJ-W3NF]. (At an even broader level, the United States also seeks to "counter both the Assad regime and Iranian influence", possibly by using US military outposts in Syria to "monitor the movement and repositioning of the jihadists, and also interdict Iranian Revolutionary Guard Corps plans to establish a direct land corridor from Iraq to Syria." This also seems to be the same with the newer leader of Syria, Ahmed Alshar'a.)

[88] Abu al-Tayyib bin Hasan bin 'Ali al-Hayyinia al-Qanuji al-Bukhari 1985, pp. 198–202, 205, 211.

immoral or unjust cannot be a Jihad."[89] This helps to explain why Islam is the most misunderstood religion by Westerners, because these forms of Jihad were seen as values and ethics in Islamic law, rather than as forms of Jihad in the sense of self-defense.[90] He further asserts that: "The *Qur'an* asserts that if it had not been for divine benevolence, many mosques, churches, synagogues, and homes would have been destroyed through violence, but Allah mercifully intervenes to put out the fires of war, and save human beings from their follies."[91] Supporting this assertion, the *Qur'anic* text states that: "Permission is now given to those who have been attacked to take up arms because they have suffered aggression, and Allah has the power to aid them."[92] According to the declarations of the Prophet, though, taking up arms essentially constitutes a taboo act of aggression unless it is an act of retaliation (self-defense).[93] Within the context of modern LoAC, therefore, the *casus belli* of ILoW stems from the concept of defensive war rather than an act of aggression.

Furthermore, according to the Prophet's sayings, which are essentially revelations of Allah's will, Jihad encompasses several levels in terms of moral necessity.[94] The highest form of Jihad is "to struggle to know oneself and cleanse oneself of moral faults,"[95] meaning that, in all aspects of life, an individual's degree of allegiance to morality and ethics forms the highest degree of Jihad. In contrast, the lowest degree of Jihad involves resorting to war as an act of self-defense.[96] Within this framework, the *last-resort* Jihad is the sole justification for war in Islam, where a Muslim must first become a jihadist with him/herself.

Despite being restricted to military operations, these rules were in fact associated with many pre-war governances.[97] In other words, resorting to war under ILoW is not a strife-armed conflict; it is contingent on an invitation to comply with Allah's commands and orders. Most importantly, however, such an invitation must be sought only after expressing the religion peacefully through the Prophet Muhammed.[98] Accordingly, this divine governance helps to explain why all prophets, including Muhammed, faced persecution. When viewed through the lens of the superior responsibility framework, a superior's order to invade or bomb a country constitutes an unlawful act (an iniquity) and is both condemnable and prosecutable and condemned under the principles of ILoW.

[89] Abou El Fadl 2017, p. 11.
[90] Cf. Firestone 1999.
[91] Abou El Fadl 2017, p. 10.
[92] Ibid.
[93] Ibid.
[94] Bonney 2004, pp. 91–92; Al-Badr 1425 AH, pp. 6–12.
[95] Abou El Fadl 2017.
[96] Bonney 2004, pp. 6, 12.
[97] Abou El Fadl 2017, p. 12.
[98] Ibid.

2.3.4 The Islamic Military System and Jus in Bello

After the death of the Prophet Muhammed, his closest companion and second superior, Abu Bakr—First Caliph—delivered an oratory to the Muslims that closely mirrors the transference of religious values and morality into legal governance in modern times. His speech also exemplifies the superior–subordinate relationship element, wherein a superior assumes the responsibility to instruct his or her subordinates on the humanitarian principles inherent in a military hierarchy.[99] Abu Bakr said:

> O people! I was elected as your governor and Caliph though I am not the best of you. If I do good deeds, help me; if I do bad deeds, show me the right way. Honesty is reliability. Telling lies is betrayal. Insha'Allah [God Willing], the weakest one of you will be the strongest one of you in my eye until I surrender him his right. Insha'Allah [God Willing], the strongest one of you will be the weakest one of you in my eye until I remove from him the rights of others. O people! Do not give up fighting in the way of Allah. Know it very well that a nation that gives up jihad will be servile. Obey me as long as I obey Allah and His Messenger; if I do not obey Allah and His Messenger, do not obey me. I ask forgiveness for me and you from Allah.[100]

Following the Prophet's death, Abu Bakr played a key role in supervising the soldiers, issuing humanitarian rules that closely align with modern *jus in bello* principles. As superior orders, the violation of these orders would be considered a prosecutable offense. Addressing the military, he declared:

> Stop, O people, that I may give you ten rules for guidance on the battlefield. Do not commit treachery or deviate from the right path. You must not mutilate dead bodies; do not kill a woman, a child, or an aged man; do not cut down fruitful trees; do not destroy inhabited areas; do not slaughter any of the enemies' sheep, cow or camel except for food; do not burn date palms, nor inundate them; do not embezzle (e.g. no misappropriation of booty or spoils of war) nor be guilty of cowardliness…You are likely to pass by people who have devoted their lives to monastic services; leave them alone[101]

In this regard, the Islamic military (including its commander) is prohibited from engaging in acts of violence, even in the context of a defensive war. In other words, even when fighting in self-defense, Muslim forces are required to adhere to humanitarian principles, to the extent that losing a battle is considered forgivable if adherence to these rules was the only reason for the conquest.[102] The rules issued by Abu Bakr were not unprecedented; rather, they are grounded in Allah's commandments and the Prophet's teachings on the conduct of defensive warfare, as noted earlier. A notable application of these rules occurred during the Battle of Uhud, where the Muslim military suffered defeat as a result of their violation of their military commander's instructions, as I shall discuss further on.

---

[99] Fenrick 1999.

[100] Ajijola 1978, p. 43.

[101] Ibid.

[102] *Qur'an*, 2:217; 17:33; 4:92.

The structure of the Islamic military is largely comparable to that of modern times. As the chief military commander, the Prophet was responsible for appointing military commanders operating under his supervision and command. Criminal prosecutions of violators of the law of war and the orders of Allah and the Prophet were, at the time, considered a form of divine sign and Allah's will to bring about the failure of disobedient soldiers during combat.[103] For example, one of the most predominant wars lost by Muslims during the Prophet's lifetime was the Battle of Uhud;[104] this was the second war during his life, in which fifty Muslim archers disobeyed their military commander's orders.[105] The battled commenced as follows: the Prophet instructed the military archers and their military commander to remain in their positions until he ordered them to move.[106] Drawn by the prospect of victory and end of the battle, however, the archers disobeyed and vacated their post.[107] Meanwhile, the opposing forces were hiding behind the mountain, waiting for the Muslim archers to descend. Once the archers descended from the hills, the enemy launched an attack, killing them. In response, Allah revealed the following verse, affirming that disobedience to orders—within the framework of religious superior responsibility—was the reason for His will to allow their defeat:

> And Allah did indeed fulfill His Promise to you when you were killing them (your enemy) with His Permission; until (the moment) you lost your courage and fell to disputing about the order, and disobeyed after He showed you (of the booty) which you love. Among you are some that desire this world and some that desire the Hereafter. Then He made you flee from them (your enemy), that He might test you. But surely, He forgave you, and Allah is Most Gracious to the believers.[108]

Regarding humanitarian orders for civilians and children, the Prophet, acting as a superior as well as the messenger, instructed his soldiers: "[n]ot to kill women, children, or the elderly, not to cut down ripe trees, burn buildings, or kill cattle or sheep except to eat."[109] He went on to command: "Do not burn palm trees and do not flood vegetation. Do not pillage or betray."[110] Moreover, the enlistment of child soldiers under the age of fifteen was prohibited in Islam.[111] If a Muslim superior ordered the recruitment of child soldiers, such an order was considered unlawful and thus prosecutable.[112] Abd Allah ibn Umar witnessed this scenario and declared:

> Allah's Apostle called me to present myself in front of him on the eve of the battle of Uḥud, while I was fourteen years of age at that time, and he did not allow me to take part in that

[103] Sahih Bukhari [….].

[104] For more details about this battle, see, generally, Afifi 2018, p. 114.

[105] Historical narratives of this war remain imprecise with respect to how the archers disobeyed their military commander.

[106] Nafziger and Walton 2003, pp. 8–9.

[107] Ibid.

[108] *Qur'an*, 3:152.

[109] Ibn Qudama 1348, p. 507.

[110] Ibid.

[111] Al-Dawoody and Murphy 2019, pp. 561–562.

[112] Ibid.

> battle, but he called me in front of him on the eve of the battle of the Trench when I was fifteen years old, and he allowed me [to join the battle]. Nafi', said, "I went to Umar bin Abdul Aziz who was Caliph at that time and related the above narration to him. He said, 'This age [15] is the limit between childhood and manhood', and wrote to his governors to give salaries to those who reached the age of fifteen."[113]

Perhaps the most predominant historical event that appears to indirectly reflect the modern-day concept of superior responsibility is the removal of Khalid Ibn Al-Waleed's command over the Islamic military. Islamic historians offer three distinct explanations for his isolation. The first narrative justified his isolation on the grounds that he was one of the bravest military commanders in Islamic history, and Muslims were struck by his status.[114] The Caliph at the time, Omar Ibn Al-Khattab, therefore ordered his isolation, fearing that he would exert a strong influence on the Muslims due to his bravery and consequently distract them from their duties toward Allah and religion. The second narrative justifies the isolation on account of the transferal of the position of Caliph from Abu Bakr to Omar Ibn Al-Khattab, both of whom took different approaches to military appointments and supervision. According to this narrative, this policy shift led the latter Caliph to isolate Ibn Al-Waleed because the former Caliph granted Ibn Al-Waleed complete authority with respect to military commandment—thus rendering him a *de facto* superior. The third narrative, which I, for one, find most accurate, suggests that Ibn Al-Waleed was isolated owing to violations of Islamic military customs, as his bravery went hand in hand with an exceptionally rigorous approach to warfare.[115] In the context of holding superiors accountable, another relevant event is the invasion of Samarkand.[116] At the time, Omar Ibn Al-Abdul-Aziz served as the Caliph (Muslim superior) in Damascus. In this capacity, with the aim of universalizing Islam, he appointed a military commander, Qutaybah ibn Muslim, to enter the country and invite its people to join Islam.[117] In terms of legitimate universalization within the context of Islamic law, ILoW requires that a superior and their military may enter non-Muslim territory only after first inviting the inhabitants to accept Islam. Alternatively, the inhabitants may choose to continue practicing their faith while paying taxes to the Islamic state in exchange for protection and public services.[118] The third and final resort would be to wage war if their actions constitute aggression against the Islamic military. The Islamic military's failure to follow these protocols would be deemed a violation of ILoW and a defiance of Allah's commands and the Prophet's sayings.

Qutaybah ibn Muslim entered Samarkand without respecting these protocols. A young man from Samarkand traveled to Damascus, home of the Muslim Caliph. He complained to him that the invasion was in violation of ILoW, because a prosecutable order had been issued by the Caliph against the military commander—Qutaybah

---

[113] See www.sahih-bukhari.com/Pages/Bukhari_3_48.php (accessed May 2021).

[114] Al Sallabi 2019.

[115] Ibid.

[116] For the full details of this invasion, see Dawod 2014.

[117] Ibid.

[118] Abou El Fadl 2017, pp. 7–8.

ibn Muslim. The Caliph ordered that a judge be appointed to preside over a trial to determine whether Qutaybah should return and carry out the proper protocols before the people of Samarkand; otherwise, the invasion would be deemed an act of aggression and thus a violation of ILoW.[119] After listening to both parties, ibn Muslim testified that he had entered Samarkand without prior warning. The judge ruled as follows:

> I rule that all armies of Muslims in this country should get out of this country and give it back to its people and give them the opportunity to prepare for war, and then make them choose between Islam, tribute or war. If they chose war then we will fight. Muslims will get out of Samarkand without anything just as they entered and deliver the city to its people, and that is the application of the law of Almighty Allah and the Sunnah of our Prophet Muhammad peace be upon him.[120]

In line with the judge's decision, the military commander returned home. Owing to the violation, the Caliph ordered his withdrawal from Samarkand and removed him from his position as commander of the Islamic military. Islamic resort to war can thus be summarized in four key points:

1. Combat in the way of Allah is synonymous with armed self-defense and aligns with Islam's broader preaching mission.
2. Universalization: Muslims are prohibited from using force and must preach Islam only through peaceful means during the process of universalization.
3. War is permissible only when an attack against Muslims is imminent.
4. If a superior order is considered taboo within the context of the *Qur'anic* text (and the Prophet's sayings), then, *a fortiori*, it is unlawful under positive law.

2.3.5 The Concept of Martyrdom as a Reward for Jihad Based on a Superior's Order

The final part of this section addresses the concept of martyrdom in Islam and its relation to superior orders. Martyrdom is most commonly understood as the granting of access to Heaven in the Hereafter to any Muslim[121] who dies for the sake of Allah (including all forms of Jihad).[122] The concept has nonetheless been criticized, particularly in relation to ILoW, in the event that a Muslim ruler declares war through a superior order rather than following divine will, which results in Muslims losing

[119] Dawod 2014.

[120] Ibid.

[121] Islamic jurists are not in agreement with respect to whether this status can also apply to non-Muslims.

[122] Islamic jurists divide this concept into two categories: "[M]inor martyrdom (al-shahada al-sughra) involves losing one's life in the course of a natural disaster or an act of Allah while major martyrdom (al-shahada al-kubra) involves sacrificing one's life defending one's life, loved ones, or property or being killed in cause of God." See Abou El Fadl 2017, p. 7, citing Abu al-Tayyib bin Hasan bin 'Ali al-Hayyinia al-Qanuji al-Bukhari 1985, pp. 179–214.

their lives owing to the ruler's command.[123] This granting of heaven in the Hereafter (martyrdom) is referenced in numerous verses of the *Qur'an*; however, three from three different *Surahs* are prominently featured in relation to a superior's orders during self-defense (in the way of God). *Surah Al-Taubah*, verse 111 provides:

> Allah hath purchased of the believers their persons and their goods; for theirs (in return) is the garden (of Paradise): they fight in His cause, and slay and are slain: a promise binding on Him in truth, through the Law, the Gospel, and the Quran: and who is more faithful to his covenant than Allah? then rejoice in the bargain which ye have concluded: that is the achievement supreme.[124]

In *Surah Al-Baqara* (The Cow), verse 154, we read: "[And] say not of those who are slain in the way of Allah: 'They are dead.' Nay, they are living, though ye perceive (it) not."[125] The final *Surah* relevant to this matter is the Family of Imran, specifically verses 157, 158, 169, 170, and 171, which express the following:

> 157. And if you are killed or die in the Way of Allah, forgiveness and mercy from Allah are far better than all that they amass (of worldly wealth's).158. And whether you die, or are killed, verily, unto Allah you shall be gathered…Think not of those who are killed in the Way of Allah as dead. Nay, they are alive, with their Lord, and they have provision. 170. They rejoice in what Allah has bestowed upon them of His Bounty and rejoice for the sake of those who have not yet joined them, but are left behind (not yet martyred) that on them no fear shall come, nor shall they grieve. 171. They rejoice in a Grace and a Bounty from Allah, and that Allah will not waste the reward of the believers.[126]

As conceptualized here with respect to superior orders in Islam, such orders may or may not entail criminally culpability, depending on whether they are lawful or unlawful in Islam. For example, if a soldier obeys his superior for the sake of God, he may be granted the status of martyrdom if his compliance with such an order results in his death during armed conflict.[127] Conversely, he may also be awarded the status of martyrdom if he disobeys a sinful order by his superior.[128] Both the superior and the subordinate are therefore bound to follow only lawful Islamic orders, and compliance with such orders may earn them the status of martyrdom in the Hereafter. Conversely, to guarantee martyrdom, these orders must not be geared toward an act of aggression, as noted earlier in this section.[129]

Based on the historical narratives of ILoW, we could therefore confer that the doctrine of superior responsibility was not meticulously codified within the framework of modern prosecutions of superiors. However, through both divine and superior orders, ILoW played a significant role in emphasizing the responsibilities borne

[123] Ibn al-Nahhas, *Mashari' al-Ashwaq*, vol. 2, pp. 1022–1023. See also Khalid 1971, pp. 71–72; al-Biqa'iyyi 2002, al-Istisshhad bi Ayat al-Jihad, p. 319; Ibn al-Nahhas, *Mashari' al-Ashwaq*, vol. 2, pp. 593–635; Abou El Fadl 2017, p. 6.

[124] *Qur'an*, 9:111.

[125] Ibid., 1:154.

[126] Ibid., 2: 157, 158, 169, 170, and 171.

[127] Abou El Fadl 2017, pp. 5–8.

[128] Ibid.

[129] Ibid.

by superiors (and even non-superiors) with respect to unlawful orders, including the imperative to protect individuals during armed conflict. These responsibilities can be aligned with superior orders in modern warfare, as reflected in the supervisory responsibilities listed in instruments such as the Lieber Code and the Hague and Geneva Conventions on humanitarian law, and the statutory interpretations of international criminal courts statutes.

In addition, the spectrum of Islamic superior orders is comparable to the concept of superior responsibility in its *latu sensu*, where a superior is held equally responsible for issuing an unlawful order (direct liability) and for failing to execute their duty to prevent subordinates from committing wrongful acts (vicarious liability). Based on the historical account of Islamic law set out above, which dates back to A.D. 610, there is clearly a remarkable similarity between Islamic law concerning the accountability of superiors and modern convictions of superior responsibility made on the same grounds—failure to execute supervisory duties appropriately. This failure to execute supervisory duties is framed through the religious concept of a superior's personal (spiritual) responsibility, "for which he would have to answer before Allah ('heavy reckoning,' 'black matter')."[130] In other words, this concept could be reflected in the Latin maxim "*sed sub Deo et sub lege, quia lex facit regem*", which deprives the superior's orders of divine legitimacy.[131]

To summarize, therefore, the narratives from antiquity exerted a remarkable historical influence on the development of superior responsibility in both the middle and modern ages, as I shall discuss hereafter. Moreover, from this historical context, one can extrapolate a broad definition of superior responsibility that encapsulates both superior orders and the narrower concept of a superior's liability for the crimes of their subordinates.

2.4 Superior Responsibility in the Middle Ages: Narratives and Codification Efforts

Particularly in Europe and Britain, the Middle Ages witnessed the development of extensive literature and regulations describing the concept of superior responsibility within the context of warfare. As previously noted, the notion of superior responsibility evolved in modern history, beginning as a domestic military concept (under the Lieber Code),[132] before being expanded into a supranational concept (according to the Yamashita Standard),[133] and ultimately becoming an internationally recognized

[130] Meron 1993, p. 72.

[131] Ibid.

[132] What I wish to underscore here is that the Hague and the Geneva Laws derived the concept of superior responsibility from the American Military Code (Lieber).

[133] The supranational stage refers to the border-crossing (extraterritorial) application of the concept of superior responsibility set out in the Lieber Code in the criminal trial of General Yamashita in the aftermath of WWII.

criminal mode of liability. It began as a domestic concept owing to its application within the confines of individual states and courts-martial, particularly through the Lieber Code. In the subsequent stage, it gained supranational status, extending beyond US borders to the Nuremberg and Tokyo Military Tribunals. Ultimately, it evolved into a fully-fledged international criminal mode of liability embedded in the statutes of *ad hoc* tribunals and the ICC. This transition from national to supranational and, finally, international status entailed significant complications regarding the legal nature and applicability of the doctrine. Considering this transition, examining the concept of superior responsibility during the Middle Ages is a crucial standpoint for understanding its legal characterization by getting to grips with the relevant normative complexities and obstacles to applicability.

2.4.1 European and British Attempts Concerning Superior Responsibility

In 1474, the Holy Roman Empire established a criminal tribunal similar to modern criminal tribunals, namely, the Breisach War Crimes Tribunal. Given its establishment on the basis of multilateral orders from Germany, Switzerland, and Alsace, and by direct order of the Archduke of Austria, it displays a clear relation to modern criminal tribunals.[134] The military commander in question, Peter von Hagenbach, was brought to trial for war crimes committed by his subordinates as a result of his failure to supervise them appropriately.[135] Although his conviction was made on the grounds of superior responsibility, he argued that the crimes had been committed under the orders of Duke Charles of Burgundy. The tribunal nonetheless proceeded to convict him as a Knight and sentenced him to death.[136] It is important to note that this criminal trial was grounded in a domestic standard of superior responsibility for an omission, which later developed into an international standard.[137]

This criminal trial was regulated by a law issued by Charles VII, King of France, in 1439.[138] The law comprised various ordinances regulating the conduct of warfare in general, and the responsibilities of military commanders in particular. Regarding superior responsibility, King Charles issued the following ordinance governing both the duties of superiors and the acts for which they could be prosecuted. The ordinance provides that:

> The king orders that each captain or lieutenant be held responsible for the abuses, ills and offences [*sic*] committed by members of his company, and that as soon as he receives any complaint concerning any such misdeed or abuse, he bring [*sic*] the offender to justice so that the said offender be punished in a manner commensurate with his offence, according

---

[134] Meloni 2010, p. 33. See also Parks 1973, pp. 4–5; Burnett 1985, pp. 78–79.

[135] Ibid.

[136] Ibid.

[137] Meloni 2010, p. 72.

[138] Green 1999, p. 283.

> to these Ordinances. If he fails to do so or covers up the misdeed or delays taking action [*sic*], or if, because of his negligence or otherwise, the offender escapes and thus evades punishment, the captain shall be deemed responsible for the offence as if he had committed it himself and be punished in the same way as the offender would have been.[139]

A century later, in 1625, Hugo de Groot (Grotius), widely recognized as the father of international law, articulated a stark interpretation of the concept that anticipates the modern understanding of superior responsibility, wherein military commanders were to be held liable for offenses committed during wartime by their subordinates. In *De Jure Belli ac Pacis*, on the liability of superiors, he asserts that: "We must accept the principle that he who knows of a crime, and is able and bound to prevent it but fails to do so, himself commits a crime."[140] However, this assertion does not fully capture the derivative nature of superior responsibility (namely, vicarious liability) because, in Grotius's formulation, the *crime* may refer to the omission itself rather than the crimes committed by others, as per the modern understanding of superior responsibility.

Subsequently, Grotius issued another text that is strictly aligned with the modern structure of superior responsibility. Here, he asserts that: "A community, or its ruler, may be held responsible *for* the crime of a subject who was able to prevent a crime but did not do so…therefore, he must have not only knowledge of it but also have the opportunity to prevent it"[141] (emphasis added). In his words, a ruler of a community may be held responsible for the crimes of his or her subordinates, provided that they had the opportunity to prevent those crimes in the first place but chose not to execute their duties to do so. He also cited the *mens rea* element of this doctrine—that is, actual knowledge of the crimes or constructive knowledge, where a superior's culpability is presumed as long as he/she is assigned the duty to supervise.[142] Therefore, as noted earlier, omission is only a proxy, which can be proven by circumstantial evidence.[143]

Unlike Alberico Gentili,[144] Grotius did not anticipate the international status later ascribed to individual criminal responsibility by modern international criminal trials. However, his writings are regarded as foundational principles in modern international law, particularly with respect to individual liability at the international level.[145] That being said, Grotius's remarkable writings, particularly his work on superior responsibility, specifically addressed individual conduct within the framework of state practice, thus reflecting a domestic standard of superior responsibility.[146] However, in

[139] Ibid., p. 283.

[140] Grotius 1964, p. 523.

[141] Ibid.

[142] Neff 2012, pp. 292–293.

[143] Damaška 2001.

[144] Alberico Gentili disagrees with Grotius with respect to the question of individual criminal responsibility versus state responsibility for the wrongful acts of its citizen. Meron 1993, p. 68.

[145] Meloni 2010, p. 34.

[146] Ibid.

international law, Grotius's *De Jure Belli ac Pacis* served as a key source for establishing legal standards to prosecute individuals internationally, moving beyond the principle of state sovereignty.[147]

Other writers in the Middle Ages also emphasized the role of superiors. For example, Alberico Gentili described the role of the superior *vis-à-vis* soldiers' crimes as follows: "[s]everity must be visited, not upon a multitude of sinners, but upon the sins of a few."[148] Cicero also asserted that: "Severity against the leaders, but generosity towards the soldiers", while Thomas More emphasized that "causing the death of the leader of the enemy, in order that in this way the harmless multitude may be spared, which is hurried into war, not of its own volition, but driven by the madness of princes."[149] Reflecting superior–subordinate roles and relationships applied in the modern understanding of superior responsibility, as described later,[150] the severity (gravity test) of a superior's failure to execute supervisory duties is proportional to the crimes of their subordinates and their consequent prosecution. This may ultimately support my theory-of-guilt proposal, which dictates vicarious liability to support superior responsibility, as opposed to personal culpability. I shall discuss this in greater detail in the next chapter.

Christine De Pizan, also known as the "mother of international law",[151] was a pioneering scholar who is often overlooked by contemporary international law scholars.[152] In the fifteenth century, she drafted military Articles of war in *The Book of Deeds of Arms and of Chivalry*,[153] a war manual presented to the Duke of Burgundy in 1410, during a period when France was embroiled in a civil war.[154] In her manual, De Pizan described the qualities required of a military commander and his responsibilities toward his subordinates, noting, importantly, that "[an] ideal military commander need not be a king or a prince but a leader with discipline and good leadership in 'training good boys.'"[155] She also argued that a just war required divine permission and could be initiated only by sovereign leaders. She sets out five lawful justifications for a just war. The first justification was "to maintain law and justice; the second is to counteract evildoers who befoul, injure, and oppress the land and the people; and the third is to recover lands, lordships, and other things stolen or usurped for an unjust cause by other who are under the jurisdiction of the prince, the country, or its subjects; the fourth is to avenge any loss or damage incurred; the fifth is to justly take over foreign lands of lordships."[156] As per modern international

---

147 Ibid., p. 35.

148 Meron 1993, p. 73.

149 Ibid.

150 See Sect. 2.3 (on the legal characterization of superior responsibility).

151 Guerra Medici 1999, pp. 15–22.

152 Latty 2019.

153 Ibid.

154 De Pizan 2003, pp. 4–6.

155 Ibid., p. 7.

156 Ibid., p. 16.

law, any act by a sovereign leader that falls outside these justifications is deemed a prohibitable act of aggression.[157]

Navigating the chronicle of English history, as portrayed by William Shakespeare, King Henry V issued a number of rules regarding warfare during the Hundred Years' War, specifically at the Battle of Agincourt.[158] In one conversation, Shakespeare depicted the king as considering the idea of donning a disguise to assume the role of a soldier in the battle.[159] In this disguise, the king entered into a conversation with a soldier named Williams and asked him whether he thought that the king's motives for waging war were just or unjust, and whether they would lead either to his reward or damnation in the Hereafter.[160] Williams responded that it was the king's responsibility alone to shoulder the reward or damnation, depending on whether or not his motives to wage war were just.[161]

The king then developed a set of rules regarding violations of the law. Of greatest relevance to superior responsibility is the assertion that: "[I]f these men [soldiers] have defeated the laws...they have no wings to fly from God."[162] The king also emphasized the role of princes as superiors within the context of superior responsibility.

In addition, the king raised some concerns with his soldiers about the religious and legal aspects of superiors' responsibilities toward their subordinates.[163] The religious concerns stemmed from fears of "eternal damnation"[164] deriving from negligence on the part of a superior that could lead to the death of his soldiers, as emphasized in Christianity.[165] The king described these religious and legal considerations as follows: "[E]very subject's duty is the King's, but every subject's soul is his own."[166] This statement epitomizes the relationship between a superior's orders and divine commandments, highlighting the distinction between the ramifications for a subordinate of violating these mandates and the superior's own responsibility.[167]

Modern commentators have suggested that, despite its natural-law origin, King Henry's statement related to an old common law principle, albeit not entirely accurately: *respondere non-sovereign*, which is an exception to the popular tort principle of *respondeat superior*.[168] Van der Vyver explained that *respondeat superior* is

[157] Ibid.

[158] Meron 1993, pp. 64–65.

[159] Ibid.

[160] Ibid.

[161] Ibid.

[162] Ibid.

[163] Ibid.

[164] Ibid.

[165] Ibid.

[166] Ibid.

[167] See, generally, Shelling 1927, p. 97. See also O'Malley 1964, pp. 46–47.

[168] White 1913, pp. 291–292.

applied in domestic legal systems, such as in common law, as a form of civil monetary damage.[169] However, contrary to domestic systems, criminal vicarious liability does not extend to monetary damages, and the superior–subordinate relationship in such matters is governed solely by domestic law.[170] In other words, *respondeat superior* has a drastically different hierarchical structure, which falls solely under the umbrella of domestic law and monetary damage reparation systems—civil responsibility.[171] Conversely, superior responsibility (vicarious liability) applies to international crimes committed by a superior's subordinates, falling within the scope of criminal prosecutions. Figuratively, the tort principle of *respondeat superior* captures the essence of superior responsibility only with respect to its modality and premise (*i.e.*, a superior as an employer and a subordinate as an employee).[172] However, the elements of these phenomena and the applicable laws are mutually exclusive. Thus, the lack of complete accuracy in modern commentators' assertions noted earlier lies in the distinction between these two legal phenomena.

In 1621, Gustavus Adolphus, the King of Sweden, promulgated a military code composed of 150 Articles, called the *Articles of Military Lawwes to be Observed in the Warres*.[173] Following its subsequent revision by his chancellor, Axel Oxenstierna, the king eventually signed the text as a binding military code.[174] This code provided a fully-fledged judicial system for prosecuting perpetrators of war crimes, with the death penalty being applied for the highest convictions.[175] Significantly, the code set out a distinct court system to prosecute superiors, composed of and decided by military judges and an auditor.[176] Regarding superior responsibility, Article 46 of the code provides that: "No Colonel or Captaine [*sic*] shall command his souldiers [*sic*] to do any unlawful thing; which who so does, shall be punished according to the discretion of the Judges…"[177] Through the application of this code, Count Rosen, an army commander of Sweden, was relieved of his duties as a military commander because of the brutal strategies employed during the unsuccessful siege of Calvinist Londonderry, which resulted in the killing of innocent civilians.[178] Regarding the rules of warfare and military commanders' responsibilities, this military code ultimately came to serve as a reference for British and US military codes.[179]

[169] Van der Vyver 2021, p. 601.

[170] Ibid.

[171] Ibid.

[172] Ibid., p. 602. (Vicarious liability in *respondeat superior* pertains to monetary damages, while vicarious liability in superior responsibility pertains to liability for crimes.)

[173] This code was a culmination of previous codes that dealt with military operation in many regions, such as the Code of Ferdinand of Hungary (1526), parts of the famous Code of Maximilian II (1570), and sections of the Code of Maurice of Nassau (1590). See Adolphus, cited in Gross 1955, p. 356.

[174] Ögren 1996, p. 438, citing Berner 1982, pp. 1611–1632; see also Roberts 1953, 1958 (text in Annex) and Brusiin 1943.

[175] Ögren 1996.

[176] Ibid., p. 439.

[177] Ibid.

[178] Hargreaves 1970, p. 44.

[179] Sherman 1970, p. 3.

According to some modern criminal justice historians, the case of *Napoleon Bonaparte* has been retrospectively cited as a proto-example of holding a leader accountable for breaching international obligations.[180] After violating the Treaty of Fontainebleau by escaping exile in *Elba* and returning to power—leading to renewed war—Napoleon was politically declared an "Enemy and Disturber of the Peace of the World" by the Allied powers.[181] Although he was not tried before an international court, his exile to *St. Helena*[182] and the justification for it foreshadowed the notion of individual responsibility under international law.[183] While the crimes committed during his renewed rule were largely war-related, some interpretations suggest that Napoleon's breach of international agreement, combined with the conduct of his forces, could be analogized to a form of superior responsibility.[184] This symbolic condemnation supports the idea that accountability for breaches of international agreements can extend beyond war crimes, potentially encompassing human rights violations and *delicta juris gentium*, as this book later proposes.[185]

In the context of the historical analysis set out in this chapter of the chain of developments leading to the modern understanding of superior responsibility, the above-mentioned event formed a key base for modern international criminal law with respect to the prosecution of superiors.[186] That being said, in the aftermath of World War I, 1914–18, the Allied States suggested, arguably based on Napoleon's proto-example, that senior leaders who had committed international crimes during the war could be convicted of such crimes.[187] I shall return to this event in the section on superior responsibility in the modern era.

2.4.2 US Approaches to Superior Responsibility

In a key moment in American warfare history, in 1775, the Provisional Congress of Massachusetts instantiated the Swedish Articles of War, called the Massachusetts

[180] Some historians, however, argue that this trial was based on an executive act made by the Allies rather than on judicial proceedings. See His Majesty's Stationery Office 1948, pp. 18–19.

[181] Green 1995, p. 322.

[182] Ibid.

[183] Ibid.

[184] His Majesty's Stationery Office 1948, p. 24.

[185] See Chap. 3, Sect. 3.2.

[186] Ibid.

[187] See Sect. 2.4.

Articles.[188] Article Eleven of this code, which specifically concerns superior responsibility; provides that:

> Every Officer commanding, in quarters, or on a march, shall keep good order, and to the utmost of his power, redress all such abuses or disorders which may be committed by any Officer or Soldier under his command; if upon complaint made to him of Officers or Soldiers beating or otherwise ill-treating any person, or committing any kind of riots to the disquieting of the inhabitants of this Continent, he, the said commander, who shall refuse or omit to see Justice done to this offender or offenders, and reparation made to the party or parties injured, as soon as the offender's wages shall enable him or them, upon due proof thereof, be punished, as ordered by General.[189]

The Massachusetts Articles were subsequently developed into a nationwide code governing American warfare, called the American Articles of War, which continued to evolve until 1920.[190] The 1806 code provided a more detailed version of Article Eleven of the Massachusetts Articles, setting out a specific mechanism for the punishment of military commanders:

> When any commissioned officer or soldier shall be accused of a capital crime, or of having used violence, or committed any offense against the person or property of any citizen of any of the United States, such as is punishable by the known laws of the land, the commanding officer and officers of every regiment, troop, or company to which the person or persons so accused shall belong, are hereby required, upon application duly made by, or in behalf of, the party or parties injured, to use their utmost endeavors to deliver over such accused person or persons to the civil magistrate, and likewise to be aiding and assisting to the officers of justice in apprehending and securing the person or persons so accused, in order to bring him or them to trial. If any commanding officer or officers shall willfully neglect, or shall refuse upon the application aforesaid, to deliver over such accused person or persons to the civil magistrates, or to be aiding and assisting to the officers of justice in apprehending such person or persons, the officer or officers so offending shall be cashiered.[191]

One significant application of this Article can be seen in the conviction of Abraham Lincoln, who was court-martialed for his failure to control his soldiers during the

---

[188] According to Bassiouni and Meloni, many domestic laws in Europe at the time dealt with warfare and war crimes; however, the most prominent among these, which dealt with *latu sensu* superior responsibility, was the Swedish Articles of War. See Bassiouni 2011, p. 530, n. 99. The other domestic laws Bassiouni referred to are the Lieber Code. Promulgated as Instruction for the Government of the United States in the Field by Order of the Secretary of War, in Washington D.C., 24 April 1863, and approved by President Lincoln. For other similar US rules, see Rules of Land Warfare, War Dept. Doc. No. 467, Office of the Chief of Staff, approved 25 April 1914 (G.P.O. 1917); Army Field Manual 27–10, Rules of Land Warfare (1956). See also, generally, Davis 1918 (tracing the history of the first Articles of War of 1775); De Hart 1846; Winthrop 1895; *The British Manual of Military Law* 1929 (revised in 1940); German Army Regulations 1902 (revised in 1911, revised in 1935) to which the 1907 Hague Convention was appended as Annex II, quoted in Lauterpacht 1944; the 1935 version; and *The Oxford Manual on the Laws and Customs of War on Land* 1880; Regolamento di Servizio in Guera, in 3 Leggi e Decreti del Regno d'Italia 3184 (1896); Meloni 2010, p. 34; and *The Judge Advocate General's School, The Background Of The Uniform Code Of Military Justice U. S. Army*, p. 2, https://www.loc.gov/rr/frd/Military_Law/pdf/background-UCMJ.pdf.

[189] Articles of War, Provisional Congress of Massachusetts Bay, 5 April 1775.

[190] Parks 1973, p. 5.

[191] Articles of War, Article 33 (1806).

Black Hawk War of 1832.[192] His sentence, however, was to step down for two days and carry a wooden sword instead of a steel one.[193] The decision against Colonel David D. Mitchell Another is another example of the conviction of a superior within the confines of the Article, which was revisited in the WWII criminal prosecutions of the High Command and Hostage cases.[194] Notably, the decision was of a civil nature; Colonel Mitchell was held responsible for illegal superior orders passed from his superior to the latter's subordinates. This decision is also relevant to the modern construction of the effective command and control test in the context of superior responsibility, where what matters in the adjudication of the doctrine is a superior's actual control over a group of subordinates, irrespective of the hierarchy of the chain of command.[195]

In 1863, the US promulgated its own military code.[196] Also controversially known either as *Instructions for the Government of Armies of the United States in the Field* or simply as the *Lieber Code*,[197] the code is attributed to Professor Francis Lieber, who at the time was a professor at Columbia College in New York.[198] The code was approved by Abraham Lincoln when the US was in a state of war—the Civil War, also referred to as The War Between the States.[199] This code addressed superior responsibility in the form of superior orders. On this note, Article 71 provides that: "Whoever intentionally inflicts additional wounds on an enemy already wholly disabled, or kills such an enemy, or who orders or encourages soldiers to do so, shall suffer death, if duly convicted, whether he belongs to the Army of the United States, or is an enemy captured after having committed his misdeed."[200]

It is noteworthy that the US Lieber Code, and the subsequent codes revising it, elicited suspicion given the role of convicted felons in drafting it.[201] John Witt supports this assertion. Witt describes the manual in the version updated by Major Glenn, with respect to the criminal prosecutions made by the US in relation to WWII, which relied heavily on the code. He explains that:

> At the war crimes trials of Nazis in American-occupied Germany from 1946 to 1949, provisions of the laws of war that Glenn had written would be cited and argued about at length by prosecutors and defense lawyers alike. No one noted that they had been crafted by a

---

[192] Sandburg and Lincoln 1961, p. 30.

[193] Ibid.

[194] Parks 1973, p. 7.

[195] See Sect. 2.3.

[196] Parks 1973, pp. 7–8.

[197] This code's rubric was altered against Lieber's wishes, as the term "code" may bear legal significance and thus required the senate's approval. As a result, it was instead modified to "Instructions" or "General Orders No 100." For more details, see Childress 1976, pp. 34, 38.

[198] Roberts 2019, p. 165.

[199] *See Instruction for the Government of the United States in the Field by Order of the Secretary of War*, in Washington D.C., Apr. 24 1863, No. 100, approved by President Lincoln, Schindler, and Toman, 3. See also Doty 1982, p. 24; O'Brien and Diefendorf 1864, vol. 2, pp. 104–116.

[200] Ibid.

[201] Ibid., p. 179.

> convicted torturer, a man whom we would today (following Lieber and Bluntschli) call a war criminal.[202]

To conclude, then, American warfare history emphasized the responsibility of superiors during wartime to properly educate their subordinates. This duty echoes the recent application requirements of the superior responsibility doctrine in relation to the superior–subordinate relationship.[203] In 1886, John Winthrop listed the responsibilities of subordinates vis-à-vis their superiors as follows:

> All officers or soldiers offending against the rule of immunity of non-combatants or private persons in war forfeit their right to be treated as belligerents, and together with civilians similarly offending, become liable to the severest penalties as violators of the laws of war... [i]t is indeed the chief duty of the commander of the army of occupation to maintain order and the public safety, as far as practicable without oppression of the population, and as if the district were a part of the domain of his own nation.[204]

During the Philippine–American War, John Smith, commander of the US Army, was court-martialed for ordering and inciting subordinates to commit war crimes on Samar Island.[205] In his conviction, President Theodore Roosevelt also emphasized the responsibility of superiors to educate their subordinates as a central aspect of superior responsibility, noting that:

> [T]he officers in high and responsible position [must be] peculiarly careful in their bearing and conduct so as to keep a moral check over any acts of an improper character by their subordinates. Almost universally the higher officers have so borne themselves as to supply this necessary check... It is impossible to tell exactly how much influence language like that used by General Smith may have had in preparing the minds of thoses [*sic*] under him for the commission of the deeds which we regret. Loose and violent talk by an officer of high rank is always likely to excite to wrongdoing those among his subordinates whose wills are weak or whose passions are strong.[206]

The American history of warfare and the regulations accompanying armed conflicts therefore played a key role in establishing the responsibilities of superiors and determining the proper punishment. The international community's efforts in shaping the doctrine of superior responsibility were thus heavily based on American history, which helped establish how a superior can be prosecuted for the crimes of his or her subordinates and what constitutes a war crime.

---

[202] Witt 2012, p. 363.

[203] See Sect. 2.3.

[204] Winthrop 1895, p. 782.

[205] Parks 1973, p. 9.

[206] S. Doc. 213, 57th Cong. 2nd Session, p. 5.

2.4.3 *The International Community's Early Attempts Apropos Superior Responsibility*

In the same vein as the US military codes, Henry Dunant, the founder of the Red Cross, also emphasized the role of military commanders through the *1864 Geneva Convention for the Amelioration of the Conditions of the Wounded in Armies in the Field*.[207] The year 1864 also marked the recognition of the Red Cross symbol, cognate to the Swiss flag, which was used as a humanitarian symbol for hospitalization purposes.[208] This Convention was codified following the Battle of Solferino in Italy, which marked the first time in history that reigning monarchs had personally commanded army units on the battlefield.[209] This Geneva Convention was designated for the *Amelioration of the Condition of the Wounded in Armies in the Field*, encapsulating the principle of superior responsibility within its subject matter—reminiscent of the American Lieber Code.[210] This alignment between the subject matter of an international treaty and a domestic military code is one reason why the US took almost twenty years to accede to it—the other reasons were more substantial. These reasons included concerns about the reaction of European states to the American Civil War and the perceived irrelevance of international law to the United States at the time.[211]

The 1864 Geneva Convention was the first in the series of Geneva Conventions, which regulated the conduct of war between contracting parties and which laid the foundation for modern international humanitarian law. Notably, this Convention did not explicitly articulate the principle of superior responsibility in the *stricto sensu*. However, it highlighted military commanders' responsibility to implement this Convention in accordance with government instructions, to ensure their military forces remained in order. Article 6 of this Convention states: "Commanders-in-Chief may hand over immediately to the enemy outposts enemy combatants wounded during an engagement when circumstances allow and subject to the agreement of both parties."[212] This Article echoes the responsibilities of military commanders in United Nations (UN) peacekeeping missions, where they are held responsible not only for the actions of their subordinates but also for their safety.[213] Another Article, related to the responsibilities of a military commander, is Article 8, which states: "The

---

[207] Roberts 2019, p. 186.

[208] The title of the convention was the "International Committee for Relief for Wounded Soldiers", which was subsequently changed to the "International Committee of the Red Cross (ICRC)". Ibid., p. 183.

[209] Ibid.

[210] Bugnion 2003, p. 13.

[211] Roberts 2019.

[212] The Geneva Convention 1864, https://ihl-databases.icrc.org/ihl/INTRO/120.

[213] See Sect. 2.1.

implementing of the present Convention shall be arranged by the Commanders-in-Chief of the belligerent armies following the instructions of their respective Governments and in accordance with the general principles outlined in this Convention."[214] This Article emphasizes the military commander's responsibility to act in good faith when implementing the rules of this Convention, particularly regarding the neutral treatment of wounded prisoners of war—an essential principle of the Convention.[215]

2.5 From Disciplinary Measure to International Criminal Liability: The Modern History of Superior Responsibility

As noted in antiquity and the Middle Ages, the doctrine of superior responsibility, in its strict and broad senses, was set up regionally as a military concept to hold superiors responsible in the context of warfare, typically through military manuals—as a military disciplinary measure.[216] The modern concept of superior responsibility also originated as a disciplinary measure, stemming from the Lieber Code and its revisions of the United States. The concept of superior responsibility then evolved, challenging state sovereignty—whereas, in cases of conflict between two or more states involving superior responsibility, the superior, as an individual, may be convicted internationally.

Accordingly, it is important to note that superiors are held responsible through two primary means: (a) court-martial (or municipal criminal court in the case of political leaders), and (b) international criminal courts.[217] Under the domestic criminal doctrine of superior responsibility, domestic courts convict superiors based on the crime of omission.[218] Conversely, as noted earlier, international criminal courts, under the international criminal doctrine of superior responsibility, convict superiors for the crimes committed by their subordinates due to the superior's failure to control the troops under their command.[219] Accordingly, the historical development of the transition between these both phenomena—the disciplinary measure of domestic superior responsibility versus the international criminal liability of international superior responsibility—will form the premise of this section on modern superior responsibility.

Thus, I shall set out to illustrate the historical evolution of superior responsibility, beginning with its application by municipal courts in military contexts, and

[214] Geneva Convention.

[215] Pictet 1960, pp. 3–6.

[216] Meloni 2010.

[217] Van der Vyver 2021, pp. 572–573.

[218] See Sect. 2.2.

[219] Ibid.

progressing to the international criminal liability of superiors, as handled by international criminal courts. In addition, as part of this discussion of the historical development, I shall explore the legal characterization of international superior responsibility and how it applies without prejudice to domestic superior responsibility.[220] I shall also address the complexities of these phenomena, which have established the international superior responsibility doctrine as a distinct mode of liability.

2.5.1 Superior Responsibility as a Disciplinary Measure

Unlike the *1864 Geneva Convention*, the Hague Conventions of 1899 and of 1907 (also known as The Hague Laws) outlined the responsibilities of military commanders within an international military framework.[221] As noted earlier, in antiquity and the Middle Ages, superior responsibility was handled as both a cultural or religious norm and a domestic standard for holding superiors liable. However, the Hague Conventions emphasized military commanders' responsibilities on the battlefield between civilized nations, noting that these provisions were framed as disciplinary measures rather than criminal prosecutions (vicarious liability). The Hague Laws consist of multiple conventions addressing various battlefield scenarios. For instance, with regard to superior responsibility, the first Article of the Fourth Hague Convention outlines the responsibilities of soldiers and their commanders concerning the determination of unlawful and lawful belligerents. Specifically, it states that, "[Soldiers] must be commanded by a person responsible for his subordinates."

Similarly, Article 19 of the Tenth Hague Convention, which addresses naval vessel bombardments, states that the military commanders of fleets must "see the execution of the details of the preceding Articles."[222] As part of the historical chain of developments, this Article could be linked to Article 8 of the 1864 Geneva Convention, which similarly holds military commanders responsible not only for maintaining law and order among troops, but also for implementing the Convention in accordance with the commander's governmental instructions.[223] These Conventions are considered customary rules in modern international law and have been reinforced by a series of subsequent conventions.[224]

---

[220] Meaning that prosecutions of superiors under domestic courts-martial do not conflict with the prosecution of these superiors at the international level. Van der Vyver 2021, p. 573.

[221] Meloni refers to a "principle of responsible command" that outlines the responsibilities of superiors towards their subordinates and includes responsibility for actions *vis-à-vis* omission. However, this principle does not appear to be an actual international norm. I would deduce that, in military law, responsible command is associated with disciplinary measures, unlike responsible command in international law, which leads to the criminal liability of others. See Meloni 2010, pp. 35–37. See also Mettraux 2009, p. 53.

[222] 36 Stat. 2277; Treaty Series No. 539; Malloy Treaties 1910, Vol. II, 2269, https://ihl-databases.icrc.org/ihl/INTRO/195.

[223] Geneva Convention.

[224] *Prosecutor v. Tihomir Blaškić*, 3 March 2000, Case No. IT-95-14-T, para 85.

With respect to trials of superiors in the early twentieth century, the Leipzig Supreme Court elected to try German leaders who had committed war crimes during and after WWI under German jurisdiction.[225] It also marked the first application of this doctrine in convicting leaders of sovereign nations, including political superiors.[226] This took place when the Allied Powers, after WWI, established the International Commission on the Responsibility of the Authors of the War and on Enforcement of Penalties to explore the possibility of international criminal trials for the war criminals. However, it faced objections from the US[227] and Japanese delegations.[228] Under international law standards, the Commission introduced a principle known as the doctrine of abstention, which supported the possibility of prosecuting both military and political superiors under the principle of superior responsibility—effectively capturing the essence of its modern form.[229] Accordingly, in 1919 the Allied States signed the Treaty of Versailles[230] in an effort to subject German war criminals to an international trial. Article 227 states:

> The Allied and Associated Powers publicly arraign William II of Hohenzollern, formerly German Emperor, for a supreme offence [*sic*] against international morality and the sanctity of treaties. A special tribunal will be constituted to try the accused, thereby assuring him the guarantees essential to the right of defence [*sic*]…. In its decision the tribunal will be guided by the highest motives of international policy, with a view to vindicating the solemnity of international undertakings and the validity of international morality.[231]

Most importantly, the crime attributed to the German Kaiser William II, involving "the sanctity of treaties", is recognized as a war crime[232] (or an act of aggression under modern international law). However, its historical roots can be traced to Napoleon's contravention of the Elba agreement, where the breach itself was considered of greater severity than the actual crimes committed.[233] Regrettably, this Article was not enforced, as at the time, William II, who was implicated in the crimes as a superior, was granted asylum in the Netherlands.[234] In addition, Germany insisted that the prosecution of these war criminals should take place solely under the jurisdiction of the Supreme Court of Leipzig, claiming that it applied international law rather than domestic governance. Nevertheless, the court tried a select few of the superiors

---

225 Parks 1973, p. 13.

226 Ibid., p. 14.

227 U.S. Delegation Memorandum to the Paris Peace Conference (1920).

228 Burnett 1985, p. 82.

229 Meloni 2010, p. 39.

230 This treaty pertains to many issues, such as the secession from Prussia; however, one of the main issues is the penalization of war criminals in Germany. For a more detailed discussion of the issues dealt with in this treaty, see Mälksoo 2019, pp. 189–190.

231 Treaty of Peace with Germany (*Treaty of Versailles*), 28 June 1919, https://www.loc.gov/law/help/us-treaties/bevans/m-ust000002-0043.pdf.

232 Meloni 2010, pp. 40–41.

233 Ibid., p. 38.

234 du Plessis 2008, p. 14.

from the list proposed by the Allied Powers, with one individual convicted under *latu sensu* command responsibility for ordering the commission of war crimes.[235]

Lastly, the second attempt by the international community to hold superiors responsible for violations in warfare came with the 1906 and 1929 Geneva Conventions, which were extensions of the 1864 Geneva Convention. These later conventions, however, also addressed violations involving naval vessels at sea.[236] Unfortunately, as a result of subsequent events—such as the Japanese crimes in Nanking in 1937 and the continued genocidal practices by the Germans[237] during WWII—the treaty became a matter of customary international law, with its subject matter left largely unaddressed in commentaries.

2.5.2 *The* **Yamashita** *Standard: A Criminal Trial Without* **Sua Sponte**

Before establishing military tribunals to prosecute WWII superiors, the United States set up a military commission in 1945 to try General Tomoyuki Yamashita of the Japanese army for the crimes committed by his soldiers.[238] This case marked a watershed moment and laid the foundation for the superior responsibility doctrine, tracing its roots to the emergence of ICL.[239] The US did not wish to wait for the formulation of the International Military Tribunals (IMTs) to begin prosecuting superiors worldwide. Instead, under the authority of the US General Douglas MacArthur, they established a commission—subject to final review by the US Supreme Court—to try General Yamashita. It is worth noting that the US initiative was prompted by the escalation of horrendous war crimes committed against American and Filipino prisoners of war in the Bataan area of Manila.[240]

Despite his claims at the trials, Yamashita was the *de facto* chief military commander and governor of the Philippines, as well as the *de jure* commander. In contrast, his *de facto* authority extended only to the police personnel and all other branches of the military branches.[241] With that in mind, this principle became part of the modern doctrine of superior responsibility, in which *de facto* authority—based

---

[235] The Leipzig Supreme Court decided in the *Llandovery Castle* case that: "[I]f the execution of an order in the ordinary course of duty involves such a violation of the law as is punishable, the superior officer issuing such order is alone responsible." The court applied their domestic penal military code, dismissing Article 227 of the Versailles Treaty. See Bassiouni 2002, pp. 244, 281. See also Bassiouni 1994, pp. 784–786, 805.

[236] Parks 1973, p. 14.

[237] Ibid.

[238] Ibid.

[239] Cf. Bassiouni 2011 2, pp. 196–197. (According to Bassiouni, the history of [inter]national criminal prosecutions began during the unjust war in Naples in 1268.) See also Philipson 1911, p. 136.

[240] Parks 1973, p. 22.

[241] Parks 1973, p. 22.

on the effective authority/command and control test—is a key component of the superior–subordinate relationship.[242] It is also noteworthy that both Yamashita and Admiral Soemu Toyoda (Commander of the Fleet) were assumed to have exercised superiority concurrently. However, the evidence against Yamashita established that, when the crimes occurred, he was the *de facto* commander of all Japanese military branches.[243] For the first time at the outset of modern ICL, the Commission explicitly applied the *strictu sensu* understanding of the doctrine of superior responsibility in its reasoning, stating that:

> Tomoyuki YAMASHITA, General Imperial Japanese Army, between 9 October 1944 and 2 September 1945, at Manila and at other places in the Philippine Islands, while commander of armed forces of Japan at war with the United States of America and its allies, unlawfully disregarded and failed to discharge his duty as commander to control the operations of the members of his command, permitting them to commit brutal atrocities and other high crimes against people of the United States and its allies and dependencies, particularly the Philippines; and he, General Tomoyuki YAMASHITA, thereby violated the law of war.[244]

The trial also found:

> It is absurd, however, to consider a commander a murderer or rapist because one of his soldiers commits a murder or a rape. Nonetheless, where murder and rape and vicious, revengeful actions are widespread offenses, and there is no effective attempt by a commander to discover and control the criminal acts, such a commander may be held responsible, even criminally liable, for the lawless acts of his troops, depending upon their nature and the circumstances surrounding them. Should a commander issue orders which lead directly to lawless acts, the criminal responsibility is definite and has always been so understood. The Rules of Land Warfare, United States Army, are clear on these points. It is for the purpose of maintaining discipline and control, among other reasons, that military commanders are given broad powers of administering military justice. The tactical situation, the character, training and capacity of staff officers and subordinate commanders as well as the traits of character, and training of his troops are other important factors in such cases.[245]

This decision underscored several key components of the modern framework of superior responsibility. Notably, it stressed that offenses committed by subordinates cannot be attributed to a superior as a matter of criminal liability. However, given the severity of the superior's "broad powers of administering military justice",[246] the attribution of such offenses to their culpability is justified—supporting the gravity test that I have proposed as a legal characterization of this doctrine in the following chapter.[247] It also established that the *mens rea* element of superior responsibility must be confined to, and thus examined in terms of, the superior's "personal neglect"—supporting the view that the required proof of *mens rea* applies only to the superior's state of mind, not to crimes committed by subordinates. In other words, the

[242] See Sect. 2.3.

[243] See Parks 1973, p. 66.

[244] The US commission based the violation of the law of war decision on the Geneva Conventions of 1907 and 1929 because Japan was a state party to them. See Parks 1973, n. 68.

[245] Ibid., p. 22.

[246] Ibid.

[247] See Sect. 2.2.

knowledge element of superior responsibility is defined as: the superior *intentional* failure to execute supervisory duties (*i.e.*, they knew) or their *negligent* failure to execute supervisory duties (*i.e.*, they had reason to know).[248]

The Commission went beyond the gravity test, however, asserting that a superior is criminally responsible for "[t]he sole fact of being the commander".[249] In this context, in light of the widespread, systematic nature of international crimes, a superior is held criminally liable regardless of their knowledge of the crimes.[250] It is important to note that this decision faced significant criticism for overlooking the knowledge element.[251] According to the interpretation of this decision, the superior's only possible rebuttal, to refute an intentional or negligent failure on their part to supervise, is to demonstrate that they performed their duties properly. In other words, the responsibility for proving *mens rea* is a matter for the prosecution, whereas proving the execution of duties—such as punishment, as inferred from the effective control test—is a matter for the defense.

Moreover, this decision could be upheld for the *but-for* test (causal link) regarding the commander's "effective attempt to discover and control [as opposed to the criminal acts]"[252] their subordinates—a requirement that is arguably now a component of superior responsibility.[253] The Commission also emphasized that: "[W]here such a duty exists, a charge alleging less than personal participation in or ordering of an act in violation of the law of war states a violation of the law of war,"[254] which highlights the nature of superior responsibility as vicarious liability. Lastly, the decision may also be linked to the recent debate over the remoteness of superiors from the location of their subordinates—a debate that, arguably, decided erroneously in the ICC's acquittal of Mr. Bemba, which further added to the complexity of this doctrine.[255]

The issue concerning the *mens rea* element in the *Yamashita* decision remains controversial, because he was convicted based on his absence of knowledge of the criminal conduct of his subordinates. However, his approval of the crimes committed by his subordinates demonstrated an intentional dereliction of duty.[256] According to this understanding of the decision, a superior may be convicted on the basis of an intentional omission, which constitutes an accessorial role rather than vicarious liability. In other words, by approving the crimes after their commission, he effectively participated in them through his intentional omission, which places him in the

248 See Sect. 2.3.

249 Meloni 2010, p. 44.

250 Parks 1973, p. 25.

251 Ibid.

252 See Chap. 4, Sect. 4.3.1.4.

253 Ibid.

254 Parks 1973, p. 35.

255 As will be discussed further on, the Appeals Chambers decided that a superior's remoteness from the location in which the crimes are committed or are to be committed constitutes a defense in favor of the superior, holding that the distance between the superior and the subordinates affects the required material ability. See Chap. 4, Sect. 4.3.2.

256 Lael 1982, p. 83. See also Parks 1973, p. 87.

role of an accessory.[257] In its review of this decision, the US Supreme Court also underscored a crucial issue regarding superior responsibility, namely, whether a superior's execution of his duties depends on his having authority or actual control over his subordinates.[258] The Court concluded that what actually matters in the fulfillment of a superior's duty is actual power, since relying on formal authority could serve as an alibi to evade accountability. In any event, the Yamashita trial ultimately resulted in the imposition of the death penalty on the grounds of vicarious liability.

In this context, it is noteworthy that, under the current ICL framework, a nuanced distinction exists between: (i) holding a superior individually responsible as an indirect participant through omission;[259] and (ii) holding a superior vicariously liable for crimes committed by their subordinates.[260] The first instance is treated as a mode of perpetration, in which the superior is held liable alongside the direct perpetrators, as a co-principal.[261] In the second instance, a superior may not directly participate in the crimes, either through their actions or omissions, yet may still be convicted for those crimes based on his knowledge of their nature coupled with the failure to discharge the entrusted duties (vicarious liability).[262] For the purposes of adjudicating superior responsibility, the key distinction lies in the fact that, in the first instance, the superior's knowledge concerns the nature of the crimes committed, whereas in the second instance, their knowledge (or negligence/recklessness/willful blindness) is connected with their duty to supervise.[263] Nevertheless, the fact that Yamashita was brought to trials does not affect its novelty as a precedent within the current framework of the superior responsibility doctrine.

2.5.3 Prosecuting Military and Political Superiors at the International Military Tribunal

The legacy of the International Military Tribunals (IMTs) and the Subsequent Nuremberg Trials (SNTs) is a significant reference in prosecuting superiors for their subordinates' crimes, particularly in Germany and in relation to those victimized during

---

[257] Parks 1973.

[258] Ibid., p. 84.

[259] *PROSECUTOR v. MIROSLAV KVOČKA, MLADO RADIĆ, ZORAN ŽIGIĆ & DRAGOLJUB PRCAĆ*, Case No. IT-98-30/1-T, para 308 (Nov. 2, 2001). See also van der Vyver 2021, pp. 437–438, 456–457.

[260] Van der Vyver 2021 5, p. 566.

[261] Ambos 2002, pp. 850–851.

[262] Ibid.

[263] See Sect. 2.3.

WWII.[264] As set out in the Moscow Declaration of the Allied Powers,[265] the criminal trials of those most responsible were conducted under a special jurisdictional structure: (i) the Nuremberg Trials, under the auspices of the US military judiciary; (ii) the Far East Military Tribunal, also known as the Tokyo Trials; and (iii) the remaining trials of "little" (or intermediate) soldiers, which were handled at the domestic level, with support from the UN War Crimes Commission's investigations and evidence collection.[266] These tribunals all operated concurrently.

Unlike the Yamashita Standard, the structure of superior responsibility adopted by the IMTs and the SNTs was shaped by the domestic criminal codes of the Allied Powers.[267] Thus, the standards by which this doctrine was implicitly defined during these trials were far removed from vicarious liability; instead, they focused on positive actions, construed as superior orders or intentional omissions.[268] For instance, under the jurisdiction of these courts, the knowledge element of superior responsibility was divided into two categories: (i) intentional knowledge, as proposed by France, Holland, and Luxembourg; and (ii) negligence, as proposed by the US, Britain, China, and Canada.[269] Accordingly, the decisions in these trials reflected a stricter standard of liability, often applying superior responsibility even in the absence of clear evidence of the superior's knowledge. In contrast, the current framework adopts a broader and more articulated mental element, requiring proof of actual or constructive knowledge.

Intriguingly, the US trials of Nazi leaders and their peers and subordinates in the SNTs witnessed a significant application of superior responsibility, though it was based on faulty reasoning again due to its origins in domestic criminal laws.[270] Before delving into the bulk of these cases, it is important to note that the IMT cases did not independently address the doctrine of superior responsibility. Rather, each case addressed a key conceptual component of the doctrine.

The trial against Field Marshal von Leeb and other commanders, acting as a unified organization of superiors (also known as the *High Command* case), resulted in different reasoning regarding the *mens rea* element, which was indicated but ultimately rejected in the Yamashita trial under the same jurisdiction—the US trials.[271] In this case, the tribunal held that a military commander at the highest level of command is not responsible for crimes committed by their subordinates, unless personal negligence is involved.[272] In other words, the tribunal limited the application of superior

---

264 Meloni 2010, p. 48.

265 This declaration was signed between the US, Britain, the Soviet Union, and China to try commanders and senior leaders following WWII, https://www.loc.gov/law/help/us-treaties/bevans/m-ust000003-0816.pdf.

266 Meloni 2010, p. 49.

267 Smidt 2000, pp. 155–175.

268 Ibid.

269 Meloni 2010, p. 49.

270 Ibid.

271 Parks 1973, pp. 38–39.

272 Ibid., p. 40.

responsibility to identifiable subordinates under the commander's supervision and to crimes that could be directly attributed to his dereliction of duty.[273] This reasoning contradicted the Yamashita decision, which upheld strict liability for superiors based on the "sole fact of being a commander".[274]

The emphasis on identifying subordinates and establishing a causal link has posed an ongoing challenge in the jurisprudence of the UN *ad hoc* tribunals.[275] Accordingly, the *High Command* case of the SNTs holds historical significance, as the tribunal determined that "these subjects are substantially free of command authority except towards the men strictly subordinates to them."[276] Under the jurisprudence of the UN *ad hoc* tribunals, the identification of subordinates was not treated as a complicating factor. Rather, the tribunals held that the existence of an unidentified group of subordinates is sufficient to establish a superior–subordinate relationship.[277] Moreover, the High Command Case also identified a bifurcated *mens rea* distinction between military commanders and other superiors, holding that the former could be prosecuted based on negligence (having reason to know), whereas the latter could be convicted for intentional knowledge, such as for consciously disregarding information. However, the *Doctors* case—also part of the SNTs and decided against Karl Brandt and others—described the duties of a military commander in a manner in line with the current jurisprudence of the UN *ad hoc* tribunals, particularly concerning the commander's entrusted duty to prevent crimes. The Tribunal held that:

> The law of war imposes on a military officer in a position of command an affirmative duty to take such steps as are within his power and appropriate to the circumstances to control those under his command for the prevention of acts which are violations of the law of war.[278]

Another important case is the *Hostage* case, which was decided against Wilhelm List and others in the Nazi military command structure. This case introduced a new standard for the *mens rea* element of superior responsibility, reminiscent of the Rome Statute of the ICC, by holding that a military commander's negligent failure to fulfill their supervisory duties could suffice. The court held that: "the German Wehrmacht was a well equipped [*sic*], well trained, and well disciplined [*sic*] army [therefore] the evidence shows that they were led by competent commanders who had mail, telegraph, telephone, radio, and courier services for the handling of communications. Reports were made daily."[279] This decision is strikingly similar to the 'should

---

[273] Un War Crimes Commission, *Law Reports Of Trials Of War Criminals, High Command case, Vol. XII*, 76 (1949), https://www.loc.gov/rr/frd/Military_Law/pdf/Law-Reports_Vol-12.pdf.

[274] Meloni 2010, p. 9.

[275] Prosecutor v. Nyiramasuhuko *et al.*, TC II Judgment, Case No. ICTR-98-42-T, para 121, 24 June 2011). See also *Prosecutor v. Bizimungu et al.*, TC Judgment, Case No. ICTR-88-50-T, para 1872, 30 September 2011.

[276] Meloni 2010, p. 54.

[277] *See Prosecutor v. Nyiramasuhuko et al.*, TC II Judgment, Case No. ICTR-98-42-T.

[278] *UNITED STATESOF AMERICA v. KARL BRANDT ET AL.*, 2 TRIALS OF WAR CRIMINALS BEFORE THE NUREMBERG MILITARY TRIBUNALS UNDER CONTROL COUNCIL LAW NO. 10 (OCT. 1946–APRIL 1949) (JUDGMENT) 171, p. 207. Washington D.C.: U.S. Gov. Printers (1950–1953).

[279] Parks 1973, p. 59. See also Burnett 1985, p. 109.

have known' standard adopted in the Rome Statute with respect to military commanders.[280] It is indisputable that a superior's absence of actual knowledge does not absolve them of their duties or criminal liability. The *indicia* of their responsibilities, including "daily reports"[281] on soldiers, are burdens that only a superior is in a position to carry out. This is also the foundation of the superior responsibility doctrine, according to which a superior cannot avoid liability unless it is proven, beyond a reasonable doubt, that they lacked material control over the actions of their subordinates.

The first international trial dealing with the superior responsibility of political leaders, which has been cited in recent international courts,[282] was held in the aftermath of WWII—specifically, the *Hirota* case.[283] Unlike the Nuremberg Trials, the Tokyo Trial involved the prosecution of both military commanders and political leaders. As Vetter explains: "The greatest inquisition of political leaders by their foreign enemies that we have seen in this century; that is both its glory and its infamy."[284] Notably, the cases of Toyoda and Koki Hirota serve as key historical references for superior responsibility under the Rome Statute of the ICC.[285]

Hirota served as a political leader of Japan from 1933 to 1938, during which time crimes were committed in China.[286] The case raises two key matters: (i) Hirota's relationship with the army and (ii) his knowledge of the crimes. In the first instance, it was clear that, owing to his military commander status, Hirota did not have effective command and control over the subordinates. However, it was later established that he did hold authority over them on account of his political leadership role.[287] In the second instance, for the purposes of adjudication under the Rome Statute of the ICC, a political leader can be convicted of superior responsibility if they knew of the crimes (intent) or consciously disregarded the information (also intent based on interpretation of willful blindness).[288] Applying the ICC's standards to Hirota would have exonerated him at the time. However, owing to his failure to act on the basis of the reports drawing attention to the atrocities committed in China, Hirota was found guilty of negligence despite being a political leader. He was also found guilty of failing to ensure that the Minister of the Japanese army fulfilled his duty to punish the soldiers responsible. As a historical reference, the outcome of this reasoning may support the view that the *mens rea* element in the Rome Statute needs to be amended

[280] Rome Statute, above n. 51, Article 28(a).

[281] See Parks 1973, p. 59.

[282] *Prosecutor v. Mucić et al*, ("Čelebići"), AC, Appeal Judgement, Case No. IT-96-21-A, paras 257–268, 20 February 2001. The Prosecutor had relied on several precedents to demonstrate that substantial influence was sufficient for establishing superior responsibility, particularly in relation to the convictions of members of the Japanese government, such as Hirota and Shigemitzu, as well as military commanders, such as Muto, chief of staff to General Yamashita.

[283] Vetter 2000, p. 128.

[284] Ibid.

[285] See, generally, Chap. 4.

[286] Meloni 2010, p. 60.

[287] Sengheiser 2007–2008, p. 706.

[288] Van der Vyver 2021, p. 562.

to equate military commanders and political superiors—namely, in relation to actual knowledge and negligence.

The *Toyoda* case marked the final judgment in the series of prosecutions conducted under the Tokyo Trial, concluding the chain of post-World War II trials concerning Japanese military leadership. The Tribunal acquitted Admiral Soemu Toyoda due to the absence of certain duties (prevent, repress, and punish) toward his subordinates. In this case, the court determined that a superior is only responsible if, by failing to take action to punish the perpetrators or permitting the atrocities to continue, he neglects his duty as a commander and must therefore be held accountable.[289] In this sense, a superior is responsible for their duty to punish only provided that they have the material ability to prevent or repress their subordinates from committing the international crimes. This reasoning aligns with the modern prosecutions of superiors under this doctrine: As I shall discuss in Chap. 3, a superior must have the material ability to collectively execute all their duties.[290] Therefore, a superior who has the authority to punish but lacks the authority to prevent may not be convicted of superior responsibility owing to a lack of material ability over their subordinates.

In light of the aforementioned historical insights from WWII trials, perhaps the only trial to address the legal characterization of superior responsibility as a distinct form of vicarious liability—despite the heavy criticism it faced—is the Yamashita trial.[291] The other trials did not adhere to a uniform standard regarding the conceptual components of superior responsibility, with their decisions fluctuating between treating superiors as principals and holding them directly responsible for actions and omissions. Despite this fluctuation, these trials marked the start of efforts to prosecute superiors at the international level, and current ICL scholarship consistently relies on them for conceptual interpretations and practical applications.

2.5.4 Post-WWII Superior Responsibility: International Treaties and Domestic Convictions

Scholars frequently overlook a key treaty that falls historically between the post-WWII military tribunals and the first codification of superior responsibility in the First Additional Protocol (API) of the Geneva Conventions; the Convention on the Non-applicability of Statutory Limitations to War Crimes and Crimes Against Humanity. This treaty is an extension of the Nuremberg Trials for those who evaded liability for WWII crimes. A close examination of Article 2 reveals that the Convention applies

[289] 19 *United States v. Soemu Toyoda* 5011 [Official transcript of Record of Trial], para 5005–6, October 1948.

[290] See Sect. 2.3.

[291] Parks 1973, p. 72.

"to representatives of the state authority who tolerate their commission".[292] While the text does not explicitly regulate criminal superior responsibility, it implicitly suggests that the failure to execute supervisory duties may be taken as toleration. This interpretation did not have any significant influence at the time, and was, accordingly, unaccounted for.

The API of the Geneva Conventions marked the first formal codification of the doctrine of superior responsibility, laying the groundwork for its modern articulation in the statutes of international criminal courts. However, during the drafting process, delegations from various countries deemed the provision applicable only within municipal legal systems—where a superior can be held criminally responsible for omissions as a disciplinary measure.[293] Notably, Article 86(2) of the API introduces a dichotomous framework for holding superiors responsible, distinguishing between the failure to act and the duty to act. It states:

> 2. The fact that a breach of the Conventions or of this Protocol was committed by a subordinate does not absolve his superiors from penal or disciplinary responsibility, as the case may be, if they knew, or had information which should have enabled them to conclude in the circumstances at the time, that he was committing or was going to commit such a breach and if they did not take all feasible measures within their power to prevent or repress the breach.[294]

The first framework holds superiors responsible for the failure to act (omission) as a disciplinary measure.[295] A commentary on this provision suggests that such disciplinary measures only apply to ordinary breaches, which should be handled under domestic laws—such as through courts-martial.[296] The second framework, however, applies to grave breaches, which constitute core international crimes, where customary international law permits universal jurisdiction. Under this framework, the state in whose jurisdiction the violation occurs must either prosecute or extradite the superior (*aut dedere aut judicare*).[297] In addition, Article 86(2) can be separated into two different avenues: (i) disciplinary measures handled domestically, based on omission; and (ii) penal sanctions, which may be handled either nationally or internationally. It is important to note that if a domestic system prosecutes a superior for an omission-based offense, this prosecution does not preclude the same superior from

[292] *Convention on the Non-applicability of Statutory Limitations to War Crimes and Crimes Against Humanity*, Article 2, https://www.un.org/en/genocideprevention/documents/atrocitycrimes/Doc.27_convention%20statutory%20limitations%20warcrimes.pdf.

[293] Gasser et al. 1987, pp. 1013–1014.

[294] *Protocol Additional to the Geneva Conventions of 12 August 1949, and relating to the Protection of Victims of International Armed Conflicts* (*Protocol I*), 1977, Article 86(2), U.N. Doc. A/32/144, 1125 U.N.T.S. 3, reprinted in 16 I.L.M. 1391 (1977).

[295] Gasser et al. 1987, p. 975.

[296] Ibid.

[297] Ibid. (*Aut dedere aut judicare* is an international law principle, according to which a state is required to either prosecute or extradite perpetrators of grave breaches. This rule is currently applied in modern international law, having first been applied in Germany for trying Syrian leaders for war crimes.)

being sanctioned before an international criminal tribunal on the basis of vicarious liability. Consequently, the superior cannot raise the *ne bis in idem* defense.[298]

This Article also addresses the *mens rea* element of superior responsibility, establishing two alternative conditions for superior liability. Firstly, a superior may be held responsible if they knew or had information that should have enabled them to conclude that the crimes were committed. The second alternative has a subject of controversy in the commentaries, particularly regarding whether it implies intent or negligence. This is due to the fact that the API was published in two official languages—English and French.[299] The English interpretation defines it as a negligence *mens rea*, which is in line with the US proposal of "should have known" in the Rome Statute, whereas the French interpretation ("*des information leur permettant de conclure*") suggests intent.[300] In the UN *ad hoc* tribunals, this interpretational discrepancy has been a significant issue, particularly for determining whether this text holds a superior responsible only for intent or a negligent state of mind.[301] As I shall discuss in Chap. 3, the second standard of *mens rea* can denote either intent, negligence, recklessness, or willful blindness. This differs from the understanding of superior responsibility outlined in the Rome Statute, which differentiates between *mens rea* for a military commander ("knew" and "should have known") and that applicable to civilian superiors ("knew" or "had reason to know").

Lastly, Article 87 of the same protocol introduced, for the first time, a text that outlines a superior's duty to provide adequate education to their subordinates. The text also underscores the superior's duty to ensure that their subordinates adhere to their responsibilities, as well as the superior's responsibility to prevent and punish subordinates by "initiating disciplinary or penal action against" them. Article 87 provides:

1. The High Contracting Parties and the Parties to the conflict shall require military commanders, with respect to members of the armed forces under their command and other persons under their control, to prevent and, where necessary, to suppress and report to competent authorities breaches of the Conventions and of this Protocol.
2. In order to prevent and suppress breaches, High Contracting Parties and Parties to the conflict shall require that, commensurate with their level of responsibility, commanders ensure that members of the armed forces under their command are aware of their obligations under the Conventions and this Protocol.
3. The High Contracting Parties and Parties to the conflict shall require any commander who is aware that subordinates or other persons under his control are going to commit or have committed a breach of the Conventions or of this, to initiate such steps as are necessary to prevent such violations of the Conventions

[298] Van der Vyver 2021, p. 8.
[299] Meloni 2010, p. 68.
[300] Gasser et al. 1987, p. 1014. See also Burnett 1985, pp. 146–147.
[301] See Sect. 2.3.

or this Protocol, and, where appropriate, to initiate disciplinary or penal action against violators thereof.[302]

As previously noted, the subject matter text of this Article has been cited throughout both ancient and recent history in the context of the superior responsibility doctrine. It mandates responsibilities for both the superior and the subordinates, reinforcing the international humanitarian law principle of Responsible Command.[303]

Regarding domestic convictions, two cases exemplify the application of the current superior responsibility doctrine, situated historically between the IMT trial and the establishment of modern international criminal tribunals. The first case involves a domestic court-martial's prosecution of US military commander Captain Medina for the crimes committed by his troops in the city of My Lai during the Vietnam War.[304] Medina was the military commander of three belligerent groups entering My Lai. Two of these groups entered the city and committed war crimes that resulted in the killing of over 500 civilians, while Medina was accompanying the third group to his headquarters, which was located near the site of the crimes.[305] The charges against Medina were for his failure to prevent his troops from committing the crimes. However, the court-martial acquitted him. This marked a critical decision, particularly given the US's recent strict stance on the Yamashita Standard. Unlike the Yamashita decision, the court ruled that superior responsibility would only apply if the superior had actual knowledge of the crimes committed.[306] The acquittal was based on the absence of Medina's actual knowledge of the crimes committed by the troops under his supervision.[307]

The second domestic conviction based on superior responsibility concerned the *Sabra and Shatila* massacre, which took place in a Palestinian refugee camp in Lebanon in 1983.[308] The Israeli Government requested the establishment of a Commission of Inquiry to investigate potential crimes committed by Israeli soldiers against Palestinians in the Sabra and Shatila refugee camp. While the Kahan Report by the Commission did not find Israeli personnel directly liable, it did hold them indirectly liable under the doctrine of superior responsibility. The outcome of this report summarized the conviction under this doctrine against the Israeli personnel as follows:

> The Commission determined that the massacre at Sabra and Shatila was carried out by a Phalangist unit, acting on its own but its entry was known to Israel. No Israeli was directly responsible for the events which occurred in the camps. But the Commission asserted that Israel had indirect responsibility for the massacre since the I.D.F. held the area. Mr. Begin was found responsible for not exercising greater involvement and awareness in the matter of introducing the Phalangists into the camp. Mr. Sharon was found responsible for ignoring

[302] See Parks 1973, Article 87.

[303] Meloni 2010, p. 35.

[304] See, generally, Linder 1999.

[305] Davanzo 1999, pp. 287–288.

[306] Lippman 1993, p. 360.

[307] Ibid.

[308] Ibid.

> the danger of bloodshed and revenge when he approved the entry of the Phalangists into the camps as well as not taking appropriate measures to prevent bloodshed. Mr. Shamir erred by not taking action [*sic*] after being alerted by communication Minister Zippori. Chief of Staff Eitan did not give the appropriate orders to prevent the massacre.[309]

In any case, the Commission was widely regarded as a sham, as it was not enforceable.[310] In conclusion, the Commission found that all the civilian superiors were responsible and should resign as part of their punishment.[311]

2.5.5 *Superior Responsibility as an International Criminal Mode of Liability*

The transitional shift from superior responsibility for omission *per se*, as addressed in international humanitarian law,[312] to a *sui generis* mode of criminal liability for international crimes has faced criticism from criminal law experts since the emergence of ICL. Such criticisms can be traced back to the drafting of the API of the Geneva Conventions of 12 August 1949, as well as the drafting of the international criminal court statutes. The central criticism of this transition relates to the absence of a domestic criminal principle that would establish the liability of a superior who did not directly participate in the commission of the crime.[313] Consequently, in this context, liability is characterized solely on the basis of the crime of omission, where an individual may be convicted for crimes based on either *actus* (acts) or *reus* (omissions).[314] This issue will be discussed in the next chapter under the legal characterization of superior responsibility. At this point, however, it is important to note that the API's commentary provided a special justification for the prosecutions of grave breaches, as opposed to normal breaches. It established that any state has universal jurisdiction to prosecute superiors responsible for such breaches.[315] *A fortiori*, ICL can provide this justification for the application of the doctrine of superior responsibility as a mode of liability, allowing for the prosecution of a superior for grave breaches committed by their subordinates.

---

[309] Meloni 2010, p. 72.

[310] Ibid.

[311] Ibid.

[312] Parks 1973, p. 20.

[313] Domestic penal codes do not feature vicarious liability within the context of the current understanding of superior responsibility; these codes convict such persons under an accomplice mode of liability. See, for example: Article 4 of the French Ordinance of August 28, 1944; Article 3 of the Law of August 2, 1947, of the Grand Duchy of Luxemburg; Article IX of the Chinese Law of 24 October 1946; and Article 8 (ii) of the British Royal Warrant.

[314] Van der Vyver reasons as to why international criminal courts' statutes, particularly the Rome Statute, did not mention the rule of act or omission in the commission the crimes. See van der Vyver 2021, p. 436. See also Parks 1973, pp. 17–19.

[315] Gasser et al. 1987, p. 975.

Another critical issue in the aforementioned mentioned transition is the *mens rea* element of superior responsibility within the context of ICL. The Articles on *mens rea* relating to superior responsibility in the statutes of the UN's *ad hoc* tribunals and the Rome Statute of the ICC only require "knowledge" for the former and "knowledge and negligence" (recklessness/willful blindness for political superiors) for the latter.[316] According to scholars and the jurisprudence of the tribunals, the controversial "had reason to know" standard is equivalent to intent, but not negligence.[317] However, I would challenge this view, and instead suggest that "had reason to know" should be based on the factual findings of each superior responsibility case.[318] In summary, if a superior is unaware of reports indicating that crimes have been or will be committed by their subordinates, then "had reason to know" merely denotes negligence. However, if the superior is aware of the reports but intentionally neglects their duties, especially their axiomatic duty to track such reports, then this constitutes an act of intentional omission. The beneficial outcome of this approach is that if the factual findings establish that the superior was genuinely unaware of the reports, they cannot rely on mere negligence as a defense.

Historically, since the *1919 Treaty of Versailles*, U.S. delegations have consistently clarified this controversy. For instance, the U.S. delegation once affirmed that: "To establish responsibility in such cases…the individual sought to be punished should have knowledge of the commission of the acts,"[319] where "should have known" denotes negligence.[320] The U.S. delegations reiterated this position during the drafting of the statutes of the UN ad hoc tribunals, where "had reason to know" denotes intelligence, as well as during the drafting of the Rome Statute of the ICC.[321] Although the US argued for a standard based on negligence, it did not foresee the prosecutions of civilian superiors, as is the case under the ICC framework. Thus, negligence was intended only for holding military commanders criminally responsible.

In sum, aside from the Yamashita Standard, one can convincingly conclude that the doctrine of superior responsibility historically emerged as a mode of criminal liability, as reflected in its modern applications. This development established the criminal liability of superiors for crimes committed by their subordinates. Notably, prosecutions of superiors during the mid-modern period—particularly between the IMTs and the advent of the UN ad hoc tribunals—were based on omissions, or omissive responsibility. Nevertheless, the legacy of the IMTs and their SNTs significantly influenced the practical evolution of superior responsibility, especially by extending its application beyond military commanders.

---

[316] In the case of a military commander, see the Rome Statute, above n. 51, Article 28(a).

[317] See Sect. 2.3.

[318] Ibid.

[319] Ibid.

[320] Ibid.

[321] Ibid.

2.5.6 Harmonizing the Doctrine of Superior Responsibility for Individuals Other Than Military Commanders

As noted earlier, following the expansion of ICL to include jurisdiction over non-military superiors, *superior responsibility* became a retronym of *command responsibility*. The idea of prosecuting political superiors can be traced back to the *1919 Treaty of Versailles*, where the Allied Powers suggested that prosecutions for German wartime offenses could extend to political leaders involved in such offenses. Based on the jurisprudence of the UN *ad hoc* tribunals, civilian superiors could also be prosecuted under the doctrine of superior responsibility, since Article 86 of the API applies penal sanctions for grave breaches of ICL to both military commanders and civilian superiors.[322]

In the case of the ICC, Article 28 explicitly outlines a bifurcated application of superior responsibility, allowing for the prosecution of individuals other than military commanders in positions of authority under the same doctrine.[323] However, the application of superior responsibility under Article 28(b) could serves as a means of defense for political leaders, since it has higher threshold which only requires intentional *mens rea*; military commanders, by contrast, may be convicted on the grounds of intent or negligence.[324] In light of this, when prosecuting political superiors, the superior may raise a defense based on *mens rea* if they negligently failed to be aware of the crimes committed.[325] Conversely, a military commander cannot raise such a defense since—if they were unaware of the crimes—they *should have known* about them based on their duty to monitor the actions of their subordinates.[326] Historically, this issue has been challenged. As noted earlier, during the drafting of the Rome State, the US, although not a state party, proposed a different approach for civilian superiors.[327] It suggested that a civilian superior could not be held liable for the crimes committed by their subordinates if they negligently failed to be aware of these offenses (*i.e.*, "should have known").[328]

This proposal stemmed from concerns over the potential prosecution of the US President and any Head of State in the political arena.[329] Along with the text regarding superior responsibility in the Rome Statute, this approach was deemed criminally unjust, because it placed the burden of proof on the military commanders for both intentional and negligent failure to execute supervisory duties, while the political

[322] See API, above n. 293, Article 86.

[323] Rome Statute, above n. 51, Article 28.

[324] Van der Vyver 2021, pp. 599–600.

[325] Ibid.

[326] Ibid.

[327] See Ambos 2002.

[328] Ibid., p. 562.

[329] See, for example, Falk et al. 1971; Knoll and McFadden 1970.

superior was held accountable only for an intentional failure to execute supervisory duties.[330]

2.6 Epilogue

Among scholars in this field, there is a general consensus that, along with case law, the history of superior responsibility played an important role in shaping the elements of this doctrine and justifying its legal characterization through a historical chain of developments. While the fluctuation of the conceptual requirements and their practical applications, as well as the absence of uniform standards documented in history, contributed to the current structure of superior responsibility, this has also led to paradoxical interpretations in scholarly discussions and judicial decisions.

In antiquity, the doctrine of superior responsibility emerged within a cultural context, as was the case with Sun Tzu's Manual, as well as through religious frameworks, where the spiritual concept of Allah's orders and commandments-imposed liability on superiors who violated both divine and human law, as noted earlier. This foundation of superior responsibility led to the notion that an individual in authority could be convicted not only for issuing superior orders (*latu sensu* superior responsibility) but also for the crimes of their subordinates (*strictu sensu* superior responsibility). As a result, according to the historical chain of developments, superior responsibility extends beyond the narrower norm of superior responsibility (vicarious liability) to also encompass the superior's positive role in the commission of crimes.

In the modern history of the prosecution of superiors for international crimes, this chapter has explored the impact of WWII tribunals on the evolution of the doctrine of superior responsibility. It has also examined the point at which the international community began to extend criminal responsibility to political leaders, as it had done for military commanders. It is also noteworthy that, during this era, the international community extended the application of the doctrine of superior responsibility to crimes other than war crimes—specifically, crimes against humanity, genocide, and the crime of aggression.

Finally, this historical evolution in the normative foundation and doctrinal development of superior responsibility—both in its conceptual components and in its practical applications—ought to provide legal and philosophical support for three key areas: (i) I introduce a third form of culpability—consequential or structural culpability—alongside personal and collective culpability, as a normative justification for this autonomous mode of liability—*i.e.*, superior responsibility. Grounded in the gravity test and a consequentialist permissive framework, this form supports reasoning that challenges the limits of contributory culpability. It may offer a principled compromise to proponents of strict personal culpability, such as those aligned

---

[330] Ibid.

with Robinson's deontic justifications, even if it introduces some acceptable discomfort within that camp; (ii) the conceptual components including their parameters governing the prosecution of superiors, as will be examined in Chaps. 3 and 4; and (iii) the prosecution of superiors for violations of human rights and treaty-based offenses, which I shall further test and evaluate in the final chapter.

References

Abou El Fadl K (2017) Islamic Law, Jihad and Violence. UCLA Journal of Islamic and Near Eastern Law 16(1), pp. 1–27

Abu al-Tayyib bin Hasan bin 'Ali al-Hayyinia al-Qanuji al-Bukhari (1985) al-'Ibra mimma Ja'a fi al-Ghazw wa al-Shahada wa al-Hijra. Dar al-Kutub al-'Ilmiyya, Beirut

Afifi A (2018) Jus in Bello and General Principles Related to Warfare According to Islamic Law. In: Gray T (ed) Islam and International Criminal Law and Justice. Torkel Opsahl Academic EPublisher, Brussels, pp. 101–120

Ajijola AD (1978) The Essence of Faith in Islam. University of Virginia Press, Charlottesville

Al Sallabi A (2019) Reasons behind the isolation of Khalid Ibn Al waleed. https://www.aljazeera.net/blogs/2019/12/12/. Accessed May 2021

al-Badr AR (1425 AH) al-Qutuf al-Jiyad min Hikam wa Ahkam al-Jihad. Dar al-Mughni, Riyadh

al-Biqa'iyyi IBUH (2002) al-Istisshhad bi Ayat al-Jihad. Dar al-Risala, Cairo

Al-bukhari M. Sahih Bukhari, Vol. 5, Book 59, Number 375. https://www.sahihbukhari.com/Pages/Bukhari_5_59.php. Accessed 22 May 2021

Al-Dawoody A (2011) The Islamic Law of War: Justifications and Regulations. Palgrave Macmillan

Al-Dawoody A (2015) Al-Sarakhsī's Contribution to the Islamic Law of War. UCLA Journal of Islamic and Near Eastern Law 14, pp. 29–55

Al-Dawoody A (2017) Islam and International Humanitarian Law: An Overview. Humanitarian Law & Policy. medium.com/law-and-policy/islam-and-international-humanitarian-law-an-overview-78d2df80712f. Accessed May 2021

Al-Dawoody A, Murphy V (2019) International humanitarian law: Islamic law and the protection of children in armed conflict. International Review of the Red Cross 101(911), pp. 551–573

Ambos K (2002) Superior Responsibility. In: Cassese A, Gaeta P, Jones JRWD (eds) The Rome Statute Of The International Criminal Court: A Commentary. Oxford University Press, Oxford, pp. 823–872

Armour (1922) Customs of Warfare in Ancient India. 8 Transactions of the Grotius Society. Grotius Society, London, pp. 71–88

Adachi S (1988) The Asian Concept. International Dimensions of Humanitarian Law. UNESCO, / Martinus Nijhoff Publishers, The Netherlands, pp. 13–19

Bassiouni MC (1994) The United Nations' Commission of Experts Established Pursuant to Security Council Resolution 780. American Journal of International Law 88, pp. 784–805

Bassiouni MC (2002) World War I: "The War to End All Wars," and the Birth of a Handicapped International Criminal Justice System. Denver Journal of International Law and Policy 30, pp. 244–291

Bassiouni MC (2011) The Theories and Elements of Criminal Responsibility. In: Crimes against Humanity: Historical Evolution and Contemporary Application. Cambridge University Press, Cambridge, pp. 472–580

Bassiouni MC (2013) The Shari'ah and Islamic Criminal Justice in Time of War and Peace. Cambridge University Press, Cambridge

Bellot HHL (1922). In: International Law Association, Report of the Thirty-First Conference, pp. 451–456

Blank LR (2021) The Use of Force to Prevent Recurrence of Conflict: Where Are the Limits of Self-Defense? Brooklyn Law Review 83, pp. 1–41
Boisard M (1987) Humanism in Islam. American Trust Publications, Indianapolis, IN
Bonaparte N (2001) Napoleon on the Art of War. In: Lavaas H (transl) Slip-Cased A (ed). Free Press
Bonney R (2004) Jihad From Qur'an to Bin Laden. Palgrave Macmillan, New York
Brand CE (1968) Roman Military Law. University of Texas Press, Austin, TX
Brusiin O (1943) Gustav Adolf krigsartiklar: några synpunkter. Tidskrift utgiven av Juridiska Föreningen i Finland 79
Bugnion F (2003) The International Committee of the Red Cross and the Protection of War Victims. Macmillan Education, Geneva
Bühler G (transl) (1886) The Laws of Manu. The Sacred Books of the East, vol 25. Clarendon Press, Oxford
Burnett WD (1985) Command Responsibility and a Case Study of the Criminal Responsibility of Israeli Military Commanders for the Pogrom at Shatila and Sabra. 107 Military Law Review, pp. 71–122
Childress JF (1976) Francis Lieber's Interpretation of the Laws of War: General Orders No 100 in the Context of His Life and Thought. American Journal of Jurisprudence 21, pp. 34–55.
Damaška M (2001) The Shadow Side of Command Responsibility. The American Journal of Comparative Law 49, pp. 455–496
Davanzo J (1999) An Absence of Accountability for the My Lai Massacre. Hofstra Law & Policy Symposium 3, pp. 287–288
Davis GB (1918) A Treatise on the Military Law of the United States, 3rd rev. edn. John Wiley & Sons, New York
Dawod F (2014) How Samarkand Was Conquered. http://islam.ru/en/content/story/how-samarkand-was-conquered. Accessed 22 May 2021
De Hart WC (1846) Observations on Military Law, and the Constitution, and Practice of Courts Martial. Wiley and Putnam, New York
De Pizan C (2003) The Book of Deeds of Arms and of Chivalry, 2nd edn. In: Willard C (ed/transl). Penn State University Press. https://books.google.fr/books?id=epXQh7B1w20C&lpg=PP1&dq=book%20of%20deeds%20of%20arms&hl=fr&pg=PP1#v=onepage&q&f=false. Accessed 22 May 2021
Donner F (1991) The Sources of Islamic Conceptions of War. In: Kelsay J, Johnson JT (eds) Just War and Jihad: Historical and Theoretical perspectives on War and Peace in Western and Islamic Traditions. Greenwood Press, New York, pp 31–70
Doty G (1982) The United States and the Development of the Laws of Land Warfare. Military Law Review 156, pp. pp. 224–255
Draper GIAD (1972) Implementation of International Law in Armed Conflict. INT'L AF 48, pp 46–58
du Plessis M (2008) The African Guide to International Criminal Justice: Purpose and Overview. In: du Plessis M (ed) (2008) African Guide to International Criminal Justice. Institute for Security Studies, pp 1–14
Falk R, Kolko G, Lifton R (eds) (1971) Crimes of War. Random House, New York
Fenrick W (1999) The Rome Statute of the International Criminal Court: Article 8 – War Crimes. In: Triffterer O (ed) Commentary on the Rome Statute of the International Criminal Court: Observers' Notes. Nomos Verlagsgesellschaft, Baden-Baden, pp 555–603
Ferencz B (2010) Preface. Available at: https://benferencz.org/articles/2010-present/illegal-armed-force-as-a-crime-against-humanity/. Accessed August 2021
Firestone R (1999) Jihād: The Origin of Holy War in Islam. Oxford University Press, Oxford
Firuzabadi M (1933) Al-Qamus al-Muhit, Cairo, vol. 1
Gasser HP et al. (1987) In: Sandoz Y, Swinarski C, Zimmermann B (eds) Commentary on the Additional Protocols to the Geneva Conventions, ICRC, pp. 1013–1014. https://www.loc.gov/rr/frd/Military_Law/pdf/Commentary_GC_Protocols.pdf. Accessed 22 May 2021

Giles L (transl) (1910) Sun Tzu on the Art of War: The Oldest Military Treatise in the World. Luzac & Co., London

Green LC (1995) Command Responsibility in International Humanitarian Law. Transnational Law & Contemporary Problems 5, pp. 319–342

Green LC (1999) War Crimes, Crimes against Humanity and Command Responsibility. In: Essays on the Modern Law of War, 2nd edn. Transnational Publisher, New York, pp. 77–117

Gross L (1955) The Punishment of War Criminals: The Nuremberg Trial. Netherlands International Law Review 11, pp. 356–370

Grotius H (1964) On the Laws of War and Peace. In: Kelsey FW (transl). Wildy Wiley & Sons, London

Guerra Medici MT (1999) The Mother of International Law: Christine de Pisan, Parliaments, Estates and Representation 19(1), pp.15–22

Hargreaves J (1970) The Rule Book of Warfare. U.S. Marine Corps Gazette, vol. 54

His Majesty's Stationery Office (1948) History of the United Nations War Crimes Commission and the Development of the Laws of War. http://www.unwcc.org/wpcontent/uploads/2017/04/UNWCC-history.pdf. Accessed 22 May 2021

Ibn al-Nahhas (2002) Mashari' al-Ashwaq, vol. 2

Ibn Qudama (1348) Al-Mughnī. Al-Manār, Egypt, vol 10, p 507. Available at: http://mc.dlib.nyu.edu/files/books/columbia_aco001735/columbia_aco001735_hi.pdf. Accessed April 2021

Kadduri M (1984) The Islamic Conception of Justice. Johns Hopkins University Press, Baltimore

Khalid H (1971) al-Shahid fi al-Islam. Dar al-'ilm li-al-Malayin, Beirut

Knoll E, McFadden J (eds) (1970) War Crimes and the American Conscience. Holt, Rinehart and Winston, New York

Lael RL (1982) The Yamashita Precedent: War Crimes and Command Responsibility. Scholarly Resources Inc., Delaware

Lanni A (2008) The Laws of War in Ancient Greece. Law and History Review 26(3), pp. 469–489

Latty F (2019) Founding "Fathers" of International Law: Recognizing Christine de Pizan. https://www.ejiltalk.org/founding-fathers-of-international-law-recognizing-christine-de-pizan/. Accessed 22 May 2021

Lauterpacht H (1944) The Law of Nations and the Punishment of War Crimes. British Yearbook of International Law 21, pp. 58–95

Linder DO (1999) An Introduction to the My Lai Courts-Martial. In My Lai: An Account Famous Trials, University of Missouri-Kansas City. http://law2.umkc.edu/faculty/projects/ftrials/mylai/Myl_intro.html. Accessed 22 May 2021

Lippman M (1993) War Crimes: The My Lai Massacre and The Vietnam War. San Diego Justice Journal, 1, pp. 360–397

Mälksoo L (2019) The Treaties of Brest-Litovsk, Versailles and Moscow: Contesting Sovereignty and Hegemony in Eastern Europe in 1918–1939. German Yearbook of International Law, pp. 189–209

Manu (Lawgiver) (1886) The Laws of Manu: Translated with Extracts from Seven Commentaries, (Bühler G (ed/transl)) (Sacred Books of the East, vol 25, Clarendon Press 1886)

Mao Z (1965) Problems of Strategy in China's Revolutionary War. In: Selected Works, vol. 1. For (for the original version, see Mao Zedong xuanji. Foreign Languages Press, Beijing)

Maridakis GS (1952) Un precedent du Procès de Nuremberg tire de l'histoire de la Grèce ancienne. Revue Hellénique De Droit International 5

McCormack T L H (1997) From Sun Tzu to the Sixth Committee: The Evolution of an International Criminal Law Regime. In: McCormack T L H, Simpson G J (eds) The Law of War Crimes: National and International Approaches. Kluwer Law International, The Hague, pp 31–63

Meloni C (2010) Command Responsibility in International Criminal Law. TMC Asser Press, The Hague

Meron T (1993) Henry's Wars and Shakespeare's Laws: Perspectives on the Law of War in the Later Middle Ages. Oxford University Press, Oxford

Meron T (2000) The Humanization of Humanitarian Law. 94 American Journal of International Law, pp. 239–278
Mettraux G (2009) The Law of Command Responsibility, Oxford University Press, Oxford
Nafziger GF, Walton MW (2003) Islam at War A History. Praeger Publishers, Westport
Naqvi AR (1974) Laws of War in Islam. Islamic Studies, 13(1), pp. 25–48
Neff SC (2012) Hugo Grotius on The Law of War and Peace. Cambridge University Press, Cambridge
O'Brien TM, Diefendorf O (1864) General Orders of the War Department Embracing the Years 1861, 1862 & 1863, vol. 2. Derby & Miller
O'Malley JM (1964) Justice in Shakespeare: The English Kings in the Light of Thomistic Thought. Pageant Press, New York
Ögren K (1996) Humanitarian Law in the Articles of War Decreed in 1621 by King Gustavus II Adolphus of Sweden. International Review of the Red Cross
Parks W (1973) Command Responsibility for War Crimes. Military Law Review 62, pp.1–104
Philipson C (1911) The International Law and Custom of Ancient Greece and Rome. Macmillan and Co., London
Pictet J (1960) Geneva Convention for the Amelioration of the Condition of Wounded, Sick and Shipwrecked Members of Armed Forces at Sea. ICRC, Geneva
Roberts A (2019) Foundational Myths in the Laws of War: The 1863 Lieber Code, and the 1864 Geneva Convention. Melbourne Journal of International Law 20(158), pp. 165–192
Roberts M (1953) Gustavus Adolphus: a history of Sweden, 1611–1632, Vol 1. Longmans, Green and Co., London
Roberts M (1958) Gustavus Adolphus: a history of Sweden, 1611–1632, Vol 2. Longmans, Green and Co., London
Sandburg C, Lincoln A (1961) The Prairie Years and the War Years. Harcourt, Brace & World, New York
Sengheiser J (2007–2008) Command responsibility for Omissions and Detainee Abuse in the "War on Terror". Thomas Jefferson Law Review, 30, pp. 1–44
Shelling F (1927) Shakespeare and 'Demi-Science'. University of Pennsylvania Press, Philadelphia
Sherman EF (1970) The Civilization of Military Law. Maine Law Review 22(1), pp. 3–40.
Smidt ML (2000) Yamashita, Medina, and Beyond: Command Responsibility in Contemporary Military Operations. Military Law Review, pp. 155–175
Solf WA, Cummings ER (1977) A Survey of Penal Sanctions under Protocol I to the Geneva Conventions of 12 August 1949. Case Western Reserve Journal of International Law 9:205–233. Available at: https://scholarlycommons.law.case.edu/jil/vol9/iss2/2. Accessed 23 April 2021
Stone J (2011) Aggression and World Order: A Critique of United Nations Theories of Aggression. Law Book Exchange edition
Sun Tzu (1963) The Art of War (Griffith SB (transl)). Oxford University Press, Oxford
Sun Tzu, Minford J (2002) The Art of War. New England Review 23(3):5
The Qur'an, https://quran.com/search?query=not+fight+them+invite+them&language=0&translation=0. Accessed 22 May 2021
UN War Crimes Commission (1949) Law Reports of Trials of War Criminals, High Command Case, Vol. XII, p. 76. https://www.loc.gov/rr/frd/Military_Law/pdf/Law-Reports_Vol-12.pdf. Accessed May 2021
United States War Department (1917) Rules of Land Warfare, Doc. No. 467, Office of the Chief of Staff, approved Apr. 25, 1914 (G.P.O. 1917)
Van Aarde TA (2018) The relation between religion and state in Islam and Christianity in the rise of ISIS. In Die Skriflig 52(1), pp. 1–8
Van der Vyver J (2015) Acts of Aggression and Prosecuting the Crime of Aggression. LAMBERT Publ., Germany
Van der Vyver J (2021) International Criminal Law: Crimes within the Jurisdiction of the International Criminal Court, vol. II. LAP LAMBERT Publ., Germany

Vetter GR (2000) Command Responsibility of Non-Military Superiors in the International Criminal Court (ICC). Yale Journal of International Law 25(89), pp. 89 149
Watt M (2018) In: Partridge C, Dowley T (eds) A Historical Overview. A Brief Introduction to Islam, vol. 4,1517 Media, Minneapolis
Weeramantry CG (1988) Islamic Jurisprudence: An International Perspective. Palgrave Macmillan Press, Basingstoke
White EJ (1913) Commentaries on the law in Shakespeare. F.H. Thomas Law Book Co., St. Louis, MO, pp 291–292
Winthrop W (1895) Military Law And Precedents, 2nd edn. Government Printing Office (G.P.O.), Washington, D.C. Available at https://archive.org/details/cu31924020024570/page/n3/mode/2up Accessed 22 May 2021
Witt JF (2012) Lincoln's Code: The Laws of War in American History. Free Press, New York
Yacoubian M (2018) A New U.S. Strategy Will Keep American Troops in Syria. U.S. Institute of Peace. https://www.usip.org/publications/2018/01/new-usstrategy-will-keep-american-troops-syria [https://perma.cc/6NSJ-W3NF]. Accessed 22 May 2021

Other Documents

Convention on the Non-applicability of Statutory Limitations to War Crimes and Crimes Against Humanity, Article 2. https://www.un.org/en/genocideprevention/documents/atrocitycrimes/Doc.27_convention%20statutory%20limitations%20warcrimes.pdf. Accessed May 2021
Instruction for the Government of the United States in the Field by Order of the Secretary of War, in Washington D.C., Apr. 24 1863, NO. 100 and approved by President Lincoln, Schindler, and Toman, 3
Memorandum of Reservations Presented by the Representatives of the United States to the Report of the Commission on Responsibilities, Annex II (1920) April 1919, 14. American Journal of International Law
Protocol Additional to the Geneva Conventions of 12 August 1949, and Relating to the Protection of Victims of International Armed Conflicts (Protocol I) (1977) Article 86(2), U.N. Doc. A/32/144, 1125 U.N.T.S. 3, reprinted in 16 I.L.M. 1391
Provisional Congress of Massachusetts Bay (1775) Articles of War, April 5, 1775
Rome Statute of the International Criminal Court (1998) 2187 U.N.T.S. 3 (entered into force 1 July 2002). http://untreaty.un.org/cod/icc/statute/romefra.htm, Art 28. Accessed May 2021
Treaty of Peace with Germany (Treaty of Versailles), 28 June 1919. https://www.loc.gov/law/help/us-treaties/bevans/m-ust000002-0043.pdf. Accessed 22 May 2021

Chapter 3
The Rudiments of the Superior Responsibility Doctrine

Contents

Abstract This chapter examines the conceptual components, legal characterization, and practical application of the doctrine of superior responsibility under the Laws of Armed Conflict (LoAC), culminating in its evolution into a mode of liability under international(ized) criminal tribunals. It distinguishes between LoAC's imposition of disciplinary responsibility on military commanders and international criminal law's (ICL) imposition of vicarious criminal liability on military and political superiors for international crimes committed by subordinates. The chapter critically explores the doctrinal and terminological ambiguities surrounding "command" and "superior" responsibility, highlighting divergent interpretations by tribunals and scholars, and the challenges posed by fragmented treaty provisions and early, also fragmented, jurisprudence. Through a comparative and critical analysis of legal texts, case law, and academic scholarship, it clarifies the doctrine's core elements and refutes the misconception that superior responsibility, for example, is merely omission-based liability.

H. Y. Al-Fadhli, *Prosecuting Superior Responsibility in International Criminal Law*,
https://doi.org/10.1007/978-94-6265-735-9_3

Rather, it supports the view that the doctrine constitutes a *sui generis* mode of liability, exclusive to ICL and grounded in a consequentialist normative framework. This theoretical approach—anchored in historical developments outlined in the previous chapter—offers a more coherent legal and moral basis for understanding superior responsibility as such, balancing liberal criminal law principles with humanitarian and human rights imperatives in addressing mass atrocity. Importantly, this chapter focuses on the jurisprudence of the *ad hoc* and hybrid tribunals, where the doctrine has developed most significantly. References to the Rome Statute are included only to establish comparative context, while a detailed analysis of its provisions is reserved for the next chapter.

Keywords Superior responsibility in international criminal law · Command responsibility in law of armed conflict · Consequential culpability · Omission liability · Modes of liability · UN *ad hoc* tribunals

3.1 Introduction

> *The common sense of mankind demands that law shall not stop with the punishment of petty crimes by little people. It must also reach men who possess themselves of great power and make deliberate and concerted use of it to set in motion evils which leave no home in the world untouched.*[1]

The aim of this chapter is to set out the basic conceptual components of the doctrine of superior responsibility. This examination will be undertaken in accordance solely with the Laws of Armed Conflict (LoAC) and the laws of the UN criminal tribunals (namely, the statutes of the *ad hoc* and hybrid criminal tribunals).[2]

On the one hand, the LoAC impose responsibility on military commanders primarily as a result of their failure to control military operations conducted by forces under their command and in instances where this failure leads to or may lead to the commission of crimes connected with the armed conflict.[3] The LoAC also impose responsibility on military commanders based on their entrusted official duties, such as issuing orders to their forces and supervising their operations during

[1] Jackson 1947.

[2] *Rome Statute of the International Criminal Court*, 17 July 1998, 2187 U.N.T.S. 3, Article 28 (entered into force 1 July 2002), http://untreaty.un.org/cod/icc/statute/romefra.htm (hereinafter Rome Statute). The Rome Statute of the International Criminal Court enshrines an elaborate structure for this doctrine, which will be examined in Chap. 4.

[3] The law of armed conflict or international humanitarian law regulates the conduct of army groups involved in an armed conflict. This regulation outlines the rights and duties of both parties, as well as civilian individuals, along with the duty to protect certain properties from attack. However, international criminal law penalizes such conduct, along with other international crimes, such as genocide, crimes against humanity, crimes of aggression, by trying and prosecuting the individuals responsible for committing these crimes. For a detailed explanation of this, see Wise and Podgor 2014, pp 496–515; Bruce 2014, p. 53; Bantekas 2006, p. 122.

the armed conflict.[4] In this context, the latter responsibility is referred to as command responsibility in its *lato sensu*. It is also known as direct command responsibility or responsible command.[5]

For the purposes of criminal prosecutions, however, ICL imposes criminal responsibility on a superior both for their own crimes[6] and/or for the crimes of their subordinates' owing to their failure to execute supervisory duties.[7] ICL draws a distinction between the criminal responsibility of military and military-like superiors and that of political superiors.[8] In contemporary practice, this distinction of criminal liability between these two categories of individuals is known as the Superior Responsibility Doctrine (a retronym for the Command Responsibility Doctrine), which encompasses both military commanders and political superiors.[9] However, with respect to the characterization of the doctrine, the key difference between these two bodies of law (LoAC and ICL) is that the former law imposes disciplinary responsibility for omissions, prosecutable at the national level, while the latter law imposes criminal liability vicariously for crimes committed as a result of omissions at the international level.[10] I shall use the term "superior" responsibility throughout this book unless the term "command" is required for the purpose of juxtaposition and further discussion.

A priori, this distinction has generated considerable challenges and complications when it comes to the legal characterization of this doctrine's nature—specifically, whether superior responsibility constitutes a distinct mode of liability or a punishable crime of omission *per se*—as well as the prevalent use of the terms *superior* and *command*.[11] Such challenges also stem from questions about how international[ized] criminal tribunals may apply this doctrine to an accused, particularly in relation to its legal requirements. Notably, most of these challenges also stem primarily from the divergent statutory (mis)interpretations of early scholarly writings, early (and ongoing) court decisions, and the opinions of commentators in this field.[12] These divergent interpretations have, in turn, led to an incoherent system of superior responsibility, either rendering the phenomenon even more complex or, worse, leading to a tendency to abolish it.[13]

---

[4] Vetter 2000, p. 99.

[5] Jackson 2019, p. 414. See also Meloni 2007, p. 622.

[6] Van der Vyver 2021, p. 568.

[7] Ibid., p. 569.

[8] *Nahimana et al. v. The Prosecutor*, Case No. ICTR-99-52-A, para 605, 28 November 2007.

[9] Meloni 2010, p. 1. See also, generally, Ambos 2002, pp. 823, 872; Guénaël 2009, p. 307; Bantekas 2002.

[10] Bruce 2014. See also van der Vyver 2021, pp. 571–572.

[11] Namely, which term—superior or command—is the correct term for this concept, and under which mode of liability it falls, as well as the various requirements for both individuals.

[12] Kortfält 2017, p. 280.

[13] In this sense, according to the statement by the former Chief Prosecutor of the ICTY, Carla del Ponte: "The ICTY has confirmed that it tends to abolish the concept of command responsibility in international criminal law as well as the concept of complicity of military and civilian leaders in systemic violence. This has rewarded the masterminds of the system who managed, through deception, to plan and organize violence on a mass scale…, making sure

These challenges associated with superior responsibility have also resulted in controversy in the laws and treaties that deal with this doctrine. The origin of these outmoded customary laws and treaties can be traced to the 1889–1907 Hague Conventions, the 1906 and 1929 Geneva Conventions, and the Geneva Conventions of August 12, 1949, from whose Articles the current parameters of command responsibility originate.[14] As these laws and treaties, which hold customary law status, refer to this doctrine in a random and non-exhaustive manner, its requirements were neither clear nor well-defined. These scattered references have resulted in challenges with drafting theory, particularly in relation to the statutes of international[ized] criminal tribunals and the practice fallacy associated with statutory-oriented decisions. Owing to these challenges, both with the drafting of theory and at the practical level, scholars have struggled to clearly define and identify this phenomenon. This is exemplified by the fact that, in the jurisprudence of these courts, political superiors are sometimes conflated with military commanders, and *vice versa*.[15] This is misleading both in terms of terminology and in terms of the essential conceptual elements of this doctrine in relation to superiors.[16]

Further adding to these challenges, perhaps the most notable, widely discussed assertion by scholars is the assumption that a superior accused on the basis of superior responsibility is criminally charged for their omission *per se*, rather than for the crimes of their subordinates.[17] Moreover, in terms of terminology, the "superior responsibility" rubric does not appear to be as popular or as well-recognized as that of "command responsibility",[18] which again results in unsystematic conclusions concerning the status of the superior who is being accused. In the statutes of many international[ized] criminal tribunals, their decisions often refer to the "command responsibility" rubric.[19] As demonstrated in the literature, this results in a theoretically misleading concept when it comes to the key distinction between the statuses of

that they did not write a direct order." Acquittal of Stanisic and Simatovic yet another blow to ICTY's credibility, DALJE.COM, http://dalje.com/en-world/acquittal-of-stanisic-andsimatovic-yet-another-blow-to-ictys-credibility/470412 (accessed 24 January 2020).

[14] The Hague Conventions impose disciplinary obligations on military commanders and their forces, while the statutes of international criminal tribunals impose criminal punishments for the crimes committed due to commanders' dereliction of their duties.

[15] *Prosecutor v. Vujadin Popović et al.*, Appeals Chamber, Case No. IT-05-88-A, para 1932, 30 January 2015.

[16] As I shall discuss further in this chapter, international case law uses both terms, particularly in relation to the *mens rea* element set out under the ICC Rome Statute.

[17] Schabas 2004, pp. 249–250. See also Damaška 2001, p. 455.

[18] Command responsibility has been widely referenced throughout history and this continues to be the case in the current literature. The misuse of the term under current international criminal law standards is problematic because it refers only to military commanders, excluding other superiors, who are as responsible as military commanders.

[19] The doctrine of superior responsibility is regulated by the statutes of international criminal courts, such as the International Criminal Tribunals of the former Yugoslavia and Rwanda: Articles 7(3) and 6(3) of the ICTY and ICTR statutes, respectively. It is also included in the statutes of hybrid criminal tribunals created through an agreement between the UN and governments that wanted their nationals to be prosecuted, such as the Special Tribunal for Lebanon and the Special Court

these two individuals concerned—*i.e.*, civilian superiors and military commanders and their subordinates.

Regarding the objective scope of superior criminal responsibility, Linnea Kortfält, along with a significant majority of scholars in this field, notes that individual criminal responsibility on the part of subordinates "corresponds to the most serious qualification of individual criminal responsibility."[20] Such a note may be acceptable—and even appropriate—within national systems and state practice.[21] However, in a *stricto sensu* ICL context, international crimes differ in nature from domestic crimes. Conceptually, international crimes are often committed within the context of a wide, systematic, organized framework,[22] with the subordinates who commit such crimes often demonstrating allegiance to their superior, who effectively controls their behavior.[23] In other words, the implementation of criminal justice in international law relies on trying those deemed the "most responsible".[24] Superiors are often at the center of international criminal proceedings because they are typically implicated in the commission of most crimes—whether directly through their own actions, indirectly through omissions, or vicariously, by being held responsible for the actions and omissions of their subordinates, as articulated by the doctrine of superior responsibility. In this latter mode, superiors have a serious legal obligation to prevent, repress, punish, or report crimes committed by those under their authority/command.[25] These duties thus underscore the importance of holding superiors criminally accountable. In this context, the nature and structure of international crimes challenge the assumption that state practice and international prosecutions operate symmetrically.

Following this overview of the phenomenon, the domain within which it emerged and the issues associated with its practice, this chapter is dedicated to a discussion of the misconception surrounding the doctrine of superior responsibility. More importantly, it will, *inter alia,* shed light on the conceptual components of the doctrine and explore the various definitions proposed by leading scholars, with a view to identifying the understanding most closely aligned with its international disciplinary and criminal character. In addition, this chapter will also explore the legal characterization of the concept through a comparative analysis of scholarly writings and case law, seeking to offer a contributory solution to this non-contributory mode of liability. I shall also analyze the key elements of this doctrine through a critical analysis focused on its codifications and jurisprudence. Through these approaches, I shall

for Sierra-Leone. It should be noted that, under Article 28, the Rome Statute still utilizes the term "command".

20 Kortfält 2017, p. 280.

21 Ambos 2009, p. 127.

22 Ibid., pp. 128–129.

23 Ibid.

24 Jackson 1947. See also the keynote speech of Stewart, Deputy Prosecutor of the ICC, on transitional justice in Colombia and the role of the ICC, organized by the Universidad del Rosario, 13 May 2015.

25 Rome Statute. See also Ambos 2002, p. 825.

seek to establish how courts have dealt (or are currently dealing) with this concept in relation to the accused, and how most scholars have presented misleading definitions of this doctrine and its elements. Ultimately, the overarching aim of this chapter is to address how the doctrine of superior responsibility has been crafted through the prosecution of superiors, resulting in a redefined concept in the contemporary period.

In terms of its scope, it is crucial to note that this chapter centers exclusively on a discussion of the conceptual components and practical applications of superior responsibility within the context of the subject-matter jurisdiction of the *ad hoc* and hybrid criminal tribunals. Therefore, I shall make only tangential reference to the Rome Statute of the ICC, to the extent necessary to establish the comparative context. Concerning the Rome Statute, Chap. 4 will explore superior responsibility within the subject-matter jurisdiction of this statute.

3.2 Superior Responsibility: Definitions, Codifications, and International Case Law

In this section, I shall examine the doctrine of superior responsibility from a comparative and critical perspective, as outlined earlier. I shall further explore the various definitions presented by leading scholars and set out in jurisprudence. In terms of descriptive and informative frameworks, I shall draw from international treaties that have promulgated this doctrine within their subject-matter, as well as briefly examining how superior responsibility is described in international instruments and case law.

3.2.1 Definitions

The doctrine of "command responsibility" was the first expression of vicarious criminal responsibility that addressed the criminality of military commanders under international law.[26] In its *lato sensu* sense, and within the military context, this doctrine relates to the criminal responsibility of a military commander for the crimes committed either by themselves or by their forces because of their failure to supervise their conduct properly.[27] The actions of these forces result in the criminal liability of their commander, which constitutes the legal justification for this distinct mode of liability in this context—according to the *stricto sensu* view (otherwise known as the military commander's vicarious liability).[28] Traditionally, this doctrine has been

26 Meloni 2010, p. 1. See also van Sliedregt 2012a, p. 63.

27 Meloni 2007. See also Damaška 2001, p. 455.

28 The legal characterization of superior responsibility will be discussed in further detail in Sect. 3.3, *infra*.

promulgated in military settings as the doctrine of command responsibility, finding its origins in the LoAC.[29]

As noted earlier, the *lato*sensu definition of command responsibility evolved through two key stages of customary international law. At the outset, it derived by analogy, from the Hague Conventions of 1899 and 1907 (hereinafter: the Hague Laws).[30] Within these conventions, command responsibility was broadly understood, referring only to the duties of both parties within the superior–subordinate relationship. In the second stage, the Hague Laws were succeeded by the first Geneva Conventions of 1906 and 1929, as well as by the 12 August 1949, Geneva Conventions and their Additional Protocols.[31] In these conventions, the doctrine of "superior responsibility" was officially structured as a well-defined, substantive law, albeit still within the context of LoAC practice. In this section, I shall therefore define the doctrine of command/superior responsibility within the context of LoAC, as well as the recently adopted framework in ICL, which builds on the former field, encompassing both military and political superiors under the framework of superior responsibility as an international criminal mode of liability.[32]

At the outset, in terms of theoretical codification and practical application guidelines, the interaction between LoAC and ICL helped to guide international judges in shaping the doctrine of superior responsibility, particularly in terms of its definition

---

[29] Jackson 1947. It should be noted that LoAC derived this doctrine from the US Lieber Code. See Roberts 2019, p. 186.

[30] Hague Convention II, Convention with Respect to the Laws and Customs of War on Land, 29 July 1899, 32 Stat. 1803, T.S. No. 403; Hague Convention IV, Convention Respecting the Laws and Customs of War on Land, 18 October 1907, 36 Stat. 2277, T.S. No. 539.

[31] Geneva Convention for the Amelioration of the Condition of the Wounded and Sick in Armies in the Field, 6 July 1906, 35 Stat. 1885, T.S. No. 464; Geneva Convention for the Amelioration of the Condition of the Wounded and Sick in Armies in the Field, 27 July 1929, 47 Stat. 2074, T.S. No. 846; Geneva Conventions of 12 August 1949, 6 U.S.T. 3114, 75 U.N.T.S. 31 (four conventions); Protocol Additional to the Geneva Conventions of 12 August 1949 and Relating to the Protection of Victims of International Armed Conflicts (Protocol I), 8 June 1977, 1125 U.N.T.S. 3; Protocol Additional to the Geneva Conventions of 12 August 1949, and Relating to the Protection of Victims of Non-International Armed Conflicts (Protocol II), 8 June 1977, 1125 U.N.T.S. 609.

[32] This section focuses on the definitions of the doctrines of command responsibility and superior responsibility within the context of international law, excluding municipal laws, which include further details and obligations according to national law. For example, the United States Military Code places more obligations on commanders than those regulated by international law, holding commanders responsible not only for international crimes but also for civil crimes. For more details, see B. U. S. Army 1971, *Responsibility for civic action training is vested in the US Army. This training responsibility is further delegated to the United States Continental Army Command*. Moreover, the Guantanamo Bay Military Tribunals have held superiors responsible for causing harm to their subordinates (positive liability), assigning them responsibility not for their subordinates' conduct but also for their criminal conduct towards those subordinates. Rosenberg, *He Waterboarded a Detainee. Then He Had to Get the C.I.A. to Let Him Stop, New York Times* (2020), https://www.nytimes.com/2020/01/22/us/politics/cia-torture-interrogation-guantanamo.html (accessed 24 January 2020).

and its central elements.[33] With this in mind, LoAC played a central role exclusively in these important formative efforts, particularly in relation to the conceptual definition of the doctrine of superior responsibility.[34]

While LoAC defined "command responsibility" as a disciplinary responsibility for omission—applicable nationally—in the early stages of ICL, the doctrine of "command responsibility" imposed criminal responsibility on a military commander (or any other individual acting in the role of a military commander)[35] for the crimes committed by forces under their command/authority and control. Intriguingly, ICL deems the commander culpable for the crimes of their subordinates, such that they may be charged for the commission of these crimes.[36] In other words, when accusing a military commander under this specific context of the doctrine in its *stricto sensu* application, they shall be responsible and charged for crimes committed by their forces, even when they did not contribute to the commission of the crimes.[37] In contemporary theory and practice, ICL applies this mode of liability both to military commanders and to political leaders in the role of Head of State, as well as to individuals who have effective authority and control over governmental personnel and police departments—under the advanced rubric of "superior responsibility".[38] Unlike the LoAC definition, ICL then defines this doctrine as a distinct-in-nature mode of liability wherein a superior can be held criminally responsible for crimes committed by their subordinates at the international level.

Before proceeding to examine the scholarly debate over how to define superior responsibility, it should first be noted that some scholars generally conceptualize this doctrine based on its municipal law context, such as the Lieber Code, US domestic military manuals, and the German Code of Crimes against international law (*Völkerstrafgesetzbuch*).[39] I would argue, however, that the attempt to apply domestic laws to international law principles in the literature has resulted in a paradoxical definition and identification of the doctrine and its elements.

---

33 Wise and Podgor 2014.

34 *Prosecutor v. Hadžihasanović et al.*, Appeals Chamber, Case No. IT-01-47-AR72, para 29, 16 July 2003. (The Tribunal decided that "[t]he Appeals Chamber affirms the view of the Trial Chamber that command responsibility was part of customary international law relating to international armed conflicts before the adoption of Protocol I. Therefore, as the Trial Chamber considered, Arts 86 and 87 of Protocol I were in this respect only declaring the existing position, and not constituting it.").

35 Rome Statute, Article 28(a).

36 Ibid.

37 See Sect. 3.3.

38 Guénaël 2009, p. 26. See also *Prosecutor v. Alfred Musema*, Judgment, Case No. ICTR-96-13-T, para 148, 27 January 2000.

39 The Lieber Code, in which command responsibility originated from this American military law. U.S. Department of War, Instructions for the Government of Armies of the United States in the Field, General Orders No. 100, 24 April 1863, https://www.loc.gov/rr/frd/Military_Law/Lieber_Collection/pdf/Instructions-gov-armies.pdf (accessed 24 January 2020). See also Meloni 2010, p. 205; Lieber 1863.

The academic literature, particularly writings relating to LoAC, defines superior responsibility in accordance with its standard military model, which has resulted in confusion when it comes to both the terminology and elements of the doctrine. For example, it has been defined as follows:

> Command (or superior) responsibility is a form of liability used in military and international law to hold an individual in a leadership position accountable for the actions of his subordinates...[t]he commander can be held [if he or she knew or should have known of unlawful actions committed by his or her troops] accountable for such actions... [a]s if those two reasons were not enough – international law may hold the commander responsible for acts he did not commit.[40]

Under ICL, this definition may result in an inaccuracy in both theoretical and practical terms. On the one hand, the author conflates military commanders and political superiors under the umbrella of the command responsibility rubric, while at the same time applying this "international" concept to domestic military laws.[41] As discussed earlier, in ICL, superior responsibility involves two different individuals: "[A]... military official who holds a high rank in a chain-of-command and has the effective *command* and control over military forces...[and] a political superior in a position of leadership and has an effective *authority* and control over either military forces or government personnel"[42] (emphasis added).

In addition, the author misinterprets the conceptual framework of the fault element of this doctrine. According to the definition given, if subordinates commit international crimes, and the superior "knew" (intent) or "should have known" (negligence) about the commission of these crimes, they will then be held accountable.[43] Assuming the other requirements are all met, this would apply only to a military commander.[44] I shall discuss this fault element further on; however, for the purposes of this paragraph, the fault element of a military commander is confined to either actual knowledge or negligence *per se*.[45] The fault element for a political superior, on the other hand, according, for example, to the Rome Statute of the ICC, requires intent when the superior "knew" (intent) or "consciously disregarded information to know", which similarly implies either recklessness or "willful blindness" (a form of intent).[46] The author may have intended to define only the military commander's responsibility under the ICC's Rome Statute, rendering the overall conclusion insufficient.

---

[40] Blank and Noone 2013, p. 653.

[41] Damaška 2001, p. 455.

[42] *THE PROSECUTOR v. CLÉMENT KAYISHEMA & OBED RUZINDANA*, Case No. ICTR-95-1-T, paras 213–215 (21 May 1999). See also *Prosecutor v. Zejnil Delalic & Others*, Case No. IT-96-21-T, para 356, 16 November 1998.

[43] Rome Statute, Article 28(a).

[44] Ibid.

[45] Ibid. See also van der Vyver 2021, p. 586.

[46] Ibid.

Mirjan Damaška defines the concept of command responsibility as "an umbrella term used in military and international law to cover a variety of ways in which individuals in positions of leadership may be held accountable."[47] While this definition captures the *lato sensu* interpretation of superior responsibility, it does not align with the doctrinal precision or analytical focus required in this book, at least with regard to its latest development. The continued use of the term "command" in place of "superior" risks conflating distinct categories of superiority and may introduce both theoretical and practical ambiguities. Nonetheless, Damaška's formulation may have been intended to highlight the dual dimensions of superior responsibility: the active role of a superior who orders the commission of crimes, and the passive role of one who incurs liability for the crimes committed by subordinates by failing to prevent or punish them.[48]

Moreover, scholars continue to confuse the subject-matter of this concept when it comes to the vicarious criminal responsibility of a superior, interpreting the doctrine as: "[s]uperior responsibility is a form of indirect liability as the superior is not held criminally liable for the acts in which he participated… but in connection with the criminal acts committed by his subordinates."[49] This definition conflicts with the premise of this doctrine, which strictly stipulates that a superior is held liable *for* crimes owing to their *failure* to control their subordinates within the confines of their legal capacity. Simply put, a superior is held criminally responsible not only because they are responsible for not controlling their subordinates' conduct—which would be handled at the domestic level on the grounds of negligent supervision of the troops under their command—but also because of their failure to fulfill the full range of their duties, ensuring genuine prevention.[50] In certain circumstances, the "in connection" assertion can imply direct liability, where a superior plays an accessorial

---

[47] Damaška 2001, p. 455.

[48] Ambos notes that the concepts of direct and indirect liabilities of a superior can take place through the following scenarios: (i) a superior is responsible for crimes committed by their subordinates *because* of the negligence aspect (indirect liability); and (ii) a superior is liable for negligence only (direct liability). In the latter scenario, a superior would be held responsible under domestic laws, although this would not necessarily be prosecutable at the international level in its own right. However, under international law, a superior is held directly responsible not only in the scenario of Ambos concerning a superior's direct liability but also if the superior orders subordinates to commit international crimes. In this case, the superior is held liable both as a superior and as a direct participant. See Ambos 2002, p. 824. In addition, in the *Čelebići* case, the Trial Chambers held that: "[i]deally a superior who participates in the actual commission of a crime should be found guilty both as a superior and also as a direct participant as any of the other participants who did so in obedience to his orders." *Prosecutor v. Zejnil Delalic & Others*, Case No. IT-96-21-T, para 1223, cf. Galand et al. 2016, p. 14. (Scholars in this edition argue that ordering, planning, or instigating all constitute a form of indirect liability. As discussed above, this is misleading and contrary to the causal link between the perpetrator and the criminal conduct in question, as applied under international case law.)

[49] Vark 2016.

[50] Van der Vyver 2021, p. 596.

role in aiding or abetting the actual perpetrators of the crimes (the subordinates who committed them).[51]

During the conference negotiations concerning the API to the Geneva Conventions of 12 August 1949, discussions were held about penalizing the passive conduct of an individual in a position of control over military troops. Notably, an Austrian representative addressed the definition of superior responsibility in the following terms:

> Penal sanctions were inevitable to ensure the implementation of Protocol I in cases of grave breaches, and in order to be effective, the system of sanctions should be as comprehensive as possible [and] should include failure to act, which could be as harmful as the commission of a breach. As a matter of law and fact, a commander is responsible for these criminal acts as if he or she physically committed it.[52]

On this basis, under international law, a superior may be charged *for* crimes committed by their subordinates in line with their failure to execute their duties toward these subordinates.

William Fenrick supports the definition presented by the Austrian representative, arguing that, "The international law doctrine of command responsibility was, in its origins, a legal vehicle whereby military commanders and certain other persons could be held liable for the criminal activities of their subordinates because they omitted or failed to control their subordinates."[53] This definition reiterates the premise of this particular form of responsibility, indicating that it is not an omission offense *per se*[54] but rather entails vicarious liability for the subordinates' criminal conduct, which is attributed to their superior owing to their failure to control the subordinates' criminal actions.[55]

Applying the doctrine of superior responsibility to peacekeeping missions' context adds another dimension. In principle, this doctrine applies to all individuals in a superior position within a military/authority context, holding them criminally responsible for crimes committed against both civilians and combatants (or those *hors de combats*) in violation of LoAC.[56] However, in the context of peacekeeping missions,[57] superior responsibility applies to the peacekeeping commander with respect to the peacekeepers' failure to protect civilians in an armed conflict.[58] In

[51] Ibid., p. 597.

[52] Summary Record of the Fiftieth Meeting, 4 May 1976, CDDH/I/SR.50, pp. 115, 120, paras 38, 68. ("By and large, implementation of [Additional] Protocol I and of the Geneva Conventions depended on commanders. Without their conscientious supervision, general legal requirements were unlikely to be effective.")

[53] Fenrick 1999, pp. 516–517. (Here, it is maintained that a superior is an accomplice to their subordinates' crimes.)

[54] Van der Vyver 2021, p. 570.

[55] Ibid.

[56] Sprik 2020, p. 5. The author reports that the concept of superior responsibility is different here because peacekeeping missions are distinct from armed conflicts within the context of LoAC.

[57] Ibid., p. 77.

[58] Ibid., pp. 100–108.

other words, during a peacekeeping mission, a superior is held criminally responsible for crimes committed by their peacekeeping subordinates only against protected civilians involved in the peacekeeping mission.

In conclusion, the definition of superior responsibility must encompass two contextual considerations: (i) the understanding of *superior responsibility*, which encompasses both military and political superiors; and (ii) its distinct characterization as vicarious liability, where a superior is charged for crimes committed by their subordinates. I shall delve further into this characterization after situating the doctrine of superior responsibility within international instruments and case law.

3.2.2 International Treaties: Situating Superior Responsibility

For the sake of this subsection, it is first worth setting out some brief historical insights regarding all the treaties that included superior responsibility within their subject-matter Articles. This section will then focus on international treaties, including the statutes of international(ized) criminal tribunals and case law, where superior responsibility is considered within their subject-matter jurisdictional Articles.

Along with customary international law, recent international treaties played a central role in the evolution of the doctrine of superior responsibility.[59] From 1864 to 2009, the international community strived to establish a clearly-defined framework to hold superiors in higher seniority ranks responsible.[60] These codification efforts took the form of international agreements, including the statutes that established international criminal courts.

At the international level, the term "command" responsibility first appeared in the First Geneva Convention of 1864.[61] Article 6 of this Convention states that, "Commanders- in-Chief may hand over immediately to the enemy outposts enemy combatants wounded during an engagement when circumstances allow and subject to the agreement of both parties."[62] Article 8 of the same Convention reads, "The implementing of the present Convention shall be arranged by the Commanders-in-Chief of the belligerent armies following the instructions of their respective Governments and in accordance with the general principles set forth in this Convention."[63]

Within its subject-matter Articles, while the First Geneva Convention of 1864 set out broad responsibilities entrusted to military commanders, it did not provide an explicit definition of superior responsibility as per its modern structure. Rather, the

---

[59] Fenrick 1999, p. 518.

[60] From the First Geneva Convention in 1864 with respect to the LoAC, up to the last statute of the *ad hoc* tribunals under ICL.

[61] Convention for the Amelioration of the Wounded in Armies in the Field, 22 August 1864, 22 Stat. 940, T.S. No. 377.

[62] Ibid., Article 6.

[63] Ibid., Article 8.

Convention merely makes occasional references to mutual obligations and martial values, on the basis of which a Commander-in-Chief should be held responsible while fulfilling his military responsibilities during an armed conflict, particularly with respect to prisoners of war (POWs) and wounded enemy soldiers.[64] By contrast, this particular Convention was established to regulate the treatment of wounded POWs and enemy soldiers under a commander's authority; this is also known as the responsible command theory as noted earlier. One commentator on the Convention, though, suggested that the identification and/or assignment of a commander would be based on bilateral agreements between the two high contracting army groups or the states in conflict with one another.[65] Such bilateral agreements would then identify the duties and rights of army groups in an armed conflict. Notably, while customary international law was the primary source when it came to the appointment of military commanders, this Convention concerned only the medicinal obligations that needed to be fulfilled toward army groups.[66]

In 1899, 1906, and 1907, on the basis of municipal laws, "command" responsibility began to take the form of an accountability mandate under international law.[67] The Hague Convention of 1899 listed the duties of a person in authority toward his subordinates, as commander-in-chief, as exemplified under its Articles. Article 1 of the Convention asserts that: "The laws, rights, and duties of war apply not only to armies but also to militia and volunteer corps fulfilling the following conditions: 1. [to] be commanded by a person responsible for his subordinates…."[68] Article 26 proclaims that, "The commander of an attacking force, before commencing a bombardment, except in the case of an assault, should do all he can to warn the authorities."[69] Article 51 stipulates that "No tax shall be collected except under a written order and on the responsibility of a commander-in-chief."[70] These Articles have closely relatable implications for the military concept of command responsibility, which, in hindsight, have influenced the formulation of the current doctrine of superior responsibility.[71] For example, the Convention suggests that a person in authority has obligations toward his or her subordinates, alluding to the superior–subordinate relationship element, which is central to the doctrine.[72]

---

64 Gasser et al. 1987, p. 688.

65 Bruce 2014, p. 11.

66 Gasser et al. 1987, p. 218.

67 For example, the Lieber Code, see n. 39. Meloni notes that the doctrine of command responsibility was first regulated in the First AP of the Geneva Conventions. This is not completely accurate, however, as the doctrine was debated and regulated on multiple occasions before this protocol. Meloni 2010, pp. 65–66.

68 Convention Respecting the Laws and Customs of War on Land, with annex of regulations, 18 October 1907, 36 Stat. 2277, Article 1.

69 Ibid., Article 26.

70 Ibid., Article 51.

71 Ambos 2002.

72 These conventions established interchangeable moral obligations between a commander and their subordinates. However, "they do not establish any sanction or consequence for the failure to do so". See Galand et al. 2016, p. 19.

Article 19 of the Second Hague Convention (1907) proceeds to state: "The commander-in- chief of the belligerent fleets must see that the above Articles are properly carried out: they will also have to see to cases not covered thereby, in accordance with the instructions of their respective Governments and in conformity with the general principles of the present Convention."[73] Article 26 of the same Convention further asserts that "The Commanders-in-Chief of belligerent armies shall arrange the details for carrying out the preceding Articles as well as for cases not provided for in accordance with the instructions of their respective Governments and in conformity with the general principles of the present Convention."[74] In the same vein as the Articles of the Hague Convention of 1899, Article 51 makes implicit reference to the superior–subordinate relationship, a central element of this doctrine. This Article highlights the authority entrusted to commanders with respect to their subordinates, asserting that, "No contribution shall be collected except under a written order, and on the responsibility of a commander-in-chief."[75] Article 52 of the Convention then proclaims that, "Requisitions in kind and services shall not be demanded from municipalities or inhabitants except for the needs of the army of occupation… [s]uch requisitions and services shall only be demanded on the authority of the commander in the locality occupied."[76]

Although the above are still considered a part of international law and the customs of war, they have, however, been affected by multiple events that have had a negative impact on their mandate.[77] For instance, the establishment of the League of Nations after WWI reshaped the customs of war and international law.[78] Nonetheless, in terms of its inherent *jus cogens* formulation, international law is exceptionally vigilant to the fact that history underpins both its substance and its objectives.

Concerning the adjudication of superior responsibility, the above conventions were again succeeded by numerous events that led to their dormancy. Similarly to the customary status of the First Hague Convention, these conventions remain part of customary international law and continue to affect superior responsibility interpretations, ultimately assisting judges with current adjudications.[79] It is worth noting that these conventions were established in the context of the laws of war and domestic martial laws, whose subject-matter did not have "a clear international criminal character".[80] Their customary and domestic status, in turn, resulted, in my view,

[73] Convention Respecting the Laws and Customs of War on Land, with annex of regulations, 18 October 1907, 36 Stat. 2277, Article 19.

[74] Ibid., Article 26.

[75] Ibid., Article 51.

[76] Ibid., Article 52.

[77] Hudson 1931, p. 1141.

[78] Ibid.

[79] *Prosecutor v. Brdanin*, Judgment, Case No. IT-99-36-T, para 720, 1 September 2004. The Tribunal decided that "superior responsibility is recognized in customary international law", para 713.

[80] Bantekas 2002. See also van der Vyver 2021, p. 573.

in conflicting views between the adjudications of the courts and academic scholarship.[81] The next in this chronicle development pertaining superior responsibility position within international law is Nuremberg Charter establishing the IMTs.

On account of the Charter's explicit reference to this concept, *lato sensu* superior responsibility was applied at the first Nuremberg IMT trials of major war criminals.[82] Article 6 of the Nuremberg Charter (otherwise known as the London Agreement) provides:

> Punishment of the major war criminals of the European Axis countries shall have the power to try and punish persons who, acting in the interests of the European Axis countries, whether as individuals or as members of organizations, …[l]eaders, organizers, instigators, and accomplices participating in the formulation or execution of a common plan or conspiracy to commit any of the foregoing crimes are responsible for all acts performed by any persons in execution of such plan.[83]

Subsequently, Article 7 addressed the responsibility of political superiors for the first time, stating that, "The official position of defendants, whether as Heads of States or responsible officials in Government Departments, shall not be considered as freeing them from responsibility or mitigating punishment."[84] Finally, Article 8 states that "[t]he fact that the Defendant acted pursuant to order of his Government or of a superior shall not free him from responsibility, but may be considered in mitigation of punishment if the tribunal determines that justice so requires."[85] The later Article deals with subordinates' allegiance to their superior in executing the latter's orders. As I shall discuss further below, the Nuremberg Charter was preceded by Control Council Law No. 10, to be relied on for the prosecution of subsequent war criminals.

As for post-WWII international treaties, the Convention for the Prevention and the Punishment of the Crime of Genocide—adopted by the UN's General Assembly on 9 December 1948—included *lato sensu* superior responsibility.[86] This Convention, in turn, indirectly referred to the responsibility of superiors with respect to the commission of genocide.[87] Similarly, the subject-matter Articles of the Convention on the Non-Applicability of Statutory Limitations to War Crimes and Crimes against Humanity also incorporated individual criminal responsibility. This Convention was adopted and entered into force in 1968 with a view to apprehending Nazi war criminals who had evaded criminal prosecution following, *inter alia*, the Nuremberg Trials. Article II of the Convention provides:

---

[81] Bantekas 2002, pp. 123, 131. See also Meron 2005, p. 817.

[82] Agreement for the Prosecution and Punishment of the Major War Criminals of the European Axis, and Charter of the International Military Tribunal, 8 August 1945, 82 U.N.T.S. 280, Articles 6–8.

[83] Ibid., Article 6.

[84] Ibid.

[85] Ibid.

[86] Van Sliedregt 2012a, pp. 62–63.

[87] Ibid.

> If any of the crimes mentioned in Article I is committed, the provisions of this Convention shall apply to representatives of the State authority and private individuals who, as principals or accomplices, participate in or who directly incite others to the commission of any of those crimes, or who conspire to commit them, irrespective of the degree of completion, and to representatives of the State authority who [tolerate] their commission.[88]

This Article makes implicit reference to the concept of superior responsibility, as a phenomenon. During the Diplomatic Conference on the Convention, it was declared, particularly by the Chilean delegation, that representatives of state authorities (*i.e.*, superiors) who "tolerate" such atrocities as well as accomplices (principal perpetrators) covered by the subject-matter jurisdiction are liable under the *stricto sensu* view of superior responsibility—namely, vicarious liability.[89] This attempt marked an initial step toward the notion of holding a superior criminally responsible for the crimes committed by his or her subordinates, at least before the establishment of the 1977 API to the Geneva Conventions of 12 August 1949.

In terms of both criminal and disciplinary responsibility, the concept of superior responsibility received its first codified recognition under the LoAC, using language similar to that employed in the Nuremberg Charter. In 1977, the API was drafted and signed as an annex to the Geneva Conventions. In addition to the principles of the Nuremberg and Tokyo Military Tribunal, this Protocol represents a clear attempt to deliver a more straightforward concept of superior responsibility. Article 86(2) of the Protocol reads:

> The fact that a breach of the Conventions or of this Protocol was committed by a subordinate does not absolve his superiors from penal or disciplinary responsibility, as the case may be, if they knew, or had information which should have enabled them to conclude in the circumstances at the time, that he was committing or was going to commit such a breach and if they did not take all feasible measures within their power to prevent or repress the breach.[90]

Despite its attractive recognition, and especially compared with the current theory and practice, Article 86(2) lacks further explanations and structure when it comes to its subject-matter. For example, the distinction between a commander and a superior and the optional punishment of superiors were the subject of debate during the drafting process.[91] This alternative approach to accountability suggests that a superior be placed under criminal trial (penal responsibility) and/or tried before a

[88] *The Convention on the Non-Applicability of Statutory Limitations to War Crimes and Crimes Against Humanity*, 26 November 1968, 754 U.N.T.S. 7, Article II.

[89] Miller 1971, p. 494.

[90] See De Preux 1987, pp. 1017–1023.

[91] ICRC 1949, *Remarks and Proposals submitted by the International Committee of the Red Cross: Documents for the Consideration of Governments Invited by the Swiss Federal Council to Attend the Diplomatic Conference at Geneva (21 April 1949)*, available at https://tile.loc.gov/storage-services/service/ll/llmlp/RC_Remarks-proposals/RC_Remarks-proposals.pdf. (accessed 21 August 2021). See also ICRC 2009, p. 461.

domestic military court for disciplinary charges stemming from omissions (disciplinary responsibility).[92] The distinction between the two forms of accountability—as set out in the proposals put forth by the delegations at the Diplomatic Conference of the API—lies in the fact that penal responsibility (the first form) involves the criminal prosecution of a superior before a criminal court. Disciplinary responsibility (the second form), on the other hand, implies that a superior is responsible and tried before a domestic court-martial.[93] More importantly, given its basic structure, the text did not clarify what a superior is charged with, failing to account for this essential component of responsibility. I shall discuss a potential interpretive solution for this *lacuna* in Chap. 4.[94] Furthermore, within this Article, the failure-to-act component of superior responsibility is restricted to the confines of the LoAC. This limitation may, in turn, indicate that other breaches of international law (beyond the context of the Geneva Conventions, such as Genocide) are exempt from superior responsibility in both *lato* and *stricto* contexts.[95]

These attempts to codify the doctrine of superior responsibility can be seen to draw on the customs and laws of war (namely, the Hague and Geneva Conventions).[96] These codifications were attempted solely for the purpose of establishing substantive laws and have not been applied internationally, except in the context of court-martial adjudications.[97] However, with the emergence of contemporary ICL, particularly with the first UN *ad hoc* tribunals (the ICTY and ICTR), the doctrine of superior responsibility began to be applied (in)consistently within the subject-matter jurisdiction of these courts. The ICTY and ICTR statutes employ identical wording to the doctrine of superior responsibility. For example, Article 7(3) of the ICTY Statute (Article 6(3) in the ICTR Statute) states:

> The fact that any of the acts referred to in articles 2 to 5 [1 to 4 ICTR Statute] of the present Statute was committed by a subordinate does not relieve his superior of criminal responsibility if he knew or had reason to know that the subordinate was about to commit such acts or had done so and the superior failed to take the necessary and reasonable measures to prevent such acts or to punish the perpetrators thereof.[98]

---

[92] Ibid. See also van der Vyver 2021, pp. 571–572.

[93] Ibid.

[94] Rome Statute, Article 28(a). Proclaiming that a superior is charged "for crimes committed by his or her subordinates".

[95] Convention on the Prevention and Punishment of the Crime of Genocide, 9 December 1948, 78 U.N.T.S. 277. See also van Sliedregt 2012a, p. 62.

[96] ICRC, *Commentary to the Protocol additional to the Geneva Conventions of 12 August 1949 (Protocol I)*, Article 87, para 3562. See also Customary International Humanitarian Law Database, Rule 153, https://ihl-databases.icrc.org/customary-ihl/eng/docs/v1_rul_rule153 (accessed 24 January 2020).

[97] For example, the Lieber and the US's Military Commissions Act of 2006, 189. 10 U.S.C. § 950q (2006).

[98] *Statute of the International Criminal Tribunal for the Former Yugoslavia*, U.N. Doc. S/25704, Annex (1993), 32 ILM 1192, Article 7(3) (hereinafter ICTY Statute); *Statute of the International Criminal Tribunal for Rwanda*, S.C. Res. 955, Annex (1994), 33 ILM 1602, Article 6(3) (1994) (hereinafter ICTR Statute).

In the same vein as the API's laconic approach to determination, these Articles do not establish what a superior is criminally charged with; however, through judges' interpretations at these institutions, it was held that a superior is to be charged with crimes committed by their subordinates (*i.e.*, vicarious liability).[99]

In relation to vicarious liability, the clearest—albeit not uncontroversial—expression of the doctrine of superior responsibility can be found in the 1998 Rome Statute of the ICC. Unlike its relatively murky status under the LoAC, the concept is treated within the ICC's subject-matter jurisdiction as a distinct and idiosyncratic mode of criminal liability, codified in Article 28.[100] Notably, the Rome Statute departs from earlier UN tribunal statutes by providing a more detailed articulation of the doctrine under the heading *Responsibility of military commanders and other superiors*. However, this formulation has not escaped criticism; it has been viewed as conceptually flawed and politically compromised—concerns that became evident in its first major application in the *Bemba* case.[101]

During the drafting of the Rome Statute, there were discussions about whether the doctrine should be titled "Superior Responsibility" rather than "Command Responsibility".[102] Notably, the Rome Statute was the first legal instrument to distinguish between two categories of superior responsibility, applying slightly different requirements to political superiors.[103] I shall engage in a more detailed discussion of the (a)symmetry of these variations between the statutes of the UN criminal tribunals and the Rome Statute's provisions in Chap. 4.

The statutes of the UN hybrid criminal tribunals, namely the Special Panels in East Timor (SPET) and the Special Court of Sierra Leone (SCSL), comprise similar Articles to those adopted within the statute subject-matter of the ICTY and ICTR.[104] The other UN hybrid criminal tribunals, however—namely, the Extraordinary Chambers in the Courts of Cambodia (ECCC) and the Special Tribunal for Lebanon (STL)—adopted the concept of superior responsibility, including both superiors and military commanders in their statutes.[105] Article 29 of the ECCC Statute addresses a military commander as a superior. Regarding a superior's material ability, it refers to the "effective command and control" of military superiors, while political superiors are

99 *Prosecutor v. Zejnil Delalic & Others*, Case No. IT-96-21-T, para 198.

100 Galand et al. 2016, p. 19. See also van der Vyver 2021, p. 570.

101 Cf. *Prosecutor v. Jean-Pierre Bemba Gombo*, Case No. ICC-01/05-01/08 A, Judgment, para 29, 8 June 2018. (In its decision, the Appeals Chamber of the ICC referred to Bemba first as a superior and later as a commander.)

102 Cryer 2015, p. 324.

103 Rome Statute, Article 28(b).

104 ICTY and ICTR Statutes.

105 *Special Tribunal for Lebanon*, S.C. Res. 1757 (2007) of 30 May 2007, U.N. Doc. S/RES/1757, Annex (2007).

referred to in relation to "effective authority and control".[106] The last UN hybrid criminal tribunal was the STL;[107] its statute referred only to political superiors, which is understandable given that defendants brought before this tribunal were non-military commanders.[108]

The elaborate codification of superior responsibility has also been integrated into international human rights law. For example, the UN's Human Rights Convention for the Protection of All Persons from Enforced Disappearance (ICPED) deals with the question of superior responsibility in its subject-matter provisions. With the exclusion of the causation link, the wording employed is very similar to that of Article 28 of the Rome Statute. Article 6(b) of the ICPED reads:

> ...[e]ach State Party shall take the necessary measures to hold criminally responsible at least...(b) [a] superior who: (i) Knew, or consciously disregarded information which clearly indicated, that subordinates under his or her effective authority and control were committing or about to commit a crime of enforced disappearance; (ii) Exercised effective responsibility for, and control over activities which were concerned with the crime of enforced disappearance; and (iii) Failed to take all necessary and reasonable measures within his or her power to prevent or repress the commission of an enforced disappearance or to submit the matter to the competent authorities for investigation and prosecution; (c) Subparagraph (b) above is without prejudice to the higher standards of responsibility applicable under relevant international law to a military commander or to a person effectively acting as a military commander.[109]

As noted, this Article is partly reminiscent of Article 28(b) of the Rome Statute. However, it also incorporates the situation of military commanders in international law, meaning that, where a crime of enforced disappearance is committed in a military setting or during an armed conflict, the prosecutor of the state concerned should refer to this doctrine in the context of international law.[110] What distinguishes this treaty is the fact that it attributes the obligation to prosecute to the state party rather than to an international criminal tribunal (with the exclusion of military commanders).[111]

---

[106] *Law on the Establishment of Extraordinary Chambers in the Courts of Cambodia for the Prosecution of Crimes Committed During the Period of Democratic Kampuchea*, NS/RKM/1004/006, 24 October 2004, Article 29.

[107] Excluding the establishment of the International Residual Mechanism for Criminal Tribunals (IRMCT), established to complete the remnant cases of ICTY and ICTR.

[108] STL Statute, Article 3(2).

[109] International Convention for the Protection of All Persons from Enforced Disappearance, G.A. Res. 61/177 (2006), Article 6(1).

[110] Galand et al. 2016, p. 22.

[111] Ibid.

3.2.3 International Case Law: Superior Responsibility Decisions

Contrary to domestic criminal law, it has been argued that the doctrine of superior responsibility has mostly been articulated through international case law, which supports its legal characterization as vicarious liability at the international level.[112] In practical terms, it has also been argued that the concept of individual criminal responsibility would effectively be elaborated through international case law than treaty law or international resolutions.[113] Such arguments should be approached with caution as they have posed a challenge to the stability of the structure of superior responsibility.[114] In light of this situation, a clear framework is required in this section to call attention to the most prominent cases that have helped shape superior responsibility under international law.

Superior responsibility was first adjudicated internationally in the aftermath of WWII, when it began to be applied pragmatically rather than serving merely as a military law theory.[115] The *Prosecution and Punishment of Major War Criminals of European Axis* was executed at the Nuremberg IMT in accordance with its Charter, where *lato sensu* superior responsibility is applied. However, in the Subsequent Nuremberg Trials (SNTs), three cases were decided strictly on the basis of superior responsibility, in accordance with *Control Council Law No. 10*.[116] These were the *Doctor* case, the *High Command* case and the *Hostages* case, where superior criminal liability was justified on the basis that superiors' failures to fulfill their duties were considered "violations of moral obligations under international law".[117] The General *Yamashita* trial, however, appears to serve as the doctrinal backbone of superior responsibility—at least with respect to its legal nature. That said, it has been subject to considerable criticism, particularly for its failure to articulate a clear *mens rea* requirement for holding superiors criminally liable under the current framework. In hindsight, albeit with some controversy, these trials formed the basis of the application of the doctrine in modern international law.[118]

In the aftermath of the WWII criminal tribunals, the UN established *ad hoc* tribunals to prosecute individuals who had committed serious violations of LoAC and

---

112 Ambos 2003, p. 247. (Ambos maintains that superior responsibility is a form of a liability for omission and labels the superior "as a direct perpetrator (principal) for the acts of third persons.)

113 For example, the Rome Statute, and the UN criminal tribunals' statutes.

114 The Nuremberg Tribunal and the Tokyo Tribunal charters did not include superior responsibility in their subject-matter jurisdiction; rather, the concept was deduced, and hence interpreted, during the trials. Williamson 2008, p. 311.

115 Van Sliedregt 2011, pp. 378–379.

116 *Allied Control Council Law No. 10: Punishment of Persons Guilty of War Crimes, Crimes Against Peace, and Crimes Against Humanity, Dec. 20, 1945*, in 3 OFF. GAZ. OF THE CONTROL COUNCIL OF GERMANY, 50 (1946).

117 *Hostage Case*, Nuremberg (February 1948), excerpted in *The Law of War, a Documentary History*, Vol. II, 1303 (Friedman ed., 1972); *High Command Case*, IXII LAW REPORTS OF THE TRIALS OF WAR CRIMINALS (1949). See also Dungel and Ghadiri 2010, p. 13.

118 Ambos 2002, p. 830.

human rights in multiple regions.[119] The first international *ad hoc* tribunal set up by the UN Security Council (SC) was the ICTY, with the purpose of prosecuting international crimes committed against three ethnic groups in the former Yugoslavia.[120] Regarding superior responsibility, the *Čelebići* case is perhaps the most compelling, detailed case.[121] This case resulted in the indictment of international criminals who were superiors and exercised authority over individuals at the *Čelebići* camp. The crimes committed by their subordinates—namely rape, torture, and the execution of detainees—were considered to result from their superiors' failure to act. This case had a significant effect on the doctrine of superior responsibility in several ways, becoming a prominently featured case cited in other superior responsibility cases at the international level.[122]

Other cases have also addressed the application of superior responsibility in ways that either overlap with the *Čelebići* case or expand on interpretations of the doctrine. For example, in the late jurisprudence of the ICTY, the court delivered a verdict that posed a major challenge to the doctrine of superior responsibility. In the *Prosecutor v. Jovica Stanišićand Franko Simatović* case, the court acquitted Stanišić and Simatović because they did not provide physical support to their subordinates in the commission of the crimes. According to this reasoning, to convict superiors either as accomplices or under superior responsibility, the Chamber held that the superior's negligence or assistance must be "specifically directed towards the commission of the crimes".[123] This jurisprudence was subsequently overturned, with the clarification that complicity through omission does not require that the act be specifically directed toward the commission of the crimes.[124] In any case, this reasoning could be problematic when it comes to understanding superior responsibility as it invalidates its distinct nature as a non-contributory mode of liability specifically designed to extend liability to the most responsible superiors as a result of their grave failure to discharge their entrusted duties. Nevertheless, the *Čelebići* case has undoubtedly influenced the adjudication of superior responsibility cases, established the modern

---

[119] I am referring here to the ICTY, ICTR, and hybrid criminal tribunals such as the ECCC and STL.

[120] Swaak-Goldman 2017, pp. 514–519.

[121] Askin 2002, pp. 908–909.

[122] Ibid.

[123] See Judgement Summary for Jovica Stanisic and Franko Simatovic, Trial Chamber, International Tribunal for the Former Yugoslavia, 30 May 2013, http://icty.org/x/cases/stanisicsimatovic/tug/en/130530summary.pdf (hereinafter Judgment Summary); see, generally, *Prosecutor v. Jovica Stanisic and Franko Simatovic*, Case No. IT 03-69, Judgement Volume II of II (International Criminal Tribute for the Former Yugoslavia, 30 May 2013), http://www.icty.org/x/cases/stanisicsimatovic/tjug/en/130530judgementp2.pdf (hereinafter Judgment Part II), at para 2360.

[124] Prosecutor v. Stanišić & Simatović, Case No. MICT-15-96-A, Appeals Judgment, para 268, 31 May 2023, United Nations Mechanism for International Criminal Tribunals.

foundations of the doctrine,[125] and proved to be a reliable framework for future cases of superior responsibility.[126]

3.3 Doctrinal Disputes over the Characterization of Superior Responsibility: Commission *v.* Omission

To determine whether superior responsibility is to be understood as a mode of liability according to which a superior is prosecuted for crimes committed by other persons or rather a separate omission-based offense or an accessorial mode of liability, it is necessary to examine the nature of this doctrine. To this end, I shall begin by distinguishing between two key concepts in the prosecution of crimes by individuals: (1) the means of perpetration or participation through which the crimes are committed, and (2) the form of criminal liability that attaches to the underlying core international crimes. This distinction is necessary for situating superior responsibility within the broader framework of modes of liability. Second, I shall, in turn, explain how the academic literature on the legal characterization of superior responsibility has approached this matter, before proceeding to set out my own analytical position in this regard.

3.3.1 Criminal Liability and Modes of Liability

In domestic criminal law scholarship, it is widely recognized that criminal responsibility is generally analyzed in two dimensions: (1) what crimes were committed (criminal liability), and (2) how those crimes were committed or intended to be committed (modes of liability).[127] Put differently, criminal liability concerns the substantive offense, while modes of liability refer to the accused's relationship to the crime—whether as a direct perpetrator or through some form of participation.[128] These modes, based on a causal link to the crime, typically include direct perpetration, indirect or direct participation through complicity, and accessory liability.[129] Under this framework, an individual may then be held responsible under one of three main labels: first, as a principal (or direct perpetrator), where they personally and

[125] Cf. Galand 2020, p. 688.

[126] More details on these overlapping opinions by judges will be discussed in the section on the elements of the doctrine.

[127] Van der Vyver 2021, p. 435. See also Al-Fadhli 2025.

[128] Van Sliedregt 2012a, pp. 64–67. (Often referred to as retributive justice, where the stigma should be proportionate to the perpetrator's culpability.)

[129] Ibid. See also Dressler 1985, p. 92; Guilfoyle 2011, p. 261 (along with the majority of scholars in the field of ICL, does not distinguish between accomplices and accessories, maintaining that both refer to the same means).

physically commit the offense; second, as an accomplice, where they participate in the commission of the offense—either directly or indirectly—by instigating, aiding or abetting others, and may be present at the scene, though physical presence is not always required; and third, as an accessory, where they assist or encourage the crime before or after its commission (commonly referred to as an accessory before or after the fact), also without necessarily being physically present.[130]

As noted, the criminal liability of an individual (*for* the crimes), therefore, refers to the attribution of the crimes that reflects such an individual's culpability (*e.g.*, if an accused is sentenced for committing murder, rape, or pillaging). In certain circumstances, modes of liability and criminal liability may not be viewed as mutually exclusive.[131] For instance, deprivation of food (a means of perpetration through omission) can result in the death of the deprived person (which results in criminal liability for murder). In some national jurisdictions, an accused in the former example would be held responsible for the crime of omission not for murder. In civil law contexts, this is sometimes legally framed as "*commissio per omissionem*"—that is, treating an omission as if it were a commission when a legal duty to act exists.[132]

In ICL scholarship, these concepts are not treated as identical and instead some possess *sui generis* characteristics.[133] The two notions—modes of liability[134] and criminal liability for international crimes—are distinct yet interconnected. Both are encapsulated within the subject-matter jurisdiction of the statutes governing international criminal tribunals. Though, there is a notable distinction in their application compared with national law practice.[135] The reason for this distinction stems from the fact that, in the first notion (modes of liability), it is necessary to call on international standards, such as the severity of the crimes, the status of such crimes under customary international law compared with national crimes, the status of the accused, and the type of victims affected (*i.e.*, a population group or the international community as a whole).[136] Both concepts—modes of liability and criminal liability for crimes—thus have different consequences, whether at the international level or national level applying international law.

Accordingly, in national trials, individuals may be convicted for international or national crimes under domestic modes of liability that emphasize how the crime was committed. For instance, an accused may be found guilty not simply of the core crime itself, but specifically as a principal, accomplice, or accessory to that crime—such

[130] The majority of ICL literature does not recognize the term "accessory" in international law simply, as it originates in various different domestic law frameworks. For example, accessories and secondary participants are derived from the common law system, while the accomplice concept is derived from a French law system and Romano-Germanic systems. See van Sliedregt 2012a, p. 67. See also van Schaack 2019, p. 8; Stahn 2019, p. 133.

[131] Van der Vyver 2021, pp. 435–436.

[132] Ibid. See also Meloni 2010, p. 206.

[133] See generally van Sliedregt 2012b.

[134] Cf. Stewart 2012, p. 165 n. 2 (noting that Stewart prefers the term "modes of attribution" over "modes of liability").

[135] ICTY and ICTR Statutes, Articles 7(1) and 6(1), respectively. Rome Statute, Article 25.

[136] Meloni 2010, pp. 14–19.

as complicity in crimes against humanity or aiding and abetting war crimes. In this sense, national courts often frame liability through the concerned mode of liability, rather than subsuming it entirely under the subject-matter crime. In comparison, courts in ICL do not place legal weight on the label of the mode of liability when it comes to establishing criminal responsibility.[137] Whether an accused is a principal, an accomplice, or held responsible under a derivative mode like superior responsibility, they are convicted of the core international crime itself.[138] The mode of liability then does not alter the nature of the crime charged but may influence sentencing, where the degree and form of perpetration or participation—such as direct perpetration *versus* omission—can mitigate or aggravate the sentence.[139] Simply put, distinctions between modes of liability—such as those assigned to principals and accessories—are often less significant at the international level in terms of conviction. The accused will typically be held liable for the underlying crimes regardless of the specific modes of liability. However, these distinctions may carry substantial weight at the sentencing stage, where the degree of blameworthiness can serve as a basis for mitigation or aggravation.[140]

To this end, within the specific context of superior responsibility, ICL uniquely attributes liability to superiors for crimes committed by their subordinates, even where those superiors did not directly contribute to the commission of the crimes—a concept often likened to vicarious liability.[141] Therefore, the distinction between ICL and domestic criminal law becomes apparent: whereas domestic systems typically require some form of contribution, either directly or through accomplice liability, ICL permits the conviction of superiors for the underlying crimes of their subordinates due to the superior's failure to prevent or punish such acts. As a result, under ICL, individuals held liable under superior responsibility may, in some cases, receive aggravated sentences[142]—unlike in many national systems, where omission-based liability often results in comparatively lesser punishment. I shall explain the reasons for such aggravated sentences later in this chapter, arguing that even without direct commission, a superior may warrant harsher punishment for the crimes due to their failure to fulfill their duties—a controversy that lies at the heart of the legal tension surrounding superior responsibility's legal characterization. This approach in ICL has sparked significant engagement in scholarly legal discourse, particularly regarding its compatibility with the concretely built principles of domestic criminal law.

---

[137] Guilfoyle 2011, p. 283.

[138] Van der Vyver 2021, p. 568. See also Jia 2000, pp. 143–144.

[139] Ibid.

[140] Al-Fadhli 2025.

[141] Ibid., pp. 569–570.

[142] Ibid., p. 571. See also *Prosecutor v. Enver Hadzihasanovic et al.*, Case. No. IT-01-47-A, para 313, 22 April 2008; *Aloys Ntabakuze v. The Prosecutor*, Case No. ICTR-98-41A-A, paras 302–305, 8 May 2012.

3.3.2 The Position of Academic Literature on the Legal Characterization of Superior Responsibility

The philosophical underpinnings of punishment demand that any pronouncement of criminal liability be logically, ethically, and legally justified.[143] While such justification has been well crafted in domestic criminal law—with relatively minor nuances depending on the jurisdiction and the legislative framework applied—the challenge becomes more complex in the context of ICL. In attempting to justify the legal characterization of superior responsibility that entails criminal liability for the crimes, scholars have adopted four key approaches in their justifications. Whether it constitutes a distinct mode of liability, an offense of omission, a hybrid form of liability, or an accessorial mode of liability, which will be addressed later in this chapter as part of my analysis of the doctrine's conceptual components.[144]

It is, first and foremost, noteworthy that while this book does not primarily focus on the nature of superior responsibility—given its curiously enduring contestation, which often diverts scholarly attention from more pressing issues—it is particularly concerned with the inconsistent patterns of reasoning in jurisprudence regarding the conceptual components that lead to either convictions or acquittals, which is a more urgent concern. Nonetheless, I shall briefly engage with principled concerns surrounding adherence to personal culpability raised by liberal accounts. Then, I shall propose a re-examination of morally grounded, historically supported, and philosophically coherent alternatives—particularly ones that challenge the dominance of deontological frameworks centered on individual blame in assessing superior responsibility. Inspired by Robinson's call for coherent legal reasoning, I introduce—by contrast—the concept of consequential culpability as a normative counterpoint to personal and collective culpability. My position is developed in two parts: first, I examine prevailing scholarly views on the nature of superior responsibility; second, I argue consequential culpability as a basis for justifying superior responsibility, arguing that the gravity of a superior's role at the international level calls for rethinking culpability in terms of institutional impact and structural consequences, rather than solely through the lens of personalized fault.

As noted earlier, the current academic literature categorizes the nature of superior responsibility based on four key perspectives: (i) as an accessorial mode of liability; (ii) as a hybrid *sui generis* mode of liability and a crime of omission; (iii) as a *sui generis* crime of omission; and (iv) as a syllogism for comprehending the gravity of the superior's failure to execute supervisory duties compared with the severity of the crimes, as well as the need to maximize victims' protection and rights, humanitarian and human rights approach.[145] The latter view, mine, is collectively conceptualized as the gravity test leading to consequential culpability rather than personal culpability. Accordingly, I shall examine the attempts set out in the canvassing literature to offer

---

[143] See generally Wood 2010.

[144] Meloni 2007, p. 620.

[145] Minkova 2023, p. 119.

a solution to these intertwining approaches and shall subsequently propose my own analytic solution in this regard.

Darryl Robinson conducted a seminal analysis of the characterization of superior responsibility based on the view set out in the ICC's Rome Statute, reflecting on the first understanding of the principle (as an accessory mode of liability).[146] First, he examined the wording used to describe the key elements of superior responsibility in the ICC Statute, which requires a causal contribution between the superior–subordinate relationship and the latter's criminal actions, which can be traced to the former's omission.[147] He then proceeds to argue that superior responsibility appears to be tantamount to an accessory mode of liability rather than a vicarious one.[148] Robinson argues that superior responsibility is not, as suggested at some of cases at *ad hoc* tribunals, a form of *suigeneris* omission offense; rather, it involves the indirect participation of a superior as a result of their omission—thereby attaching the superior's accessorial role (omission) to the commission of the crimes.[149] He also argues that, both at its outset and throughout history, the doctrine of superior responsibility has served as a form of liability with an accessorial character, until it was misinterpreted and misconstrued by the *ad hoc* tribunals.[150] He proceeds to explain that this misconception of the nature of superior responsibility may be attributable to the wording employed to describe superior responsibility in the statutes of the *ad hoc* tribunals, which was copied from the API to the Geneva Conventions of 12 August 1949.[151] In this context, it was unclear whether superiors were subject to criminal or disciplinary responsibility—two distinct forms of liability.[152] As noted earlier, disciplinary responsibility is intended to be applied within domestic legal frameworks,

---

[146] Robinson 2020.

[147] Robinson 2012, p. 3. It should be noted, however, that Robinson maintains that superiors are directly liable and does not recognize indirect liability in this particular mode of liability.

[148] Ibid.

[149] Cf. ibid. (It should be noted, however, that he maintains that superiors are directly liable and does not recognize indirect liability of this particular mode of liability.)

[150] Ibid.

[151] Ibid.

[152] Article 82(2) of the 1977 Protocol I to the Geneva Conventions addresses two types of responsibilities: first, disciplinary responsibility, which is designed for military domestic courts, wherein omission is treated as a disciplinary matter to be dealt with domestically; and second, penal responsibility, which has a criminal character and pertains to criminal adjudications at the international level for the violations of LAOC (core international crimes). For the second type of responsibility, international courts charge superiors for crimes committed by their subordinates, which is referred to as indirect liability. Van der Vyver 2021, p. 568. He notes: "failure of a superior…to exercise proper control over the troops under his or her command is indeed an offence that is to be dealt with internally, as a matter of disciplinary responsibility…[s]uperior responsibility [in ICL] holds the person in authority vicariously liable as a matter of 'penal responsibility' for offences within the jurisdiction of the ICC or other international criminal tribunals committed by his or her subordinates." See also Damaška 2001, p. 486. Therefore, a superior cannot raise the *ne bis idem* claim before an international tribunal, even if they were prosecuted under this doctrine before a national court.

where a military commander may be held liable for offenses of omission, again, a prevailing approach to view ICL through the lens of domestic criminal law.

Robinson also argues that the adjudications of international criminal tribunals target military commanders (and non-military superiors) when they are party to the crimes committed by their subordinates. In other words, in this context, a superior's liability stems from his or her contribution to the crimes.[153] He affirms that, on this view, the superior's omission is based on an active role on their part, wherein they indirectly contribute to the crimes.

Robinson also reiterates the superior's accessorial role through their omission as a form of liability associated with other contributory modes of liability. He notes that omission is an integral part of superior responsibility as this mode of liability would not exist in its own right if such an omission had not occurred. However, it constitutes the *actus reus* of superior responsibility only if it would not arise without the commission of crimes by the superior's subordinates. Therefore, a superior's omission (or failure to fulfill their duties) would appear to be a causal contribution to the crimes committed by their subordinates, guided by the superior's accessorial role. In other words, this form of indirect liability is synonymous with accessory or complicity liability and must therefore be interpreted as such. According to this analysis, the superior "played a part"[154] in the crimes committed by their subordinates, and their "failure to know of the subordinate crimes is a sufficiently blameworthy state of mind to ground accessory liability".[155] To situate this suggestion within the context of individual criminal responsibility, a direct order contributes to the crimes, rendering the superior a direct principal perpetrator. Whereas aiding or abetting constitutes an indirect perpetration (a means of participation) of and direct liability for the crimes, superior responsibility is understood as an accessory mode of liability that indirectly contributes to the commission of the crimes.

William Schabas,[156] Chantal Meloni, and Elies van Sliedregt (along with the majority of scholars in this field) reflect on the second instance—the hybrid mode of liability that encompasses both an accessorial role and a crime of omission *per se*.[157] They justify this mode of liability as a hybrid, *sui generis* mode liability and liability for omission, which is applicable only when the superior's state of mind was based on negligence (*i.e.*, they should have known). On this point, citing the majority view, Meloni notes that:

> The nature of superior responsibility in these cases should thus be more conveniently found in the mere failure to act under a duty to do so. Consequently, the superior should not bear responsibility for the subordinates' crimes 'as if he had committed them' on the sole basis of his failure to punish them.[158]

---

[153] See Ambos 2009, p. 823; see also Meloni 2015, p. 4.

[154] See *Prosecutor v. Enver Hadzihasanovic et al.*, Case. No. IT-01-47-A, para 193, 15 March 2006.

[155] Robinson 2012, p. 12.

[156] Schabas 2004.

[157] Van Sliedregt 2011, p. 388.

[158] Meloni 2007, p. 637.

She notes that if a superior "knew", then that would make them an accessory to the crimes committed by their subordinates.[159] Meanwhile, Mirjan Damaška, Robert Cryer, and Antonio Cassese reflect on the third instance, according to which the doctrine is understood as "a distinct crime, consisting of the failure to discharge supervisory duties".[160]

My position only within the previous principled context shall fall within with a fourth instance, a *sui generis* (as opposed to classic modes of liability) vicarious mode of liability. Superior responsibility is then not a form of criminal liability based on omission, nor does a superior's failure to execute supervisory duties automatically render them an accessory to the crimes. In short, in terms of its rationality, the doctrine of superior responsibility can only be classified as a *sui generis* international criminal mode of liability that vicariously attributes criminal liability for subordinates' crimes to their superior.[161] The attribution of subordinates' crimes to a superior, as proposed in this book, rests on a bifurcated test: it weighs the gravity and hierarchical significance of the superior's entrusted duties against the severity of their failure to act—assessed through a consequentialist lens and grounded in historical precedent—as a permissive event enabling the commission of the crimes. As noted in the history chapter, dated legal support dictates that: "command is severity".

On the one hand, as already noted, this rationally justified test reflects the superior's failure to prevent and punish their subordinates' grave crimes. On the other hand, it supports the mandate to maximize victims' rights through various prosecutions of superiors, "who under *traditional criminal law principles* would escape justice".[162] Judicial support for this view can also be found in the Appeals judgment in the Čelebići Case, where it was decided that: "[a] failure to prevent or punish murder or torture committed by a subordinate must be regarded as being of greater gravity than a failure to prevent or punish an act of plunder."[163] In addition, this decision supports the broad advocacy for the noted gravity test set out in this study, asserting that: "The Appeals Chamber's conclusion, however, is not based on any such reasoning [*i.e.*, omission per se] but simply recognizes the inevitable relationship between the gravity of the superior's failure to prevent or punish criminal conduct and the criminal conduct to which that failure relates."[164]

Based on this syllogism of attributing the crimes committed by a subordinate to their superior—vicarious liability—it cannot be deemed correct that superiors incur criminal responsibility based solely on omission. Alleging such would lead to a fallacious understanding of a specific crime, an omission, for which criminal

---

[159] Ibid.

[160] Cassese et al. 2013, p. 192; Damaška 2001; Cryer 2014, p. 394.

[161] Van der Vyver 2021, p. 568.

[162] *Prosecutor v. Laurent Gbagbo and Charles Blé Goudé*, Case No. ICC-02/11-01/15-1263-AnxC-Red (Separate dissenting opinion of Judge Herrera Carbuccia), para 492, 16 July 2019. See also Mégret 2011, pp. 1011–1052, esp. p. 1046; Galand 2020, p. 675; Robinson 2008, pp. 936–937.

[163] *Prosecutor v. Zejnil Delalic & Others*, Case No. IT-96-21-T, Appeals Chamber, Case No IT-96-21-A, para 732, 20 February 2001.

[164] Ibid.

accountability is typically applied at the national level.[165] That being said, if the superior were charged and tried for an omission *per se*, their condign punishment (often a mitigated sentence based on omission) would not reflect the gravity of their failure to discharge their entrusted duties (*e.g.*, a ten-year sentence for the crime of rape). Furthermore, the judgment in the *Čelebići* case specifies that: "[i]t would be incorrect to state that, as a matter of law, responsibility for criminal conduct as a superior is less grave than responsibility as the subordinate perpetrator."[166] In light of this conclusion, superior responsibility cannot be doctrinally characterized as a criminal liability of omission *per se*, because if it were, it would need to have its own usually mitigated punishment, which is currently not included in the subject-matter jurisdiction of criminal institutions at the international level.[167]

Furthermore, given that omission is recognized as a national offense and often associated with less severe domestic crimes, interpreting superior responsibility as a crime of omission is both misleading and fraught with uncertainty.[168] Such a characterization is also misleading at the international level, because a superior's failure to execute proper control over his or her subordinates can sometimes constitute a direct mode of liability, as if he or she were a principal/accessory.[169] As this passive role constitutes a crime in its own right, the superior is deemed an aider or abettor, depending on the facts of the case concerned.[170] In contrast, omission *per se* is more widely recognized as a disciplinary offense subject to the jurisdiction of municipal courts (and sometimes forming an accessorial mode of direct/indirect liability at the international level, as observed earlier by Robinson).[171] Thus, within the confines of ICL adjudication, superior responsibility is a form of derivative responsibility for crimes committed by a superior's subordinates.[172]

Douglas Guilfoyle explains that superiors' criminal responsibility is inherently derivative—*i.e.*, a superior's liability derives from the acts of their subordinates.[173] In other words, superiors are held responsible for the criminal actions of their subordinates' criminal actions, not based on their failure to perform an assigned duty or the superior's *de facto* material control over them. This is also consistent with the purpose of ICL, which, contrary to domestic criminal legal systems, is intended to prosecute the criminals deemed most responsible for the crimes concerned, even if they are not the physical perpetrators. However, they incur criminal responsibility for

[165] Van der Vyver 2021, pp. 569, 570, 572.

[166] *Prosecutor v. Delalic et al.*, Case No. IT-96-21-T, para 735.

[167] Van der Vyver 2021, p. 570. See also Triffterer 2002, pp. 179, 187, 195.

[168] Van der Vyver 2021, p. 570.

[169] Ibid., p. 569.

[170] Ibid.

[171] Damaška 2001, p. 458 (analyzing the role of courts-martial with regard to the disciplinary responsibility of superiors).

[172] A superior can be accused of multiple alternative modes of liability. See Chap. 5, Sect. 5.2.

[173] Guilfoyle 2011, p. 283.

acts over which they could have exercised control and failed to do so.[174] Ultimately, this is in line with the interpretation of superior responsibility as a form of omission. Superior responsibility does not arise solely on the basis of omission, however, if the superior's subordinates committed no crimes. On the contrary, in cases of omission, superior responsibility applies only when crimes have been committed by the superior's subordinates, casting aside inchoate offenses as will be note later. Axiomatically, the commission of crimes by subordinates is considered to be the determinative element of superior responsibility. The ICTY reinforced this rationale in the *Prosecutor v. Hadžihasanović* case, where it held that "a superior who exercises effective control over his subordinates…incurs responsibility…[i]n that sense, the superior has substantially played a part in the commission of those crimes."[175]

To conclude this omission-based counterargument: under the domestic principle of culpability, if superior responsibility is characterized strictly as liability for omission, then the superior should not be held responsible for the crimes committed by subordinates, but only for the omission itself—*i.e.*, the failure to prevent or punish. However, this view is not sustained by international criminal jurisprudence and the enabling statutes of its institutions. According to the case law of international tribunal—the system that found this principle—superior responsibility attaches not merely to the omission but to the core crimes themselves, provided they fall within the tribunal's subject-matter jurisdiction. As aptly summarized, "[i]f the commander is not culpable for the core crime, then it is impossible to convict him for that crime—which constitutes 'justice.'"[176]

The absence of a clear contribution element in the doctrine of superior responsibility calls for a philosophical grounding, especially given the traditional non-consequentialist, deontological foundations of criminal law that prioritize individual fault and its respective punishment. To this end, I now turn to the introduction of consequentialism to support what I term consequential or structural culpability (as opposed to personalized forms of culpability)—an invitation to scholars and judges to perhaps reconsider superior responsibility beyond the strict confines of personal culpability, or at least to view it alongside personal culpability and collective culpability as part of a broader justificatory framework.

This shift toward a consequentialist or structural model of culpability emphasizes the institutional role of superiors, focusing on the justifiability of holding them accountable not solely for their subjective blameworthiness—as is the case with direct or indirect (co-)principals and accessories—but for their objective position of

---

[174] *Prosecutor v. Jean-Pierre Gombo* (Decision Pursuant to Article 61(7)(a) and (b) of the Rome Statute on the Charges against Jean-Pierre Bemba Gombo), Case No. ICC-01/05-01/08-424, para 371, 15 June 2009.

[175] *Prosecutor v. Enver Hadzihasanovic et al.*, Case. No. IT-01-47-A, para 193.

[176] Cf. ibid., p. 19: "A non-contributory failure to punish is still serious, and can and should be taken up by national legal systems, whose mandate is not restricted to the most serious international crimes…[n]ational systems are free to adopt the 'separate offence' [*sic*] approach and thus prosecute non-contributory derelictions as derelictions" (maintaining that negligence is a contributory factor in superior responsibility).

authority.[177] Specifically, it centers on their capacity to either negligently or intentionally fail to discharge their duties to prevent, repress, punish, or report crimes committed by subordinates. While Robinson advocates for deontic constraints—arguing that personal culpability, rooted in non-consequentialist reasoning, is essential even in the context of superior responsibility[178]—this approach, by contrast, offers a normative alternative. Consequential or structural culpability, as grounded in consequentialism, does not constrain responsibility to individual contribution or intent.[179] Rather, it permits a principled basis for vicarious liability, justifying responsibility based on role-sourced obligations and the consequences of failing to discharge them, even in the absence of a direct contribution to the crime that, nonetheless, justifies imputation of principal punishment.[180]

This approach arguably aligns with the function of punishment in ICL, not only to reflect individual guilt but to deter and prevent systemic atrocities. I develop this further through what I term the gravity test, which evaluates the legitimacy of superior responsibility in light of the seriousness and systemic nature of the crimes involved. When viewed through the combined lens of the gravity test and consequentialist reasoning, superior responsibility emerges as a *sui generis* mode of liability—distinct from classical forms in that it does not require direct contribution to the crime yet remains proportionate to the gravity of the superior's failure. This failure, situated within a position of authority, functionally justifies punishment as though the superior had committed the crime themselves. Importantly, this *sui generis* designation should not be confused with omission-based liability in the domestic sense.[181] Instead, it reflects a unique construct of ICL, shaped by the superior's authoritative position, knowledge, and material ability to prevent or punish crimes.

This doctrinal distinctiveness is then affirmed that superior responsibility is not accessory as conceptualized by Robinson and other scholars noted earlier, but a tailored form of accountability suited to the realities of mass criminality that has relatively no parallel in a domestic setting.[182] In other words, culpability based on consequentialist reasoning would regard a superior's failure to properly control their subordinates—including the duties to prevent, repress, or submit the matter to competent authorities—as wrongful, insofar as adherence to a rule requiring such control tends to produce better systemic outcomes (such as deterrence of future crimes and

[177] For more reading on these concepts, see van Sliedregt 2012a, pp. 61–75. See also van Sliedregt et al. 2019, pp. 85–120.

[178] Robinson 2020.

[179] See Hooker 2000, pp. 32–47.

[180] Ibid.

[181] See Mégret 2011. See also Galand 2020, p. 675.

[182] It is worth noting that some common law jurisdictions have accepted criminal liability theories that depart from strict personal culpability. For example, under the Pinkerton Doctrine in U.S. federal law, a co-conspirator may be held criminally liable for substantive offenses committed by another member of the conspiracy, even without direct participation, provided the acts were reasonably foreseeable and in furtherance of the conspiracy. This demonstrates that the notion of holding individuals accountable absent direct involvement—while controversial—is not alien to well-established criminal systems. *Pinkerton v. United States*, 328 U.S. 640 (1946).

preservation of humanitarian norms) than would a rule criminalizing only personal neglect of those duties. Alongside the gravity test discussed later, the consequences of a superior's failure to discharge their entrusted duties can be considered as morally and legally grave as the crimes committed by their subordinates. As such, superiors may justifiably be punished for the principal crimes—particularly where they enjoy immunity or where national jurisdictions fail due to impunity. In laboring on this point, immunity often shields for high-ranking superiors and the *unwilling* or *unable* limitations of domestic jurisdictions function as *de facto* protections, often frustrating accountability efforts. While these privileges do not, on their own, justify the doctrine of superior responsibility, they help explain why it cannot rest solely on deontic constraints such as personal culpability. Instead, it calls for a hierarchical model of culpability—one grounded in consequentialist reasoning—that responds to the unique structural challenges international criminal law seeks to overcome. In this context, immunity privileges and impunity barriers frequently converge and, in some cases, extend downward to shield subordinates, ultimately floating above the reach of conventional criminal liability.[183]

While I depart from Robinson's deontological insistence on personal culpability, I find myself, however, deeply influenced by his methodological commitment to moral clarity. My own approach, though structurally grounded, is shaped by a similar engagement with non-consequentialist reasoning—one that seeks fairness but without relying solely on individual blameworthiness.[184] Robinson explains, "deontic reasoning focuses not on what texts and precedents allow or how to maximize beneficial impact, but on the principled constraints arising from respect for the personhood or agency of accused persons as moral agents."[185] This type of reasoning, he argues, requires us to consider the limits of personal fault and the respective punishment. Robinson thus criticizes early international criminal law jurisprudence for failing to meet deontic thresholds.[186] In contrast, culpability based on consequentialist reasoning, as noted earlier, offers an alternative—but still principled—justification: one rooted not in the accused's contribution, but in the superior's position to control structures of violence under their authority/command.[187]

As outlined in Chap. 2, this rationale has historical precedent. From Sun Tzu and Hugo Grotius to early modern and medieval laws of war, the idea of holding leaders accountable for the acts of subordinates has deep roots, even where direct involvement was lacking.[188] These traditions often embraced a form of vicarious or structural punishment, grounded in duty and authority rather than personal fault. Recognizing this history—along with the influence of consequentialist reasoning—I argue that superior responsibility then should not be viewed as a deviation from

---

[183] See Scharf and Morris 1995, pp. 100–101.

[184] Robinson 2020, p. 15.

[185] Ibid., p. 11.

[186] Ibid.

[187] *Prosecutor v. Hadžihasanović et al.*, Case No. IT-01-47-T, Trial Judgment, 25 March 2006, paras 94–102 (on the nature of effective control and lawful orders).

[188] See Chap. 2.

personal culpability, but rather as a historically grounded anomaly: a *sui generis* principle justified by systemic concerns and consistent with ICL's preventive aims, especially in addressing mass criminality.

Of an important note, this argument is not an appeal to punish superiors at all costs, nor does it claim that ICL entirely disregards deontic constraints. On the contrary, ICL has acknowledged the importance of fairness, due process, legality, and moral restraint—though primarily because these principles align more naturally with the structures of both national and international criminal law.[189] Rather, this argument offers an alternative framework—rooted in both history and philosophy—that explains why superior responsibility resists full assimilation into either domestic criminal law or traditional liberal models of culpability. Its justification is *sui generis*: individuals—particularly those in positions of authority in circumstances that trigger the application of superior responsibility—often benefit from structural privileges embedded in national legal and political systems, such as immunity and systemic impunity.

To this end, given that domestic criminal law often fails to provide an adequate account for addressing mass criminality—the recurring theme in which superior responsibility typically operates—the previously proposed solution offers a potential compromise between two competing regimes: nationalists, which insist on deontic constraints such as personal culpability, and retentionists, which emphasize international authority and accountability grounded in consequentialist reasoning.[190] My proposal, in turn, offers a middle ground. It reassures those who favor nationalists that deontic constraints—such as personal culpability—remain essential, particularly for example in some cases involving principal and accessory liability. At the same time, it proposes that culpability grounded in hierarchical, immunity-privileged, and consequentialist reasoning provides a valid and doctrinally sound reasoning for superior responsibility as an exceptional case—one that, in this limited context, sets aside the strict requirement of personal culpability.

Regardless, in my view, both regimes might instead benefit from shifting the focus toward questions such as why political leaders are subject to a lower fault threshold under Article 28(b) of the Rome Statute, while military commanders face stricter standards under Article 28(a).[191] Or, whether there is a limit for a superior to take all or some necessary measures to prevent and punish the crimes of their subordinates, This inconsistency—embedded within the same vicarious liability structure—then calls for the urgent need for a principled and consistent account of superior responsibility, one grounded in the equality of the gravity of the crimes that follows from immunity privileges, the authority of the superior, and the systemic consequences of their failure to act. These substantive issues, in my view, warrant greater scholarly attention than the continued effort to develop an abstract philosophical account of the doctrine's nature.

---

[189] Cryer et al. 2019, p. 23.

[190] Minkova 2023, p. 71.

[191] See Rome Statute, Article 28.

In addition to the consequentialist culpability proposition, I now introduce what I term the gravity test as an additional analytical layer to that proposition. This test functions to evaluate the doctrinal legitimacy of superior responsibility within ICL. I argue that, when a case involving superior responsibility is adjudicated, the doctrine should be understood as a *sui generis* mode of liability—a distinct and autonomous legal construct within ICL, as rightly promulgated in the laws enabling international tribunals outside the individual criminal responsibility clauses (even though some strands of that tradition continue to place significant weight on personal culpability).[192] The gravity test highlights the qualitative and systemic seriousness of the crimes for which the superior is held accountable, thereby justifying the imposition of liability regardless of the superior's absent contribution to the underlying acts. An important caveat must be made, however: the designation *sui generis* should not be taken to equate superior responsibility with a mere crime of omission, as that concept is typically understood in domestic legal systems—or even in some scholarly attempts to frame it as a hybrid *sui generis* mode of liability.[193] Rather, it reflects the unique legal and structural character of the doctrine within ICL, where liability is premised not on passive failure alone but on the superior's authoritative position, their duty to act, and the broader consequences of their inaction in the context of mass atrocity.

This doctrinal uniqueness grounded in the gravity test affirms that superior responsibility is not simply a derivative or accessory form of liability, but a standalone legal category, tailored to the demands and realities of international criminal adjudication.[194] It has, again, no parallel application in criminal law. Rather, it is purposefully established to address a specific accountability gap, where the accused is charged for grave international crimes committed by their subordinates, notwithstanding the absence of their contribution to and, in some cases, knowledge of these crimes.[195] Needless to say, the key factor when it comes to incriminating a superior is the emphasis on culpability, which is criminally decisive when it comes to determining the severity of the punishment.[196] It is legally plausible to later impose a sentence on a superior in line with the one allocated to their subordinates—the direct perpetrators—on the grounds that the crimes would not have been committed if their superior had prevented them in the first place. In this regard, superiors may bear more responsibility and should, consequently, be sentenced with an aggravated punishment commensurate with their subordinates' culpability.[197]

[192] Van Sliedregt 2012b.

[193] Van Sliedregt 2012a, p. 196.

[194] Cf. Meloni 2007, p. 637 (where she refers to the *sui generis* nature of superior responsibility as a crime of omission in its own right).

[195] The *sui generis* solution may be required to address the distinct nature of ICL. See Damaška 2001, p. 457. See also Meloni 2007, p. 632.

[196] Van der Vyver 2021, p. 58.

[197] See *Prosecutor v. Stakić*, Appeals Chamber, Case No. IT-97-24-A, para 380, 22 March 2006; *Prosecutor v. Muhimana*, Appeals Chamber, Case No. ICTR-95-1B-A, para 234, 21 May 2007; *Prosecutor v. Ndindabahizi*, Appeals Chamber, Case No. ICTR-01-71-A, para 138, 3 July 2007; see, e.g., *Prosecutor v. Munyakazi*, Appeals Chamber, Case No. ICTR-97-36A-A, para 185, 28

To demonstrate, a superior is not charged with the failure to act specifically, but rather for the crimes committed or about to be committed by their subordinates, which is considered as grave as the actual commission of the crimes. Otto Triffterer rightly argued that this distinct mode of liability was created "to put an end to impunity for those who do not fulfill their legal obligation to prevent unlawful acts and thus, at least by silent toleration, abuse their power over subordinates, which they have because of their higher position in a very strict hierarchical system."[198] Simply put, under superior responsibility, the crimes for which subordinates may be charged (*e.g.*, torture) correspond to what the superior may be charged for (again, torture).[199] As such, superior responsibility cannot be combined with modes of perpetration or participation requiring an actual act of perpetration or co-perpetration or participation through complicity. This may explain why the Rome Statute of the ICC addresses the question of superior responsibility under a specific article.[200]

Lastly, within the confines of superior responsibility, the failure to act (omission) is regarded as an inherently grave offense on the part of the superior compared with the principal crimes committed by their subordinates. The gravity test was also implicitly supported in the *Ntabakuze* case, where the ICTR decided that "the seriousness of a superior's conduct in failing to prevent or punish crimes must be measured to some degree by the nature of the crimes to which this failure relates, *i.e.*, the gravity of the

September 2011; *Prosecutor v. Rukundo*, Appeals Chamber, ICTR- 2001-70-A, para 243, 20 October 2010; *Prosecutor v. Aleksovski*, Appeals Chamber, Case No. IT-95-14/1-A, para 182, 24 March 2000; *Prosecutor v. Zejnil Delalic & Others*, Case No. IT-96-21-T, para 732; *Prosecutor v. Milošević*, Appeals Chamber, Case No. IT-98-29/1-A, para 334, 12 November 2009. Cf. *Prosecutor v. Strugar*, Appeals Chamber, Case No. IT-01-42-A, paras 353–354 (17 July 2008); *Prosecutor v. Kalimanzira*, Appeals Chamber, Case No. ICTR-05-88, para 236, 20 October 2010; Kortfält notes that a superior would be held more liable than the principle perpetrator; however, if the superior does not complete the crime (voluntarily withdraws), then neither the superior nor the subordinate would be liable. Kortfält 2017, p. 261.

198 Triffterer 2002, p. 186.

199 *Prosecutor v. Tharcisse Renzaho*, Case No. ICTR-99-31-T, para 811, 14 July 2009.

200 As noted earlier, under superior responsibility, failure to act can be confused with other modes of liability where a superior may be held responsible as an accomplice to the crimes. In such cases, the superior is charged for the crimes (direct liability) as an accomplice (aider or abettor) by omission if their omission constituted the *actus reus* elements of an aider and abettor. In other words, if the superior's intention, as an accomplice by omission, "[was] *directed* to assist, encourage or lend moral support to the perpetration of a crime and have a substantial effect upon the perpetration of the crime" (emphasis added). In superior responsibility (vicarious liability), by contrast, the superior's mental element is limited to the *mens rea* required for the failure to discharge their entrusted duties. This mental element is typically assessed through a factual inquiry into what the superior knew, had reason to know, or should have known/consciously disregarded information as promulgated in the Rome Statute, and what measures were available and taken to prevent or punish the crimes. See *Prosecutor v. Naser Orić*, Appeals Chamber, Case No. IT-03-68-A, para 43, 3 July 2008; *Prosecutor v. Seromba*, Appeals Chamber, Case No. ICTR-2001-66-A, para 56, 12 March 2008; *Prosecutor v. Blagojević & Jokić*, Appeals Chamber, Case No. IT-02-60-A, para 127, 9 May 2007; *Prosecutor v. Aleksovski*, Appeals Chamber, Case No. IT- 95-14/1-A, para 162, 24 March 2000.

crimes committed by the direct perpetrators."[201] Accordingly, ICL[202] justifies the use of the gravity test *in lieu* of a causal contribution to the superior's failure to act, to the extent that this test is applied as if the superior had themselves committed the crimes of their subordinates.[203] With that in mind, in the *Čelebići* Case, the ICTY decided that the superior's failure to act was *as serious as* the actual commission of the crimes by their subordinates, and that the they should therefore be charged with those crimes, just like their subordinates.[204] According to this analysis, the gravity test can justify the ICL principle of derivative liability, as previously advocated by Guilfoyle.[205]

To simplify this analysis, a brief explanation may prove helpful here: as a general rule, individual criminal responsibility requires the following two elements: (i) means of perpetration/participation; and (ii) the attribution of the crimes to the individual concerned (criminal responsibility). In ICL, these two requirements are addressed in the laws of international criminal tribunals as follows:

- Articles 7(1) of the ICTY Statute, 6(1) of the ICTR Statute, and 25 of the ICC Statute refer to the means of perpetration and participation by which an individual may be held criminally responsible. This includes both principal liability—whether through direct contribution or indirect modes developed through jurisprudence, such as Joint Criminal Enterprise (basic, systemic, or extended)—and accomplice liability through indirect contributions, such as aiding and abetting. In each of these instances, the individual bears *direct criminal responsibility* for the commission of the core crimes.
- In terms of the extended modes of liability umbrella, Articles 7(3) of the ICTY Statute, 6(3) of the ICTR Statute, and 28 of the ICC Statute do not require direct or indirect contribution by the superior; however, the Articles attribute the crimes committed by subordinates to their superior (*vicarious criminal responsibility*).

On the second point, as noted earlier, my justification for the absence of a specific means of perpetration or participation in cases of superior responsibility lies in the fact that, through the application of the gravity test—combined with consequentialist reasoning—ICL effectively downplays the contribution requirement. Instead, it emphasizes the gravity of the superior's failure to discharge duties that could have prevented the commission of international crimes, thereby elevating superior responsibility to a principle in its own right. Consequently, attempts to reframe superior responsibility in terms of personal culpability—so as to justify what is essentially

[201] *Prosecutor v. Ntabakuze*, para 302 (affirming the same judgment of the Trial Chamber, which further decided: "[Ntabakuze's omission] is equivalent to other senior regional authorities who have also received life imprisonment"). It should be noted that, here, the court supports the view that a superior should receive a higher sentence than the default sentence of the principle criminals, as this is treated as an aggravated circumstance inferred from the severity of the omission. *Prosecutor v. Bagosora et al.*, Judgment, Case No. ICTR-98-41-T, paras 2267–2268, 18 December 2008.

[202] Referring to the recent judgments on superior responsibility in the ICTY and ICTR.

[203] *Prosecutor v. Zejnil Delalic & Others*, Case No. IT-96-21-T, para 732.

[204] Ibid.

[205] Guilfoyle 2011, p. 284.

a form of vicarious liability—become less persuasive and conceptually misaligned with the structural logic and goals of ICL. In turn, the superior's failure to act is considered *as grave as* their subordinates' means of perpetration/participation.

In conclusion, the only logical description of superior responsibility then is as a distinct mode of liability wherein, to result in the superior's criminal responsibility,[206] the broader meaning of the rule of "*nulla persona sine culpa*"[207] does not require participation but merely an intentional negligent/recklessness mental status toward the failure to discharge the duties, which is deemed as grave as the crimes committed by others.[208] Thus, superior responsibility constitutes a *sui generis* mode of liability, where culpability arises not from participation but from negligence of such gravity that it substitutes for direct involvement—provided all legal requirements are met, an imperative that is neither easily satisfied nor clearly and coherently articulated in jurisprudence.

3.4 Elements of Superior Responsibility

For prosecution purposes, the superior responsibility doctrine requires the prosecutor to prove beyond reasonable doubt that all the elements of this doctrine are met, lock, stock, and barrel, as regards the accused superior.[209] However, the Articles concerning superior responsibility included in the subject-matter jurisdiction in the statutes of the UN *ad hoc* tribunals lack the prerequisite construction regarding the conceptual elements of the doctrine. For example, the text of these Articles does not distinguish between military and political superiors, nor does it specify the required statuses relating to their subordinates, namely whether they should possess *de jure* or *de facto* effective command/authority and control over their subordinates. These Articles also lack an essential requirement of superior responsibility, namely, what the superior is criminally charged with (*i.e.*, crimes committed by the subordinates). Given the brevity of the language employed in these articles, the judges of the UN *ad hoc* tribunals, particularly the ICTY, played a commendable interstitial role in

[206] Van der Vyver 2021.

[207] *Prosecutor v. Mpaambara*, Judgement, Case No. ICTR-01-65-T, para 26, 11 September 2006 (here, under superior responsibility, the gravity of the superior's negligence is equated with participation and co-participation in the actual commission of the crimes).

[208] It should be noted that, here, negligence refers to the dereliction of a superior's duty with respect to their subordinates. However, it does not refer to the *mens rea* element. *Mens rea*, as an element of superior responsibility, pertains to whether a superior knew about the crimes (intent) or should have known (negligence). For more detail, see Sect. 3.4.3.

[209] *Prosecutor v. Orić*, Appeals Chamber, Case No. IT-02-68-A, para 18, 3 July 2008). See also *Prosecutor v. Nahimana*, Appeals Chamber, Case No. ICTR-99-52-A, para 484, 28 November 2007; *Prosecutor v. Halilović*, Appeals Chamber, Case No. IT-01-48-A, para 59, 16 October 2007; *Prosecutor v. Blaškić*, Appeals Chamber, Case No. IT-95-14-A, para 484 (29 July 2004); *Prosecutor v. Aleksovski*, Appeals Chamber, Case No. IT-95-14/1-A, para 72, 24 March 2000; *Prosecutor v. Aleksovski*, Judgement, Case No. IT-95-14/1-T, para 294, 25 June 1999.

developing the law by deconstructing the elements of the doctrine, resulting in a three-prong test.

Scholars have also attempted to deconstruct these elements, giving rise to some additional sub-elements (or parameters) within the confines of these elements in their writings.[210] If any of these parameters are not satisfied, its concomitant element will also not be satisfied, which precludes the possibility of applying superior responsibility to the accused superior.[211] In other words, the elements of superior responsibility (and the parameters they generate) are intrinsically intertwined and interdependent. In terms of securing a conviction, their collective substantiation thus forms the basis of an indictment against a superior.

To this end, the essential elements are: (i) the superior–subordinate relationship; (ii) fault (*mens rea*); and (iii) failure to discharge the superior's duties.[212] This three-prong test was established in the statutes of the ICTY and ICTR, with the case law of these tribunals stemming from the text of API Article 86(2). In the following sections, I shall take a pedagogical approach to each element, engaging in a more detailed discussion of the parameters of each element.

3.4.1 Superior–Subordinate Relationship Parameters: **De Jure v. De Facto** *Superiors; Subordinates* **v.** *Army Forces; Effective Command and Control* **v.** *Effective Authority and Control*

In the history of international criminal tribunals' adjudications, the superior–subordinate relationship element has been applied in divergent ways. Scholars and judges have challenged this element on multiple grounds,[213] most notably in relation to the distinction between the superior–subordinate relationship in a military framework and a non-military, political framework, particularly in terms of Command and Control *v.* Effective Authority and Control. The challenge lies in determining

---

[210] Kortfält 2017, p. 280.

[211] Contra, ibid. (Here, it is correctly noted that the satisfaction of any element of superior responsibility gives rise to criminal responsibility.)

[212] Ibid. See also *Prosecutor v. Gacumbitsi*, Appeals Chamber, Case No. ICTR-2001-64-A, para 143, 7 July 2006; *Prosecutor v. Nahimana et al.*, Appeals Chamber, Case No. ICTR-99-52-A, para 484, 28 November 2007. Failure to act means that a superior must prevent, repress, or investigate and punish their subordinates, and must take necessary and reasonable measures to comply with these duties. However, the Rome Statute of the ICC sets out a different set of rules: in this respect, a superior must take "*all* necessary and reasonable measures within his or her power to prevent or repress their commission or to submit the matter to the competent authorities for investigations and prosecution." [emphasis added] Rome Statute, Article 28(a)–(b) (emphasis added).

[213] Scholars have presented various categorizations of the elements of superior responsibility. Most notably, they categorize them in accordance with two main factors: objective and subjective elements. See Galand 2020, pp. 7–8; Ambos 2002; Kortfält 2017, p. 280.

the status of the subordinates concerned (Civilian Subordinates *v.* Army Forces),[214] both in relation to their superior and their means of perpetration or participation in the crimes (as principals or accomplices). In the latter context, a key issue concerns whether, under this doctrine, a superior may be prosecuted only in cases in which subordinates committed the crimes as principals, or whether this also extends to accomplice subordinates.[215] A further challenge relates to the prosecutor's task of proving whether a superior holds (or held) a *de jure* or *de facto* status, and, based on this distinction, whether the superior–subordinate relationship was formal or informal.

A *de jure* position means that the superior is appointed by law or competent authorities to supervise a group of subordinates.[216] In other words, a superior is legally entitled to exercise control over their subordinates' actions. In the case of a *de facto* superior, on the other hand, the superior "act" as they are in the position of a *de jure* superior and exercises actual control over their subordinates by discharging their duties without a formal legal appointment.[217] Although it has been argued that *de jure* status may provide a *prima facie* indication of this relationship, it should not be taken as determinative of this relationship. The prosecutor must therefore investigate whether the superior exercised effective command/authority and control (*i.e.*, material ability),[218] and, in the case of the ICC, whether the superior's negligence led directly to the commission of the crimes (thereby establishing a causal link).[219]

As a general rule, a superior's *de jure* or *de facto* position may be identified through their relationship with their subordinates. As suggested earlier, in relation to the superior–subordinate relationship requirement, the statutes of the *ad hoc* tribunals (the ICTY and ICTR) do not distinguish between these two positions of superiors.[220]

---

214 Whether the subordinate should be considered as a principal to the crimes or an accomplice.

215 On the legal characterization of superior responsibility, see Sect. 3.3.

216 Guénaël 2009, pp. 138–139.

217 Ibid.

218 See *Prosecutor v. Enver Hadzihasanovic et al.*, Case. No. IT-01-47-A, para 17, 7 December 2001. See also *Prosecutor v. Zejnil Delalic & Others*, Case No. IT-96-21-T, para 197; *Prosecutor v. Orić*, Appeals Chamber, Case No. IT-03-68-A, para 91; *Prosecutor v. Sefer Halilović* (AC), Case No. IT-01-48-A, para 85, 16 November 2005.

219 Rome Statute, Article 28 ("as a result of").

220 Statute of the International Criminal Tribunal for the Former Yugoslavia (ICTY), Article 7(3); Statute of the International Criminal Tribunal for Rwanda (ICTR), Article 6(3). (Unlike the Rome Statute, the statutes of the ICTY and ICTR do not explicitly distinguish whether the accused is a military commander or a political superior, nor do they clarify whether the superior holds a de jure or de facto position. Additionally, they do not set out whether there must be a well-defined relationship between the superior and their subordinates or the extent of control exercised. Instead, these parameters have been developed through the jurisprudence of these tribunals. The ICTY and ICTR jurisprudence has recognized that a superior may be held criminally responsible for crimes committed by their subordinates if they fail to fulfill their duties, regardless of whether their authority is formal or informal. International law, therefore, does not focus on official titles when assessing superior responsibility. Rather, it considers the material ability of the superior to control their subordinates, their knowledge of the relationship, and whether they took reasonable measures to prevent or punish the crimes committed.)

The Rome Statute of the ICC, however, explicitly distinguishes this element by extending criminal responsibility to political superiors under the doctrine, as set out in its text.[221] In this context, it is noteworthy that both the ICTY and ICTR Statutes employed the exact wording used to describe superior responsibility in Article 86(2) of the API, which does not explicitly distinguish between military commanders and political superiors.[222] Unlike the parameters of superior responsibility set out under Article 28 of the Rome Statute of the ICC, the unsatisfactory characterization of superior responsibility in the ICTY and ICTR Statutes (along with those of other *ad hoc* tribunals)[223] compelled judges at these institutions to progressively interpret whether superiors held a *de jure* or *de facto* position, as well as addressing the lack of clarity regarding the criminal responsibility of political superiors.[224]

While some earlier interpretative attempts were helpful, in some cases they were either too strict or overly vague. It appears that, to establish the superior–subordinate relationship, not only is *de jure* and *de facto* control important but also seniority and rank. The rank element is required to trace the criminal acts of subordinates to their *de jure* or *de facto* superior, which is essential for employing an effective command/authority and control test.[225] As such, a *de jure* superior must meet two essential requirements: they must hold a position of seniority with respect to their assigned subordinates, and they must exercise actual control over their subordinates.

In addition, a superior's position within a hierarchical system does not legally need to be proven by a court of law. As long as the superior exercises "actual" power over their subordinates, this automatically results in a *prima facie* finding that they have effective command and control (military commanders) or effective authority and control (political superiors).[226] Accordingly, a superior will be held responsible only on the substantiated finding that they possessed material ability, irrespective of their official capacity within this system.[227] It has been argued that, in both military and non-military settings, a superior must occupy a certain level of seniority. Contrary to this argument, however, a superior may be held accountable even if they do not hold such a rank.[228] In the *Blaškić* case, the court ruled that "the commander need not have

---

221 Rome Statute, Article 28.

222 *Protocol Additional to the Geneva Conventions of 12 August 1949, and relating to the Protection of Victims of International Armed Conflicts (Protocol I)*, 1977, Article 86(2), U.N. Doc. A/32/144, 1125 U.N.T.S. 3, reprinted in 16 I.L.M. 1391 (1977).

223 SCSL & STL Statutes, STL Statute; Report of the Secretary-General on the Establishment of a Special Court for Sierra Leone, U.N. Doc. S/2000/915, Annex (4 October 2000), *the Special Court for Sierra Leone Statute*, Article 6(3).

224 Guénaël 2009, p. 143.

225 Ibid. Here, seniority rank is key to establishing the relationship linking the superior to their subordinates.

226 Ibid.

227 Ibid., p. 101.

228 Arnold and Triffterer 2008, p. 830. In principle, seniority rank (chain-of-command) is not a pre-existing condition required to give rise to a superior's criminal responsibility; however, it becomes necessary during the prosecution process, when a superior may be absolved of responsibility if they were not the direct superior of the subordinate who committed the crimes. Guénaël begs to

any legal authority to prevent or punish acts of his subordinates." Rather, they held that "[w]hat counts is his material ability" to control a subordinate's actions.[229] In this context, then, a superior must be aware of two facts—their hierarchical position in relation to the criminal acts committed by their subordinates and their "awareness" of their to prevent, repress, and or punish such acts.[230]

I shall engage in a more detailed discussion of the fault element of superior responsibility further on. For the purposes of the discussion here, however, the superior's awareness of the relationship with their subordinates may serve as a substantiating finding regarding the "had reason to know" element of *mens rea*.[231] That being said, when a superior is aware of their position and the duties entrusted to them, this provides a *prima facie* indication that they had reason to know about the misconduct of their subordinates. Conversely, the absence of such awareness (*i.e.*, *de facto* or *de jure* relationship) will undermine their indictment under the doctrine of superior responsibility.[232]

Another pertinent issue concerning a superior's *de jure* appointment is that, although it may not be difficult to identify a superior's legally assigned position within a hierarchical military structure, identifying such a position may prove more complicated for political superiors. Most domestic martial laws assign a military commander to supervise their forces; however, in the case of political superiors, such a formal designation is not always clear. Although a superior's *de jure* position establishes a *prima facie* basis for establishing superior responsibility, this must be accompanied by proof beyond a reasonable doubt that the *de jure* political superior exercised effective authority over their subordinates. It is important to note that this is not the only element that needs to be considered; what also matters is the superior's actual material ability. In the *Čelebići* case, the Trial Chamber held that: "… the factor that determines liability for [superior] criminal responsibility is the actual possession or non-possession of powers of control over the actions of subordinates."[233]

The Appeals Chamber in the *Blaškić* case supported the view taken in the *Čelebići* case, adding that "disobedience of the subordinates can instead be counted as evidence of the lack of effective control."[234] The material ability mentioned in these decisions refers to the superior's certainty that their orders will be executed by their

differ, however, noting that "[t]he first requirement of superior responsibility relationship between the accused and the perpetrator, *demands* a hierarchical relationship" (emphasis added). Guénaël 2009, p. 146.

229 *Prosecutor v. Blaškić*, Judgement, Case No. IT-95-14-T, paras 300–301, 3 March 2000.

230 *See* Guénaël 2009, pp. 139–140.

231 Wu and King 1997, p. 290.

232 *Prosecutor v. Limaj*, Judgment, Case No. IT-03-66-T, para 522, 30 November 2005. (The appeals decision in Nahimana rejects the notion that proof of such a relationship is not required.) See *Nahimana et al. v. The Prosecutor*, Case No. ICTR-99-52-A, para 605, 28 November 2007.

233 *Prosecutor v. Mucić et al.*, Judgment, Case No. IT-96-21-T, para 370, 16 November 1998.

234 Kortfält 2017, p. 288 (citing *Prosecutor v. Blaškić*, Appeals Chamber, Case No. IT-95-14-A, para 69–399, 29 July 2004.

subordinates.[235] Therefore, in principle, in the absence of a superior *de facto* position, a *de jure* position is deemed sufficient if it is accompanied by effectiveness and material ability, assuming the other essential elements are met. However, if both *de facto* and *de jure* positions are present, the *de facto* status of the superior prevails for accusation purposes.

Concerning the effective command/authority and control parameter of this element, a prosecutor must prove that the superior has or had the effective command/authority to exercise control over their subordinates.[236] To put this bluntly, the superior–subordinate relationship is "interpersonal" and therefore confined to the superior's position (acting in an effective capacity) with respect to their subordinates.[237] Accordingly, for the purposes of establishing superior responsibility, proving the effectiveness and material ability within a superior–subordinate relationship is a *sine qua non*.[238] In other words, in the absence of this effectiveness and material ability, a prosecutor cannot secure an indictment even if the superior had knowledge of the commission of the crimes.[239] Indeed, effective authority/command and control is the cornerstone of the superior–subordinate relationship, which ultimately places the superior in a blameworthy position. It should also be noted that the doctrine of superior responsibility is not triggered merely by a superior's "substantial influence".[240]

Ultimately, the effective control parameter can indicate conformity with the gravity test described earlier in this chapter. To render the superior's dereliction of duties grave, it must be established that they hold genuine effective command/authority control. In other words, because superiors are entrusted with dominant obligations, which are presumed to entail effectiveness and material ability within the relationship, their failure to discharge these duties may result in their liability for grave crimes.

To comply with this test, a superior's effective command/authority and control over their subordinates consists of three prerequisite requirements:

1. mutual awareness of both the duties and obligations characteristic of the superior–subordinate relationship;
2. certainty on the part of the superior that their orders will be executed by their subordinates; and

---

[235] In the *Čelebići* case, the prosecutor, citing the *Hostage* case, claimed otherwise; however, both the Trial and Appeals Chambers rejected this claim, holding that it was contrary to customary international law and the Statute of the Court. *Prosecutor v. Zejnil Delalic & Others*, Case No. IT-96-21-T, para 266. See also Heller 2016–17; Fenrick 1999, at 518.

[236] *Prosecutor v. Zejnil Delalic & Others*, Case No. IT-96-21-T, para 303.

[237] Ibid.

[238] Kortfält 2017, p. 288. (Meaning "without which it could not be requirement".) See also Ambos 2002, p. 860.

[239] *Prosecutor v. Ndindiliyimana et al.*, Judgment, Case No. ICTR-00-56-T, paras 126, 1916, 17 May 2011.

[240] *Contra*, Fenrick 1999, p. 520. (Maintains that business influence may be taken into account in determining the *de facto* status of a superior.)

3. the superior's material ability to prevent or punish the crimes committed by their subordinates. In other words, the superior must be aware of their power to prevent and/or punish the crimes resulting from their subordinates' conduct.[241]

To substantiate a finding regarding the existence of a superior–subordinate relationship, the prosecutor must furnish proof of all three of these constituent parameters.[242] It will also demonstrate the severity of their duties to prevent or punish their subordinates' crimes. To summarize, concerning the superior–subordinate relationship, what matters most is the effective command/authority and control (and the material ability) parameter. In other words, the superior–subordinate relationship must be based on a two-fold parameter: effective command/authority and control, and the assurance that the superior has material ability over their subordinates through complete adherence to their orders.

Regarding subordinates, in the *Nyiramasuhuko et al.* case, the ICTR decided that it is a requirement that "subordinates [are] sufficiently identified".[243] As a general rule, to attribute the criminal liability of subordinates to the superior, the subordinates must be identified within the confines of the superior–subordinates relationship.[244] However, there is some disagreement on this point in jurisprudence concerning this doctrine.[245] As explained earlier, ICL does not chiefly intend to prosecute "little people", and in this respect, when it comes to prosecutions, it is not as vital to identify subordinates as it is their superior.[246] To this end, what matters under the doctrine of superior responsibility is that beyond-reasonable-doubt proof is provided of the crimes committed by the superior's subordinates, irrespective of their scale. In support of this assertion, in the *Orić* case, the Trial Chamber of the ICTY held that, "The direct perpetrators of a crime punishable under the Statute *do not need to be* identical to the subordinates of a superior. It is only required that the relevant subordinates, by their own acts or omissions, be criminally responsible for the acts and omissions of the direct perpetrators."[247] It is noteworthy that the Appeals Chamber reversed the trial decision based on the absence of Orić's *mens rea*, rather than on the basis of the subordinates not being identified.[248]

---

[241] Guénaël 2009, p. 188.

[242] Van der Vyver 2021, p. 575.

[243] *Prosecutor v. Nyiramasuhuko et al.*, Judgment, Case No. ICTR-98-42-T, para 121, 24 June 2011. See also *Prosecutor v. Bizimungu et al.*, Judgment, Case No. ICTR-88-50-T, para 1872, 30 September 2011.

[244] For the purpose of establishing a causal link; however, the jurisprudence of the *ad hoc* tribunals does not support the necessity of a causal link to apply superior responsibility. See van der Vyver 2021, p. 584. See also Triffterer 2002, p. 189.

[245] Van Sliedregt 2011, pp. 384–385.

[246] May and Fyfe 2018, p. 95.

[247] *Prosecutor v. Naser Orić*, TC Judgment, Case No. IT-03-68, para 478, 30 June 2006.

[248] Van Sliedregt 2011, p. 385.

By the same token as in the *Orić* case, the Trial Chamber of the ICTY in the *Hadžihasanović* case held that an exact identification of subordinates is not required, provided that the subordinates are identified as a group.[249]

In summary, the chain of command/authority between the accused superior and the perpetrator subordinate need not be strictly formal or informal. However, identifying such a chain will help the prosecutor establish the remaining requirements for proving the superior's criminal responsibility.[250] In any case, what matters with respect to this element is establishing the existence of actual and effective command/authority and control. It is crucial to note that, in the case of political superiors, the degree of effective control over their subordinates—that triggers their supervisory duties—needs to be parallel to that of military commanders.[251] Put simply, the aforementioned parameters should be applied proportionally to both military commanders and political superiors.

3.4.2 Failure to Execute Supervisory Duties: The Duty to Prevent, Repress, and Punish

To prosecute a superior under the superior responsibility doctrine, the prosecutor must prove that they failed to carry out their entrusted duties to prevent or punish subordinates, resulting in the commission of crimes.[252] The prosecutor must also prove that the superior did not take necessary, reasonable measures in line with their duties to prevent or punish the crimes committed by subordinates under their command or control.[253] In other words, to fulfill their duty to take necessary and reasonable measures, a superior must execute their duties to prevent, repress, and punish, in that order.

These duties are rooted in the LoAC, according to which a superior incurs criminal and/or disciplinary responsibility for violating this law owing to their failure to prevent or punish the principal (or accomplice) perpetrators.[254] These duties are also an integral part of their duties as part of the chain of command/authority, which requires them to guide their subordinates' conduct; this, in turn, establishes their awareness of these duties under international law.[255] That being said, a superior does not incur criminal liability solely on account of failing to comply with their entrusted duties. Rather, the prosecutor must also establish that, as part of these

---

[249] *Prosecutor v. Hadžihasanović & Kubura*, TC Judgment, Case No. IT-01-47-T, para 90, 15 March 2006.

[250] Report of the International Commission of Inquiry on Darfur to the United Nations Secretary-General, paras 558, 561, 25 January 2005.

[251] *Prosecutor v. Delalic*, Case No. IT-96-21-T, para 377–8.

[252] *Prosecutor v. Aleksovski*, Judgment, Case No. IT-95-14/1-T, para 76, 25 June 1999.

[253] Sadat 2002, p. 203.

[254] *PROSECUTOR v. BLASKIC*, para 290.

[255] Mettraux 2009, p. 126.

necessary and reasonable steps, the superior failed to take necessary and reasonable measures (*i.e.*, involving guidance and awareness) to prevent or punish. In other words, the superior's failure to act comprises two failures: (i) failing to instruct their subordinates about violations of international law, and (ii) failing to take necessary and reasonable measures to repress and punish.[256]

However, before elaborating on this requirement, it is important to note that a superior's failure to carry out these entrusted duties stems from the effective command/authority and control requirement. In other words, these aspects are not mutually exclusive. Indeed, the ICTY decided that the use of force by a superior to prevent and/or punish their subordinates "may demonstrate material ability", which denotes effective command/authority and control.[257] That being said, if a superior lacks the prescribed degree of effective command/authority and control and material ability[258] over their subordinates, the prosecutor cannot assume that the superior would have been capable of preventing or punishing the crimes if their subordinates do not comply with their command/authority and control. In other words, "a [superior] cannot be blamed for not having done something he or she had no power to do".[259] Therefore, a superior's failure to act must stem from their actual effective command/authority and control. In the absence of such control, the former alone is not sufficient to establish the superior's criminal responsibility.[260]

3.4.2.1 Duty to Prevent

As part of the necessary and reasonable measures required under the law of superior responsibility, a superior is required to prevent subordinates from committing crimes.[261] As previously noted, the superior must be aware of the obligations set out in international law toward their subordinates, and they are responsible for extending this awareness to their subordinates.[262] Such awareness is conveyed by training subordinates on LoAC, with the establishment of a reporting system to track their actions and take corrective measures, where necessary, in respect of their conduct.[263] This duty is not explicitly outlined in the law and jurisprudence of the *ad hoc* tribunals;

[256] Fenrick 1999, p. 521.

[257] *Prosecutor v. Aleksovski*, para 81.

[258] Again, effective command/authority and control here must be accompanied by the subordinates' material ability to execute the superior's orders.

[259] *Prosecutor v. Aleksovski*, para 81.

[260] In such cases, effective command/authority and control must be recognized at the international level and the superior cannot raise the argument that they had no effective command/authority and control based on municipal laws. Kortfält 2017, p. 293. See also van der Vyver 2021, p. 572.

[261] Kortfält 2017, p. 279.

[262] Mettraux 2009, p. 126. Fenrick differentiates between two types of superiors and their obligations within this duty. While a senior superior "may convene martial courts", a junior superior may recommend that their subordinates be subjected to disciplinary action. Fenrick 1999, p. 520.

[263] Fenrick 1999, p. 519.

rather, it was extracted from LoAC and customs and laws of war.[264] In turn, the API dictates that a superior must establish a system for reporting subordinates' actions and inform the authorities of any breaches of LoAC.[265] Under both international treaty and customary law, a superior is required to ensure that subordinates are neither committing nor about to commit breaches of LoAC.[266] Ultimately, as a corrective measure to prevent violations of this law, a superior must provide more training in LoAC.[267] In addition to stepping in and ordering subordinates not to commit such breaches, all of these measures satisfy the superior's duty to prevent violations. As noted earlier, there are subsequent duties that must also be executed.

3.4.2.2 Duties to Repress and Punish

By the same token, in the statutes of the *ad hoc* tribunals, the duties to prevent and repress are not explicitly identified as separate but related duties. However, the tribunals have held that this duty constitutes an auxiliary duty to punish, as inferred from LoAC.[268] On the basis of the customary nature of superior responsibility, a superior was indicted in the aftermath of WWII for not repressing crimes committed by his subordinates.[269] In the *Von List* case, the Military Tribunal held that, "failure to terminate these unlawful killings and take adequate steps to prevent their recurrence constitutes a serious breach of duty and imposes criminal responsibility."[270] In addition, the duty to repress must be carried out jointly with the duty to punish. In this context, as part of the duty to punish, the duty to repress is required at the time at which the crime is committed.[271]

For a prosecutor to substantiate a finding, it is noteworthy that, for the purpose of establishing a superior's criminal responsibility, these duties—to prevent, repress, and punish—are treated as a single cluster. It follows that a prosecutor must investigate whether a superior failed first to prevent, second to repress, and third to punish. However, in the context of an ongoing hostility, these duties must be executed by the superior either before, during, or after the commission of their subordinates' crimes.

---

[264] Ibid.

[265] Ibid., p. 521.

[266] *Prosecutor v. Pavle Strugar*, Judgement, Case No. IT-01-42-T, para 374, 31 January 2005.

[267] Fenrick 1999, p. 520.

[268] The duty to repress (or suppress) was adopted from the AP of the Geneva Conventions, which distinguishes between two kinds of LoAC violations: grave breaches and any other type of breach. In both cases, the commander must repress these breaches by imposing either penal or disciplinary actions on their subordinates. See ICRC Commentary, para 3539.

[269] It should be noted that, according to the *ad hoc* tribunals, the duty to repress appears to be a sub-category of the duty to punish. However, according to the Rome Statute, depending on the stage at which the violations take place, the duty to repress can be part of the duty to prevent and the duty to punish. See Kortfält 2017, p. 296.

[270] *U.S. v. Wilhelm von List et al.*, Trials of War Criminals before the Nuernberg Military Tribunals under Control Council Law No. 10, vol. xi, p. 1272 (hereinafter "U.S. v. von List et al").

[271] ICRC Commentary, para 3400.

For example, a superior cannot be absolved of criminal responsibility merely because they repressed the commission of crimes or punished the subordinates. In this scenario, the superior must definitively prove that they pursued their first duty (the duty to prevent). Kortfält notes that the wording of the statutes of the *ad hoc* tribunals regarding this matter suggests the opposite, however. He notes that: "the superior['s] fail[ure] to take the necessary and reasonable measures to prevent such acts *or* to punish…are thus two-fold"[272] (emphasis added). This statement is misleading and inaccurate for several reasons. First, the word "or" in the Article does not indicate an alternative. Rather, it reflects the legislator's intent to underscore that a superior's duty to prevent does not absolve them of criminal liability for failing to punish perpetrators "even" if they fulfilled their duty to prevent or repress.[273] In other words, the superior must abide by a consecutive series of duties in a sequential manner, commencing with the duty to prevent and concluding with the duty to punish. Based on these consecutive duties, the accused cannot plead innocence solely for executing one of these duties. In the *Blaškić* case, the ICTY supported this view, holding that:

> [T]he Trial Chamber stresses that the obligation to "prevent or punish" does not provide the accused with two alternative and equally satisfying options. Where the accused knew or had reason to know that subordinates were about to commit crimes and failed to prevent them, he cannot make up for the failure to act by punishing the subordinates afterwards.[274]

Second, these duties have long been part of customary international law, on the basis of which the jurisdictions of the *ad hoc* tribunals were defined.[275] In the aftermath of WWII, customary and international case law suggested that, although these duties are interdependent, they must be carried out in a step-by-step manner by the superior.[276] Therefore, a superior has a duty to prevent subordinates from committing crimes (before) and to repress the commission of such crimes (during/after if there was an indication of ongoing hostility), and finally, to punish them after their conclusion (after). In this scenario, the superior cannot rely on having carried out only one of these duties as a basis for pleading innocence. The superior must also have access to the knowledge element of superior responsibility—that is, whether they knew or had reason to know—while carrying out their duties to prevent and punish, as will be discussed further below.[277]

Regarding the duty to punish, a superior may use legal force to carry out this duty. For instance, in the *Hadžihasanović* case, the ICTY decided that: "a superior may….use force to prevent or punish the commission of crimes by subordinates…[t]his kind of force is legal under international humanitarian law."[278]

---

[272] Kortfält 2017, p. 292.

[273] ICRC Commentary, para 3400.

[274] *Prosecutor v. Blaškić*, Appeals Chamber, Case No. IT-95-14-A, para 336.

[275] Ibid., para 85.

[276] *U.S. v. Wilhelm von List*. See also Tokyo War Crimes Trial, pp. 49, 847, where the Court held that: "Tojo [is] guilty for the failure to punish, in addition to his being found guilty for the failure to prevent."

[277] Van der Vyver 2021, p. 598. Certain domestic criminal jurisdictions strictly require intent only.

[278] *Prosecutor v. Enver Hadzihasanovic et al.*, Case. No. IT-01-47-A, para 228.

However, this conclusion appears to apply only in the case of military commanders, given their martial rights and military structural capacities to effectively use such force. Such a situation would be inconceivable in the case of political superiors, however, who presumably would not be able to use such force against subordinates to prevent and punish. This issue remains unaddressed by international criminal tribunals. However, drawing on the language employed in the *Hadžihasanović* case, the tribunal did note that this mode of preventing and punishing subordinates is one of the 'modalities' that can be used to fulfill these duties.[279]

Therefore, on the one hand, this use of force appears to be applicable—on a case-by-case basis—only to military commanders, and not to non-military superiors. On the other hand, political superiors may apply other "modalities" to prevent and punish when "formally" issuing orders to prevent the commission of crimes and/or submitting the matter to the competent authorities after the commission of the crimes.[280] According to this syllogism, Fenrick argues that: "[Political] superiors…are unlikely to have substantial disciplinary powers…[t]hey, therefore, have to submit the matter to the competent civil authorities for investigation and prosecution."[281] In itself, such an approach may satisfy the political superior's duty to punish. As a result, such a superior may not be prosecuted under the doctrine of superior responsibility if they submitted the matter to the competent authorities, thereby discharging their duty to punish.[282]

3.4.3 Mens Rea *in Superior Responsibility: Intent* v. *Negligence* v. *Recklessness* v. *Willful Blindness*

As an essential element of *mens rea*, criminal law requires that—for the accused to be held criminally responsible—crimes must be committed with awareness and/or intent on the part of the perpetrator.[283] However, under ICL the distinctive features of superior responsibility, as noted earlier, extend beyond its fault element.[284] Accordingly, an international criminal offense requires intent and/or knowledge on the part of the accused, meaning that they were either aware of the consequences of their conduct (knowledge) or had a deliberate intention to partake in the commission of the crime and bring it to fruition (*dolus directus*).[285] In the context of superior responsibility, ICL imposes the fault element of intent when the superior knew about their

279 Ibid.

280 Ibid.

281 Fenrick 1999, p. 522.

282 See van der Vyver 2021, p. 593.

283 Ibid., pp. 61–64.

284 Here, a superior's failure to act, owing to negligence, renders them equally criminally responsibility for the crimes committed by their subordinates as would be the case if they had intentionally failed to act.

285 See van der Vyver 2021.

subordinates' criminal acts but failed to prevent or punish them.[286] Ambos asserts that, in superior responsibility, the required *mens rea* must be based on both the superior's failure to act and on the crimes committed by their subordinates.[287] This dichotomous assertion is inaccurate under the law of participation in ICL, where a prosecutor's proof of *mens rea* must reflect the perpetrator's mode of liability in the commission of the crimes.[288] To elaborate on this, for an aider, the required *mens rea* is their intent and/or knowledge that their role in the crime (as an accomplice) may subject them to criminal responsibility, as long as they are aware of the direct perpetrator's intent.[289] In the context of superior responsibility, the fault element must be interpreted within the confines of the subject-matter of this doctrine. The superior's knowledge of their duties—and failure—to act may therefore subject them to criminal liability for their subordinates' crimes, thereby establishing the fault element of superior responsibility.[290]

It is important to note that the statutes of the *ad hoc* tribunals regarding superior responsibility were not analogous to the Rome Statute of the ICC. Moreover, under the statutes of the *ad hoc* tribunals, the wording and structure of this doctrine were not set out in the same way as in the Rome Statute. For example, the ICTY and ICTR Statutes do not differentiate between military and non-military superiors, while the jurisprudence of the tribunal does make such a distinction.[291] In the case of the ICC, the Rome Statute explicitly addresses the position of a military commander compared with their political superior counterparts, as well as their associated elements of responsibility.[292] For example, under the subject-matter jurisdiction of the tribunals, the *mens rea* element of superior responsibility was drawn from the Article on superior responsibility in the API, which requires preconceived knowledge or reason to know, both of which arguably denote intent. In contrast, for military or military-like commanders, the ICC Statute refers to a "should have known" state of mind (denoting negligence), while for political superiors it refers to "consciously disregarded information" (denoting intent).[293]

---

[286] Ibid., p. 586.

[287] Ambos 2002, pp. 851–852.

[288] Depending on the jurisdiction of the case. The ICTY and ICTR differ from the ICC in this regard. See *infra.*

[289] Van Sliedregt 2012a, p. 69.

[290] See the discussion *infra*: on certain occasions, the *ad hoc* tribunals decided that, under the doctrine of superior responsibility, the required *mens rea* element for accusations relating to the crime of genocide pertains to the superior's failure to prevent and punish, and not their intent to destroy a group, either in whole or in part.

[291] *Prosecutor v. Delalic*, Case No. IT-96-21-T, para 356. See also *Prosecutor v. Musema*, para 148; *Prosecutor v. Ferdinand Nahimana, Jean-Bosco Barayagwiza & Hassan Hgeze*, Case No. ICTR-99-55-T, para 976, 3 December 2003.

[292] Van der Vyver 2021, p. 569.

[293] Rome Statute, Article 28(a): i; (b): i. The ICTY and ICTR Statutes refer to the *mens rea* requirement as 'had reason to know'. ICTY and ICTR Statutes, Article 7(3) and Article 6(3), respectively.

In this context, the superior's negligence arises where they "should have known" (in the case of the ICC Rome Statute) or "had reason to know" (in the case of the statutes of the *ad hoc* tribunals) about the crimes being committed or about to be committed by their subordinates.[294] Accordingly, the superior's *mens rea* can be described on the basis of two fault scenarios: (i) they knew that the crimes were about to be committed or were being committed, indicating intent; and (ii) they had reason to know about the crimes but failed to execute their duties to prevent or punish, indicating either intent or negligence, depending on the factual findings of the case.[295]

At one end of the spectrum, the superior "knew", and this state of mind standard is, to some extent,[296] uncontroversial. The superior's knowledge that crimes were being committed or about to be committed and the failure to execute their duties provides certain proof that they intentionally neglected their duty, indicating intent. At the other end of the spectrum, however, the second instance of fault—wherein the superior *had reason to know*—is more controversial, raising the question of whether this denotes intent or negligence. Legal academic literature and international case law have both struggled to determine whether "had reason to know" signifies intent or negligence *per se*.[297] Accordingly, academic literature either equates "had reason to know" with the "should have known" standard (negligence),[298] sets a higher standard for "should have known", or describes it as willful blindness (a form of intent).[299] Kai Ambos and Thomas Weigend suggested that "had reason to know" and "should have known" reflect the same state of mind standard, namely, negligence.[300] Van Sliedregt argues that "had reason to know" denotes intent but often closely resembles "should have known" (negligence).[301] Sadat, on the other hand, suggests going further, arguing that both "knew" and "should have known" or, in the case of a political superior, "consciously disregarded information" should be viewed exclusively as criminal negligence.[302] She argues that the superior responsibility doctrine is based institutionally and exclusively on culpable negligence.[303]

---

[294] Among scholars and tribunal jurisprudence, there is some controversy surrounding whether the had-reason-to-know standard denotes intent or mere negligence or a willful blindness. See van der Vyver 2021, pp. 586–587.

[295] *See infra* for a discussion on whether had reason to know denotes intent.

[296] Ambos does not endorse the view that superior responsibility may entail criminal responsibility for the crimes committed by a superior's subordinates; rather, he considers a superior's failure to execute their duties as a separate crime of omission. Ambos 2002, pp. 852–853. Damaška, on the other hand, endorses the standard pertaining to intentional neglect and objects to the one pertaining to negligent neglect. See Damaška 2001, p. 44.

[297] Ibid.

[298] Ambos 2002, p. 864. See also Levie 1997–1998, p. 10; Landrum 1995, p. 300; Vetter 2000, pp. 122–123.

[299] Van Sliedregt 2003, p. 188.

[300] Ambos 2002, p. 864 (a).

[301] Van Sliedregt 2003, p. 186.

[302] Sadat 2002, p. 207.

[303] Ibid.

The bulk of the *ad hoc* tribunals' jurisprudence has held that "had reason to know" is "...considered as having the required knowledge",[304] which denotes intent.[305] The one exception may be the *Blaškić* case, where the tribunal held that "'had reason to know'...is the result of negligence in the discharge of his [or her] duties."[306]

My position on the controversial "had reason to know" standard is based on an assessment of the factual findings of the case, through a case-by-case approach.[307] In turn, to determine whether the superior's having "reason to know" is associated with intent or negligence, the court's assessment must take into account two factors:

1. their duty to gather relevant information about their subordinates' actions;[308]
2. the severity of the risk posed by their subordinates' actions leading to the commission of the crimes.[309]

Accordingly, depending on the scenario in question, the "had reason to know" standard could be interpreted as either intentional or based on mere negligence. Therefore, as suggested by Ambos and in the *Blaškić* case, this standard may therefore denote a "stronger" state of mind of negligence but a "weaker" form of intent.[310] This understanding of the significance of negligence in relation to the "had reason to know" standard seems appropriate for three reasons. First, if the drafters of the *ad hoc* tribunals' statutes had intended to equate "had reason to know" with willful blindness (a form of intent), then basing superior responsibility exclusively on "an actual knowledge" (state of mind) about the commission of the crimes would suffice in the context of this doctrine.[311] Second, the "had reason to know" standard in the statutes of the *ad hoc* tribunals originates from a US proposal, as does the "should have known" (negligence) standard in the Rome Statute.[312] The origin of the standard invoked by the US proposal for both bodies could plausibly indicate that the drafters intended "had reason to know" to denote negligence. Third, the distinct nature of

---

[304] *Prosecutor v. Delalic*, Case No. IT-96-21-T, para 238.

[305] It should be noted that, in the *Strugar* and *Hadzihasanovic* cases, "had reason to know" is viewed as intentional only if the superior had knowledge of past crimes committed by their subordinates and failed to prevent or punish them; the reoccurrence of new crimes would place the superior in an intentional state of mind of "had reason to know".

[306] *Prosecutor v. Blaškić*, Appeals Chamber, Case No. IT-95-14-A, para 332.

[307] *Prosecutor v. Hadžihasanović*, Appeals Chamber, Case No. IT-01-47-AR72, 16 July 2003, paras 30, 31. See also *Prosecutor v. Strugar*, Appeals Chamber, Case No. IT-01-42-A, paras 353–354, 17 July 2008, para 31.

[308] Fenrick 1999, pp. 522–523.

[309] *Prosecutor v. Strugar*, Appeals Chamber, Case No. IT-01-42-A17, paras 303–304, July 2008. It should be noted that the court decided that a superior's failure to prevent or punish previous crimes forms an intention state of mind in relation to future crimes. Accordingly, the superior's "had reason to know" standard in respect to the latter crimes is deemed intentional.

[310] Ibid.

[311] This Article, along with the identical Articles concerning superior responsibility applied by the *ad hoc* tribunals, are rooted in the API of the Geneva Conventions. See *Protocol Additional to the Geneva Conventions of 12 August 1949, and relating to the Protection of Victims of International Armed Conflicts* (*Protocol I*), Article 86(2).

[312] Ambos 2002, p. 866.

superior responsibility (as a form of negligent liability)[313] allows criminal responsibility for a subordinate's crime to extend to the superior because of the latter's negligence. Therefore, based on an assessment of the factual findings of the case, the two standards (intent and negligence) are both applicable for proving "had reason to know".

In a nutshell, the fault element requires that if the superior "knew", then they intentionally neglected their duties. However, if they had access to information that should have alerted them to the possibility of unlawful acts being carried out, to establish liability it is necessary to assess whether the possession of such information entails intent or negligence. The "had reason to know" standard could thus be metaphorically understood as a pendulum. The pendulum swings toward negligence if the superior's awareness was inadequate—in terms of the validity of the reports in their possession—while it swings toward intent if the superior knowingly turned a blind eye to their subordinates' explicitly alarming conduct, which indicates intent.

The fault element of superior responsibility must be strictly interpreted with respect to the superior's own culpability—that is, their failure to act. The superior's intentional failure to act (knew/had reason to know, where applicable) or neglect of their duty to act (had reason to know/should have known) should not be conflated with their subordinates' intent to commit crimes.[314] By contrast, Ambos and Damaška associate the fault element of subordinates' crimes with the fault element embodied in the doctrine of superior responsibility.[315] Ambos suggests that "it would be more logical not to find the superior criminally liable for the intent crime of the subordinates at all" when the subordinates are prosecuted on the basis of intent and the superior is prosecuted on the basis of negligence for the same crime.[316] Damaška, meanwhile, argues that "a commander's [negligent] liability is divorced from his culpability to such a degree that his conviction no longer mirrors his underlying conduct or his actual *mens rea*."[317] Both views are logically valid, but only if the interpretation relates to a national common law criminal justice system, where modes of liability, perpetrators, and crimes are confined to legislator's or courts' *stare decisis* interpretations.[318]

Accordingly, in both theory and practice, it is essential to establish an idiosyncratic distinction between the superior's *mens rea* and the subordinates' intent in relation to the crimes. As a matter of statutory interpretation, the distinction between these two states of mind is not only necessary to achieve a theoretical understanding of the matter but also has significant legal repercussions in practice. Theoretically, in line with the personal culpability principle, an accusation made against a superior under this doctrine must be supported by proof of the state of mind underpinning their *failure to execute supervisory duties*—namely, whether this was intentional or

313 Sereni 2004, p. 117.

314 Ibid.

315 Ambos 2002, p. 853. See also Damaška 2001, p. 455.

316 Ibid.

317 Ibid.

318 Van der Vyver 2005, p. 58.

negligent.[319] In other words, the fault element here must be interpreted only within the confines of the superior's failure to act.[320] In practical terms, if this interpretation suggested otherwise—such as suggesting that the superior and the actual perpetrator both had the intent to commit the crime, for example a murder—this could generate confusion with other modes of liability. In this case, the superior could be prosecuted directly as an accomplice to the crimes (as an aider or abettor) if it were proven that they intentionally set out to bring about the subordinates' crimes. This narrower interpretation could result in difficulties and, consequently, create unintended gaps in the superior responsibility doctrine.[321]

Conclusively, in both the literature and case law, concerns were raised about the application of a negligence standard when a superior is accused, under the doctrine of superior responsibility, of crimes based on *dolus specialis* (such as genocide, persecution, and terrorism).[322] Under international law, the crime of genocide requires that the perpetrator have a specific genocidal intent to destroy a group of people, either in whole or in part.[323] The controversy arises if the superior is accused of superior responsibility based on the should have known/had reason to know standard (negligence), while accusing a perpetrator of genocide requires proof of *dolus specialis*.[324] The majority of case law holds that, to trigger superior responsibility, the special intent behind such crimes must also extend to the superior's *mens rea*.[325] As discussed earlier in this chapter and as reiterated here, superior responsibility relates to the subordinates' crimes, which are attributed vicariously to the superior as if they were the actual physical perpetrator. As far as *mens rea* is concerned, the fault element of superior responsibility must be interpreted as a requirement within the confines of the doctrine. In the *Brdanin* case, the ICTY held that "superior responsibility ... does not require proof of intent to commit a crime on the part of the superior...[i]t is, therefore, necessary to distinguish between the *mens rea* required for the crimes perpetrated by the subordinates and that required for the superior."[326]

Based on personal culpability, a superior's criminal responsibility, by contrast, does not extend to the *mens rea* connected with the subordinates' intent to commit the crime (and their means of perpetrating—or participating in—it).[327] In other words,

---

319 Guilfoyle 2011, p. 283.

320 Ambos 2002, pp. 852–853.

321 Ibid.

322 See van der Vyver 2021, p. 598.

323 Ibid.

324 Van der Vyver 2005, p. 71.

325 Cassese et al. 2013, p. 190.

326 *Prosecutor v. Brdanin*, Judgment, Case No. IT-99-36-T, para 720, 1 September 2004. See also Nerlich 2007, p. 672.

327 Here, the question concerns whether the proof required to determine the subordinate's intent is confined to their contribution to the crime (as a principal/accomplice) or also to the intent behind the crime. The *ad hoc* tribunals do not all concur on this matter; in some cases, to accuse a person of aiding and abetting, they have required knowledge of the means of perpetration, in addition to the intent behind the crime committed. It should be noted that this view was reversed in the *Prosecutor v. Šainović et al.* case, Appeals Chamber, Case No. IT-05–87-A, 23 January 2014. The

if a superior is accused of genocide under the doctrine of superior responsibility, the prosecutor is not required to prove their intent to destroy a group of people, either in whole or in part, as may be the case with actual perpetrators of genocide. Instead, proof of *indicia* (direct or circumstantial evidence of the superior's intentional or negligent failure to act)[328] is sufficient to establish their vicarious liability for the crime of genocide according to the fault element of superior responsibility. Ultimately, this interpretation by the tribunal[329] can also support the gravity test analysis proposed in this study as a means of justifying the legal characterization of superior responsibility. In this context, the superior's negligence is considered as grave as the subordinates' intent,[330] meaning that a superior's duty to prevent or punish acts of genocide by subordinates is as serious as if the superior had themselves committed the genocide.

3.4.4 Other Jurisprudential Elements

Scholars and case law[331] have underscored an additional element for both theoretical and practical purposes—namely, the "crimes committed".[332] While this may be viewed as an axiomatic requirement for triggering superior responsibility and may not be classified as an element within the confines of the doctrine, it is commonly regarded as a default requirement.[333] However, the debate surrounding this element here centers on the understanding of "committed", *i.e.*, whether the crimes were completed by the superior's subordinates or were inchoate offenses that are sufficient to hold the superior responsible,[334] as well as whether the subordinates were sufficiently identified to substantiate their superior's vicarious liability.[335]

Rome Statute clearly sets out that these means of perpetration must be based on the knowledge and purpose (intent) of the crimes committed by an accomplice. See Stahn 2019, p. 139.

328 Fenrick 1999, p. 519.

329 *Prosecutor v. Brdanin*, Judgment, Case No. IT-99-36-T, 1 September 2004 para 715. See also *Prosecutor v. Ntagerura t al.*, Judgment, Case No. ICTR-99-46-T, paras 653–654, 694–695, 25 February 2004.

330 The gravity of the superior's failure to act as opposed to the gravity of the actions of the physical perpetrator of the crimes.

331 *Prosecutor v. Orić*, Judgment, Case No. IT-03-68-T, para 294, 30 June 2006.

332 Van Sliedregt 2011, p. 378. See also Meloni 2010, pp. 83–84. It should be noted that the commission of the crimes is a default rule in this concept, as discussed earlier in relation to the legal characterization of superior responsibility, where a superior is charged for crimes only when they have been committed (or about to be committed/attempted).

333 *Prosecutor v. Orić*. It should be noted that the court indicated that this requirement was first embodied within the superior responsibility doctrine in this judgment, while the jurisprudence of the court had previously not accounted for this requirement.

334 Inchoate offenses include attempts, voluntarily withdrawal, solicitation, incitement, complicity, etc. Kortfält 2017, p. 284.

335 Ibid. See also Arnold and Triffterer 2008, p. 827.

Regarding the first issue, concerning the understanding of "committed", Arnold suggests that to trigger a superior's criminal responsibility, the crimes committed by their subordinates must be brought to completion.[336] Regarding the second issue, the ICTY decided in the *Hadžihasanović* case that the superior responsibility doctrine is not applicable to inchoate offenses committed by subordinates.[337] However, Ambos, along with the ICTY in its decision in the *Naser* case, noted that, theoretically, in the framework of superior responsibility, all inchoate offenses and their corresponding modes of perpetration/participation are prosecutable under international law.[338] Accordingly, a superior can be held criminally responsible for offenses committed by their subordinates even if they are viewed as inchoate offenses.[339] Ambos's assertion and the reasoning in the *Naser* case reasoning are both valid with respect to the applicability of superior responsibility to inchoate offenses. That being said, for the purposes of prosecutions and given the derivative nature of the superior's liability according to this doctrine, what applies to subordinates in terms of convictions for international crimes also applies to their superior's criminal responsibility. Therefore, international law does not focus on whether the subordinates brought the criminal act to completion; and, in the case of inchoate offenses, in line with the fundamental concept of vicarious liability, their superior's criminal responsibility aligns with their own criminality. On the third issue, regarding the identification of subordinates, in *Naser*'s case the ICTY held that their position within the superior–subordinates relationship is sufficient to establish their superior's criminal responsibility, without necessitating their specific identification.[340]

Another dimension to this requirement concerns timing: at what stage in the commission of the crimes should a superior be accused of the failure to discharge their duties?[341] If the superior retained effective command/authority and control over their subordinates before, during, and after the commission of the crimes, accusing a superior in this context may not prove problematic.[342] However, in cases in which the superior's position undergoes a transformative shift during these stages, jurisprudence appears to present a bifurcated view regarding superior responsibility. The first opinion on this issue can be seen in the *Orić* case before the ICTY, where, in a partially dissenting opinion, it was held that: "If a commanding officer assumes effective control after a crime was committed, he should be held criminally responsible as a superior."[343] The conclusion was that a superior's duty in the third stage is a sufficient

[336] Ibid.

[337] *Prosecutor v. Enver Hadzihasanovic et al.*, Case. No. IT-01-47-A, para 204.

[338] Ibid.

[339] See Ambos 2002, pp. 747, 765–767. See also *Prosecutor v. Orić*, paras 301, 328. The Appeals Judgment of this trial also supports this conclusion. See *Prosecutor v. Orić*, para 47.

[340] *Prosecutor v. Orić*, paras 35, 48.

[341] Van der Vyver 2021, p. 593.

[342] Ibid. See also Kortfält 2017, p. 292.

[343] Van der Vyver 2021, p. 593, quoting *Prosecutor v. Orić*, Partially Dissenting Opinion and Declaration of Judge LIU, para 2.

basis to establish their criminal responsibility.[344] At this point, therefore, they have a duty to punish or submit the matter to the competent authorities. The Special Court for Sierra Leone (SCSL) also supported this view.[345] The second opinion, by contrast, does not differentiate between these three stages when it comes to establishing a superior's criminal responsibility. Instead, on the one hand, it considers that a superior may be charged for crimes committed by their subordinates when these crimes first took place.[346] On the other hand, if the superior assumed command/authority and control after the commission of the crimes, they are not deemed criminally responsible for these crimes even though they have a duty to punish the perpetrators or submit the matter to the competent authorities.[347] Van der Vyver appears to support the view that a superior's criminal responsibility may be triggered only when they exercised command/authority and control before the commission of the crimes.[348]

3.5 Conclusion

In this chapter, I have introduced the doctrine of superior responsibility, under which international criminal tribunals prosecute superiors for the crimes of their subordinates. The most defining feature of this doctrine, in terms of legal characterization, is the imputation of subordinate crimes to the superior's culpability, even in the absence of any direct contributory link. This feature reflects the historical evolution of international law. Since the emergence of ICL, however, the prosecution of superiors under this doctrine has produced significant practical challenges arising from theoretical misunderstandings, largely due to its complex functionality. Within this instance alone, the central theoretical challenge then lies in the legal conceptualization of the doctrine, which originated in the context of military governance but has since been transposed into the broader framework of international criminal governance. With this transformation in mind, given that legal principles are well established within the borders of nation-states, national legislation has historically bound the scope of offenses committed within those borders. These principles, embedded in the minds of domestic scholars and tied closely to state sovereignty, have contributed to the decline in the functional recognition of superior responsibility at the international level. Consequently, offenses, together with the means by which they are executed, are adjudicated primarily within the framework of national legislation and criminal justice systems.

---

344 Ibid.

345 *Prosecutor v. Sesay et al.*, Judgment, SCSL-04-15-T, paras 299, 306–7, 2 March 2009.

346 *Prosecutor v. Orić*, para 335. See also *Prosecutor v. Hadzihasanovic*, Decision on Interlocutory Appeal Challenging Jurisdiction in Relation to Command Responsibility, Case No. IT-01-47-AR72, Partial Dissenting Opinion of Judge Shahabuddeen, para 32, 16 July 2003.

347 Ibid.

348 Van der Vyver 2021, p. 593.

These original deontological restrictions, as termed by Robinson, have accompanied domestic scholars in their efforts to analyze the theoretical understanding of this doctrine with a view to identifying its underlying justification—an undertaking widely regarded as indispensable within legal scholarship. Yet this pursuit has often resulted in imprecise definitions of the doctrine and a failure to clearly delineate its conceptual elements. Consequently, in my view, when applied before international criminal courts (by means of statutory interpretations), this doctrine has produced contradictory judicial interpretations, and scholarly discourse has remained divided, giving rise to contentious and often polarized debates on the subject.

Against this backdrop, this chapter engaged in a theoretical and critical examination of the conceptual foundations and practical applications of the doctrine of superior responsibility in international law, seeking to clarify inconsistencies in jurisprudence and to shed light on the controversies in scholarly debate. Through such an approach, I have examined the doctrine from its definition to its application. To narrow the discussion, I have focused on the law of the *ad hoc* and hybrid criminal tribunals. The Rome Statute of the ICC is excluded from the discussion because the doctrine has a different structure under this statute, which warrants a separate discussion.

In Sects. 3.1 and 3.2, I systematically reviewed the academic literature and the jurisprudence of the *ad hoc* and hybrid criminal tribunals with the aim of defining this doctrine on the basis of its practical application at the international level. The objective behind this critical analysis of scholarly writings concerning this doctrine is to achieve a better understanding of the vicarious liability of superiors, in relation both to its actual conceptual components and to its practical application. In addition, concerning the informative framework approach, in Sect. 3.2, I examined treaties that include this doctrine within their subject-matter, as well as international case law adjudicating superior responsibility, with a view to providing guidelines for its application. In Sect. 3.3, I analyzed the academic literature on this subject to contribute to the doctrinal dispute over the legal characterization of superior responsibility—specifically, whether it constitutes a crime of omission or a vicarious mode of liability. I concluded that the justification for the nature of superior responsibility stems from ICL, which equates the severity of the crimes committed by a superior's subordinates with the gravity of the superior's failure to discharge their entrusted duties. This nature thus resolves the accountability gap at the international level, according to which a superior may escape criminal responsibility were they to be tried at the national level. It therefore constitutes a distinct, unparalleled mode of liability that does not apply at the national level and should not be interpreted through those legal systems. Lastly, in Sect. 3.4, I discussed the conceptual components of superior responsibility with a view to providing a guideline.

As mentioned earlier, it is crucial to note that this chapter has centered on a discussion of the fundamental elements of superior responsibility within the context of the practice of the UN tribunals. However, the conceptual components of the law of superior responsibility have undergone an advanced development. This is exemplified, for instance, under Article 28 of the Rome Statute of the ICC, which will be further explored in the following chapter.

References

Al-Fadhli H (2025) From Nuremberg to the Hague and beyond: Reincorporating "taking a consenting part" into international criminal modes of liability. Netherlands International Law Review, 72(2)

Ambos K (2002) Superior Responsibility. In: Cassese A, Gaeta J, Jones J (eds) The Rome Statute of the International Criminal Court, 2nd edn. Oxford University Press, Oxford, pp. 823–871

Ambos K (2003) Current Issues in International Criminal Law. Criminal Law Forum, vol. 14, Springer, pp. 225–260

Ambos K (2009) Command responsibility and Organisationsherrschaft: Ways of attributing international crimes to the 'most responsible'. In: Nollkaemper A, van der Wilt H (eds) System Criminality in International Law. Cambridge University Press, Cambridge, pp 127–157

Arnold R, Triffterer O (2008) Article 28: Responsibility of Commanders and Other Superiors. In: Triffterer O (ed) Commentary on the Rome Statute of the International Criminal Court: Observers' Notes, Article by Article, 2nd edn. Beck, Munich, pp. 795–843

Askin KD (2002) Reflections on Some of the Most Significant Achievements of the ICTY. New England Law Review 37(903), pp. 903–933.

Bantekas I (2002) Principles of Direct and Superior Responsibility in International Humanitarian Law. Manchester University Press, Manchester

Bantekas I (2006) Reflections on some sources and methods of international criminal and humanitarian law. International Criminal Law Review 6, Brill, pp. 121–135

Blank L, Noone G (2013) International Law and Armed Conflict Fundamental Principles and Contemporary Challenges in the Law of War. Kluwer Press, Dordrecht

Bruce M (2014) International humanitarian law and criminal justice: An introductory handbook. Commonwealth Secretariat. Available at: https://production-new-commonwealth-files.s3.eu-west-2.amazonaws.com/migrated/inline/Law%2BIntroductory%2BHandbook%2BEB.pdf (accessed 21 August 2021)

Cassese A et al (2013) Cassese's International Criminal Law. Oxford University Press, Oxford

Cryer R (2014) An Introduction to International Criminal Law and Procedure. Cambridge University Press, Cambridge

Cryer R (2015) International Criminal Law: General Principles of Liability in International Criminal Law, vol. II. Routledge, UK

Cryer R et al. (2019) An Introduction to International Criminal Law and Procedure, 4th edn. Cambridge University Press, Cambridge

Damaška M (2001) The Shadow Side of Command Responsibility. The American Journal of Comparative Law 49, pp. 455–496

De Preux (1987) The Affirmative Duties Established by Article 87 Additional Protocol I of 1977 and its Commentary. In: Pilloud C et al. (eds) Commentary on the Additional Protocols of 8 June 1977 to the Geneva Conventions of 12 August 1949, pp. 1017–1023

Dressler J (1985) Reassessing the Theoretical Underpinnings of Accomplice Liability: New Solutions to an Old Problem. Hastings Law Journal 37(91), pp. 91–138

Dungel J, Ghadiri S (2010) The Temporal Scope of Command Responsibility Revisited: Why Commanders Have a Duty to Prevent Crimes Committed After the Cessation of Effective Control. U.C. DAVIS Journal of International Law & Policy 17(1), pp. 3–61

Fenrick W (1999) In: Triffterer O (ed) Commentary on the Rome Statute of the International Criminal Court: Article by Article, pp. 515–522

Friedman L (ed) (1972) The Law of War: A Documentary History (Vol. II). Random House, New York, NY

Galand A S (2020) Bemba and the Individualisation of War: Reconciling Command Responsibility under Article 28 Rome Statute with Individual Criminal Responsibility. International Criminal Law Review 20, pp. 688–725

Galand A S, Hunter E, Utmelidze I, Bekou O (2016) International Criminal Law Guidelines: Command Responsibility, 2nd edn. Centre for International Law Research and Policy (CILRAP), Florence

Gasser H P et al. (1987) Commentary on the Additional Protocols of 8 June 1977 to the Geneva Conventions of 12 August 1949. ICRC/Martinus Nijhoff Publishers

Guénaël M (2009) The Law of Command Responsibility. Oxford University Press, Oxford

Guilfoyle D (2011) Responsibility for Collective Atrocities: Fair Labelling and Approaches to Commission in International Criminal Law. Current Legal Problems 64, pp. 255–286

Heller K J (2016–17) Taking a Consenting Part: The Lost Mode of Participation. Loyola University of Los Angeles International & Comparative Law Review 39, pp. 247–257

Hooker B (2000) Ideal Code, Real World: A Rule-Consequentialist Theory of Morality. Oxford University Press

Hudson M O (1931) The Ninth Year of the Permanent Court of International Justice. The American Journal Of ICRC (1949) Remarks and Proposals submitted by the International Committee of the Red Cross: Documents for the Consideration of Governments Invited by the Swiss Federal Council to Attend the Diplomatic Conference at Geneva (21 April 1949). https://www.loc.gov/rr/frd/Military_Law/pdf/RC_Remarks-proposals.pdf

ICRC (2009) Analysis of the Punishments Applicable to International Crimes (War Crimes, Crimes Against Humanity and Genocide) in Domestic Law and Practice. International Review of the Red Cross 90

Jackson M (2019) Command Responsibility. In: de Hemptinne J, Roth R, van Sliedregt E (eds) Modes of Liability in International Criminal Law. Cambridge University Press, Cambridge, pp. 409–431

Jackson R H (1947) Opening statement before the International Military Tribunal, 21 November 1945. In: Trial of the Major War Criminals before the International Military Tribunal: Nuremberg, 14 November 1945–1 October 1946, vol 2. International Military Tribunal, Nuremberg

Jia B B (2000) The Doctrine of Command Responsibility. Yearbook of International Humanitarian Law 3(131), pp. 131–165

Kortfält L (2017) Individual Criminal Responsibility. In: Klamberg M (ed) Commentary on the Law of the International Criminal Court. Torkel Opsahl Academic EPublisher, Brussels, pp. 279–304

Landrum B D (1995) The Yamashita War Crimes Trial: Command Responsibility Then and Now. Military Law Review 149(293), pp. 293–322

Levie S (1997/1998) Command Responsibility. Journal of Legal Studies 8(1), pp. 1–19

Lieber F (1863) Instructions for the Government of Armies of the United States in the Field (24 April 1863) [The Lieber Code]

May L, Fyfe S (2018) International Criminal Tribunals: A Normative Defense, Cambridge University Press, Cambridge

Mégret F (2011) The Legacy of the ICTY as Seen Through Some of its Actors and Observers. Goettingen Journal of International Law 3, pp. 1011–1052

Meloni C (2007) Command Responsibility: Mode of Liability for the Crimes of Subordinates or Separate Offence of the Superior? Journal of International Criminal Justice 5(3), pp. 619–637

Meloni C (2010) Command Responsibility in International Criminal Law. TMC Asser Press, The Hague

Meloni C (2015) The Evolution of Command Responsibility in International Criminal Law. FICHL Publication Series No. 22

Meron T (2005) Revival of customary humanitarian law. American Journal of International Law 99(4), pp. 817–834

Mettraux G (2009) The Law of Command Responsibility. Oxford University Press, Oxford

Miller RH (1971) The Convention of the Non-Applicability of Statutory Limitations to War Crimes and Crimes against Humanity. American Journal of International Law 65, pp. 494–508

Minkova L G (2023) Responsibility on Trial: Liability Standards in International Criminal Law. Cambridge University Press

Nerlich V (2007) Superior Responsibility under Article 28 ICC Statute - For What Exactly Is the Superior Held Responsible? Journal of International Criminal Justice 5(3), pp. pp. 665–682
Roberts A (2019) Foundational Myths in the Laws of War: The 1863 Lieber Code, and the 1864 Geneva Convention. Melbourne Journal of International Law 20(158), pp. 165–192
Robinson D (2008) The Identity Crisis of International Criminal Law. Leiden Journal of International Law 21, pp. 925–963
Robinson D (2012) How Command Responsibility got so Complicated: A Culpability Contradiction, its Obfuscation, and a Simple Solution. Melbourne Journal of International Law 13(1), pp. 3–28
Robinson D (2020) Justice in Extreme Cases: Criminal Law Theory Meets International Criminal Law. Cambridge University Press
Rosenberg C (2020) He waterboarded a detainee. Then he had to get the C.I.A. to let him stop. The New York Times. https://www.nytimes.com/2020/01/22/us/politics/cia-torture-_ interrogation-guantanamo.html. Accessed 21 August 2021
Sadat LN (2002) The International Criminal Court and The Transformation of International Law: Justice for The Millenium. Transnational Publishers, Ardsley, NY
Schabas W (2004) The Right to a Fair Trial. In Lattanzi F, Schabas WA (eds) 2 Essays on the Rome Statute of the International Criminal Court, pp. pp. 241–278
Scharf M P, Morris V (1995) An insider's guide to the International Criminal Tribunal for the Former Yugoslavia. Transnational Publishers, Irvington-on-Hudson, NY
Sereni A (2004) Individual Criminal Responsibility. In: Lattanzi F, Schabas WA (eds) Essays on the Rome Statute of the International Criminal Court, 2nd edn. Editrice il Sirente, Ripa di Fagnano Alto, Italy, pp 139–146
Sprik L (2020) Protection of Civilians and Individual Accountability: Obligations and Responsibilities of Military Commanders in United Nations Peacekeeping Operations. Routledge, UK
Stahn C (2019) A Critical Introduction to International Criminal Law. Cambridge University Press, Cambridge
Stewart J G (2012) The end of 'modes of liability' for international crimes. Leiden J Int Law 25(1), pp. 165–219
Swaak-Goldman O (2017) Prosecutor v. Delalic. No. IT-96–21-T, The American Journal Of International Law 93(2), pp. 514–519
Triffterer O (2002) Causality, A Separate Element of the Doctrine of Superior Responsibility as Expressed in Article 28 of the Rome Statute? Leiden Journal of International Law 15(179), pp. pp. 179–205
Van der Vyver J (2005) The International Criminal Court and the Concept of Mens Rea in International Criminal Law. University of Miami International & Comparative Law Review 12, pp. 57–95
Van der Vyver J (2021) International Criminal Law: Crimes within the Jurisdiction of the International Criminal Court, vol. II. LAP Lambert Publishing, Germany
Van Schaack B (2019) House Foreign Affairs Committee Tom Lantos Human Rights Commission Hearing on Ending Genocide: Accountability for Perpetrators
Van Sliedregt E (2003) The criminal responsibility of individuals for violations of international humanitarian law. T.M.C. Asser Press, The Hague, Netherlands
Van Sliedregt E (2011) Command Responsibility at the ICTY—Three Generations of Case-law and Still Ambiguity. In: Swart B, Zahar A, Sluiter G (eds) The Legacy of the International Criminal Tribunal for the Former Yugoslavia. Oxford University Press, pp 367–390
Van Sliedregt E (2012a) Individual Criminal Responsibility in International Law. Oxford University Press, Oxford
Van Sliedregt E (2012b) The curious case of international criminal liability. Journal of International Criminal Justice 10(5), pp. 1171–1188
Van Sliedregt E et al. (2019) Co-perpetration Based on Joint Control over the Crime. In: Cupido M, Ventura MJ, Yanev L (eds) Modes of Liability in International Criminal Law. Cambridge University Press, Cambridge, pp 85–120

Vark K (2016) Superior Responsibility and Indirect Liability. Occasional Paper No. 2/06, Eur. Network of Diplomatic & Sec. Stud.
Vetter G R (2000) Command Responsibility of Non-military Superiors in the International Criminal Court (ICC). Yale Journal of International Law 25(90), pp. 89–149
Williamson J A (2008) Some Considerations on Command Responsibility and Criminal Liability. International Review of the Red Cross 90(870), pp. 303–326
Wise E M, Podgor E S (2014) International Criminal Law: Cases and Materials, 3rd edn. LexisNexis Matthew Bender, New Providence, NJ, pp 496–515
Wood D A R (2010) Punishment: consequentialism. Philosophy Compass 5(6), pp. 455–469
Wu T, King Y S (1997) Criminal liability for the actions of subordinates: The doctrine of command responsibility and its analogues in United States law. Harvard International Law Journal, 38(1), pp. 272–294

Legislation

Allied Control Council Law No. 10: Punishment of Persons Guilty of War Crimes, Crimes Against Peace, and Crimes Against Humanity (1945), 20 December 1945, Official Gaz. of the Control Council of Germany, 3(50)
Law on the Establishment of Extraordinary Chambers in the Courts of Cambodia for the Prosecution of Crimes Committed During the Period of Democratic Kampuchea (2004) NS/RKM/1004/006
Statute of the International Criminal Tribunal for Rwanda (1994) S.C. Res. 955, Annex, 33 ILM 1602, Article 6(3) (1994)
Statute of the International Criminal Tribunal for the Former Yugoslavia (1993) U.N. Doc. S/25704, Annex, 32 ILM 1192
The Convention on the Non-Applicability of Statutory Limitations to War Crimes and Crimes Against Humanity (1968) 754 U.N.T.S. 7, Article II. The Lieber and the US's Military Commissions Act of 2006 (2006) 189. 10 U.S.C. § 950q

Other Documents

Protocol Additional to the Geneva Conventions of 12 August 1949, and Relating to the Protection of Victims of International Armed Conflicts (Protocol I) (1977). Article 86(2), U.N. Doc. A/32/144, 1125 U.N.T.S. 3, reprinted in 16 I.L.M. 1391
Report of the International Commission of Inquiry on Darfur to the United Nations Secretary-General, paras 558, 561 (Jan. 25, 2005) Report of the Secretary-General on the Establishment of a Special Court for Sierra Leone, U.N. Doc. S/2000/915, Annex (Oct. 4, 2000), the Special Court for Sierra Leone Statute, Article 6(3)

Chapter 4
The Uncertain Application of Superior Responsibility at the International Criminal Court

Contents

Abstract This chapter critically examines the evolving and uncertain application of the doctrine of superior responsibility within the framework of the Rome Statute, with particular focus on the implications of the *Bemba* Appeals Chamber judgment. While the jurisprudence of the UN *ad hoc* tribunals significantly shaped the doctrine—anchoring it in the Laws of Armed Conflict—the International Criminal Court (ICC) has adopted a structurally distinct and arguably narrower approach under Article 28. This divergence raises pressing questions about the ICC's conceptualization of superior responsibility, particularly in light of the recent acquittal and prosecutorial caution. This chapter contends that the ICC's main challenge lies in its fragmented interpretation of the doctrine's elements, including the introduction of acquittal-enabling factors such as the remoteness of superiors from the scene of the crimes. Through analysis of key cases—especially Prosecutor v. Bemba—this chapter explores how institutional and doctrinal shifts have affected the standards for conviction and accountability. Furthermore, in light of their normative parallels, the chapter considers the broader relationship between superior responsibility, the crime of aggression, and superior orders, and concludes with recommendations aimed at enhancing doctrinal clarity and prosecutorial consistency in future ICC practice.

Keywords Superior responsibility · Rome Statute Article 28 · International Criminal Court (ICC) · Bemba judgment · Crime of aggression · Superior orders

H. Y. Al-Fadhli, *Prosecuting Superior Responsibility in International Criminal Law*,
https://doi.org/10.1007/978-94-6265-735-9_4

4.1 Introduction

A slap on the wrist of the offender is a slap in the face of the victims.[1]

The doctrine of superior responsibility remains one of the most debated and evolving areas of international criminal law (ICL), even following the efforts of the UN *ad hoc* tribunals to refine its contours.[2] Chapter 3 addressed the doctrine within the framework of the Laws of Armed Conflict and the ensuing jurisprudence of the UN *ad hoc* tribunals. While that chapter provided essential philosophical, doctrinal, and rudimentary grounding, it was not intended to extend beyond those tribunals, even though its jurisprudence continues to resonate.

Against this backdrop—and given both the doctrinal complexity of Article 28 of the Rome Statute[3] and the ongoing controversy surrounding the *Bemba* Appeals Judgment (hereinafter, *Bemba* AC judgment),[4] which remains relatively underexplored in the scholarly literature[5] in the way this chapter seeks to address[6]—a separate chapter is then warranted to undertake a deeper analysis of the doctrine's crystallization and its contested interpretation within the International Criminal Court (ICC) framework.

---

[1] Harmon and Gaynor 2007, p. 712.

[2] This chapter offers a holistic assessment of the elements of superior responsibility as set out under the Rome Statute of the International Criminal Court, with a primary focus on an analysis of the *Bemba* case. Most importantly, this chapter also seeks to build on the previous discussion of the doctrine of superior responsibility in Chap. 3, with the ultimate aim of providing a more clearly defined, unified source of law for the doctrine of superior responsibility.

[3] Rome Statute of the International Criminal Court, 17 July 1998, 2187 U.N.T.S. 3 (entered into force on 1 July 2002), http://untreaty.un.org/cod/icc/statute/romefra.htm (Rome Statute).

[4] *Prosecutor v. Jean-Pierre Bemba Gombo*, Case No. ICC-01/05-01/08 A, Judgment, 8 June 2018. (Hereinafter *Bemba* AC Judgment.)

[5] Jackson 2022. I am particularly struck by the fact that, even in the aftermath of the *Bemba* AC Judgment, a number of scholarly works continue to revisit and extrapolate the legal characterization of superior responsibility. In my view, however, the more urgent task is no longer to reaffirm its status as a *sui generis* mode of liability—a classification that has achieved broad consensus at the ICC, as Jackson himself aptly observes—but to shift the scholarly lens toward the misapplication that follows from its misinterpreted conceptual components. This deeper inquiry would more effectively illuminate the doctrine's normative function and clarify its place within the broader framework of international criminal responsibility.

[6] Cf. Ibid. Notably, Jackson, in this paper published in May 2022—after the final submission of this chapter in December 2021 as part of my doctoral thesis—pursued an analytical approach closely aligned with that taken here, seeking to extrapolate the nature of the doctrine of superior responsibility from the *Bemba* AC Judgment, including the separate opinions of the judges. Drawing on interpretative tools grounded in Article 38 of the Vienna Convention on the Law of Treaties (VCLT), his contribution commendably engages with the legal tensions surrounding the doctrine. Nevertheless, as noted above, I maintain the position developed throughout this book: that the more urgent issue lies not in interpretative methodology alone, but in the persistent conceptual misunderstandings that continue to shape—and often distort—the doctrine's application in international criminal law.

Since the commencement of its prosecutorial activities in 2002,[7] the ICC acquitted one of its first cases involving war crimes and crimes against humanity under the doctrine of superior responsibility. Given the ICC's lofty mandate and strongly supported credibility, this judgment raised significant concerns. Particularly given its impact on the ICC's reputation, which could cast doubts on the theorization of legal precedents in future cases, this decision could influence the development of the law of superior responsibility in decades to come.[8] For instance, one particularly less compelling aspect of the reasoning in the *Bemba* AC judgment concerns how Bemba's physical separation, or remoteness, from the scene of the insubordinations constituted adequate exculpatory evidence to overrule the charges in the case. Thus, even when a superior has neglected the commission of heinous crimes, the remoteness argument serves as a protective barrier around the superior, shielding them from accountability under international law.

In addition, the inconsistent reasoning expressed by the majority of judges in the AC (hereinafter, the majority), *inter alia,* was based on a divergent interpretation of the "all necessary and reasonable measures" element of the doctrine, failing to engage in an assessment of the other requisite elements.[9] In its own right, this questionable practice could constitute an error of law pursuant to the ICC's practice. The judgment may therefore affect the future development of the doctrine, serving as a secondary source for the ICC.[10] This is particularly noteworthy because the ICC previously emphasized that: "[the Appeals Chamber] does not change its jurisprudence lightly".[11]

The key issue with this outcome is that, unlike other international criminal tribunals, the ICC is a permanent international criminal court that is charged with administering the contemporary practice of international criminal justice.[12] Such a pattern of adjudication runs the risk of undermining efforts to deter international crimes and could instead promote the practice of impunity, which runs contrary to the ICC's mission. Furthermore, because the goal of ending impunity was specifically promulgated under the Rome Statute, it could also override existing jurisprudential rules designed to construct the doctrine of superior responsibility.[13]

---

[7] Van der Vyver 2021, pp. 1–2. See also Sadat 2019, p. 353.

[8] Statement by the ICC Prosecutor, Fatou Bensouda, on the recent judgment of the ICC AC acquitting Mr Jean-Pierre Bemba Gombo (13 June 2018), https://www.icc-cpi.int/Pages/item.aspx?name=180613-OTP-stat.

[9] *Prosecutor v. Jean-Pierre Bemba Gombo*, Case No. ICC-01/05-01/08-3636-Anx1-Red 08-06-2018 1/269 EC A, (Dissenting Opinion of Judge Sanji Mmasenono Monageng and Judge Piotr Hofmański), para 46, 8 June 2018.

[10] Rome Statute, Article 21 (Applicable Law) (As will be explained further on this chapter, although the ICC is not a court based on precedents, it may still apply precedents as a secondary source of law, in accordance with Article 21(2) of the Rome Statute.)

[11] *Prosecutor v. Jean-Pierre Bemba*, Case No. ICC-01/05-01/08-3636-Anx1-Red 08-06-2018 1/269 EC A, para 5.

[12] Sadat 2002a, p. 47.

[13] *Prosecutor v. Jean-Pierre Bemba*, Case No. ICC-01/05-01/08 Pre-Trial Chamber, para 3 (20 April 2009). (AMICUS CURIAE OBSERVATIONS ON SUPERIOR RESPONSIBILITY SUBMITTED

Thus, these discouraging applications of superior responsibility, as reflected in the current practices of the ICC, signal the deficiencies when it comes to ending the impunity of superiors. Notably, the *Bemba* AC judgment, along with various other cases, resulted in dismissals without convictions,[14] at either Pre-Trial[15] or Trial stages. For example, in the *Prosecutor v. Ongwen* case, the Pre-Trial Chamber found substantial grounds to believe that Dominic Ongwen was criminally responsible for international crimes under various modes of liability, including the possibility of superior responsibility.[16] However, the Trial Chamber ultimately declined to convict Ongwen under Article 28 of the Rome Statute, instead relying on other forms of individual criminal responsibility under Article 25, such as direct perpetration, ordering, and indirect co-perpetration.[17] This may reflect the ongoing interpretive difficulties surrounding superior responsibility, particularly in the aftermath of the Bemba Appeals Chamber's acquittal, which significantly raised the threshold for establishing

PURSUANT TO RULE 103 OF THE RULES OF PROCEDURE AND EVIDENCE) (holding that "[the] intended policy choice of the drafters of the Statute to strengthen commanders' obligations [as opposed to deterrence] beyond those under customary international law".) See also Hibbert 2019, p. 97.

[14] *Prosecutor v. Bosco Ntaganda*, Case No. ICC-01/04-02/06, 9 June 2014; *Prosecutor v. Dominic Ongwen*, Case No. ICC-02/04-01/15, 23 March 2016; *Prosecutor v. Laurent Gbagbo & Charles Blé Goudé*, Case No. ICC-02/11-01/15-1263-AnxC-Red, 16 July 2019; *Prosecutor v. Alfred Yekatom & Patrice-Edouard Ngaïssona*, Case No. ICC-01/14-01/18, 11 December 2019.

[15] The Pre-Trial Chambers are tasked with confirming the charges brought against the accused before the Prosecutor of the ICC, which are subject to the vetting of the Trial Chamber. See van der Vyver 2021, pp. 250–251.

[16] *Prosecutor v. Dominic Ongwen*, Case No. ICC-02/04-01/15, 23 March 2016, para 36.

[17] Ibid.

liability under Article 28.[18] For example, a superior may be prosecuted for international crimes under Article 25 for their direct involvement in the commission of crimes by their subordinates, while simultaneously being held liable under Article 28 for the same crimes due to their failure to prevent, punish, or report those crimes as a superior.

Accordingly, the following questions remain: How has the ICC reshaped the doctrine of superior responsibility in terms of its conceptual elements in ways that are inconsistent with the original Rome Statute? How will this impact the legacy of the jurisprudence of the UN *ad hoc* tribunals regarding the parameters of superior responsibility? In this chapter, I shall explore these questions, with a view to addressing future challenges relating to the legal theory and practical application of this doctrine. The aim of this chapter is therefore to examine the doctrine of superior responsibility within the confines of the Rome Statute and to critically analyze the *Bemba* case, which may be interpreted as an example of unjust adjudication.

To get to grips with the distinction between the UN *ad hoc* tribunals and the ICC, it is important to understand how each of these institutions operates in relation to the doctrine of superior responsibility.[19] As noted earlier, although the inclusion of this

[18] An example of a case where the test of superior responsibility was not met at the ICC as a result of a misunderstanding of this doctrine is the *Gbagbo & Goudé* case. Both defendants were charged with crimes under Article 28 of the Rome Statute (superior responsibility). However, they were acquitted at both the trial and appeal stages. In the Trial Chamber (which the AC upheld), the court decided that: "It bears mentioning, however, that the Prosecutor has failed to explain, for each of the charged crimes, precisely when Mr Gbagbo had knowledge or should have been aware of impending or completed criminal behavior." *Prosecutor v. Laurent Gbagbo & Charles Blé Goudé*, Case No. ICC-02/11-01/15-1263-AnxC-Red, 16 July 2019, para 2031. The reasons given by Judge Geoffrey Henderson are available at https://www.icc-cpi.int/RelatedRecords/CR2019_07450.PDF. According to the doctrine of superior responsibility, as will be discussed in Sect. 4.2.2, the Prosecutor is not required "to explain, for each of the charged crimes, precisely when Gbagbo had knowledge or should have been aware of impending or completed criminal behavior." As long as crimes were committed and the other requirements of superior responsibility are met, the burden of proof lies only in establishing that there are actual victims of crimes committed by the defendants' subordinates, because the crimes are jurisdictional in nature. The prosecutor is therefore not required to carry out a specific examination of the superior's knowledge of the crimes or their material elements with respect to the superior. However, the dissenting opinion in this case underscored this flawed interpretation in accordance with the law of superior responsibility. Judge Herrera Carbuccia held that, "In cases where article [*sic*] 28 is applicable, it is not necessary to show that the accused fulfilled the remaining *mens rea* requirement in relation to the material elements of crimes against humanity [as long as knowledge or reason to know evidence is available to the superior to adduce]." *Prosecutor v. Laurent Gbagbo & Charles Blé Goudé*, Case No. ICC-02/11-01/15-1263-AnxC-Red (Dissenting Opinion Judge Herrera Carbuccia), para 73, 16 July 2019, https://www.icc-cpi.int/RelatedRecords/CR2019_07451.PDF. See, generally, Guilfoyle 2019, p. 401. (For a general discussion on the reasons behind the obstacles to securing convictions.)

[19] This comparison examines the structural, legal, and interpretative frameworks of the UN *ad hoc* tribunals (ICTY and ICTR) and the ICC in their treatment of superior responsibility. While the formers were reactive institutions created under Chapter VII of the UN Charter to address atrocities in the Balkans and Rwanda, the ICC emerged from a treaty-based process with a permanent, forward-looking mandate. The *ad hoc* tribunals, operating under Articles 7(3) (ICTY) and 6(3) (ICTR), developed pioneering jurisprudence on superior responsibility *ex nihilo*, notably in cases such as Čelebići, *Delalić*, *Bagilishema*, and *Kayishema*, emphasizing "effective control" as the

discussion may appear to diverge from the chapter's primary focus, it is nonetheless essential for presenting a complete picture of how the UN *ad hoc* tribunals developed the doctrine of superior responsibility. These tribunals adopted the doctrine from the Laws of Armed Conflict and, through judicial lawmaking, progressively developed its conceptual components *ex nihilo*, embedding it within the broader framework of individual criminal responsibility. By contrast, the Rome Statute of the ICC—as well as its jurisprudence, particularly in *Bemba* case—treats superior responsibility as a distinct mode of liability, articulated separately from the provisions on individual criminal responsibility.[20] This structural distinction may suggest that the doctrine resists full alignment with a traditional personal culpability analysis and instead reflects a more institutional, role-based theory of liability.

Finally, this chapter will shed light on prosecutable criminal acts historically associated with the doctrine of superior responsibility in its *latu sensu* interpretation—*to wit*, superior orders and the crime of aggression.[21] While the inclusion of these topics may also appear to diverge from the chapter's primary focus, it in fact serves to illuminate the nuanced relationship between this leadership crime, superior orders, and the doctrine of superior responsibility—particularly insofar as the perpetrator of aggression is, by definition, someone occupying a superior position. Together—and especially in light of the ICC's privileged, though limited, jurisdiction over this crime—these elements ultimately aim to provide a clear understanding of superior responsibility under the Rome Statute.

---

material ability to prevent or punish crimes. The ICC codifies these standards in Article 28 but introduces asymmetry: Article 28(a) requires that military superiors "knew", while Article 28(b) only requires civilian superiors to have "should have known". This political compromise during Rome's negotiations has drawn criticism (Van Schaack 2021). Unlike the flexible, jurisprudence-driven practice of the *ad hoc* tribunals, the ICC's treaty-bound nature restricts interpretive creativity. For instance, in Bemba, the Appeals Chamber overturned a conviction due to strict application of causality and control, diverging from the *ad hoc* tribunals' more pragmatic standard. Despite these challenges, all three courts somewhat affirm that superior responsibility is a sui generis mode of liability grounded in vicarious liability. While the ICC offers a broader victim-centered potential due to its permanence, its effectiveness depends on flexible interpretation and state cooperation. The *ad hoc* tribunals, though limited in time and scope, demonstrated greater adaptability in addressing systemic atrocities. These differences ultimately reflect the varying political mandates and enforcement mechanisms of the tribunals and the ICC, underscoring the tension between legal rigidity and pragmatic justice.

[20] I would align with the body of literature that normatively argues superior responsibility may be conceptualized either as an omission-based offense or as a form of accessory liability, particularly in contexts where the Rome Statute might have incorporated superior responsibility as a subset of individual criminal responsibility, as was the case under the statutes of the UN *ad hoc* tribunals. In such a framework, there would be a stronger basis for requiring adherence to personal culpability. However, the Rome Statute appears to adopt a more precise and appropriate approach: it treats superior responsibility as a *sui generis* mode of liability, assigning it a distinct and separate provision—Article 28—thereby conceptually distancing it from the general framework of individual criminal responsibility.

[21] See Chap. 3 for details on the distinction between the *latu* and *strictu* senses of superior responsibility.

Excluding the introduction and conclusion, this chapter is structured into three main parts. The first part provides an overview of the establishment of the International Criminal Court (ICC), with the aim of identifying potential parallels—if any—with the UN *ad hoc* tribunals and examining the institutional and legal nexus between them as it pertains to the doctrine of superior responsibility. The second part focuses on the doctrine of superior responsibility under the Rome Statute. It outlines the structural similarities in how superior responsibility is articulated within the subject-matter jurisdiction of both the UN *ad hoc* tribunals and the ICC. It then breaks down the elements of superior responsibility, aligning this analysis with the unique structure and interpretation of Article 28. More significantly, this part undertakes a critical examination of the *Bemba* AC judgment, assessing whether it aligns with Article 28 of the Rome Statute and established jurisprudence. The third part turns to the conceptual relationship between the crime of aggression and superior orders—two dimensions that further inform the broader designation of superior responsibility under the Rome Statute. This discussion is essential for achieving a comprehensive understanding of the doctrine's current scope and future philosophical development, particularly given that the crime of aggression did not fall within the jurisdiction of previous tribunals. The chapter concludes with proposed corrective measures aimed at enhancing the interpretation and application of superior responsibility within the ICC framework.

4.2 The Creation of the ICC and Its Functions: An Overview

From the outset, some saw the ICC (an institution that enjoys universality and permanency) as an overbearing establishment that contested states' sovereign powers.[22] Others, however, argued that it represented a revitalized effort to legislate ICL.[23]

---

[22] Ibid. See also Sadat 2002b, pp. 1073, 1074.

[23] In this sense, James Crawford summarized this endeavor at the Rome Conference, months before the formal adoption of the Rome Statute. His summary reads as follows: "First, it was to be a permanent Court which would sit as required; thus, it had to have an in-built flexibility to work as required. Second, it was to be a Court created by a treaty under the control of the States Parties to the treaty, but in a close relationship to the UN, including the Security Council. It would thereby obviate the need for further *ad hoc* tribunals. The creation of *ad hoc* tribunals by emergency resolution after the crimes have started to be committed may be necessary, but it is legally undesirable. Third, it would be a Court of defined jurisdiction over grave crimes of an international character under *existing* international treaties. It relied on a substantive *droit acquis*, an existing body of laws, in the field of international criminal law, although it was recognized that in certain areas, especially crimes against humanity and war crimes in internal armed conflict, the *droit* is only *partiellement acquis*, only partially acquired, and is still unsatisfactory. Fourth, the Court's jurisdiction—with the significant exception of genocide—would be dependent on the acceptance of States or on triggering by the Security Council under Chapter VII. Fifth, the Court would be integrated with the existing system of international criminal assistance. It was not intended to displace existing domestic systems in cases where those systems were capable of working property. Hence the principle of

The controversial initiative of the ICC has its origins in the efforts of the ILC after WWII.[24] The ILC was established by the UN's General Assembly.[25] It was tasked, in particular, with developing international law, determining rules of criminal law with an international character, and establishing a permanent international criminal court.[26] In 1981, thanks to the work of an *ad hoc* Working Group, the ILC's efforts led to the creation of a code of crimes, culminating from the Nuremberg Principles, the principles in *the UN Convention for the Prevention and the Punishment of the Crime of Genocide*, and similar domestic criminal codes geared at defining crimes.[27] Moreover, it contained rules of criminal procedure and evidence, which contributed to the drafting of the Rome Statute.[28]

It is noteworthy that a General Assembly resolution initially encouraged the establishment of a permanent international criminal court in response to requests from the President of Trinidad and Tobago.[29] Transnational crimes, taking place in the Caribbean states at the time, particularly narcotics smuggling and human trafficking, had raised increasing concerns for the President of Trinidad and Tobago.[30] In 1993–4, James Crawford, who was appointed Special Rapporteur for the UN, took the pledge to complete a draft for an international criminal court, which was finalized and submitted for adoption and agreement to the General Assembly in 1996.[31] Following the adoption of the draft, a drafting committee, chaired by M. Cherif Bassiouni, was established and tasked with reviewing the final draft of the Rome Statute.[32] The Rome Statute was adopted by the *Rome Diplomatic Conference* on 17 July 1998 and entered into force on 1 July 2002.[33]

The establishment of a permanent court provoked strong reactions—as had occurred with the establishment of the Tribunals—particularly by diplomats and practitioners, who viewed it as an unorthodox imposition on their *inviolable* sovereign

---

complementarity. Sixth, it was to be a Court which would offer full guarantees of due process as recognised by international law. This is vital." Crawford 1997, p. 255.

[24] Schabas 2007, pp. 15–21.

[25] Ibid.

[26] Van der Vyver 2021, p. 29.

[27] Ibid., p. 9.

[28] Sadat 2002b, p. 1074.

[29] A.N.R. Robinson (Prime Minister of Trinidad and Tobago), speech calling on the UN General Assembly to consider establishing a permanent international criminal court, 1989, leading to GA Resolution 44/141.

[30] Schabas 2007, p. 10. See also van der Vyver 2021, p. 85; Trinidad and Tobago, in ASSEMBLY OF STATES PARTIES TO THE ROME STATUTE OF THE INTERNATIONAL CRIMINAL COURT, EIGHTH SESSION, THE HAGUE, NOV. 18-26, 2009, Annex II, Report of the Working Group on the Review Conference, Appendix IV, at 68. (This proposal, drafted by Trinidad and Tobago in 2009, was to be revisited during the 2010 Kampala Review Conference of the ICC, reiterating their position on the prosecution of drug trafficking before a permanent international criminal court.)

[31] For a further discussion of the historical procedure of the creation of the ICC, see van der Vyver 2021, pp. 29–35.

[32] Ibid.

[33] Sadat 2002b, p. 1077.

powers.[34] As Crawford has noted, perhaps one of the chief reasons why it was necessary to establish such a permanent court was: "[to] obviate the need for further *ad hoc* tribunals",[35] which could have encountered legality issues, as was the case with the Tribunals' critiques.[36]

Unlike the statutes of the *ad hoc* tribunals, the Rome Statute of the ICC contains well-crafted criminal rules of an international character and was explicitly crafted to overcome the challenges associated with the statutes of such tribunals, which were criticized for being overly *laconic* principled rules. The Rome Statute, however, contains explicit rules of jurisdiction, sources of law, and interpretation mechanisms.

4.2.1 Jurisdiction, Sources of Law, and Statutory Interpretations

Given their differing founding instruments, the *ad hoc* tribunals and the ICC adopted divergent approaches to exercising jurisdiction and rely on differing sources of law and varying venues of statutory interpretation. The statutes of the *ad hoc* tribunals, for instance, adopt flexible interpretative avenues that permit the judges to exercise judicial creativity.[37] However, the judges of the said tribunals also interpret issues by relying on sources other than the enabling statute.[38] The *ad hoc* tribunals' statutes present a limited timeframe for exercising jurisdiction over specific individuals, and customary international law plays a central role as a source of law. The ICC, on the other hand, is a treaty-based institution; the Rome Statute legitimizes its jurisdiction, governs its sources of law and interpretative abilities, and defines its scope of jurisdictional powers independently.[39] This section will explore these two divergent approaches.

4.2.1.1 Jurisdiction of the *Ad Hoc* Tribunals and the ICC

Under international law, jurisdiction refers to multi-normative applications. A general rule of thumb, in hypothetical terms, would be that if State A's courts exercise jurisdiction over State B's territories and/or nationals, according to the *Lotus* case[40] such

[34] Ibid., p. 1079.

[35] Report of the *Ad Hoc* Committee on the Establishment of an International Criminal Court, UN GAOR, 50th Sess., Supp. No. 22 (UN Doc. A/50/22, 1995), p. 3.

[36] Ibid.

[37] Van Schaack 2008, p. 120. See also Shahabuddin 2004, p. 1007.

[38] *Prosecutor v. Zlatko Aleksovski*, Case No. IT-95-14/1-A, Judgment, para 127, 24 March 2000.

[39] Van der Vyver 2021, p. 179.

[40] The Lotus principle is a general principle that cannot be triggered by states if a treaty exists that limits it. For example, the treaty concerning high seas grants the flag state of ships exclusive

an exercise of jurisdiction is legitimate on the end of State A.[41] Only State B may argue for the (il)legality of this jurisdiction.[42] Similarly, the interaction between these states may also include criminal jurisdiction over universally condemned offenses deriving from customary international law,[43] as well as compensations over civil-like damages, such as tort claims (*viz.*, the *US Alien Tort Claims Act*).[44]

Under ICL, jurisdiction calls for a closer look at the confines of this regime. Regarding the practice of the court, criminal jurisdiction encompasses two key norms. First, the competency of the court's "power to prosecute responsible persons [*i.e.*, the exercise of jurisdiction]".[45] Second, this competency also gives rise to authoritative jurisdictional powers over particular individuals and territories, which are further defined by a time-span factor, as well as over specific offenses.[46] As noted, these jurisdictional powers stem from the founding statutes of the *ad hoc* tribunals, which constitute legally binding instrument for their parties and derive their legitimacy from their subject matter.[47] In this context, the competency to exercise jurisdiction extends beyond the courts' relationship within the territory, government, and individuals of the victim states concerned.[48] To underscore this point, acting on behalf of the parties of the victim states (referred to formally as concurrent jurisdiction), the said tribunals exercise their jurisdiction through a full compliance mandate authorized by the UN Security Council (SC).[49]

However, while the ICC's jurisdiction is both spatiotemporally universal and permanent, it remains contingent upon the principle of complementarity, with specified limitations.[50] In short, as an international criminal institution, this means that the ICC is intended to complement the criminal jurisdiction of domestic courts.[51] Accordingly, it can operate as a last resort only in cases in which States' Parties are "unable or unwilling"[52] to prosecute, or where prosecutions by these states appear to be a sham.[53] Moreover, by principle, the ICC's jurisdiction must be exercised

jurisdiction over its ships, even if it has committed violations in a sovereign state. Case of the S.S. "Lotus", P.C.I.J. (Series A) No. 9, pp. 18–21, 7 September 1927.

41 Van der Vyver 2021, p. 270.

42 Ibid.

43 There is an exceptionally fast-growing body of literature on the legality of exercising universal jurisdiction over international crimes by domestic courts. See Stahn 2018, p. 414; Henkin et al. 1987, p. 821.

44 *Alien Tort Claims Act*, 28 U.S.C. § 1350. Available at: https://crsreports.congress.gov/product/pdf/R/R44947.

45 ICTY Statute, Article 1.

46 Van der Vyver 2021, p. 303.

47 Sadat 2002a, p. 112. See also Simonovic 1999, p. 444.

48 Ibid.

49 ICTY Statute, Article 9.

50 See, generally, Sadat 2002a, pp. 103, 27.

51 It is important to note that, in this context, a domestic court must be from a state party to the Rome Statute, with the exception of a UN SC referral.

52 Rome Statute, Article 17/1 (a).

53 Ibid., Article 17/2.

over States' Parties in accordance with the Rome Statute; it may also investigate crimes by nationals of non-State Parties or crimes committed in their territories in the case of a referral to the UN SC.[54] In both of these instances, the ICC may step in to investigate and prosecute.[55] The second definition of jurisdiction concerns the various subdivisions deriving from the exercise of jurisdiction mantle, wherein the scope of these jurisdictional powers is authorized by the founding statutes.[56] These subdivisions of jurisdictional power can be divided into the following four instances:

1. Subject-matter jurisdiction (*ratione materiae*). This jurisdictional power refers to the court's exercise of jurisdiction in relation to certain crimes, namely, within the context of ICL, war crimes, crimes against humanity, genocide, and acts of aggression—collectively referred to as core international crimes.[57]
2. Location-based jurisdictional power (*ratione loci*). This jurisdictional power allows the court to prosecute within the geographical boundaries of states where the violations were committed and/or where the perpetrators are situated.[58]
3. Jurisdictional power over individuals (*ratione personae*). This jurisdictional power means that the court can only prosecute natural persons, not abstract entities.[59]
4. Jurisdictional power and timeframe (*ratione temporis*). This jurisdictional power defines the period of time during which the court can prosecute; this is also referred to as non-retroactivity under the Rome Statute.[60]

There is extensive discussion of these jurisdictional powers within scholarly writings;[61] however, the following discussion will be restricted to a brief comparison between the *ad hoc* tribunals and the ICC regarding the exercise of jurisdiction.

The first jurisdictional power, *ratione materiae*, differs significantly with respect to the *ad hoc* tribunals and the ICC, in many respects, first and foremost in relation to the scope of the crimes the two institutions can prosecute.[62] For instance, given the specific situation in the former Yugoslavia, the ICTY was authorized to exercise jurisdiction over war crimes and their definitions, as set out under Article 2, as well as violations of the laws of custom and war.[63] It is worth noting here that this Article provides a legal basis for judges to prosecute non-codified, universally condemned offenses through interpretations of customary law and the laws of war.[64] As noted earlier, to address the unique situation at the time, the judges of the said tribunals

[54] Ibid., Article 13.

[55] Ibid.

[56] Sadat 2002a, pp. 104–106.

[57] Van der Vyver 2021, pp. 270–280.

[58] Ibid., pp. 280–287.

[59] Ibid., pp. 287, 302.

[60] Non-retroactivity is confined to the ICC. Ibid., pp. 302, 316.

[61] Ibid., pp. 270, 316.

[62] Cassese 2002, pp. 13–15.

[63] Ibid.

[64] Meron 2004, p. 47.

were given the flexibility to exercise lawmaking through interpretative analysis.[65] The ICTR differs slightly from the ICTY when it comes to *ratione materiae* because most of the crimes it dealt with concerned genocide, and the perpetrators were nationals of Rwanda (thus deemed an internal armed conflict).[66]

As the ICC is legally bound by the Rome Statute, in handling crimes and their definitions, ICC judges must rely on Articles 5–8bis.[67] In this regard, the ICC strongly opposes the creation of offenses through interpretation.[68] On one occasion, the ICC held that: "[it] considers that when a matter [offense] is regulated in the primary sources of law of the Court, there is…no room for chambers to rely on purported 'inherent powers' to fill in non-existent gaps".[69]

The *ad hoc* tribunals' statutes comprise thirty-four substantive criminal law Articles; however, owing to the "*laconic* approach" adopted by the drafters, rules on criminal procedure and evidence were excluded.[70] Accordingly, the judges were granted discretionary lawmaking powers to craft such rules.[71] The ICC, by contrast, enjoys a broader, more elaborate *ratione materiae* over crimes other than breaches of the LoAC.[72] For instance, in addition to war crimes, crimes against humanity, and genocide, the ICC also exercises jurisdiction over the crime of aggression.[73] In this context, it is noteworthy that, in an attempt to attract powerful states, the framers of the Rome Statute elected to include an opt-out option for the crime of aggression under Article 124,[74] according to which a state may be excluded from jurisdiction over its nationals or territory for seven years after the Rome Statute's entry into force.[75] Some analysts argued that this option was intended to encourage the US and France to accede to the Rome Statute.[76]

Regarding the second jurisdictional power, *ratione loci*, from a geographical perspective, the *ad hoc* tribunals are limited to exercising jurisdiction within the territories where the violations took place, namely, the former Yugoslavia for the ICTY and Rwanda for the ICTR.[77] An important caveat needs to be made here, however: in the case of the *ad hoc* tribunals, all UN members are obliged to comply

---

[65] Watson 2002, p. 872.

[66] ICTR Statute, Article 2.

[67] However, in certain strict situations, judges may be allowed to redefine offenses in accordance with customary international law if a significant lacuna was encountered before the Court. *Prosecutor v. Jean-Pierre Bemba Gombo et. al.*, Case No. ICC-01/05-01/13 A6 A7 A8 A9, para 2, 8 March 2018.

[68] *Contra.*, Sadat 2002b, p. 1078.

[69] *Prosecutor v. Bemba*, para 76.

[70] Sadat and Dixon 1997, p. 81. See also Mundis 2001, p. 191; Nsereko 1994, p. 507.

[71] Meron 2004, p. 521. See also the ICTY Statute, Article 15; ICTR Statute, Article 14.

[72] Sadat 2002b, p. 1073.

[73] Rome Statute, Article 8bis.

[74] Van der Vyver 2021, p. 211.

[75] Ibid.

[76] Ibid. At the Review Conference in Kampala, Uganda, this option was advocated by the US. See also Sadat 2002a, p. 106.

[77] Ibid., p. 105.

with the territorial jurisdiction of the said tribunals.[78] This requirement deviates from the *ratione loci* jurisdiction set out in the ICC's Rome Statute.

Given its treaty-based constitution, while, in principle, the ICC exercises jurisdiction over the territories of states that are parties to it, it may also exercise such jurisdiction universally over a non-state party's territory and/or nationals. In these cases, either the UN SC must first assess the situation and make a referral, or the non-State Party must consent to the ICC's jurisdiction to investigate and prosecute.[79] These unique forms of *ratione loci* proved controversial and were challenged before the adoption of the Rome Statute.[80]

It is important to underscore that the third instance of jurisdictional power, *ratione personae*, constitutes a putative jurisdictional power, according to which ICL can hold only natural persons criminally responsible at the international level.[81] However, *ratione personae* specifically addresses targeted persons subject to the court's jurisdiction.[82] While, in the case of the *ad hoc* tribunals, nationals of the former Yugoslavia and Rwanda are subject to their jurisdiction, the ICC, as a permanent and universal institution, prosecutes virtually all nationals of its States Parties, as well as persons referred by the UN SC or a consenting state.[83] Finally, in an armed conflict of a non-international character, the ICC also exercises jurisdiction universally over non-military soldiers, such as freedom fighters.[84]

The fourth and final instance of jurisdictional power, *ratione temporis*, was in fact the most controversial as its legality was challenged.[85] The *ad hoc* tribunals exercise jurisdiction during a pre-established time frame, which is usually restricted to the period during which the crimes were committed.[86] The ICC, on the other hand, in its capacity as a permanent court, applies a different interpretation of *ratione temporis*.

---

78 *Prosecutor v. Tihomir Blaškić*, Case No. IT-95-14-AR108bis, Judgment on the Request of the Republic of Croatia for Review of the Decision of Trial Chamber II of 18 July 1997, paras 13, 32, 33, 29 October 1997.

79 Rome Statute.

80 The US challenged this conclusion, advocating that "it is not a principle accepted in the practice of most governments" Discussion Paper, U.N. Doc. A/CONF.183/C.1/L.53, 6 July 1998.

81 States' responsibility for international crimes is considered in a narrower sense, where the international community may impose punitive and compensatory measures. This matter was considered in the *Prosecutor v. Furundžija* case at the ICTY, where the Court held that: "Under current international humanitarian law, in addition to individual criminal liability, State responsibility may ensue as a result of State officials engaging in torture or failing to prevent torture or to punish torturers. If carried out as an extensive practice of State officials, torture amounts to a serious breach on a widespread scale of an international obligation of essential importance for safeguarding the human being, thus constituting a particularly grave wrongful act generating State responsibility." *Prosecutor v. Anto Furundžija*, Case No. IT-95-I-T, at 142 (10 December 1998). See also Case Concerning the Application of the Convention of the Prevention and Punishment of the Crime of Genocide (Bosnia *v.* Serbia and Montenegro), 2007 I.C.J., para 166.

82 Van der Vyver 2021, p. 287.

83 Rome Statute, Article 13.

84 Ibid., Article 8 (c); (d); (e); (f).

85 Schabas 2007, p. 65.

86 Ibid.

In principle, the ICC is bound by the non-retroactivity clause, according to which jurisdiction can only be exercised after the entry into force of the Rome Statute. As such: "[n]o person shall be criminally responsible under [the Rome Statute] for conduct prior to the entry into force of the Statute".[87] It is important to note, however, that the non-retroactivity principle applies only to the entry into force of the Rome Statute, not to the acceding state.[88] In other words, if a state decided to accede to the Rome Statute four years after the Rome Statute's entry into force in 2006, the non-retroactivity principle would apply only to crimes committed before 2002. In other words, based on the Rome Statute's entry into force in 2006, the ICC could prosecute crimes committed from 2002 until the accession date in 2006, and onwards.[89]

Finally, the relationship between the jurisdictions of the *ad hoc* tribunals and the ICC and the admissibility of cases should not be viewed as mutually exclusive. The admissibility of cases at the ICC involves many stages.[90] The principle of *ne bis in idem* (which means that the accused cannot be convicted twice unless the conviction at the domestic level fell outside the scope of the Rome Statute's subject-matter jurisdiction) may obstruct the ICC from exercising jurisdiction.[91] This principle may restrict the ICC's competency to exercise jurisdiction to evade double jeopardy.[92] Accordingly, the *ne bis in idem* principle could be seen as a double-edged sword: if domestic prosecutions do not adhere to rules of the Rome Statute with respect to international perpetrators, the ICC may step in and prosecute, and *vice versa.*

4.2.1.2 Sources of Law and Statutory Interpretations (Applicable Law)

There are significant differences when it comes to the sources of law and statutory interpretations applied by the *ad hoc* tribunals and the ICC, which, as I shall discuss later, affects the application of superior responsibility in broad terms.

Unlike the more restrictive rules of the ICC, the construction of the *ad hoc* tribunals' statutes extended beyond the applicable law and interpretations, prompting the said tribunals to rely on established rules of public international law.[93] On this point, international law provides that sources of law are to be drawn from Article 38 of the International Court of Justice (ICJ) Charter.[94] Article 38 lists the following sources: "treaties, customary international law, general principles of law created by world legal systems and, as a subsidiary means for the [*sic*] determining the law,

[87] Van der Vyver 2021, p. 304. See also Rome Statute, Article 24.

[88] Ibid., p. 310.

[89] Ibid., p. 311.

[90] Sadat 2002a, pp. 125–127.

[91] Van der Vyver 2021, pp. 5–11.

[92] Ibid.

[93] Grover 2014, p. 44.

[94] *Statute of the International Court of Justice*, 26 June 1945, 59 Stat. 1055, 33 U.N.T.S. 933, Article 38.

judicial decisions and scholarly writings of publicists."[95] Although these sources were originally designed for the ICJ's practice, the *ad hoc* tribunals have viewed them as generally accepted laws at the international level.[96] Moreover, the *ad hoc* tribunals' statutes are not treaty-based instruments; rather, they should be viewed, *obiter dictum*, as "proximate in nature to [treaties]".[97]

The ICC, on the other hand, follows a strict yet pragmatic methodology for identifying sources of law. The ICC is confined to Article 21 (Applicable Law) of its Rome Statute, which exclusively enumerates its hierarchy of sources of law.[98] This article is divided into primary sources and last-resort sources. ICC judges and the Office of the Prosecutor (OTP) are primarily required to apply the crimes (including their definitions) and rules of procedure and evidence that are comprehensively outlined in the Rome Statute.[99] When necessary, the ICC and the OTP can also make use of the following sources:

> [A]pplicable treaties and the principles and rules of international law, including the established principles of the international law of armed conflict; Failing that, general principles of law derived by the Court from national laws of legal systems of the world including, as appropriate, the national laws of States that would normally exercise jurisdiction over the crime, provided that those principles are not inconsistent with this Statute and with international law and internationally recognized norms and standards.[100]

In the hierarchy of sources of law for the ICC and the OTP, the final resort is its own jurisprudence, particularly that of the AC, as well as internationally recognized human rights that may stem from treaties and customary international law.[101] It must also be emphasized that although the ICC does not follow the precedent system (as practiced under the common law of many nations), in the final stage of this hierarchy of sources of law, it may, by virtue of *ratio decidendi*, base its reasoning on its own precedents as its source of law.[102] These sources of law may also be used by judges as an interpretative mechanism for resolving situations, particularly interpretations of ambiguous provisions.[103]

The interpretation mechanisms employed by the *ad hoc* tribunals are not explicitly set out in their statutes. Rather, they were implicitly shaped through their jurisprudence.[104] In the said tribunals' early jurisprudence, they followed interpretative

---

95 Akande 2009, pp. 41–43.

96 Murphy 2012, p. 14.

97 *Prosecutor v. JOSEPH KANYABASID*, Case No. ICTR-96-15-A, (Dissenting Opinion of Judge Shahabuddeen) para 21 (3 June 1999). See also *Prosecutor v. Zlatko Aleksovski*, Case No. IT-95-14/1-A, n. 364, 24 March 2000; *Prosecutor v. Dražen Erdemovic*, Case No. IT-96-22-A (Joint Separate Opinion of Judge McDonald and Judge Vohrah), para 40, 29 November 1996.

98 Schabas 2007, p. 76.

99 Rome Statute, Article 21(1).

100 Ibid.

101 Ibid., Article 21(2,3). See also Bitti 2009, pp. 281–95 (where it is maintained that Article 38 of the ICJ must not be applied by the ICC judges in terms of interpretations).

102 Ibid.

103 Grover 2014, pp. 6–7.

104 Ibid., p. 9.

approaches exemplified under Articles 31–33 of the *Vienna Convention on the Law of Treaties* (VCLT),[105] viewing their statutes as international treaties in essence (Treaty-like statutes).[106] The VCLT Articles specify that, in principle, provisions should be interpreted in accordance with their literal meaning.[107] However, in cases where the provision concerned is ambiguous, it could be interpreted teleologically—[108] a form of consequentialism-based reasoning.[109] In such cases, the interpreter—by means of reasoning—may take into account the purpose and spirit of a provision to support their interpretation.[110] For example, when following a teleological approach, an interpreter may consider *addenda* to the original provision. These include, but are not limited to, the preparatory work of the founding instrument; the marginal contractual agreements demonstrating the parties' intentions to give the provision in question a specific effect; customary international law; and the preamble to the text of the instrument.[111]

Antecedently, Theodor Meron, proposed a *sui generis* rape crime in 1993.[112] Despite not being codified as such, said crime was to be interpreted as an offense under customary international law, primarily stemming from the grave breaches enumerated in the *1949 Geneva Conventions*.[113] Article 8(2)(a)(iii) of Geneva Convention I teleologically supports such an interpretation, which penalizes offenses that "willfully caus[e] great suffering or serious injury to body or health".[114] With respect to the admissibility of interpretations at the *ad hoc* tribunals, based on a teleological interpretation of Article 8(2)(a)(iii), the uncodified rape crime was eventually incorporated into the said tribunals' subject-matter jurisprudence.[115] In comparison, domestic criminal systems do not tolerate such a broad approach owing to the principle of the impediment of legality (*nullum crimen sine lege*), which can be summarized as: No law, no crime, no conviction.[116]

From an interpretative perspective, the ICC also follows the *nullum crimen sine lege* principle with respect to its subject-matter jurisdiction (concerning the core

[105] *Vienna Convention on the Law of Treaties*, Article 31–33, U.N. Doc. A./CONF.39/27 (22 May 1969), 1155 U.N.T.S. 331, 8I.L.M. 679 (1969).

[106] Akande 2009. See also Schabas 2003, p. 850.

[107] Young 2001, pp. 319–320. See also van der Vyver 2021, p. 187.

[108] Van der Vyver 2021, p. 180.

[109] Cryer et al. 2019, p. 23.

[110] Ibid.

[111] Ibid., p. 181. See also Sadat and Jolly 2014, p. 763.

[112] Meron 2021, p. 46.

[113] Under Israeli law, the 1949 Geneva Conventions are not considered to hold a customary international law nature; however, international law and its community consider these conventions as customary international law. See van der Vyver 2021, p. 272. See also *PROSECUTOR v. ANTO FURUNDZIYA*, Case No. IT-95-T, para 138, 10 December 1998.

[114] Meron 2021, pp. 46–47. Such fluidity is intolerable under the Rome Statute, given its fully codified criminal law concerning only the crimes and their definitions.

[115] Ibid.

[116] Rome Statute, Article 22.

crimes and their definitions).[117] However, this principle should not be understood in terms of the principle of legal limits. In all respects, the judges still have the power to interpret issues other than the crimes and their definitions.[118] In this sense, because the principle of legality relates to the crimes and their definitions, it does not apply to modes of liability outlined under the Rome Statute. Instead, these modes of liability (including their conceptual components) can be interpreted in accordance with both Articles 31–33 of the VCTL and Article 21 of the Rome Statute.[119] For example, if ICC judges interpreted the nature of superior responsibility—to determine whether it constitutes a nationally oriented offense of omission though in my view only with regard to the duty to prevent, as will be explained later, which typically incurs a mitigated sentence or vicarious liability for the subordinates' crimes—they may rely on teleological interpretations as their point of departure, for instance based on the Preamble of the Rome Statute.[120] In laboring on this point, the Rome Statute was created with a view to ending the impunity of superiors and prioritizing victims' rights while continuing to ensure fair and reasonable prosecutions and sentences.[121] These goals (fairness and reasonableness) can be achieved only through only a strict literal interpretation mechanism (*in dubio mitius*),[122] which is explicitly described in Article 21 with respect to international crimes and their definitions, which must be interpreted in favor of the accused.[123] However, the former goal (ending the impunity of superiors) may be interpreted teleologically. The ICC must therefore interpret this doctrine in a manner that prioritizes victims' rights and aligns with its primary purpose, namely, the imposition of vicarious liability.[124] In this sense, superior responsibility as a mode of liability cannot be confined to a strictly literal interpretation. Contrary to the position advanced by some commentators, it is not a sui generis omission offense; if it were, it would necessarily be subject to literal interpretation.[125] To this end, the ICC clearly, though only partially, adopted such an approach.

---

[117] *PROSECUTOR v. ALI MUHAMMAD ALI ABD-ALRAHMAN* ("ALI KUSHAYB"), Case No. ICC-02/05-01/20 OA8, para 91, 1 November 2021. See also Sadat and Jolly 2014, p. 763.

[118] Ibid. See also Robinson 2008, pp. 925, 933–938.

[119] Cf. Sadat and Jolly 2014. (Where, according to the reasoning applied in this study, it is argued that the exhaustive list of interpretations set out in the VCTL, which somehow resembles Article 21 of the Rome Statute, could serve as an effective framework for interpreting the Rome Statute as regards superior responsibility.)

[120] Van der Vyver summarizes a portion of the Preamble of the Rome Statute in relation to its teleological sense: "The Preamble furthermore outlines the general purpose of an international criminal court. It Proclaims that the most serious crimes of concern to the international community as a whole, must not go unpunished. Impunity of perpetrators of such crimes must come to an end. This in turn might contribute to the prevention of such crimes and lasting respect for the enforcement of international justice." Van der Vyver 2021, p. 188.

[121] Powderly 2010, pp. 17–44, esp. pp. 41–42. See also Grover 2010, p. 554.

[122] Baragwanath 2014, p. 482.

[123] Ibid.

[124] See Sect. 3.3 on the legal characterization of superior responsibility in Chap. 3.

[125] Van der Vyver 2021.

Judge Herrera Carbuccia helpfully summarized the form of interpretation in accordance with the goal of superior responsibility:

> The essence of article 28 is that it holds responsible those who, under the veil of the rule of law, in fact abuse the rule of law against the population they are supposed to protect. The application of traditional criminal law standards (*lex generalis*) in proceedings where article 28 of the Statute is applicable (*lex specialis*) is a perversion of this norm and invalidates its existence. Such an interpretation of the law, together with the de facto or de jure position of command or authority of the accused vis-à-vis the victims of the crimes, can only lead to unreasonable conclusions. Judicial analysis of article 28 must pierce this veil of "strict" application of criminal law that ignores the object and purpose of international criminal law, and particularly of article 28 of the Statute. Unless article 28 of the Statute is analyzed with this in mind, those holding power and authority who commit crimes against those they are supposed to protect will be acquitted, and victims will be denied justice.[126]

He further asserted that:

> Unlike other concepts used at international criminal trials, which emanate directly from criminal law (*e.g.* the principle of legality), the concept of command and superior responsibility is an original creation of international criminal law and international human rights law... [superior responsibility] allows judges to hold responsible not only military commanders but also civilian authorities (constituted de jure or de facto), who under *traditional criminal law principles* would escape justice.[127] [emphasis mine]

Another customary and VCLT-based teleological interpretative method that can be applied by ICC judges centers on interpreting the elements of the doctrine of superior responsibility, as outlined under Article 28, for instance in accordance with the *travaux préparatoires* of the Rome Statute, which make peripheral reference to the intentions of states' delegations.[128] Within this context, some delegations to the Rome Statute shared their views on what they intended the fault element of this doctrine to mean with respect to military (or military-like) commanders.[129] As noted earlier, although the US was not a state party, its delegation insisted that the "should-have-known" state of mind of military (or military-like) commanders signifies pure negligence.[130] This *mens rea* requirement thus characterizes superior responsibility as a relaxed form of liability.[131]

In conclusion, the completion of the *ad hoc* tribunals' mission should not be seen as synonymous with its perennial jurisprudence within the ICL regime. In addition to the jurisprudence of the ICC, the case law of the *ad hoc* tribunals has provided both formative and normative sources of ICL—contributing interpretations that will

---

[126] *Prosecutor v. Laurent Gbagbo and Charles Blé Goudé*, Case No. ICC-02/11-01/15-1263-AnxC-Red (Separate dissenting opinion of Judge Herrera Carbuccia), para 494, 16 July 2019 (where it is argued that it is a form of liability for omission).

[127] Ibid., para 492.

[128] Van der Vyver 2021, pp. 182–184.

[129] Levie 1997–1998, p. 10. See also Landrum 1995, p. 300.

[130] U.N. Diplomatic Conference of Plenipotentiaries on the Establishment of an International Criminal Court, Summary Records of the 1st Meeting of the Committee of the Whole, U.N. Doc. A/CONF.183/C.1/SR.1, 20 November 1998, para 67.

[131] Ibid. See also Sect. 4.3.1.3.

continue to serve as reference points for future tribunals.[132] Prospective tribunals—whether they are established through the same approach, a UN SC resolution, or a unilateral treaty—may draw on the jurisprudence of the earlier tribunals as a source of law, particularly with respect to the jurisprudentially generated parameters of the doctrine of superior responsibility, which is what renders the outcome of the AC's judgment in the *Bemba* case so critical for international criminal justice.[133]

4.3 *The Bemba* Judgments: Concerns About the Theorization of Fallacious Legal Practice

In this section, I shall first set out to critically analyze the transcendence and/or misapplication of the doctrine of superior responsibility at the ICC, as demonstrated by the AC's judgment in the *Bemba* case. As noted earlier, this judgment concerns Article 28 of the Rome Statute of the ICC, which will also be examined in this section for theoretical and practical purposes.

The AC's judgment in the *Bemba* case was broadly contested in relation to many aspects of its reasoning, particularly the arguably misleading understanding of the Appellate Review Standard and the limitations of the Scope of Charges at the Pre-Trial phase.[134] Accordingly, in the following analysis, I shall explore aspects of the reasoning behind this judgment, together with the conceptual components presented in this book, for the purpose of demonstrating how the ICC has retouched the doctrine of superior responsibility.

4.3.1 Prosecuting Superiors at the ICC Under Article 28 of the Rome Statute

As outlined in the Rome Statute of the ICC, the compartmentalization of individuals' criminal modes of liability is quite elaborate and should not be seen as being on a par with the *ad hoc* tribunals' provision concerning modes of liability.[135] Under the Rome Statute, a superior may be charged with international crimes in the following ways: (i) as a principal following physical action (or omission), as a result of a superior order;[136] or by jointly participating in a criminal enterprise (Claus Roxin's control over the crime theory); (ii) as an accomplice, in cases in which the superior conspires

[132] Pjic 1997, p. 860.

[133] Pruitt 2014, p. 375.

[134] For a more discussion on these aspects of the judgment, see Sadat 2019, pp. 357, 360; Powderly 2018, pp. 1031–1079, esp. 1032–1033.

[135] Van der Vyver 2021, p. 566. See also ICTY Statute, Article 7; ICTR Statute, Article 6.

[136] Rome Statute, Article 25 (a); (b).

with or aids and abets subordinates to commit crimes;[137] and/or (iv) by failing to fulfill their duties to supervise, which leads to the commission of crimes (superior responsibility).[138] Article 25 of the Rome Statute addresses the first two instances (under the *individual criminal responsibility* rubric), while Article 28 covers the third instance (under the *other grounds of criminal responsibility* rubric). These modes of liability under the Rome Statute were not specified in the *ad hoc* tribunals' statutes. Instead, under Article 7 of the ICTY Statute (and Article 6 of the ICTR Statute), modes of liability are combined with superior responsibility, upholding, *inter alia*, the primacy of their jurisdiction over all prosecutions, concurrently with those of the victim states.[139]

Before elaborating on the structure of Article 28, I shall make a brief digression here to discuss the omission liability of superiors under the Rome Statute. Some analysts have argued that, during the drafting process,[140] the framers of the Rome Statute felt "uncomfortable" with explicitly submitting omission (as opposed to action) to the jurisdiction of the ICC, considering Article 28 as a form of omission that could fill the perceived gap in relation to culpability of omission.[141] As discussed in the section on *Sources of Law and Interpretation*, this argument can be strongly refuted on both conceptual and practical grounds. Practically speaking, in the *Bemba* case, the ICC's Pre-Trial Chamber held that "acts of murder of civilians as a war crime can be committed through an act or an omission".[142] As a matter of law, omission was implicitly incorporated into the definitions of crimes under the Rome Statute, like, for example, starvation that can be committed through omission.[143] If the framers of the Statute had included an exclusive provision for omission, this would have rendered the subsequent provision "superfluous"[144] or redundant to the Rome Statute.[145]

Conversely, Article 28 of the Rome Statute clearly establishes that this provision is designed for charging a superior "for" crimes committed or about to be committed by the superior's subordinates, which the superior failed to prevent, repress, and/or

---

[137] Ibid., Article 25 (c). See also *PROSECUTOR v. THOMAS LUBANGA DYILO* (Decision on Confirmation of Charges), Case No. ICC-01/04-01/06-803-tEN, para 318, 29 January 2007; Van der Vyver 2021, p. 568.

[138] Ibid., Article 28.

[139] ICTY Statute, Article 9; ICTR Statute, Article 8.

[140] Draft Statute for the International Criminal Court, Article 28, U.N. Doc. A/CONF.183/2/Add.1, 14 April 1998.

[141] Sadat 2002a, p. 203. See also see Ambos 2002, pp. 823, 850–851; Ambos 1999b, pp. 475, 492; Eser 2002, pp. 818–819; Schabas 1998, pp. 400, 412.

[142] *PROSECUTOR v. JEAN-PIERRE BEMBA GOMBO* (Decision Pursuant to Article 61(7)(a) and (b) of the Rome Statute on the Charges against Jean-Pierre Bemba Gombo), Case No. ICC-01/05-01/08-424, para 274, 15 June 2009 (hereafter Bemba Pre-Trial Judgment).

[143] Van der Vyver 2021, p. 436.

[144] Ibid. See also Draft Statute for the International Criminal Court, UN Doc. A/CONF.183/2Mdd.l.

[145] See *Chairman's Suggestion for Articles 21, 26 and 28*, Article 28, U.N. Doc. A/CONF.183/C.1/WGGP/L.1, 15 June 1998. See also Cryer 2004, pp. 236–240; Clark 2001, pp. 303–304.

submit to the competent authorities.[146] Therefore, omission as a prosecutable offense is not entirely excluded from the Rome Statute. Rather, it is incorporated into the definitions of the crimes, which contradicts the characterization of Article 28 as a form of omission liability.[147] To this end, and in response to persistent scholarly resistance to the individualization of superior responsibility, Miles—potentially misinterpreting the partially unanimous Bemba AC judgment concerning its *sui generis* nature[148]—concludes that superior responsibility "operate[s] as to render the commander a party to the crimes of their subordinate".[149] This is a striking and potentially problematic interpretation, at least against the central thesis of this book. In the context of ICL, some modes of liability, *a priori*, do not necessarily render an accused a party to the crime. This distinction is crucial, as it guards against the mistaken assumption that individuals held liable under *sui generis* modes of liability, such as superior responsibility, are automatically considered participants in the commission of the crimes themselves. Superior responsibility does not require that the superior be deemed a co-perpetrator or accomplice, as would be the case under the more (in)direct modes outlined in Article 25. Rather, it is sufficient to establish that the superior failed to discharge their legal duties toward their subordinates' crimes—provided that the other elements of the doctrine are satisfied. Treating the superior as a party to the crime, even hypothetically, would conflate superior responsibility with principal or accessory liability, thereby eroding its distinct normative and legal essence.

In addition, it should also be underscored here that a superior may be held criminally responsible "for not executing his or her duties to supervise",[150] as an omission offense.[151] This offense may give rise, in its own right, to criminal responsibility for omission at the domestic level (in a domestic court or court-martial).[152] However, under the doctrine of superior responsibility as set out in the Rome Statute (ICC), domestic prosecutions for omission shall not jeopardize the possible conviction of a superior for the ensuing crimes resulting from their omission.[153] To elaborate on this point, according to the complementarity principle, the ICC serves as a supplemental international criminal institution for domestic courts, for instance when the ICC conducts an investigation and prosecutes if the domestic prosecution appears to be a sham or is based on omission *per se* in this case.[154] In the latter scenario, the superior then "cannot raise the defense of *ne bis in idem* [double convictions on the same conduct] if he or she were to be subsequently charged to stand trial in the ICC [under superior responsibility]".[155]

146 Rome Statute, Article 28.

147 For a detailed discussion on the nature of superior responsibility, see, generally, Chap. 3.

148 Jackson 2022, p. 438.

149 Ibid.

150 Van der Vyver 2021, p. 568.

151 Ibid., p. 570.

152 Van Sliedregt 2018, pp. 740–742.

153 Van der Vyver 2021, p. 572.

154 Ibid.

155 Ibid.

In any case, given the *laconic* articulation of superior responsibility under the *ad hoc* tribunals' statutes, the framers of the Rome Statute set out to address superior responsibility as a self-explanatory concept—as set out idiosyncratically under Article 28—in contrast to the modes of perpetration/*participation* outlined under Article 25.[156] Article 28 of the Rome Statute, titled *Responsibility of Military Commanders and Other Superior Officials*, reads:

> In addition to other grounds of criminal responsibility under this Statute for crimes within the jurisdiction of the Court:
>
> (a) A military commander or person effectively acting as a military commander shall be criminally responsible for crimes within the jurisdiction of the Court committed by forces under his or her effective command and control, or effective authority and control as the case may be, as a result of his or her failure to exercise control properly over such forces, where:
> (i) That military commander or person either knew or, owing to the circumstances at the time, should have known that the forces were committing or about to commit such crimes; and
> (ii) That military commander or person failed to take all necessary and reasonable measures within his or her power to prevent or repress their commission or to submit the matter to the competent authorities for investigation and prosecution.
>
> (b) With respect to superior and subordinate relationships not described in paragraph (a), a superior shall be criminally responsible for crimes within the jurisdiction of the Court committed by subordinates under his or her effective authority and control, as a result of his or her failure to exercise control properly over such subordinates, where:
> (i) The superior either knew or consciously disregarded information which clearly indicated that the subordinates were committing or about to commit such crimes;
> (ii) The crimes concerned activities that were within the effective responsibility and control of the superior; and
> (iii) The superior failed to take all necessary and reasonable measures within his or her power to prevent or repress their commission or to submit the matter to the competent authorities for investigation and prosecution.[157]

The conceptual components of superior responsibility described here are specifically worded to correspond to the criminal responsibility of military commanders in accordance with the customary and modern application of command responsibility, with a distinction drawn between *de jure* and *de facto* military commanders.[158] It is also important to note that—on an initial inspection of the *ad hoc* tribunals' provision of superior responsibility compared with that of the Rome Statute—the latter identifies what the superior is criminally charged for (the subordinates' crimes) in more specific terms.[159] The provision of the *ad hoc* tribunals, by contrast, does not explicitly indicate what the superior may be charged for.[160] It was therefore left up to the judges of the *ad hoc* tribunals to determine the indirect liability principle, along

---

[156] *Prosecutor v. Jean-Pierre Bemba Gombo*, Case No. ICC-01/05-01/08, Judgment Pursuant to Article 74 of the Statute, para 16, 21 March 2016; Bemba Appeals chamber judgment, para 173.

[157] Rome Statute, Article 28.

[158] Kortfält 2017, p. 279.

[159] *Contra*, ICTY Statute, Article 7; ICTR Statute, Article 6.

[160] Ibid. See, generally, Chap. 3.

with the elements of this doctrine, through teleological statutory interpretations.[161] Article 28 also encapsulates two types of failures that the prosecutor must prove in a superior criminal responsibility case: a *chapeau* failure to properly control subordinates and a narrower form of failure to take all necessary and reasonable measures to fulfill their duties.[162]

Jurisprudentially, Article 28 covers three key elements that apply, albeit somewhat unequally, to both military and political superiors[163]: (i) the superior–subordinate relationship; (ii) the failure to supervise; and (iii) the fault (*mens rea*) of the accused superior.[164] Following further interpretations by jurisprudence and scholars, however, a fourth element (causation) was introduced.[165] According to the rationale of this book, I would argue that this element is not a core constituent element of superior responsibility, based on some scholarly attempts to interpret the phrase "as a result of" in the *chapeau* of Article 28.[166] Rather, it should be understood as a putative parameter applicable only in evaluating whether or not the superior exercised proper control.

With this semi-clear group of elements in mind, ICC judges are not required, for example, to determine whether the accused is a military commander or a political superior, as was the case in the *ad hoc* tribunals' jurisprudence.[167] ICC judges are also not required to differentiate between the duty to submit the matter to the competent authorities and the duty to punish, as the case was in the said tribunals' jurisprudence.[168] I shall explore each of these elements in further detail in the following subsections.

---

[161] *Prosecutor v. Delalić & Others*, para 198.

[162] Van Sliedregt 2011, p. 20.

[163] Ibid., p. 27. In their interpretations, both scholars and judges at the Tribunals have classified these elements based on customary international law.

[164] Van der Vyver 2021, p. 573. See also *FERDINAND NAHIMANA, JEAN-BOSCO BARAYAGWIZA & HASSAN NGEZE v. THE PROSECUTOR*, Case No. ICTR-99-52-A. para 484, 28 November 2007; *PROSECUTOR v. AUGUSTIN NDINDILIYIMANA*, Case No. ICTR-00-56-T, para 1916, 17 May 2011; *SYLVESTRE GACUMBITSI v. THE PROSECUTOR* (Separate Opinion of Judge Schomberg on the Criminal Responsibility of the Appellant for Committing Genocide), Case No. ICTR-2001-64-A, para 143, 7 July 2006.

[165] See, for example, Ambos 2002, p. 860 (where it is stated that Article 28 "implies a causal relationship between the superior's failure and the subordinate's commission of crimes"). See also Triffterer 2002, p. 197 (where causation is described as a "constituent element" of Article 28); Osiel 2005, p. 1779.

[166] See, e.g., Jackson 2022.

[167] Van Sliedregt 2011, p. 25.

[168] Ibid., p. 18 (although she maintains that the duty to submit the matter to the competent authorities applies only to future crimes).

4.3.1.1 Superior–Subordinate Relationship

In Chap. 3, I examined this element, including all its features and parameters, in depth.[169] However, the provision on this element set out under the Rome Statute takes an asymmetrical approach to the superior–subordinate relationship, particularly in relation to the status of the superior. For example, the provision draws a distinction between a military commander (*de jure*), a person acting as a military commander (*de facto*), and a political superior.[170] The provision also describes two slightly different relationships with respect to *de jure* or *de facto* military commanders and political superiors: a relationship based on command and control on the one hand, and a relationship based on authority and control on the other.[171] The first relationship (based on command and control) requires that there be a connection between the *de jure* military commander and their *forces*. For example, in cases of armed conflict not of an international character, soldiers or militias, such as freedom fighters, are considered to be subject to effective command and control.[172] The second relationship (based on authority and control) relates to the relationship between *de facto* military commanders and their *forces*, as well as between political superiors and their *subordinates*. In the ordinary course of events, this refers to political/civilian subordinates subjected to effective authority and control.[173] I would argue that, in matters of authority and control, superior responsibility applies "*mutatis mutandis*" to both *de facto* military commanders and political superiors.[174] Accordingly, to secure a conviction under the Rome Statute, political superiors need not qualify as *de facto* military commanders. For liability to attach, it is sufficient to establish a stricter *mens rea* threshold against the political superiors—namely, negligence (should have known)—rather than the higher standard of intent (consciously disregarded information).[175]

[169] See, generally, Chap. 2.

[170] Rome Statute, Article 28(a) and (b). See also Kortfält 2017; Van der Vyver 2021, pp. 572–573.

[171] Ibid. See also Ambos 2002, p. 856.

[172] See Galand 2020, p. 693.

[173] *Contra* van der Vyver 2021, p. 582; *Prosecutor v. Jean-Pierre Bemba Gombo*, Judgment (8 June 2018), Case No. ICC-01/05-01/08 A, para 413. (Van der Vyver, along with the Pre-Trial Chamber in Bemba's case, concur in equating *de jure* and *de facto* military commanders, noting that the relationship should be based on effective command and control.)

[174] Based on a literal interpretation of the text concerning superior responsibility, Article 28 (a) addresses both *de jure* and *de facto* military commanders. *De jure* military commanders are assigned orders of a military nature. Such an assignment implies a command-and-control relationship, to be exercised effectively. *De facto* military commanders, on the other hand, are individuals who, despite not being assigned a role of, appear to carry out the role of military commanders, and are therefore not assigned military orders. However, because they are not assigned a military position, they instead exercise authority and control, *i.e.*, possessing the material ability to command the execution of and obedience to their orders. In short, while *de jure* military commanders appear to function as military commanders, they also exercise authority and control owing to the fact that they are not assigned military status. See, for example, Sadat 2019, p. 205. See also Pigeau and McCann 2002, pp. 53–63. In any case, this would not affect the application of superior responsibility, as it is simply a linguistic, *obiter dictum* matter.

[175] See Sect. 4.3.1.3. See also van der Vyver 2021, p. 599.

The asymmetrical approach by Rome Statute in the differentiation between *de jure* and *de facto* military commanders may stem from the fact that, within a military institution, *de jure* military commanders were assigned a militant capacity to issue their orders, particularly in relation to orders corresponding to the duty to punish, as opposed to the more *civilized* duty of submitting the matters to the competent authorities. Historically, this text can be linked to the *Yamashita* trials. In this instance, the Commission held that, as a general, Yamashita's *de jure* status over the Japanese military, along with his *de facto authority* over police personnel, established his culpability as a superior, irrespective of his *de jure* status.[176] This *de facto* status of a military commander can apply to a range of police personnel and all branches of the military apparatus.[177] In the *Bemba* case, the Pre-Trial Chamber did not define this relationship; instead, the term "forces" was used to refer to subordinates serving military and military-like superiors.[178] This failure to provide an explicit definition could lead to confusion in the application of superior responsibility, which will be discussed further below. Furthermore, the doctrine of superior responsibility does not require that subordinates be identified within the superior–subordinate relationship.[179] Just as the provision under Article 28 does not specify that subordinates need to be explicitly identified, the jurisprudence also stipulates that it is not necessary to identify subordinates as long as they can be linked to the superior's material ability to control them.[180] Thus, in the analysis of the *Bemba* case provided here, the specificity of subordinates (and their crimes) does not affect the applicability of superior responsibility.

As a guideline, the superior–subordinate could be considered within the context described above: hypothetically, the status of this relationship (command and control *v.* authority and control) determines the relationship between a political leader and their military soldiers (or freedom fighters), and, *vice versa*, between a military commander and their civilian subordinates (*i.e.*, farmers by day, soldiers by night). However, could this hypothetical application of superior responsibility under the Rome Statute differentiate between the two superiors, especially when the fault element in each of the applications is mutually exclusive? Unfortunately, this question has not been addressed either by the Rome Statute or by practitioners. According to Leila Sadat, however, as a result of this potential *lacuna*, it is left to the ICC "to interpret these provisions in light of their object and purpose [*i.e.*, to perhaps teleologically commensurate these instances of control]".[181] This question could also be addressed analytically by considering the status assigned to superiors in the Article. On the one hand, if a political leader takes on the role of a military commander

---

[176] See Chap. 3.

[177] Van der Vyver 2021, p. 573 (n. 34).

[178] *Prosecutor v. Bemba*, para 407.

[179] Cf. *ALOYS SIMBA v. THE PROSECUTOR*, Case No. ICTR-01-76-A, para 70–75, 29 November 2007 (where it is argued that the specific identity of direct perpetrators or subordinates is not required, particularly in the large-scale commission of crimes).

[180] Ibid.

[181] Ibid.

(*i.e.*, a *de facto* military commander), the provision on the criminal responsibility of military commanders (Article 28(a)) alone would apply to them, irrespective of their status or that of their subordinates.[182]

In addition, according to Article 28, the superior–subordinate relationship must be interpreted based on the effectiveness of the command/authority and control. In this context, a superior who lacks the material ability to execute their duties may not be criminally responsible for the crimes committed by their subordinates.[183] Thereby, the prosecutor must adduce evidence beyond a reasonable doubt that the relationship between the accused superior and their subordinates is based on such a material ability—that is, the ability to issue orders, which is also associated with the superior's duty to ensure their subordinates' adherence to and execution of those orders.[184] Such material ability can be interpreted as evidence or *indicia* of the superior's practice of effective command/authority and control over their subordinates.[185] As will be critically analyzed in the context of the AC's judgment in the *Bemba* case below, effective command and control results in duties that are purposefully assigned and therefore must be fulfilled, as ordered by the superior. Failure to enforce these duties (a *chapeau* omission) may result in the superior's criminal responsibility if it is also established that the superior also failed to take all necessary and reasonable measures (narrowed omission).[186]

4.3.1.2 Failure to Execute Supervisory Duties

Under the Rome Statute, the failure to execute supervisory duties is also fundamentally different from the provisions concerning superior responsibility under the *ad hoc* tribunals' statutes. Before examining the failure to take all necessary and reasonable measures to execute these duties, however, it is first necessary to consider the nature of these duties, as set out under the Rome Statute. Customarily, the duty to supervise can be separated into three inextricably interconnected obligations assigned to the superior[187]: (i) the duty to prevent; (ii) the duty to repress; and (iii) the duty to submit

[182] Cf. *Prosecutor v. Bemba*, para 264. (The Trial Chamber held that "the Commander is held responsible with [crimes] committed by forces, or subordinates", indicating that, in this context, the provision of military commander responsibility also applies, from an interpretive perspective, to civilian subordinates.) See also Sadat 2002a, p. 207; *Prosecutor v. Ntaganda*, para 166.

[183] Van der Vyver 2021, pp. 576–577. See also *THE PROSECUTOR v. RASIM DELIĆ* (Decision on Interlocutory Appeal Challenging the Jurisdiction of the Tribunal), Case No. IT-04-83-AR72, para 10, 8 December 2005.

[184] *Prosecutor v. Dario Kordić & Mario Čerkez*, Case No. IT-95-1A-A, para 46, 26 February 2001. See also *Prosecutor v. Tihomir Blaškić*, Case No. IT-95-14-A, para 69, 29 July 2004.

[185] Van der Vyver 2021, pp. 590–591.

[186] Triffterer 2002, p. 193.

[187] *United States of America v. Karl Brandt et el., 2 Trials of War Criminals Before the Nuremberg Military Tribunals Under Control Council Law No. 19* (October 1946–April 1949) (Judgment) 171, p. 207. Washington D.C.: U.S. Gov. Printers (1950–3). See also Chap. 3 on such obligations.

the matter to the competent authorities.[188] The first duty—the duty to prevent—is an obligation entrusted to the superior on account of their predetermined capacity to control their subordinates in the ordinary course of events. It also underscores the importance of their collective responsibilities under international law and the repercussions of violating it (consequentialism).[189] Pragmatically, the duty to prevent can be fulfilled, for instance, through a system designed for monitoring subordinates' activities. For example, to fulfill their duty to monitor their subordinates, a superior could implement, *inter alia*, a remote reporting system that supports their superiority status, especially if they are geographically removed from their subordinates[190] (This is a rebuttal to "remoteness" alibi voiced by the AC judges in the *Bemba* case). Such a monitoring system would need to be sufficiently effective not only to keep track of subordinates' activities but also to serve as a deterrence incentive.[191] Ultimately, the superior's duty to prevent is synonymous with their duty to exercise proper control over subordinates. It follows that if a superior fails to train their subordinates, they also fail to discharge their duties to exercise proper control, assuming that crimes were committed or about to be committed.[192]

The second duty—the duty to repress—is somewhat controversial. It encompasses a superior's duty to halt the commission of crimes while they are being committed or about to be committed, as well as their duty to punish.[193] The third duty—to submit the matter to the competent authorities—is a novel addendum to the doctrine of superior responsibility under the Rome Statute. The second and third duties are not mutually exclusive; as such, in cases in which the superior carried out the first duty but failed to fulfill their duty to repress, they are still required to carry out the third duty—namely, to submit the matter to the competent authorities.[194]

Interestingly, the judges at the ICC are not faced with the challenge of elucidating and examining these duties separately and collectively, as is the case in the *ad hoc* tribunals' adjudication.[195] For example, the duty to submit the matter to the competent

---

[188] *Prosecutor v. Bemba*, para 435. See also van der Vyver 2021, pp. 578–579.

[189] Some *indicia* of proving this duty were drawn from the jurisprudence of the Tribunals, including the following: "Did the superior impose measures to ensure that the forces under his or her authority has been properly trained in humanitarian law; Did he or she make provision for reports showing that military that military actions were carried out in accordance with the laws and customs of international humanitarian law; Did he or she issue orders for bringing for bringing the relevant practices into conformity with the laws and customs of armed conflict; Did he or she take disciplinary action to prevent the commission of the atrocities by troops under his or her effective command and control?" See van der Vyver 2021, pp. 590–591. See also *Protocol Additional to the Geneva Conventions of 12 August 1949, and relating to the Protection of Victims of International Armed Conflicts* (Protocol I), 1125 UNTS 3, adopted 8 June 1977, entered into force 7 December 1978, Article 86.

[190] Fenrick 1999, n. 9.

[191] Ibid.

[192] Van der Vyver 2021, p. 583. See also Chap. 3, Sect. 3.4.2.

[193] Ibid., p. 591. See also *Prosecutor v. Bemba*, para 439; *Prosecutor v. Tihomir Blaškić*, Case No. IT-95-14-T, Trial Judgment, 3 March 2000, para 446 (ICTY).

[194] Ibid., p. 593.

[195] Ibid., p. 591, n. 144.

authorities was not available to the *ad hoc* tribunals; rather, it was established through a teleological interpretation as a corollary parameter of the duty to punish.[196] In this case, the *ad hoc* tribunals' jurisprudence determined that, in cases in which the superior holds a political status, they may sometimes not possess the capacity to punish available within military settings. Alternatively, therefore, they may discharge their duty by submitting the matter to the competent authorities for investigation and potential prosecution.[197] From a normative perspective, the framers of the Rome Statute set out to clarify the controversy surrounding the duties to repress and to submit the matter to the competent authorities. Consequently, the judges of the *ad hoc* tribunals were tasked with identifying the key parameters of this element within the confines of the doctrine of superior responsibility.[198] In doing so, to ensure that the superior's duties were fully discharged, the framers in the case of the Rome Statute explicitly included the duty to submit the matter (*i.e.*, the commission of crimes by subordinates) to the competent authorities for investigation and prosecution, so as to establish the superior's culpability.[199]

Another crucial dimension concerning the execution of these duties arose when a debate developed over the interpretation of the word "or" in Article 28 during the Pre-Trial Chamber Confirmation of Charges trial in the *Bemba* case.[200] The debate concerned whether the word "or" implied that the superior needed to carry out a variety of duties alternatively (*i.e.*, "prevent *or* repress their commission *or* to submit the matter to the competent authorities for investigation and prosecution").[201] Alternatively, there were discussions as to whether "or" should be taken to denote a separate but collective discharge of duties. As noted earlier,[202] historically, the doctrine of superior responsibility constitutes an enactment of customary international law that can be interpreted teleologically through the Second AP to the 1949 Geneva Conventions.[203] With respect to customary interpretations of international law, the superior's duties must not reflect the alternative ideologies that were selected and drafted. Rather, they should reflect "the full range of his or her duties in respect of subordinate criminal conduct".[204] In addition, some analysts have argued that the addition of the word "or" in this provision was intended to address cases where the duty to repress, for example, is unavailable to the superior, in which case, to avoid culpability for significant offenses, the superior is obliged to submit the matter to the

196 Ibid.

197 Ibid.

198 Van Sliedregt 2011, p. 18.

199 Ibid. See also *Prosecutor v. Jean-Pierre Bemba Gombo*, Judgment, 8 June 2018, Case No. ICC-01/05-01/08 A, para 440.

200 *Prosecutor v. Jean-Pierre Bemba Gombo*, Judgment, 8 June 2018, Case No. ICC-01/05-01/08 A, para 435.

201 Ibid.

202 Ibid.

203 See Protocol Additional to the Geneva Conventions of 12 August 1949, and relating to the Protection of Victims of Non-International Armed Conflicts (Protocol II), 1125 UNTS 609, adopted 8 June 1977, entered into force 7 December 1978.

204 *Prosecutor v. Bemba*, para 48.

competent authorities.[205] It is important to note that the unavailability of proof of duties may indicate that the superior was assigned such a role only after the crimes were committed.[206] This subsequent assignment does not imply liability for offenses *ex post facto*, and consequently does not impose on the superior a duty to discharge their duties even if the fault state of mind is later established on their part.[207]

4.3.1.3 The Fault Element

Compared with the provisions of the tribunals, the fault element of superior responsibility under the Rome Statute is also controversial. To trigger the application of superior responsibility, it is necessary to establish that a military (or military-like) commander either knew about the crimes that have been committed or that were about to be committed or, owing to the circumstances, should have known about them.[208] For this to be applied to political superiors, however, it is necessary to establish that the superior, again, either knew, or, "consciously disregarded information which clearly indicated, that his or her subordinates committed or were about to commit crimes".[209] To this end, the fault state of mind required for military (or military-like) commanders could consist of an intentional failure to carry out their duties (where they knew about the crimes, but did nothing to repress or report them), or mere negligence—should have known.[210] For example, to fulfill their duties, a military (or military-like) commander is expected to acquire knowledge of crimes.[211] The fault state of mind required of a political superior is based only on an intentional failure to carry out their duties, despite their knowledge of the crimes (knew or consciously disregarded information about them).[212]

Accordingly, the framers of the Rome Statute imposed a more stringent fault requirement on military (or military-like) commanders, mitigating this requirement in the case of political superiors.[213] As such, securing a conviction against military (or military-like) commanders is viewed as less challenging, because it requires only the establishment of a negligent state of mind, whereas securing a conviction against a political superior requires evidence of the superior's actual knowledge or awareness that their subordinates had committed or were about to commit crimes. To sum up, under Article 28 (a) and (b), the "knew" standard of the *mens rea* in both clauses and

[205] Van der Vyver 2021, pp. 592–593.

[206] Ibid.

[207] Ibid.

[208] Rome Statute, Article 28 (a).

[209] Ibid., Article 28 (b).

[210] Recklessness is also controversial in this context because it may indicate intent. See Ambos 2009, p. 719. See also *Prosecutor v. Tihomir Blaškić*, Case No. IT-95-14-T, para 249, 3 March 2000; Cassese 2002, pp. 905–906; Van der Vyver 2004, pp. 66–67; Saland 1999, p. 206.

[211] Damaško 2001, p. 483.

[212] Van der Vyver 2021, p. 586.

[213] Ibid., p. 599.

consciously disregarded information have a commensurate effect—actual knowledge (intent). The "should-have-known" standard of the *mens rea* element set out in Article 28(a) simply indicates a military (or military-like) commander's duty, as part of their duty to prevent, to acquire knowledge, through a recognition of *indicia* relating to their subordinates' behavior, indicating that they either committed or were about to commit the crimes—that is, constructive knowledge.[214]

The fault element of superior responsibility is not to be confused either with the nature of the crimes or with the intent behind the subordinates' criminal acts, because a superior is removed (but informed) from the scene of the crimes. Rather, it must be assessed within the confines of its description in Article 28.[215] Some analysts have argued that, when securing a conviction against a superior under the doctrine of superior responsibility, the cognitive aspect in Article 30[216] and the *mens rea* embedded in Article 28 of the Rome Statute should be read in conjunction with one another.[217] They argue that, to secure a conviction against a superior, the latter must have obtained knowledge about the intent behind the crimes committed by their subordinates.[218] For example, in the event that subordinates have committed the offense of rape, the prosecutor must present evidence that the superior either intended to facilitate this act or was aware of the conduct in a way that associates them with their subordinates.[219]

Additionally, they argue that, within the context of Article 30, for crimes that require intent, convicting a military commander based on a negligent state of mind (should have known) undermines the principle of culpability.[220] Thus, Article 28 (pertaining to superior responsibility) and Article 30 (concerning the mental element of the subject-matter core crimes) must be assessed together. In my view, this interpretation is untenable, given that Article 30 of the Rome Statute explicitly states, "unless otherwise provided",[221] thereby allowing for the possibility that other provisions—such as Article 28—may establish distinct mental element standards. This indicates then that, if any Article in the Rome Statute includes a concomitant *mens rea*

---

214 Ibid., p. 588.

215 Badar and Porro 2017, p. 279. See also Sadat 2002a, p. 208; *Prosecutor v. Bemba*, para 479; Werle and Jessberger 2005, pp. 47–48.

216 Rome Statute, Article 30. Article 30 reads: "1. Unless otherwise provided, a person shall be criminally responsible and liable for punishment for a crime within the jurisdiction of the Court only if the material elements are committed with intent and knowledge. 2. For the purposes of this article, a person has intent where: (a) In relation to conduct, that person means to engage in the conduct; (b) In relation to a consequence, that person means to cause that consequence or is aware that it will occur in the ordinary course of events. 3. For the purposes of this article, 'knowledge' means awareness that a circumstance exists, or a consequence will occur in the ordinary course of events. 'Know' and 'knowingly' shall be construed accordingly."

217 Sadat 2002a, p. 207.

218 Van Sliedregt 2011, p. 20.

219 Ibid. See also Howard 1972, p. 20; Schabas 1998, p. 417.

220 Ibid.

221 Rome Statute, Article 30.

element, as does Article 28, then the subject-matter of Article 30 does not apply.[222] This argument—wherein the subject-matter of Articles 28 and 30 are equated in terms of proving the fault element of superior responsibility—is inaccurate and should not necessarily be accepted.

In addition to fulfilling other elements, Article 28 explicitly requires that a military (or military-like) commander knew or should have known, or that a political superior knew or consciously disregarded information about the crimes in question, and failed to execute their duties, irrespective of the nature of the crimes.[223] Thus, Article 28 does not require the specific identification of the crimes, and the intent to commit them is not, *a fortiori*, required. Therefore, the fault element of superior responsibility must be established within the confines of the superior's failure to execute their duties, not based on the specific nature of the crimes committed by their subordinates.

4.3.1.4 Causation Is (Not) an Element of Superior Responsibility

Causation is a highly contentious issue in ICL scholarship, perhaps overly so.[224] Causation, within the specific context of Article 28, refers to the existence of a provable link between the crimes committed by the subordinates and the superior's failure to exercise proper control over them.[225] Although causation is clearly set out under Article 28, using the wording "as a result of", in terms of practical applications, it must not be taken as a core constituent requirement of superior responsibility *vis-à-vis* the superior–subordinate relationship, fault, and failure to act elements.[226] From a certain vantage point, causation may be viewed as a putative condition—incorporated not as a strict legal requirement, but rather to inform the theoretical understanding of superior responsibility. Whether one interprets the superior's liability as stemming from their failure to prevent crimes, or as causally linked to the crimes committed by subordinates, the doctrine remains a distinct mode of liability in its own right (*conditio sine qua non*).[227]

The majority of academic literature, however, maintains that causation is required to prove that crimes committed by subordinates are the result of the superior's failure to discharge all of their duties (*i.e.*, the duty to prevent, repress, and/or submit the matter to the competent authorities).[228] However, a minority of scholars question

---

222 Ibid.

223 *Prosecutor v. Bemba*, para 494.

224 *Prosecutor v. Jean-Pierre Bemba Gombo*, Case No. ICC-01/05-01/08-3636-Anx3 (Concurring Separate Opinion of Judge Eboe-Osuji), para 156, 8 June 2018.

225 Van der Vyver 2021, pp. 583–584. See also *Prosecutor v. Bemba*, para 423; Triffterer 2002, p. 197.

226 *Prosecutor v. Dario Kordić & Mario Čerkez*, para 830–832; *Prosecutor v. Tihomir BLAŠKIĆ*, para 77. (According to the Tribunals' jurisprudence, causation is not an element, and, thus, not a constituent requirement.)

227 *Cf.* van der Vyver 2021 p. 583 (asserting that "[l]iability for an omission presupposes a duty to act).

228 Ibid., p. 584.

whether a link must be established between the crimes committed and one or more of the duties listed under Article 28, relying on interpretative tools to support their reading of the provision, as this chapter did.[229] For example, Jackson, in his paper contesting Judge Ozaki's position, rightly concludes that the VCLT applies as an interpretive tool.[230] However, although his interpretive approach closely mirrors that taken in this chapter, he—like Judge Ozaki—appears to suggest that Article 22 of the Rome Statute is available for resolving textual ambiguities. This overlooks the fact that Article 22 pertains exclusively to the interpretation of crimes and their definitions, not to provisions on modes of liability.

Van der Vyver suggested a compromise here, arguing that causation should need to be established only in accordance with the superior's failure to execute their duty to prevent, because the duty to repress or to submit the matter to the competent authorities does not require a causal link to crimes already committed by their subordinates.[231] This proposal coincides with the wording of Article 28, which renders commanders or superiors liable for crimes committed by their subordinates as a result of their "failure to exercise control" over the subordinate perpetrator, which clearly means that the "negligence of duty by the person in authority must precede the commission of the crimes."[232] For example, the duty to prevent usually sets before the commission of the crimes by means of training and monitoring. Requiring a causal link between a superior's failure to exercise proper control toward the duty to prevent—such as through training and monitoring—and the commission of crimes is legally sound. However, requiring a causal link between the superior's failure to punish or to submit the matter to the competent authorities after the crimes have been committed would render the requirement superfluous, as the crimes have already occurred and such *post-facto* actions would neither prevent nor decisively influence the outcome.

4.3.2 Critical Analysis of the AC's Judgment in the Bemba *Case*

The facts of the *Bemba* case were, arguably, not adequately presented before the ICC. Indeed, had the historical facts concerning Bemba's caliber been presented before the ICC, it could have changed the course of his acquittal.[233]

Bemba was the founder and president of the *Movement for the Liberation of the Congo* (MLC) and the Commander-in-Chief of its military wing, the *Armée de Libération du Congo* (ALC).[234] This Ugandan-backed party operated from the

[229] Ibid., p. 585.

[230] Jackson 2022, pp. 450–451.

[231] Ibid.

[232] Ibid. See also *Prosecutor v. Bemba*, para 424.

[233] See, generally, Stearns 2011, Chap. 15.

[234] Ibid. See also van der Vyver 2021, p. 241.

northwest region of the Democratic Republic of the Congo (DRC) and supported the government of Ange-Félix Patassé during the conflict in the Central African Republic (CAR).[235] Patassé was then the sitting president of the CAR. Bemba controlled significant parts of the DRC and was linked to routes used for military operations and alleged looting in the CAR.[236] During this intervention, armed conflict between African militias and the ALC led to the commission of war crimes and crimes against humanity against civilian populations.[237] During this period, the UN and regional actors, including South Africa, facilitated peace initiatives—namely, the *Pretoria and Sun City Agreements*—which were eventually undermined by continued hostilities involving Bemba's forces.[238]

Although serving as a senator in the DRC at the time of his arrest, Bemba was not in Patassé's government.[239] He was arrested in Belgium in response to an ICC arrest warrant[240] issued following the CAR's self-referral of the situation in 2004.[241] The ALC comprised approximately 20,000 soldiers, including many mid-level commanders who served as direct intermediaries to Bemba.[242] He equipped the ALC with modern communication technologies, including Thuraya satellite phones, before deploying his forces.[243] It is also important to note that Bemba visited his troops sporadically and maintained operational involvement—physically or through communication—throughout their deployment in the CAR.[244]

Drawing on its jurisdiction over the CAR, the ICC initiated a lengthy trial against Bemba, involving both the Pre-Trial and Trial Chambers. After hearing testimonies from more than 77 witnesses and assessing 733 items of evidence, both chambers found Bemba guilty pursuant to Article 28 (superior responsibility).[245] He was charged with war crimes and crimes against humanity of murder, pillaging, and sexual violence committed by his troops during the period of 26 October 2002, to 15 March 2003. He was sentenced to 18 years' imprisonment.[246]

On 4 April 2016, Bemba and his defense team filed an appeal with the AC. Their case was based on six grounds for appeal, in accordance with Article 82 of the Rome Statute (the Standard of Appeals Review), which allows the AC to reconsider a trial

[235] See Taulbee 2018, pp. 362–363.

[236] Ibid., p. 361.

[237] Ibid. see also *Prosecutor v. Jean-Pierre Bemba Gombo*, Judgment, 8 June 2018, Case No. ICC-01/05-01/08 A, para 72.

[238] Taulbee 2018, p. 362.

[239] Ibid.

[240] Van der Vyver 2021, p. 240.

[241] Ibid.

[242] Taulbee 2018, p. 363.

[243] Ibid. See also Hibbert 2019, p. 99.

[244] Ibid. See also Sadat 2019, p. 358.

[245] *Prosecutor v. Bemba*, 205.

[246] Ibid.

judgment based primarily on an error of law.[247] In narrower circumstances, such a reconsideration also extends to errors of fact that materially affected the fairness of the trial, namely, "misappreciated…facts", the taking into account of "irrelevant facts", or the failure "to take into account relevant facts".[248] In any case, the grounds for appeal put forward by Bemba's team were: (i) mistrial; (ii) conviction exceeding the charges; (iii) nonliability under superior responsibility; (iv) failure to establish the contextual elements of the crimes; (v) laconic identification of evidence; and (vi) other procedural errors that invalidated the conviction.[249]

On 8 June 2018, the AC reversed the Trial judgment, criticizing its reasoning as "tainted with errors of [law]".[250] Surprisingly, however, the AC's acquittal judgment focused primarily on *purported* errors of fact.[251] This judgment was warranted by three concurring judges (hereafter referred to as the majority): Judges Christine van den Wyngaert, Howard Morrison, and Chile Eboe-Osuji (who, despite holding a separate view, concurred with the outcome).[252] By contrast, the remaining two judges—Judges Sanji Mmasenono Monageng and Piotr Hofmański—dissented, expressing a separate opinion. In brief, the reasoning behind the majority's acquittal was based on the following errors, which will be analyzed in detail:

(i) The Trial Chamber erred by failing to properly appreciate the limitations that Mr. Bemba would have faced in investigating and prosecuting crimes as a remote commander sending troops to a foreign country;
(ii) The Trial Chamber erred by failing to address Mr. Bemba's argument that he sent a letter to the CAR authorities before concluding that Mr. Bemba had not referred allegations of crimes to the CAR authorities for investigation;
(iii) The Trial Chamber erred in considering that the motivations that it attributed to Mr. Bemba were indicative of a lack of genuineness in adopting measures to prevent and repress the commission of crimes;
(iv) The Trial Chamber erred in attributing to Mr. Bemba any limitations it found in the mandate, execution, and/or results of the measures taken;
(v) The Trial Chamber erred in finding that Mr. Bemba failed to empower other MLC officials to fully and adequately investigate and prosecute crimes;

---

247 *See Prosecutor v. Simone Gbagbo*, Case No. ICC-02/11-01/12-75-Red (OA) Judgment on the appeal of Côte d'Ivoire against the decision of Pre-Trial Chamber I (Decision on Côte d'Ivoire's challenge to the admissibility of the case against Simone Gbagbo), para 40, 27 May 2015.

248 Ibid., para 38. See also *Prosecutor v. Mathieu Ngudjolo Chui*, Case No. ICC-01/04-02/12-271 (A), (Judgment pursuant to Article 74 of the Statute", para 22, 27 February 2015; *Prosecutor v. Germain Katanga & Mathieu Ngudjolo Chui*, Case No. ICC-01/04-01/07-572 (OA4) (Judgment in the Appeal by Mathieu Ngudjolo Chui of 27 March 2008 against the Decision of Pre-Trial Chamber I on the Application of the Appellant for Interim Release), para 25, 9 June 2008.

249 *Prosecutor v. Bemba*, para 29.

250 Ibid., para 166.

251 Ibid., para 189.

252 Ibid., para 1. See also van der Vyver 2021, p. 567.

(vi) The Trial Chamber erred in failing to give any indication of the approximate number of crimes committed and to assess the impact of this on the determination of whether Mr. Bemba took all necessary and reasonable measures; and

(vii) The Trial Chamber erred by taking into account the redeployment of MLC troops, for example, to avoid contact with the civilian population as a measure available to Mr. Bemba.[253]

In my view, the central question arising from this judgment is whether a finding on superior responsibility can rest solely on an assessment of a single element of the doctrine—*i.e.*, whether *all necessary and reasonable measures* were taken. The short answer is that it cannot. As demonstrated above, all exculpatory findings revolve around this element and whether the measures taken were sufficient. However, it is important to note that the doctrine of superior responsibility is structured as a cumulative chain of elements. These elements are interdependent and cannot be selectively applied to justify acquittal. This also applies to the fact that those findings do not, as a matter of law, satisfy the requirement of all necessary and reasonable measures, as they fail to reflect the full scope of duties imposed on the superior—namely, the duty to prevent, the duty to repress or punish, and the duty to submit the matter to the competent authorities. Accordingly, the outcome of this judgment appears misaligned with the doctrinal integrity of superior responsibility as recognized in international criminal law.

Nevertheless, just as the court is obliged to examine all the elements, so too is the prosecutor obliged to examine all elements of superior responsibility to secure a conviction against an accused superior (as was the case here).[254] Accordingly, the prosecutor in this case issued the following statement following the acquittal judgment:

> It is clear that serious crimes were committed in the Central African Republic ("CAR") by Mr. Bemba's forces. My first thoughts are with the victims of those terrible crimes, their families and communities. Last Friday's judgement indeed confirms that Mr. Bemba's troops committed grave crimes, which resulted in great suffering in the CAR. The carnage and suffering caused by those crimes were very real. My Office has been in touch with the Legal Representative of Victims in the case, and we join her in her disappointment over this decision and its impact, first and foremost, on the victims…[t]he level of detail that the Prosecution may now be required to include in the charges may render it difficult to prosecute future cases entailing extensive campaigns of victimisation, especially where the accused is not a direct perpetrator, but a commander remote from the scene of the alleged crimes but who may bear criminal responsibility as the superior having effective control.[255]

Such a statement should raise concerns among the international community about the efficiency of the ICC, which is designed to serve as a sanctuary for victims of international crimes (which were indisputably committed by Bemba's troops).[256]

[253] Ibid., para 189.

[254] See van der Vyver 2021, p. 567.

[255] Statement of the ICC Prosecutor.

[256] Van der Vyver 2021, p. 567. See also Hibbert 2019, p. 97.

At the outset, it is essential to point out that a verdict reached by a court of law comprises, *a priori*, two lines of reasoning: *ratio decidendi* and *obiter dicta*.[257] *Ratio decidendi* concerns the judges' duty to address the facts in their decisions, which must be based on the applicable law, whereas *obiter dicta* is defined as "such a statement of legal principle which goes beyond what was necessary for the disposal of the case".[258] Accordingly, in the Bemba AC judgment, as noted earlier, the majority relied heavily on the duty to take all necessary and reasonable measures as an exonerating element of the judgment (*ratio decidendi*), considering the other requirements as *obiter dicta*, although they should be viewed as *ratio decidendi*.[259] The conceptual elements were therefore entirely marginalized at the Appeals level. As already noted, to fully satisfy the *ratio decidendi* aspect of a superior responsibility decision and to determine the applicability of the doctrine to the accused, the essential elements of the doctrine of superior responsibility must all be examined in full.

As the reasoning put forward by the majority pivoted chiefly around the *all necessary and reasonable measures* element of superior responsibility, it extended this element to fit multifaceted novel dimensions, which were viewed as integral parts of the element.[260] The reasoning of the majority was filled with factual endorsements that appeared to stem from a fallacy geared at absolving Bemba of his failure to take all necessary and reasonable measures.[261] To this end, the majority decided that a superior's geographical remoteness could impose an obstacle to ensuring proper supervision of their subordinates, which impedes their duty to take all necessary and reasonable measures to prevent, punish, and submit the matter to the competent authorities for investigation and prosecution.[262] As such, in this case, the all necessary and reasonable measures element of superior responsibility is not satisfied. Constituting a novel approach to this element, this interpretation is inconsistent with the Rome Statute and existing jurisprudence and is, therefore, inaccurate.[263] At its core, this doctrine hinges on the fact that, in the ordinary course of events, a superior is physically distant from the scene of the crimes.[264] Conversely, if a superior's physical presence at the crime scene were proven, this position would, in principle, subject them to liability on the grounds of direct (co)perpetration.[265]

---

[257] For a thorough discussion on these two elements of a judgment, see *Prosecutor v. Alekosvski*, para 113. See also *Prosecutor v. Milan Milutinovic el.*, Case No. IT -99-37-AR72 (SEPARATE OPINION OF JUDGE DAVID HUNT ON CHALLENGE BY OJDANIC TO JURISDICTION JOINT CRIMINAL ENTERPRISE), para 3, 21 May 2003.

[258] *Prosecutor v. Milan Milutinovic.*

[259] Robinson 2020, p. 258.

[260] Ibid.

[261] Ibid.

[262] *Prosecutor v. Bemba*, para 191.

[263] Powderly 2018, p. 1033.

[264] *Prosecutor v. Delalić & Others*, paras 377–378.

[265] Van der Vyver 2021, pp. 568–569. See also *Prosecutor v. Tihomir Blaškić*, para 337.

The rationale underpinning the *ad hoc* tribunals' jurisprudence refutes such an outcome, establishing that remoteness is to be taken into account only when determining the fault element of superior responsibility (*mens rea*), not the *all necessary and reasonable measures* element.[266] Thus, any means of communication would negate the suggestion that a superior's physical remoteness imposes an obstacle that hinders them from carrying out all necessary and reasonable measures. What is more, Bemba was in fact connected to his troops by means of modern communication equipment. In addition, it was evident that he made sporadic visits to the location of his troops.[267] Further—and perhaps more importantly—Bemba was a military commander, not a political superior. This distinction undermines any argument based on remoteness, which might have held more weight had he been a political superior.

The majority held that the Trial Chamber had erred in its consideration of Bemba's letter to the UN requesting that the crimes be investigated; according to their reasoning, this exonerated him by demonstrating that he had fulfilled his duties to prevent, punish, and submit the matter to the competent authorities.[268] I would argue that this reasoning is inaccurate and deviates from the jurisprudence concerning superior responsibility. First, Bemba sent this letter two months after his troops committed the crimes. And second, the fact that he sent the letter does not demonstrate that he fulfilled his duty to prevent future crimes or submit the matter to the competent authorities. As noted earlier, these duties—that is, the duties to prevent, repress, and submit the matter to the competent authorities—need to be fulfilled in conjunction with one another. In this case, Bemba failed to do so. Moreover, sending a letter to the competent authorities two months after these atrocious crimes had been committed by his troops does not cancel out his duty to prevent future crimes, particularly as the crimes continued to be committed. Assuming that he had already complied with the other aforementioned duties, this letter should have been sent promptly after his troops committed the crimes.[269]

The majority held that the prosecutor failed to adequately define the scope of the crimes committed by Bemba's troops, which obstructed their assessment of whether he carried out his duty to take all necessary and reasonable measures.[270] However, this assertion must be approached with care and requires further consideration. It is essential to reiterate that even if some of the crimes could not be identified, that does not, as a matter of law and justice, result in complete exoneration based on the absence of individualized crimes.[271] Leila Sadat has presented a thought-provoking

[266] Cf. *Prosecutor v. Delalić & Others*, para 373. (The defendant argues remoteness only in relation to his lack of knowledge of the crimes committed by his subordinates.) See also Van Sliedregt 2011, p. 27; Aloys *NTABAKUZE v. THE PROSECUTOR*, Case No. ICTR-98-41A-0012/1, paras 199–200, 8 May 2012.

[267] Hibbert 2019, p. 97. See also Taulbee 2018, p. 363.

[268] *Prosecutor v. Bemba*, paras 174–175.

[269] See van der Vyver 2021, p. 592.

[270] *Prosecutor v. Bemba*, para 184.

[271] See, generally, Peniguet, *CPI: Jean-Pierre Bemba, chronique d'un acquittement surprise*, DALLOZ, ACTUALITÉ, 22 June 2018.

perspective in this regard, maintaining that the specificity of international crimes is "jurisdictional in nature".[272] On this point, Sadat argues that, according to the Rome Statute, the prosecutor is required only to present proof beyond reasonable doubt that the crimes concerned form part of a *course of conduct* (*e.g.*, war crimes and crimes against humanity).[273] Accordingly, establishing such a course of conduct is "not an invitation to the judges to require that every subsidiary act giving rise to the finding of the 'course of conduct' be *independently* established beyond a reasonable doubt"[274] (emphasis added). Elaborating on this point, she offers the following example:

> If a defendant is accused of dispatching a train carrying civilians and deporting them to a concentration camp, that would represent a "course of conduct" involving the multiple commission of 'acts' establishing one of the context elements; it would be impossible to establish each individual act of deportation in most situations, nor does the case law require the prosecutor to do so. Indeed, given the practical reality of mass atrocity prosecutions, it is unsurprising that the ad hoc tribunals have not adopted the Separate Opinion's interpretation of Article 7(2)(a), which seems grounded in neither the text of the Statute nor customary international law.[275]

Sadat's "course of conduct" argument has previously been relied on by Mark Ellis in his review of the *Milošević* case.[276] In his assessment, Ellis asserts that the identification of a consistent pattern of conduct constitutes sufficient evidence of Milošević's responsibility under superior responsibility.[277]

I believe that Sadat's and Ellis's perspectives are sound and fully in line both with prosecutions in ICL in general and with the specific wording used to define superior responsibility under the Rome Statute in particular. By means of analogy, according to the *ad hoc* tribunals' jurisprudence, the specific identification of subordinates does not affect the criminal liability of their superior.[278] *A fortiori*, it follows that it is not necessary to prove the extent of the crimes individually, provided that it is evident which war crimes and crimes against humanity were committed. An interpretation of the text concerning superior responsibility set out in the Rome Statute highlights the absence of a definite article (*the* crimes). Rather, to trigger the doctrine of superior responsibility, the text merely requires that "crimes" were committed or about to be committed.[279] Based on the reasoning of the majority, Article 28 is to be understood as a double-edged sword: needlessly raising the burden of proof required for the prosecutor to identify the crimes, and allowing criminal acts under superior responsibility to go unpunished if they were not specifically identified.[280]

---

[272] Sadat 2019, p. 358. See also Sadat 2002a, pp. 146–148.

[273] Ibid.

[274] Sadat 2019, p. 359.

[275] Ibid.

[276] Ellis 1999, Non-Negotiable; War Criminals Belong in the Dock, Not at the Table, WASH. POST, p. B I.

[277] Ibid.

[278] *SIMBA v. THE PROSECUTOR*, paras 70–75.

[279] Rome Statute, Article 28.

[280] Powderly 2018, pp. 1032–1033. See also SáCouto and Viseur Sellers 2019, p. 612.

In addition, the majority held that probing the all necessary and reasonable measures element is contingent upon "considerations of what crimes the commander knew or should have known about and at what point in time".[281] Hypothetically, if, to secure a conviction against a military (or military-like) commander, it were necessary to identify the kinds of crimes committed and at what point in time, it follows that it would be necessary to establish the fault element of these crimes. Conversely, under Article 28 (concerning intent, or negligence), the doctrine of superior responsibility demands only the fault element embodied in that Article.[282] In this sense, if establishing the fault element of these crimes is required to support the majority's reasoning—which requires the identification of the crimes within a specific timeframe—this requirement may redirect the conviction from one based on superior responsibility to one based on complicity, where the superior partakes in the crimes as an accessory, alongside the subordinates.[283]

Another counterargument to the identification of crimes is that specifying the kinds of crimes also entails identifying the criminals as well as the victims. For the latter, this could place them at risk through the disclosure of their identities.[284] In this sense, the majority must have relied on the fact that the crimes were committed as a result of Bemba's failure to execute his duties, rather than on "the focus of Article 28 of the [Rome] Statute, namely holding a commander responsible for his failures and not for his actions".[285] Moreover, the crimes committed by Bemba's troops should not be assessed from the perspective of convictions or acquittals under the doctrine of superior responsibility, but rather on the basis of whether Bemba executed his duties to prevent and repress these crimes and to submit the matter to the competent authorities. The former approach to such an assessment may be relevant only in the case of a domestic conviction, which could hinge on Bemba's failure to fulfill his duty to supervise (constituting omission). In such cases, to secure a domestic conviction based on omission *per se*, crimes committed as a result of such a failure on Bemba's part must be assessed independently.[286] However, under the doctrine of superior responsibility, a superior is held liable for crimes committed by his troops and their overall nature, *e.g.*, war crimes involving murder, crimes against humanity, rape, and pillaging, etc. Lastly, the fact that international crimes are committed as part of a wide-scale, systematic pattern distinguishes them from domestic offenses, potentially rendering the specific identification of the subordinates or their crimes impossible to achieve.

Therefore, the factor triggering this element lies in the absence of the full range of measures that Bemba should have taken, as he himself testified.[287] It appears

---

[281] *Prosecutor v. Bemba*, para 168.

[282] Van der Vyver 2021, p. 598.

[283] Triffterer 2002, pp. 187, 195.

[284] Vetter, Command Responsibility of Non-Military Superiors in the International Criminal Court (ICC), p. 140. See also Robinson 2008, pp. 936–937.

[285] *Prosecutor v. Bemba*, para 45.

[286] Van der Vyver 2021, p. 598.

[287] *Prosecutor v. Bemba*, para 48.

surprising that the majority took a *lenient* view when establishing whether the accused superior had taken all necessary and reasonable measures, while imposing a *strict* approach by demanding that the prosecutor present numerical, independent proof of the crimes committed by the superior. Pursuant to the Rome Statute, the majority could have ordered a retrial to address the new accusations instead of dismissing the application for additional evidence.[288]

Another peculiar aspect of their reasoning is their view that Bemba's motivation to protect the image of his troops does not mean that he failed to discharge his duty to take all necessary and reasonable measures.[289] While motivation is not a constituent part of the mental element requirement that must be met,[290] it is not excluded entirely when establishing a superior's liability under the doctrine of superior responsibility.[291] In this sense, van der Vyver has argued that while a superior is required to execute his or her duties genuinely, their motivations to execute such duties "could signify a particular mental disposition on his or her part".[292] When it comes to the case in question here, Bemba testified that he was motivated by the desire to protect the image of his troops, which is not a prosecutable offense.[293]

The majority pointed out, by means of *obiter dictum*, that a superior responsibility case must be established solely on the provision of evidence beyond reasonable doubt, satisfying all elements of the doctrine.[294] In principle, it is true that—at both the domestic and international levels—a conviction must be secured based on evidence beyond a reasonable doubt. However, there are certain exceptions to the subject-matter of this principle with respect to the doctrine of superior responsibility. Although ICL does not exclude the use of circumstantial evidence by prosecutors to secure a conviction, this evidence must be the only evidence available to the prosecutor.[295] As far as superior responsibility is concerned, circumstantial evidence may be presented in relation to the fault element of the superior, which may be satisfied through the provision of *indicia* that the superior had knowledge of the crimes committed by their subordinates.[296] For example, given that superior responsibility under the Rome Statute constitutes a *sui generis* mode of liability, circumstantial evidence indicating that the superior knew about the commission of the crimes based

[288] Sadat 2019, p. 360.

[289] *Prosecutor v. Bemba*, para 179.

[290] Van der Vyver 2021, p. 589.

[291] Ibid.

[292] Ibid.

[293] *Prosecutor v. Jean-Pierre Bemba Gombo*, Case No. ICC-01/05-01/08-3472-Corr-Red, Public Redacted Version of "Corrected Version of 'Prosecution's Response to Appellant's Document in Support of Appeal'", para 213, 19 January 2017.

[294] *Prosecutor v. Bemba*, para 3.

[295] *Prosecutor v. ANDRE NTAGERURA e al.*, Case No. ICTR-99-46-A, para 306 (Jul. 7, 2006).

[296] *Prosecutor v. Bemba*, paras 431, 489. See also, *Prosecutor v. Fatmir Limaj & others*, Case No. IT-03-66-T, para 524 (Nov. 30, 2005); *Prosecutor v. Naser Orić*, Case No. IT-03-68-T, para 319 (Jun. 30, 2006); *Prosecutor v. Rasim Delić*, Case No. IT-04-83-T, para 64, 15 September 2008).

on their widespread occurrence could be accepted as evidence of the accused's state of mind.[297]

The majority also referred to the doctrine of superior responsibility as a non-strict mode of liability, where, according to Cherif Bassiouni, non-strictness is to be understood as "responsibility without intent".[298] Although the cornerstone case of superior responsibility (the *Čelebići* case) endorsed the view that the doctrine is "not a form of strict liability",[299] a historical examination and rational analysis of vicarious liability—as set out in this book—suggests the opposite. This analysis may find its origin in the provision on superior responsibility set out in the statutes of the *ad hoc* tribunals, where the fault element requires intent (knew/had reason to know).[300] However, the Rome Statute of the ICC opposes such a conclusion.[301] To clarify, under Article 28, the fault element of superior responsibility indicates that superiors may be charged for crimes under this mode of liability even in the absence of their knowledge, employing the standard of "should have known".[302] Notably, as opposed to the state-of-mind requirements imposed on political superiors, this form of fault is unjustly imputed to military commanders and persons acting in that capacity.[303]

While I would argue that it is illogical to purport that a superior lacks material control over the institutional setting of their own troops,[304] the majority held, conversely, that "a commander is [not] required to employ every single conceivable measure within his or her arsenal, irrespective of considerations of proportionality and feasibility."[305] As a matter of both theoretical and practical importance, the doctrine of superior responsibility contains no corroborated basis for arguing for a minimum standard of duty on the part of superiors to take *limited* necessary and reasonable measures. This suggests that a superior may fail to carry out their full range of duties while protecting their own risky position. The wording of Article 28 concerning this reasoning is self-explanatory, setting out that a superior is required to take *all* necessary and reasonable measures. This contrasts with the wording used to describe superior responsibility in the *ad hoc* tribunals' Articles, where such argument could align. The actions for which Bemba was acquitted involved vouching for the image of his troops, irrespective of the crimes that were evidently committed and tolerated by him. This certainly falls short of the requirement to take all necessary

---

297 Van der Vyver 2021, p. 588.

298 Bassiouni 2011, p. 516.

299 *Prosecutor v. Zdravko Mucić aka "Pavo", Hazim Delić, Esad Landžo aka "Zenga", and Zejnil Delalić*, Case No. IT-96-21-A, Appeal Judgment, 20 February 2001, para 239 (ICTY).

300 ICTY Statute, Article 7(3); ICTR Statute, Article 6(3).

301 Ambos 1999a, p. 19.

302 Ibid.

303 Ibid. I discuss this issue in Chap. 5.

304 Sadat 2019, p. 358.

305 *Prosecutor v. Bemba*, para 169.

and reasonable measures. Ultimately, a superior must take all necessary and reasonable measures with a view to preventing and repressing crimes; it is not sufficient to demonstrate that the superior did not initiate the crimes.[306]

Another divergent aspect of the reasoning can be found in the separate opinion voiced by Judge Eboe-Osuji, who argued that superior responsibility is incompatible with vicarious liability under Article 28 of the Rome Statute. Rather, he conceptualized superior responsibility as a mode of complicity whereby the superior partakes in the commission of the crimes committed by their subordinates.[307] It follows that, to accuse a superior under superior responsibility, the prosecutor must put forward an accusation based on Article 25 of the Rome Statute.[308] This reasoning, which establishes a connection between complicity and vicarious liability, may result in unjust prosecutions. For example, if Bemba were to be characterized as an accomplice, he would be liable only for the crimes in which he played an accessorial role. Conversely, owing to the absence of any accessorial role on his part, other crimes that were supposed to be imputed to Bemba vicariously would not result in his criminal liability.[309] Paradoxically, in the *Yekatom* case, the Pre-Trial Chamber held that "the narrative of the relevant events as emerging from the available evidence is such that Yekatom's conduct resulted in the realization of the objective elements of the crimes, rather than only consisting in the mere failure to prevent or repress crimes committed by other persons."[310] The Chamber thus framed his responsibility under Article 25, effectively distancing the case from Article 28. The case could thus be seen as a rejection of the normative position advanced by Judge Eboe-Osuji and Jackson.[311] However, this interpretation is problematic. When a superior is actively involved in the criminal conduct of their subordinates, such involvement does not negate—but rather coexists with—liability under Article 28. A superior can be both a direct perpetrator and an accomplice (under Article 25) and concurrently liable under Article 28 for failing to prevent or punish the broader pattern of crimes committed by subordinates.[312] The Chamber's rigid separation overlooks this duality and risks narrowing the scope of superior responsibility unjustifiably.

The final critical analysis of the majority's decision concerns the criminal procedure and evidentiary *lacuna* of the acquittal.[313] Most of the documented evidence presented by the prosecutor was challenged at the AC as hearsay evidence, which is

---

[306] Van der Vyver 2021, p. 593. See also *Prosecutor v. Bemba*, para 436; *Prosecutor v. Tihomir Blaškić*, para 336; *Prosecutor v. Dario Kordić & Mario Čerkez*, para 444.

[307] *Prosecutor v. Bemba*, para 198.

[308] Rome Statute, Article 25(b).

[309] Triffterer 2002, pp. 187, 195.

[310] International Criminal Court, 11 December 2019. *Decision on the confirmation of charges against Alfred Yekatom and Patrice-Edouard Ngaïssona* (ICC-01/14-01/18-403-Conf-Corr). Pre-Trial Chamber II, para 58.

[311] Jackson 2022.

[312] Bradfield 2020. Alternative charges and modes of liability in the latest CAR case at the ICC – Trouble ahead? EJIL: Talk! https://www.ejiltalk.org/alternative-charges-and-modes-of-liability-in-the-latest-car-case-at-the-icc-trouble-ahead/. Accessed 16 June 2025.

[313] *Prosecutor v. Bemba*, para 183.

considered of low value.[314] However, the admissibility of hearsay evidence "is not automatically excluded in international criminal law". Rather, "it is for the Prosecution to prove its relevance and probative value".[315] Accordingly, a complete acquittal based on the judges' discretionary decision regarding the indirect nature of hearsay evidence is legally questionable and adds to the surprising nature of this acquittal. As a matter of principle, the fact that hearsay evidence is indirect does not minimize its probative value and relevant weight.[316] Furthermore, the AC is not tasked with evaluating evidence to determine its value. It is the responsibility of the Trial Chamber's to assess and evaluate such evidence, on account of its authority to do so and its direct contact with witnesses.[317] Nevertheless, the AC did not assess the value of the hearsay evidence; it was simply discarded as such.[318]

In my view, as well as in that of Amann, the majority may have overlooked their interpretative duty to delineate the specific measures a superior must undertake to fulfill their obligation to take all necessary and reasonable steps—a gap in reasoning that, if addressed, could have clarified the practical contours of the doctrine.[319] Applying a consequentialist approach, the judges could have articulated an illustrative—if not exhaustive—list of such measures, including issuing clear and lawful orders, removing implicated subordinates, initiating prompt investigations, reporting crimes to competent authorities, deploying monitoring mechanisms, restricting troop movements, and limiting access to weapons where foreseeable risks arise. The *ad hoc* tribunals' jurisprudence, by contrast, offers a more diligent example of *a superior's execution of necessary and reasonable measures*.[320] It would therefore have been a legally constructive endeavor to try to define, and possibly restrict, these measures for future reference. On the strength of their position as lawmakers, the majority could have established an *in concreto* baseline for what measures the superior should have taken to execute their duties. Instead, they simply denounced the Trial Chamber's allegation for undertaking a task that essentially falls to the Appeal Chamber—a court of law.

In conclusion, the majority judgment raised controversial issues regarding the role of the AC acting as an authoritative source for future cases of superior responsibility at the ICC.[321] The case was decided by a split bench, with a three-judge majority and

---

[314] Ibid.

[315] *Prosecutor v. Naser Orić*, para 23. See also *Prosecutor v. Brdjanin*, Case No. IT-99-36, Judgement, Trial Chamber, para 29 (1 September 2004), holding: "[w]ith respect to documentary hearsay evidence, the Prosecution must prove its relevance and probative value beyond reasonable doubt, whereas the Defence is only required to prove the relevance and probative value of such evidence on a balance of probabilities."

[316] Ibid.

[317] SáCouto and Viseur Sellers 2019, p. 612.

[318] Ibid., p. 613.

[319] Amann DM (2018) In Bemba and beyond, crimes adjudged to commit themselves. EJIL: Talk! https://www.ejiltalk.org/in-bemba-and-beyond-crimes-adjudged-to-commit-themselves/ (accessed 16 June 2025).

[320] Van der Vyver 2021, pp. 590–593.

[321] Peniguet 2018.

a two-judge minority, each of whom held separate opinions. None of the majority addressed the elements of superior responsibility themselves, for example, a superior's authority to prevent, repress, and submit matters to the competent authorities. The ICC thus finds itself in a critical position, as it did not assist in forming an interpretation of this key component of the doctrine of superior responsibility and its ensuing measures. Instead, the majority reached an acquittal based on a preponderance of facts, overlooking their obligations toward the necessary interpretations of this inherently complex mode of liability. The ICC AC's delivered a counterproductive judgment on superior responsibility that is not based on any visible authoritative citations regarding the doctrine of superior responsibility.[322] In the absence of a consensus on the essential elements of this law and the international community's frustration in relation to this judgment, we could conclude that "the ICC still has many miles to run".[323]

4.4 Superior Orders and the Crime of Aggression

In addition to providing a better understanding of the doctrine of superior responsibility in its *latu sensu* view, this section is intended to offer a concise discussion of other forms of superior criminal responsibility, such as superior orders and the crime of aggression. It is not the aim of this section, however, to enter into the details of all these forms. Rather, it seeks to answer the following question: How might superior orders and the crime of aggression converge with respect to the application of superior responsibility under the Rome Statute?

The crime of aggression, otherwise known as the "leadership crime",[324] was added to the Rome Statute of the ICC following the Review Conference held in Kampala, Uganda, in 2010.[325] While incorporating discussions on various issues, the conference chiefly focused on the inclusion of the crime of aggression.[326] As per Article 121, the Rome Statute allows amendments to its subject-matter on a case-by-case basis, as brought to it by States Parties through the UN SC. However, such amendments are restricted to a period of seven years after the entry into force of the ICC Statute.[327]

Within the ICC's subject-matter jurisdiction, the *chapeau* definition provided for the crime of aggression is, "the planning, preparation, initiation or execution, by a

[322] Sadat 2019, p. 357.

[323] Van der Vyver 2021, p. 602.

[324] Politi 2004, p. 46.

[325] REVIEW CONFERENCE OF THE ROME STATUTE OF THE INTERNATIONAL CRIMINAL COURT in Kampala, Uganda (2010). Available at https://asp.icc-cpi.int/iccdocs/asp_docs/ASP9/OR/RC-11-ENG.pdf. (hereinafter Kampala Review Conference).

[326] Suggestions were made during the Kampala Review Conference that treaty crimes should be included. See Boister 2009, p. 345. See also van der Vyver 2021, p. 77.

[327] Rome Statute, Article 121.

person in a position effectively to exercise control over or to direct the political or military action of a State, of an act of aggression which, by its character, gravity, and scale, constitutes a manifest violation of the Charter of the United Nations."[328] The ICC's definition of the crime of aggression is a verbatim reflection of the definition of the crime of aggression provided by the UN SC.[329] As such, at the outset, the delegations at the Review Conference found its addition to the Rome Statute challenging given that the Statute's substance jurisdiction is restricted to natural persons (*materiae personae*), not abstract entities.[330] In this sense, the crime of aggression holds a special status compared with other core international crimes, as the latter may be prosecuted under domestic courts, while the crime of aggression can be prosecuted either through a UN SC subsidiary organ or, with certain limitations, the ICC.[331]

Regarding superior responsibility, the prosecution of the crime of aggression must, in principle,[332] be based on an order issued by a superior to their forces to initiate aggression against the territorial integrity or the political independence of a state, or against people seeking self-determination.[333] In this case, the leader is charged with a crime of aggression as a co-principal.[334] Although, in the context of the crime of aggression, the pattern of a superior order subjects the accused superior to the *latu sensu* application of superior responsibility, an act of aggression, normatively, entails crimes either committed or about to be committed by the superior's subordinates. As such, a superior accused of the crime of aggression may be prosecuted directly as a principal or co-principal perpetrator and may also face liability for the crimes of their subordinates under superior responsibility.[335] For example, a superior may be charged with a crime of aggression under Article 25 (concerning superior orders and/or complicity or conspiracy), as well as with international crimes resulting from such aggression under Article 28 (superior responsibility). Notably, a superior in this case will receive an aggravated sentence due to their additional criminal responsibility under the doctrine of superior responsibility.[336] To sum up, the crime of aggression

---

[328] Ibid., Article 8bis.

[329] G.A. Res. 3314 (XXIX) of 14 Dec. 1974, 29 U.N. GAOR Supp. (No. 31), at 142, U.N. Doc. A/9631 (1974).

[330] Ibid., Article 25 (1). See also van der Vyver 2021, p. 215.

[331] Cf. Stahn 2018, p. 99. (Stahn asserts that the only "forum" available to prosecute acts of aggression is the ICC.)

[332] All the modes of liability under Article 25, namely, orders, aiding and abetting, etc., apply to the leader; however, an act of aggression normally occurs as a result of a superior order. Cassese asserts that crimes of aggression are mostly committed through joint criminal enterprise (conspiracy). See Cassese 2002, p. 145.

[333] Ibid. See also Drumbl 2009, pp. 306–307, 313, 318.

[334] Van der Vyver 2021, p. 215.

[335] Cf. Kampala Review Conference, p. 45 (para 5). (The Working Group noted that the prosecution of the crime of aggression does not affect the investigation of the other crimes under the Rome Statute, which may be committed by the leader's subordinates.)

[336] *Prosecutor v. Ratko Mladić*, Case No. IT-09-92-A, Appeals Judgment, 8 June 2021, International Residual Mechanism for Criminal Tribunals, para 529. (Notably, the Court in this case emphasized an alternative approach—abuse of authority—as a conceptual replacement for the doctrine of superior responsibility.)

and superior orders can be viewed as a two-fold, *latu sensu* understanding of superior responsibility that, in addition to vicarious liability, also encompasses criminal responsibility for direct perpetration.

4.5 Conclusion

This chapter began by introducing some preliminary discussions on criminal institutions at the international level. Through an analysis of the key similarities and differences between the asymmetrical structures of these institutions, it has become clear that each charge plays an important role in the application of the doctrine of superior responsibility. Consequently, this juxtaposition has proved important in characterizing the doctrine of superior responsibility, which reached its most developed form at the ICC. However, synergistically with the ICC, the jurisprudence of the earlier *ad hoc* tribunals also contributed to the development of this doctrine. Regrettably, in the ICC's first superior responsibility case, the majority elected to overlook that jurisprudence, which could have provided meaningful precedents for the ICC. There were high expectations that this case would result in a verdict affirming superior responsibility charges; disappointingly, however, it resulted in an acquittal.

Unlike domestic criminal law, the premise of ICL does not allow for the acquittal of individuals proven to have committed crimes.[337] This is reiterated in the jurisprudence of the *ad hoc* tribunals, which has been viewed as an extension of the legacy of the Nuremberg Military Tribunals and the Tokyo Tribunals. In the *Bemba* case, both the court and the prosecutor concluded that Bemba was responsible for war crimes and crimes against humanity, and that the victims needed to be compensated accordingly. In my view, the anomalous outcome of the examination of the *all necessary and reasonable measure* element was the result of differing opinions on the nature and elements of superior responsibility expressed in scholarly writings, which were admitted into the ICC records. These can be found in the annex exhibits deposited to the Court's records as evidence and a list of authorities.[338]

According to van der Vyver's *obiter dictum* view of the *Bemba* case, one of the reasons that may have led to the unpromising application of superior responsibility at the ICC, particularly with Bemba's acquittal, is the focus on the prosecution of African leaders in the early stages. The Court has thus made a point of overturning this stigma.[339] In this case, Bemba's acquittal would have been guided by political

---

[337] *Contra*, Sadat 2019, p. 361.

[338] Annex A to the Prosecution's Response to Appellant's Document in Support of Appeal. Available at https://www.legal-tools.org/doc/bffba9/.

[339] In support of van der Vyver's assertion, see Allo, The ICC's Problem Is Not Overt Racism, It Is Eurocentrism, *Al Jazeera* (28 July 2018), https://www.aljazeera.com/indepth/opinion/iccproblem-simple-racism-eurocentricism-180725111213623.html. See also Fritz, The ICC: A Common Cause Between John Bolton and Africa? *Al Jazeera* (16 September 2018), https://www.aljazeera.com/indepth/opinion/icc-common-johnbolton-africa-180915095755954.html; Zavis and Dixon, Only

considerations rather than objective legal arguments, at the expense of the victims' rights.

The ICC AC has yet to overthrow the arguably irrelevant factual examination of superior responsibility in the *Bemba* AC's judgment. It could be argued that it should accept the Rome Statute's invitation to apply more constructive rules through teleological interpretations in favor of ending the impunity of superiors. As a permanent international criminal court of law geared at administering justice and ending impunity, the ICC needs to emancipate itself from politically motivated reproaches driven by political authorities and policymakers. The ICC AC's judgment in Bemba raises significant concerns regarding the interpretation and application of the doctrine of superior responsibility under Article 28 of the Rome Statute. While the majority emphasized the need for proof beyond a reasonable doubt, they failed to clearly define the evidentiary thresholds and specific measures a superior must take to meet their *inter alia* duties. Although circumstantial evidence is admissible under ICL, its dismissal by the AC—particularly the treatment of hearsay—suggests a problematic evidentiary standard that deviates from established procedural norms. The judgment's rejection of strict liability contrasts with the Rome Statute's "should-have-known" standard for military commanders, which arguably expands the doctrine beyond mere intent-based culpability.

Moreover, divergent judicial views—as well as scholarship, including Jackson's, and Judge Eboe-Osuji's conflation of superior responsibility with complicity under Article 25—reflect a deeper conceptual misalignment that risks distorting the *sui generis* nature of the doctrine. Notably, the AC missed a vital opportunity to offer interpretative clarity by failing to articulate an illustrative set of necessary and reasonable measures grounded in either practice or theory—something a consequentialist judicial approach could have addressed. In doing so, the Chamber overlooked its normative role in shaping future jurisprudence. Instead of providing a doctrinal anchor for superior responsibility, the judgment relied heavily on factual reconsiderations, undermining legal certainty and institutional coherence tasked to the ICC. With a split bench and no majority consensus on the elements of superior responsibility, the ICC AC's decision in Bemba stands as a missed opportunity to clarify a core mode of liability within ICL. Absent a unified and well-reasoned articulation of the doctrine's content and thresholds, the ICC risks further eroding confidence in its authority. As such, the case underscores the urgent need for jurisprudential consistency and conceptual clarity in future applications of superior responsibility.

The following concluding chapter reflects on the doctrine of superior responsibility and proposes refinements to enhance its conceptual consistency. A uniform application of the doctrine across all categories of superiors—by the ICC and other judicial bodies—is essential not only for fairness, legality, and doctrinal coherence but also for strengthening accountability in prosecuting core international crimes and serious human rights violations at both domestic and international levels.

Africans Have Been Tried at the Court for the Worst Crimes on Earth, *LA Times*, http://www.latimes.com/world/africa/la-fg-iccafrica-snap-story.html.

References

Akande D (2009) Sources of International Criminal Law. In: Cassese A, Akande D, Acquaviva G (eds) The Oxford Companion to International Criminal Justice. Oxford University Press, Oxford, pp 41–53

Allo A K (2018) The ICC's Problem Is Not Overt Racism, It Is Eurocentrism. Al Jazeera, 28 July 2018. https://www.aljazeera.com/indepth/opinion/iccproblem-simple-racism-eurocentricism-180725111213623.html (accessed 16 June 2022)

Amann D M (2018) In Bemba and beyond, crimes adjudged to commit themselves. EJIL: Talk! https://www.ejiltalk.org/in-bemba-and-beyond-crimes-adjudged-to-commit-themselves/ (accessed 16 June 2025)

Ambos K (1999a) General Principles of Criminal Law in the Rome Statute. Criminal Law Forum 10, Kluwer, Dordrecht, pp. 1–32

Ambos K (1999b) General Principles of Criminal Law. In: Triffterer O (ed) Commentary on the Rome Statute of the International Criminal Court. Nomos Verlagsgesellschaft, Baden-Baden, pp. 475–492

Ambos K (2002) Superior Responsibility. In: Cassese A, Gaeta P, Jones JRWD (eds) The Rome Statute of the International Criminal Court: A Commentary, Vol. 3, 823–872. Oxford University Press, Oxford, pp. 823–871

Ambos K (2009) Critical Issues in the Bemba Confirmation Decision. Leiden Journal of International Law 22, pp. 715–726

Badar M E, Porro S (2017) Article 30 Mental Element. In: Klamberg M (ed) Commentary on the Law of the International Criminal Court, FICHL Publ. Series No. 29, pp. 314–322

Baragwanath D (2014) The Interpretative Challenges of International Adjudication across the Common Law/Civil Law Divide. Cambridge Journal of International and Comparative Law 3, pp. 472–494

Bassiouni C (2011) Crimes against Humanity Historical Evolution and Contemporary Application. Cambridge University Press, Cambridge

Bitti G (2009) Article 21 of the Statute of the International Criminal Court and the Treatment of Sources of Law in the Jurisprudence of the ICC. In: Stahn C, Sluiter G (eds) The Law and Practice of the International Criminal Court. Oxford University Press, pp. 281–295

Boister N (2009) Treaty Crimes, International Criminal Court? New Criminal Law Review: An International and Interdisciplinary Journal 12(3), pp. 341–385

Bradfield P (2020) Alternative charges and modes of liability in the latest CAR case at the ICC – Trouble ahead? EJIL: Talk! https://www.ejiltalk.org/alternative-charges-and-modes-of-liability-in-the-latest-car-case-at-the-icc-trouble-ahead/. Accessed 16 June 2025

Cassese A (2002) Crimes Against Humanity. In: Cassese A, Gaeta P, Jones JRWD (eds) The Rome Statute of the International Criminal Court: A Commentary, vol. 1, pp. 1–20. Oxford University Press, Oxford

Clark R S (2001) The Mental Element in International Criminal Law: The Rome Statute of the International Criminal Court and the Elements of Offences. Criminal Law Forum: American International Journal 23, pp. 291–334

Crawford J (1997) An International Criminal Court? Connecticut Journal of International Law 12, pp. 255–278

Cryer R (2004) General principles of liability in international criminal law. In McGoldrick D, Rowe P, Donnelly E (eds) The Permanent International Criminal Court: Legal and policy issues. Hart Publishing, Oxford/Portland, pp 233–254

Cryer R et al. (2019) An Introduction to International Criminal Law and Procedure, 4th edn. Cambridge University Press, Cambridge

Damaško M (2001) The Shadow Side of Command Responsibility. American Journal of Comparative Law 49(3), pp. 455–496

Drumbl M (2009) The Push to Criminalize Aggression: Something Lost Amid the Gains? Case Western Reserve Journal of International Law 41, pp. 291–316

Ellis M S (1999) Non-Negotiable; War Criminals Belong in the Dock, Not at the Table. Washington Post. Available at https://www.congress.gov/106/crec/1999/05/10/145/66/CREC-1999-05-10.pdf (accessed 16 June 2022)

Eser A (2002) Individual Criminal Responsibility. In: Cassese A, Gaeta P, Jones JRWD (eds) The Rome Statute of the International Criminal Court: A Commentary, vol 1. Oxford University Press, Oxford, pp 767–822

Fenrick W J (1999) Responsibility of Commanders and Other Superiors. In: Triffterer O (ed) Commentary on the Rome Statute of the International Criminal Court. Nomos Verlagsgesellschaft, Baden-Baden, pp. 515–522

Fritz F (2018) The ICC: A Common Cause Between John Bolton and Africa? Al Jazeera, 16 September 2018. https://www.aljazeera.com/indepth/opinion/icc-common-johnbolton-africa-180915095755954.html (accessed 16 June 2022)

Galand A S (2020) Bemba and the Individualisation of War: Reconciling Command Responsibility under Article 28 Rome Statute with Individual Criminal Responsibility. International Criminal Law Review 20, pp. pp. 688–725

Goldstone R J (2018) The International Criminal Tribunals for the Former Yugoslavia and Rwanda. In: Crane D M, Sadat L N, Scharf M P (eds) The Founders: Four Pioneering Individuals Who Launched the First Modern-Era International Criminal Tribunals. Cambridge University Press, pp 57–84

Grover L (2010) A call to arms: Fundamental dilemmas confronting the interpretation of crimes in the Rome Statute of the International Criminal Court. European Journal of International Law, 21(3), pp. 543–583

Grover L (2014) Interpreting Crimes in the Rome Statute of the International Criminal Court. Cambridge University Press, Cambridge

Guilfoyle D (2019) Lacking Conviction: Is the International Criminal Court Broken? An Organisational Failure Analysis. Melbourne Journal of International Law 20, pp. 401–429

Harmon M B, Gaynor F (2007) The Sentencing Practice of International Criminal Tribunals: Ordinary Sentences for Extraordinary Crimes. Journal of International Criminal Justice 5(683), pp. 683–71

Henkin L, Pugh R C, Schachter O, Smit H (1987) International Law: Cases and Materials, 2nd edn. West Publishing, St. Paul, MN

Hibbert S (2019) The Bemba Acquittal: A Blow to the ICC's Legitimacy in a Time of Crisis. Temple International & Comparative Law Journal 34, pp. pp. 95–121

Howard K (1972) Command Responsibility for War Crimes. Journal of Public Law 21, pp. 20–44

International Criminal Court (ICC) (2018) Statement of ICC Prosecutor, Fatou Bensouda, on the recent judgment of the ICC AC acquitting Mr Jean-Pierre Bemba Gombo. https://www.icc-cpi.int/Pages/item.aspx?name=180613-OTP-stat (accessed 16 June 2022)

International Criminal Court (ICC) (2019) Decision on the confirmation of charges against Alfred Yekatom and Patrice-Edouard Ngaïssona (ICC-01/14-01/18-403-Conf-Corr). Pre-Trial Chamber II (11 December 2019)

Jackson M (2022) Causation and the Legal Character of Command Responsibility after Bemba at the International Criminal Court. Journal of International Criminal Justice 20(2), pp. 437–458

Kortfält L (2017) Responsibility of commanders and other superiors. In: Klamberg M (ed) Commentary on the Law of the International Criminal Court. FICHL Publ. Series No. 29, pp. 279–304

Landrum B D (1995) The Yamashita War Crimes Trial: Command Responsibility Then and Now. Military Law Review 149, pp. 293–322

Levie H S (1997–1998) Command Responsibility. Journal of Legal Studies 8, pp. pp. 1–19

Meron T (2004) Procedural Evolution in the ICTY. Journal of International Criminal Justice 2, pp. 521–539

Meron T (2021) Standing Up for Justice: The Challenges of Trying Atrocity Crimes. Oxford University Press, Oxford

Mundis D A (2001) The Legal Character and Status of the Rules of Procedure and Evidence of the Ad Hoc International Tribunals. International Criminal Law Review 1, Brill, pp. 191–214
Murphy S D (2012) The International Court of Justice. In: Giorgetti C (ed) The Rules, Practice, and Jurisprudence of International Courts and Tribunals. Brill, Leiden, pp 11–35
Nsereko D D (1994) Rules of Procedure and Evidence of the International Tribunal for the Former Yugoslavia. Criminal Law Forum 5, pp. 507–552
Osiel M (2005) The Banality of the Good: Aligning Incentives against Mass Atrocity. Columbia Law Review 105, pp. 1751–1862
Peniguet M (2018) CPI: Jean-Pierre Bemba, chronique d'un acquittement surprise. Dalloz, Actualité. Available at https://www.dalloz-actualite.fr/flash/cpi-jean-pierre-bemba-chronique-d-un-acquittement-surprise (accessed 16 June 2022)
Pigeau R, McCann C (2002) Re-conceptualizing Command and Control. Canadian Military Journal 3(1), pp. 53–63
Pjic J (1997) The Tribunal and the ICC: Do Precedents Matter? Albany Law Review 60, pp. 861–872
Politi M (2004) The Debate within the Preparatory Commission for the International Criminal Court. In: Politi M, Nesi G (eds) The International Criminal Court and the Crime of Aggression. Ashgate, Hants/Burlington, pp 43–46
Powderly J (2010) Judicial Interpretation at the Ad Hoc Tribunals: Method from Chaos. In: Darcy S, Powderly J (eds) Judicial Creativity at the International Criminal Tribunals. Oxford University Press, pp. 17–44
Powderly J (2018) Introductory Note to Prosecutor v. Jean Pierre Bemba Gombo. International Legal Materials 57(6), pp. 1031–1035
Pruitt K (2014) Destroying the Legacy of the ICTY: Analysis of the Acquittals of Jovica Stanisic and Franko Simatovic. 15 San Diego International Law Journal 15, pp. 15–47
Robinson D (2008) The Identity Crisis of International Criminal Law. Leiden Journal of International Law 21, pp. 925–963
Robinson D (2020) Justice in Extreme Cases: Criminal Law Theory Meets International Criminal Law. Cambridge University Press, Cambridge
SáCouto S, Viseur Sellers P (2019) The Bemba Appeals Chamber Judgment: Impunity for Sexual and Gender-Based Crimes? William & Mary Bill of Rights Journal 27, pp. 1–52
Sadat L N (2002a) The International Criminal Court and the Transformation of International Law: Justice for the New Millennium. Transnational Publishing, New York
Sadat L N (2002b) The Legacy of the ICTY: The International Criminal Court. New England Law Review, pp. 1073–1090
Sadat L N (2019) Prosecutor v. Jean-Pierre Bemba Gombo. American Journal of International Law 113, pp. 353–361
Sadat L, Dixon R (1997) Developing International Rules of Evidence for the Yugoslav and Rwanda Tribunals. Transnational Law and Contemporary Problems 7, pp. 81–120
Sadat L N, Jolly J M (2014) Seven Canons of ICC Treaty Interpretation: Making Sense of Article 25's Rorschach Blot. Leiden Journal of International Law 27, pp. 755–778
Saland P (1999) International Criminal Law Principles. In: Lee RS (ed) The International Criminal Court: The Making of the Rome Statute. Brill, Leiden, pp. 189–216
Schabas W A (1998) The General Principles of the Rome Statute. European Journal for Crime, Criminal Law, and Criminal Justice 6, pp. 417–440
Schabas W A (2003) Interpreting the Statutes of the Ad Hoc Tribunals. In: Vohrah LC et al. (eds) Man's Inhumanity to Man, Essays on International Law in Honour of Antonio Cassese. Kluwer Law International, The Hague, 847–888
Schabas W A (2007) An Introduction to the International Criminal Court, 3rd edn. Cambridge University Press, Cambridge
Shahabuddin M (2004) Does the Principle of Legality Stand in the Way of Progressive Development of Law? Journal of International Criminal Justice 2, pp. 1007–1028
Simonovic I (1999) The Role of the ICTY in the Development of International Criminal Adjudication. Fordham International Law Journal 23(2), pp. 440–474

Stahn C (2018) A Critical Introduction to International Criminal Law. Cambridge University Press, Cambridge

Stearns J K (2011) Dancing in the Glory of Monsters: The Collapse of the Congo and the Great War of Africa. Public Affairs, New York

Taulbee J L (2018) War Crimes and Trials: A Primary Source Guide, ABC-CLIO Publishing

Triffterer O (2002) Causality, a Separate Element of the Doctrine of Superior Responsibility as Expressed in Article 28 Rome Statute? Leiden Journal of International Law 15(1), pp.179–197

Van der Vyver JD (2004) The International Criminal Court and the concept of mens rea in international criminal law. University of Miami International and Comparative Law Review 12, pp. 57–94

Van der Vyver J (2021) International Criminal Law: Crimes within the Jurisdiction of the International Criminal Court, Vol. II. LAP Lambert Publishing, Germany

Van Schaack B (2008) Crimen sine lege: Judicial Lawmaking at the Intersection of Law and Morals. Georgetown Law Journal 97(1), pp. 119–192

Van Schaack B (2021) Animating the U.S. War Crimes Act. International Law Studies 97, pp.1585–1586

Van Sliedregt E (2011) Command Responsibility at the ICTY Three Generations of Case Law and Still Ambiguity. In: Swart A H et al. (eds) The Legacy of the ICTY. Oxford University Press, Oxford, pp. 367–390

Van Sliedregt E (2018) Criminalization of Crimes Against Humanity under National Law. Journal of International Criminal Justice 16(4), pp. 717–743

Vetter GR (2000) Command Responsibility of Non-Military Superiors in the International Criminal Court (ICC). Yale Journal of International Law 25, pp. 89–143

Watson G R (2002) The Changing Jurisprudence of the International Criminal Tribunal for the Former Yugoslavia. New England Law Review 37, pp. pp. 871–878

Werle G, Jessberger F (2005) Unless Otherwise Provided: Article 30 of the ICC Statute and the Mental Element of Crimes under International Criminal Law. Journal of International Criminal Justice, Vol. 3, Issue 1, pp. 35–55

Young S (2001) Surrendering the Accused to the International Criminal Court. The British Yearbook of International Law, Oxford 71(1), pp. 319–392

Zavis A, Dixon R (2018) Only Africans Have Been Tried at the Court for the Worst Crimes on Earth. Los Angeles Times. Available at https://www.latimes.com/world/africa/la-fg-icc-africa-snap-story.html (accessed 16 June 2022)

Case Law

Aloys Ntabakuze v. The Prosecutor, Case No. ICTR-98-41A-0012/1, 8 May 2012

Aloys Simba v. The Prosecutor, Case No. ICTR-01-76-A

Ferdinand Nahimana, Jean-Bosco Barayagwiza & Hassan Ngeze v. The Prosecutor, Case No. ICTR-99-52-A, 28 November 2007

Prosecutor v. Alfred Yekatom & Patrice-Edouard Ngaïssona, Case No. ICC-01/14-01/18, 11 December 2019

Prosecutor v. Ali Muhammas Ali Abd-Alrahman ("Ali Kushayb"), Case No. ICC-02/05-01/20 OA8, para 91, 1 November 2021

Prosecutor v. ANTO FURUNDZIYA, Case No. IT-95-T, 10 December 1998

Prosecutor v. AUGUSTIN NDINDILIYIMANA, Case No. ICTR-00-56-T, 17 May 2011

Prosecutor v. Bosco Ntaganda, Case No. ICC-01/04-02/06, 9 June 2014

Prosecutor v. Dario Kordić & Mario Čerkez, Case No. IT-95-1A-A, para 46, 26 February 2001

Prosecutor v. Dominic Ongwen, Case No. ICC-02/04-01/15, 23 March 2016

Prosecutor v. Dražen Erdemovic, Case No. IT-96-22-A (Joint Separate Opinion of Judge McDonald and Judge Vohrah), para 40, 29 November 1996

Prosecutor v. Germain Katanga & Mathieu Ngudjolo Chui, Case No. ICC-01/04-01/07-572 (OA4) (Judgment in the Appeal by Mathieu Ngudjolo Chui of 27 March 2008 against the Decision of Pre-Trial Chamber I on the Application of the Appellant for Interim Release), para 25, 9 June 2008

Prosecutor v. Jean-Pierre Bemba Gombo, Case No. ICC-01/05-01/08 A, Judgment, 8 June 2018

Prosecutor v. Jean-Pierre Bemba Gombo (Decision Pursuant to Article 61(7)(a) and (b) of the Rome Statute on the Charges against Jean-Pierre Bemba Gombo), Case No. ICC-01/05-01/08-424, para 274, 15 June 2009

Prosecutor v. Joseph Kanyabasid, Case No. ICTR-96-15-A, (Dissenting Opinion of Judge Shahabuddeen) para 21, 3 June 1999

Prosecutor v. Laurent Gbagbo & Charles Blé Goudé, Case No. ICC-02/11-01/15-1263-AnxC-Red, 16 July 2019

Prosecutor v. Mathieu Ngudjolo Chui, Case No. ICC-01/04-02/12-271 (A), (Judgment pursuant to Article 74 of the Statute", para 22, 27 February 2015

Prosecutor v. Milan Milutinovic el., Case No. IT -99-37-AR72, para 3, May 21, 2003

Prosecutor v. Rasim Delić (Decision on Interlocutory Appeal Challenging the Jurisdiction of the Tribunal), Case No. IT-04-83-AR72

Prosecutor v. Simone Gbagbo, Case No. ICC-02/11-01/12-75-Red, 27 May 2015

Prosecutor v. Tihomir Blaškić, Case No. IT-95-14-AR108bis, Judgment on the Request of the Republic of Croatia for Review of the Decision of Trial Chamber II of 18 July 1997

Prosecutor v. THOMAS LUBANGA DYILO (Decision on Confirmation of Charges), Case No. ICC-01/04-01/06-803-tEN, para 318, 29 January 2007

Prosecutor v. Zdravko Mucić aka "Pavo", Hazim Delić, Esad Landžo aka "Zenga", and Zejnil Delalić, Case No. IT-96-21-A, Appeal Judgment, 20 February 2001, para 239 (ICTY)

Prosecutor v. Zlatko Aleksovski, Case No. IT-95-14/1-A, Appeal Judgment, 24 March 2000

Prosecutor v. Zlatko Aleksovski, Case No. IT-95-14/1-A, Judgment, para 127, 24 March 2000

SYLVESTRE GACUMBITSI v. THE PROSECUTOR (Separate Opinion of Judge Schomberg on the Criminal Responsibility of the Appellant for Committing Genocide), Case No. ICTR-2001-64-A, para 143, 7 July 2006

Statute of the International Court of Justice, June 26, 1945, 59 Stat. 1055, 33 U.N.T.S. 933, Article 38

United States of America v. Karl Brandt et el., 2 Trials of War Criminals Before the Nuremberg Military Tribunals Under Control Council Law No. 19 (October 1946–April 1949) (Judgment) 171, p 207. Washington D.C.: U.S. Gov. Printers (1950–1953)

Vienna Convention on the Law of Treaties, Articles 31–33, U.N. Doc. A./CONF.39/27, 22 May 1969, 1155 U.N.T.S. 331, 8I.L.M. 679 (1969)

Other Documents

Alien Tort Claims Act (28 U.S.C. § 1350). https://crsreports.congress.gov/product/pdf/R/R44947

Convention (No. IV) Respecting the Laws and Customs of War on Land, with Annex of Regulations, 1907, Article 25, 36 Stat. 2277, U.S.Y. 539, reprinted in 1 BEVANS 631 and 2 AM J. INT'L L. (Supp.) 90 (1908)

Prosecutor v. Ratko Mladić, Case No. IT-09-92-A, Appeals Judgment, 8 June 2021, International Residual Mechanism for Criminal Tribunals

Prosecutor v. Zdravko Mucić aka "Pavo", Hazim Delić, Esad Landžo aka "Zenga", and Zejnil Delalić, Case No. IT-96–21-A, Appeal Judgment, 20 February 2001, (ICTY)

Protocol Additional to the Geneva Conventions of 12 August 1949 and relating to the Protection of Victims of International Armed Conflicts (Protocol I), 1125 UNTS 3, adopted 8 June 1977, entered into force 7 December 1978

Report of the Ad Hoc Committee on the Establishment of an International Criminal Court, UN GAOR, 50th Sess., Supp. No. 22 (UN Doc. A/50/22, 1995)
Statute of the International Criminal Tribunal for Rwanda (1994) S.C. Res. 955, 33 ILM 1602

Chapter 5
Epilogue: Superior Responsibility Plot Twist and Concluding Remarks—The Proof Is in the Pudding

Contents

Abstract Although this may appear to diverge from the book's central focus—the doctrine of superior responsibility—this chapter wishes to explore its application beyond the traditional scope of core international crimes. This is justified by the fact that such crimes are, at their core, grave human rights violations. Accordingly, where additional categories of human rights violations are recognized as international crimes, superior responsibility remains applicable. This chapter then investigates whether, and under what legal grounds, a superior may be held criminally responsible for human rights violations committed, or about to be committed, by their subordinates. Using syllogistic reasoning and a victim-centered lens, it explores the doctrine's potential extension to gross violations beyond core crimes. The analysis targets three regimes: United Nations *ad hoc* tribunals, the International Criminal Court (ICC), and national jurisdictions. These mechanisms increasingly demonstrate the feasibility of prosecuting military and political superiors for serious violations such as rape and enforced disappearance, particularly when linked to failures to prevent or punish. A normative framework based on a severity scale is introduced to assess whether specific violations meet the threshold for superior responsibility under international law. The chapter argues that this expansion is both legally grounded and normatively necessary for enhancing accountability and victim access to justice. In conclusion, it offers concluding reflections for the book as a whole, synthesizing its legal, normative, and institutional insights to inform future applications of superior responsibility across a wider spectrum of (inter)national criminal justice.

H. Y. Al-Fadhli, *Prosecuting Superior Responsibility in International Criminal Law*,
https://doi.org/10.1007/978-94-6265-735-9_5

Keywords Superior responsibility · Human rights violations · Legal syllogistic reasoning · Treaty crimes · Universal jurisdiction · Victims' rights/humanitarian account

5.1 Introduction

Where law ends, tyranny begins.[1]

As a point of departure, this chapter seeks to examine, through syllogistic reasoning, whether or not a superior may be charged with human rights violations that have been committed, or that are about to be committed, by their subordinates, and on what grounds. It should be noted that the analysis centers on victims' rights, rather than on those of the accused.[2] This chapter also seeks to further clarify the doctrine of superior responsibility, the current conceptual components of which may be subject to reform, focusing on the three regimes in which this phenomenon is applied.

As noted throughout this book, the doctrine of superior responsibility has undergone various changes, which have expanded its subject-matter mandate beyond the context of war crimes, to also include other similar-in-essence violations.[3] For instance, the establishment of the Military Tribunals and the UN *ad hoc* tribunals provided a forum for international institutions to hold political superiors criminally responsible for gross human rights violations other than war crimes.[4] In laboring on this point, rape—a gross human rights violation under customary law—was teleologically incorporated into the criminal jurisdiction of the UN *ad hoc* tribunals, as per the UN's mandate to provide redress for victims in this regard.[5] In addition, the Rome Statute of the ICC addresses a range of gross human rights violations that can be attributed to a superior's culpability owing to their failure to prevent and punish such actions by their subordinates.[6] The Rome Statute also extends liability to superiors for gross human rights violations during armed conflicts of a non-international character.[7] From a jurisdictional perspective, domestic criminal systems also serve

[1] Locke 1690/1988, § 202.

[2] For a thorough discussion of the difference between the rights of an accused, see generally Danner and Martinez 2005.

[3] Walsh and Berry 2016, p. 424.

[4] *Statute of the International Criminal Tribunal for the Former Yugoslavia*, U.N. Doc. S/25704, Annex (1993), 32 ILM 1192 (hereafter ICTY Statute); *Statute of the International Criminal Tribunal for Rwanda*, S.C. Res. 955, Annex (1994), 33 ILM 1602 (1994) (hereafter ICTR Statute).

[5] Meron 2021, p. 46. See also Reinisch 2001, p. 851; Seibert-Fohr 2010, p. 207.

[6] Cf., Rome Statute of the International Criminal Court, 17 July 1998, 2187 U.N.T.S. 3 (entered into force 1 July 2002), available at: http://untreaty.un.org/cod/icc/statute/romefra.htm (hereafter Rome Statute). (Namely, codified core crimes, their elements, and their definitions.)

[7] Ibid., Article 8 (c); (d); (e); (f).

as a unique tool to prosecute superiors for human rights violations by their subordinates, where such violations are criminalized at the national (or international)[8] level.[9] Given the proven ability of the three regimes—the UN, the ICC, and domestic judiciaries[10]—to revolutionize convictions for gross human rights violations under superior responsibility, I would argue that such convictions are feasibly attainable and may be achieved in the short run. It is nonetheless important to note that such an application must hinge on at least one defining feature of a human rights violation, compared with core international crimes, which will be discussed in further detail below. One example that supports this syllogistic test is the existing human rights treaty, which incorporated superior responsibility into its subject matter—*The International Convention for the Protection of All Persons from Enforced Disappearance* (ICPPED).[11]

To meet these objectives, this chapter contains two main sections. In Sect. 5.2, I introduce the notion of a severity scale for human rights and its relationship to international crimes to determine whether or not superior responsibility could apply to such violations. I will then explore how international law regimes could address (or are already addressing) these situations, with an emphasis on the importance of prosecuting superiors for human rights violations committed by their subordinates. Given the lack of academic literature on this progressive test, this section not only serves as a conclusion to this holistic study but also contributes—from a normative perspective—to enhancing the protection of victims of human rights violations, through an optimistic approach. In other words, human rights protection can be enhanced only if prosecution venues for such violations are expanded. In Sect. 5.3, I will draw concluding remarks and appraisals of the current conceptual and practical framework, with a view to providing guidance for superior responsibility practitioners.

5.2 Criminal Superior Responsibility and Human Rights Violations

Given the ongoing, disturbing state of affairs worldwide, the scope of human rights varies across different regions, and violations are not equally criminalized in different areas. In Europe, the scope of human rights could be compared to a pendulum oscillating between the Margin of Appreciation and the Principle of Proportionality,

---

[8] Some states currently practice universal jurisdiction. On 30 November 2021, Germany reached a verdict against an Iraqi nationals and ISIS member for committing genocide against the Yazidi community in Iraq. See https://www.amnesty.org/en/latest/news/2021/11/germany-iraq-worlds-first-judgment-on-crime-of-genocide-against-the-yazidis/.

[9] Stahn 2018, pp. 164, 241. See also Damrosch et al. 2009, p. 1307.

[10] The ICC is bound by its subject-matter jurisdiction over core crimes; however, there are ways through which its jurisdiction could be extended to include human rights violations.

[11] *International Convention for the Protection of All Persons from Enforced Disappearance*, A/RES/61/177, 20 December 2006.

which either limits or expands this scope.[12] In Asia, the scope of human rights is often connected with tribalism and cultural and religious relativism.[13] For example, in some societies, women's face-covering in public may be a prosecutable offense, while in others it may be seen as an advocated human right. Nevertheless, the human rights criteria applied in these regions, along with the associated cultural and religious relativism, *inter alia*, may serve as a springboard for developing a severity scale for human rights violations. In accordance with domestic and international human rights instruments, such violations may—based on their defining features—amount to international crimes.[14]

To this end, except for those that have attained a *jus cogens* status at the international level (*i.e.*, state practice and *opinion juris*), not all human rights are universally promoted, nor are their violations universally condemned.[15] However, the severity scale for human rights violations—promoted or condemned—and the defining features of criminality play a key role in their universal criminalization at the international level, in light of the rapidly developing *jus cogens* norms.[16] Therefore, if these gross human rights violations are to be labeled as such, the proposition of applying superior responsibility may neatly fit within this context, especially as many of these offenses are committed as a result of a superior's failure to supervise their subordinates. In this section, I shall first define the close association between international crimes and human rights violations, before proceeding to examine current human rights instruments and how, taken together, the governance of the three regimes may apply superior responsibility, with a view to extrapolation.

5.2.1 Human Rights Violations **v.** *International Crimes*

At the international level, a distinction can be drawn between identifying an offense as a gross human rights violation and a core international crimes. Within the context of superior responsibility, it is with the latter that a superior may be criminally charged.[17] Core international crimes (*delicta juris gentium*) and gross human rights violations are not mutually exclusive. In fact, they can be seen to reflect each other.[18] More precisely, all core international crimes can be viewed as a narrower instance of gross human rights violations. In terms of ICL, however, the distinction hinges

---

[12] For a more detailed discussion of these two concepts, see, generally, Letsas 2006, p. 705.

[13] For further discussion of these factual impacts, see *Amnesty International Report Asia-Pacific 2020*. Available at: https://www.amnesty.org/en/location/asia-and-the-pacific/report-asia-pacific/.

[14] *Universal Declaration of Human Rights* Article 11, G.A. Res. 217(III), UN GAOR, 3d Sess., U.N. Doc. A/810 (1948); International Covenant on Civil and Political Rights Article 14, 19 December 1966, 999 U.N.T.S. 171, 6 I.L.M. 368.

[15] Pérez-León Acevedo 2017, p. 147.

[16] Ibid., p. 148.

[17] Pérez-León Acevedo 2017, p. 152.

[18] Powderly 2010, p. 1. See also Meron 2003, p. 165.

on the defining features of these offenses, for instance whether they are grossly and systematically executed.[19] In terms of ICC adjudication, international crimes and human rights violations have been addressed interchangeably in decisions.[20] Human rights violations can therefore be conceptualized as an umbrella category, which includes offenses committed during an armed conflict, as well as crimes against humanity committed during times of peace and during wartime.

This narrower instance of gross human rights violations (core international crimes) can be traced back to WWII, when movements began to defend their human rights against Nazi brutality.[21] For this reason and others,[22] the victorious Allied States entered into agreements to establish the IMTs, with a view to bringing those most responsible for gross human rights violations to international criminal justice. Notably, these violations were codified for the first time as war crimes, crimes against humanity, genocide, and crimes against peace (now referred to as the crime of aggression, with subtler nuances).[23] As a result, some analysts assert that ICL precedes contemporary international human rights law (IHRL).[24] In their view, contemporary IHRL emerged based on the UN's *Universal Declaration of Human Rights* (UDHR), which sets out the rights that were violated internationally and prosecuted at the IMT. However, the UDHR became a key reference point for domestic and international advocacy and accountability instruments, representing contemporary ICL.[25] For example, the Rome Statute included many gross human rights offenses that were codified as crimes against humanity, with specific defining features outlined under the rubric concerning the elements of the crimes. Moreover, regional and international human rights instruments such as the European Convention on Human Rights are inherently centered on the human rights subject-matter provisions of the UDHR.[26] The *International Covenant on Civil and Political Rights* (ICCPR) also includes corresponding provisions to the UDHR, to be implemented at the domestic level by its States Parties.[27]

---

[19] Chehtman 2020, pp. 3–4.

[20] *SITUATION IN THE PEOPLE'S REPUBLIC OF BANGLADESH/REPUBLIC OF THE UNION OF MYANMAR*, Case No. ICC-01/19 (Decision Pursuant to Article 15 of the Rome Statute on the Authorisation of an Investigation into the Situation in the People's Republic of Bangladesh/ Republic of the Union of Myanmar), para 64, 19 November 2019.

[21] Clapham 2016, p. 12.

[22] Moreover, war crimes committed against soldiers of the Allied forces. See Clapham 2015, pp. 34–39.

[23] Pérez-León Acevedo 2017, p. 151. See also van der Vyver 2021, p. 53.

[24] Clapham 2016.

[25] It is worth noting that some scholars establish a vertical hierarchy among core international crimes with respect to their severity. For example, genocide is situated at the top of the hierarchy, followed by crimes against humanity, with war crimes at the bottom. See Sadat 2002, p. 170. Van der Vyver notes that the crime of aggression is, however, the "crime of all crimes". See van der Vyver 2021, pp. 75–76 (quoting the *Trial of the Major War Criminals* at Nuremberg).

[26] THE PROSECUTOR *v. GEORGES ANDERSON NDERUBUMWE RUTAGANDA*, Case No. ICTR-96-3-A (Dissenting Opinion of Judge Pocar), para 2, 26 May 2003.

[27] *International Covenant on Civil and Political Rights*, G.A. Res. 2200 (XXI), U.N. Doc. A/6316 (1966), 999. U.N.T.S. 171, 6 I.L.M. 368 (1967).

Currently, gross human rights violations—to be prosecuted internationally—must be assessed on the basis of defining features that may establish them as high-profile offenses.[28] In terms of the current conceptualization of these defining features, gross human rights offenses must (1) be committed against a group of the population, whether in times of peace or war (as part of a course of conduct); (2) be severe in nature or *non-derogable*; and (3) in the context of the ICC's adjudication, be codified within the subject-matter jurisdiction of its statute.[29] Conversely, a human rights violation against one individual arguably does not class as an international crime even if it were found to satisfy the criterion concerning severity. As such, not all human rights violations are criminalized. Rather, most shockwave-provoking offenses that threaten human security, in whole or part, are subject to criminalization.[30] Andrew Clapham addresses the association between gross human rights and international crimes, noting that an international crime is "the ultimate enforcement of the criminalisation of a human rights violation".[31] Moreover, a report by the UN *War Crimes Commission* characterized war criminals' criminal responsibility as "individual responsibility for violations of human rights in wartime".[32] We could therefore conclude that international crimes are to be understood as high-profile examples of gross human rights violations, provided that all the defining features feature collectively.

Crimes against humanity constitute the closest conceptualization of gross human rights violations, but they are committed by individuals rather than states.[33] If we strip away their international criminal defining features, a closer observation of these offenses indicates that they fall within the broader category of gross human rights violations.[34] Theodor Meron has noted that crimes against humanity "overlap with some violations of fundamental human rights (such as torture, rape or enslavement), which thus become criminalized under a multilateral treaty".[35] For instance, under the Rome Statute, in the event that the deprivation of food (the right to food) were inflicted on a group of prisoners, this would be classified as an international crime. Equally, the denial of political rights could also amount to genocide if the intent to destroy a political group—even though it is not often substantiated—could be established.[36] Fortunately, most states around the world either entered into multilateral or smaller-scale agreements to criminalize human rights violations, supporting those individuals who pursue such rights and/or seek redress for victims of such violations.

---

[28] Chehtman 2020, p. 2.

[29] *Prosecutor v. Jean-Pierre Bemba Gombo et. al.*, Case No. ICC-01/05-01/13 A6 A7 A8 A9, para 76, 8 March 2018. See also Sadat 2017, p. 212.

[30] Parker 2012, p. 2.

[31] Clapham 2016, p. 13.

[32] *Information Concerning Human Rights Arising from Trials of War Criminals*, UN Doc. E/CN.4/W.19, at ii, 15 May 1948.

[33] Pérez-León Acevedo 2017, p. 150.

[34] Ibid., p. 152.

[35] Meron 2003, p. 165.

[36] Van Schaack 1997, p. 2263.

Given its *jus cogens* status, treaty crimes such as human trafficking are implemented and criminalized at the domestic level but are generally addressed through thematic sanctions. Only by considering the importance of measuring the severity of human rights violations can the international community act collectively and synergistically to create the impetus needed to ensure their prosecution.

Regrettably, certain human rights violations that are "non-derogable" in nature are exempt from the defining features of core international crimes and are thus often overlooked at the international level.[37] For instance, individuals who exercise political rights or academic/journalistic freedom of expression are often subject to bodily harm from authoritarian state and non-state actors.[38] By the same token, advocates for self-determination are often subjected to abuse and, in some cases, ethnic cleansing. Because most abused advocates are either nationals of authoritative legal regimes, living under occupying powers, or their tyrannical state systems are not accountable, their lives are excluded from protection and redress.[39]

The predictability of both state and non-state perpetrators, who often act *ultra vires* in committing gross human rights violations—even against a small number of individuals—is concerning and must be emphatically addressed by the above-mentioned three regimes of governance.[40] These state and non-state perpetrators rely on receiving permissibility signals from their superiors, particularly political superiors, who either intentionally or negligently facilitate their criminal offenses. In other words, the origin of these human rights violations can in some cases be traced to the political superior's failure to properly oversee their subordinates, who thus enjoy a form of extended immunity.[41] As such, prosecuting superiors not only strengthens deterrence and the associated stigma of offenders but also encourages the international community to close the gap (of non-criminalized offenses) through criminal accountability. In the long run, such accountability mandates may help to bridge the divide between domestic, regional, and international regimes, with respect to the differing views of what constitutes a gross human rights violation.

5.2.2 *The Superior's Responsibility for Human Rights Violations and the Competency of Accountability* Fora

As noted, superior responsibility may be applied through the trio of regimes responsible for redressing victims of human rights violations and maintaining public order, namely the ICC, the UN SC's accountability fora, and individual states. However, to avoid criticisms from advocates of national sovereignty, it is always favorable to

[37] Stahn 2018, p. 61.

[38] Bassiouni 2011c, p. 51. Office of the United Nations High Commissioner for Human Rights 2015, pp. 30–31.

[39] Bassiouni 2013, p. 1018.

[40] Ibid., p. 51. See also Milanovic 2020, p. 33.

[41] Ibid., p. 37.

prosecute crimes at the national level.[42] Accordingly, many states have entered into agreements to prosecute superiors who are either directly or vicariously involved in the commission of human rights violations. For example, in 2006, the UN adopted the ICPPED, with the purpose of holding accountable those responsible for the enforced disappearance offense.[43] This Convention obliges States Parties to implement accountability measures within their national legislation, in accordance with the Convention's subject-matter.

In terms of *strictu sensu* superior responsibility, the 2006 UN ICPPED is, to date, the sole international instrument that, under Article 6, obliges States Parties to prosecute superiors for human rights violations, similarly to the approach to the accountability of superiors under ICL.[44] Given that the offense of enforced disappearance is invariably committed against victims by political/civilian superiors, this Article targets political superiors, mirroring the wording of Article 28 of the Rome Statute. The accountability of military and military-like superiors may—where applicable—be addressed through prosecutions under the ICL regime. Article 6 of the ICPPED provides as follows:

1. Each State Party shall take the necessary measures to hold criminally responsible at least:
   (a) Any person who commits, orders, solicits or induces the commission of, attempts to commit, is an accomplice to or participates in an enforced disappearance;
   (b) A superior who:
      (i) Knew, or consciously disregarded information which clearly indicated, that subordinates under his or her effective authority and control were committing or about to commit a crime of enforced disappearance;
      (ii) Exercised effective responsibility for and control over activities which were concerned with the crime of enforced disappearance; and
      (iii) Failed to take all necessary and reasonable measures within his or her power to prevent or repress the commission of an enforced disappearance or to submit the matter to the competent authorities for investigation and prosecution;
   (c) Subparagraph (b) above is without prejudice to the higher standards of responsibility applicable under relevant international law to a military commander or to a person effectively acting as a military commander.
2. No order or instruction from any public authority, civilian, military or other, may be invoked to justify an offence of enforced disappearance.[45]

---

[42] *International Convention for the Protection of All Persons from Enforced Disappearance*, A/RES/61/177, 20 December 2006.

[43] Ibid.

[44] Jerončič and Moreno 2016, p. 21.

[45] *International Convention for the Protection of All Persons from Enforced Disappearance*, A/RES/61/177, 20 December 2006, Article 6(1).

Although this remains the only single international human rights instrument to date, in 2019 the ILC prepared some draft Articles concerning the punishment and prevention of crimes against humanity, which was intended to be universally open for accession by states.[46] If adopted and brought into force, the draft treaty on "Crimes Against Humanity" would be the first endeavor to criminalize such crimes at the domestic level, obligating States Parties to implement it within their domestic criminal law systems. Article 6(3) of the text explicitly deals with the vicarious criminal responsibility of superiors, stating that:

> Each State shall…take the necessary measures to ensure that commanders and other superiors are criminally responsible for crimes against humanity committed by their subordinates if they knew, or had reason to know, that the subordinates were about to commit or were committing such crimes and did not take all necessary and reasonable measures in their power to prevent their commission, or if such crimes had been committed, to punish the persons responsible.[47]

In the context of this prospective treaty, human rights abuses committed by a superior's subordinates—either nationally or internationally—would not escape criminal justice, even in the case of perpetrators who enjoy domestic immunity. It is important to note that there could be some confusion between the Rome Statute's provision on crimes against humanity and this draft treaty, which could lead one to assume that the latter is superfluous given the Rome Statute's existing provision.[48] Contrary to this assumption, however, the Rome Statute is not entirely universal and, in principle, is binding only for States Parties.[49] Moreover, the Rome Statute establishes cooperation between States Parties and the ICC, not compliance among sovereign states with respect to the prosecution of such crimes.[50] In addition, as a draft UN treaty, the draft text on crimes against humanity is designed to be universal as well as to promote the legitimate exercise of universal jurisdiction by all States Parties in relation to such crimes.

Various other UN treaties also obligate States Parties to implement measures to punish those responsible for offenses included within their subject-matter. However, the criminal responsibility of superiors, as per these mandates, applies only to the application of *latu sensu* superior responsibility, namely ordering, aiding or abetting, or co-perpetrating. For instance, the *Convention against Torture and Other Cruel, Inhuman or Degrading Treatment or Punishment* prohibits superior orders (*latu sensu* superior responsibility) in committing torture, whether during times of peace

---

[46] It should be noted that this draft is a lengthy, dated approach to codifying crimes against humanity. See van der Vyver 2021. See also *Code of Offenses Against the Peace and Security of Mankind*, U.N. GAOR, 9th Sess., U.N. Doc. A/2693 (1954).

[47] *International Convention for the Protection of All Persons from Enforced Disappearance*, A/RES/61/177, 20 December 2006, Article 6(3).

[48] UN Member States have expressed both positive and negative reactions with respect to this difference and the definitions. See: https://cpb-us-w2.wpmucdn.com/sites.wustl.edu/dist/b/2004/files/2021/08/Compilation-of-6th-Committee-Responses-to-CAH-2013-2020.pdf.

[49] Bassiouni 2011b, pp. 649–723, esp. 721.

[50] Ibid.

or wartime.[51] Article 2 of this Convention states: "No exceptional circumstances whatsoever, whether a state of war or a threat of war, internal political instability or any other public emergency, may be invoked as a justification of torture". It proceeds to specify that "[a]n order from a superior officer or a public authority may not be invoked as a justification of torture".[52] With respect to regional treaties, the *Inter-American Convention to Prevent and Punish Torture* criminalizes torture committed either as a result of a public official's order or jointly with other officials.[53]

In the context of the UN accountability fora, the SC has played a key role in prosecuting gross human rights violations, both during wartime and in times of peace, against groups or individuals, and whether as core international crimes or human rights violations.[54] The *ad hoc* tribunals are one example of these accountability fora. Furthermore, hybrid criminal tribunals established jointly with the victim state represent another way of holding superiors criminally responsible under the doctrine of superior responsibility.[55]

Regarding accountability fora in the context of domestic regimes, the United States also played a central role in emphasizing the criminal responsibility of superiors rather than that of their subordinates, both in terms of case law and enacted bills. The US federal law system and its case law have integrated superior responsibility in many areas, with a specific focus on addressing international human rights violations at the domestic level.[56] For example, based on the *Victims of Trafficking and Violence Protection Act*, the *US Court of Appeals for the Ninth Circuit* found, in *Hilao v. Estate of Marcos*, that:

> The United States has moved toward recognizing... command responsibility for torture that occurs in peacetime, perhaps because the goal of international law regarding the treatment of noncombatants in wartime-to protect civilian populations and prisoners ... from brutality, is similar to the goal of international human-rights law.[57]

Furthermore, based on the *Alien Tort Claims Act* and the *Torture Victim Protection Act*, in *Ford v. Garcia* and *Romagoza v. Garcia*, US courts applied the doctrine of superior responsibility to human rights violations, but in the form of monetary

[51] *Convention against Torture and Other Cruel, Inhuman or Degrading Treatment or Punishment*, 10 December 1984, G.A. Res. 39/46, U.N. GAOR, 39th Sess., Supp. No. 51, U.N. Doc. A/39/ 57 (1984), entered into force on 26 June 1987, draft reprinted in 23 ILM 1027 (1985), with final changes in 24 ILM 1027.

[52] Ibid., Article 2.

[53] See, generally, Gomez 2001.

[54] Violations of gross human rights have been prosecuted under the UN SC hybrid criminal tribunals. For example, the Special Tribunal for Lebanon was established between the UN and the Government of Lebanon to prosecute the criminals responsible for the assassination of Rafiq Al Hariri, Prime Minister of Lebanon. See Yun 2010, pp. 181–182.

[55] Ibid.

[56] Van Schaack 2021, pp. 1585–1586. See also van Schaack 2019, pp. 8–10.

[57] *Hilao v. Estate of Marcos*, 103 F.3d 767, 777 (9th Cir. 1996).

compensations (thematic sanctions) rather than criminal sentences for these violations.[58] Moreover, in 2011, President Obama promulgated a Presidential Proclamation regarding individuals (encompassing superiors) to be banned from entry to the United States for their violations of core international crimes and fundamental human rights.[59] Section 2 (a) of the Proclamation sets forth that:

> Any alien who planned, ordered, assisted, aided and abetted, committed or otherwise participated in, including through command responsibility, widespread or systematic violence against any civilian population based in whole or in part on race; color; descent; sex; disability; membership in an indigenous group; language; religion; political opinion; national origin; ethnicity; membership in a particular social group; birth; or sexual orientation or gender identity, or who attempted or conspired to do so.[60]

Clause (b) adds: "Any alien who planned, ordered, assisted, aided and abetted, committed or otherwise participated in, including through command responsibility, war crimes, crimes against humanity or other serious violations of human rights, or who attempted or conspired to do so."[61] These clauses apply to superiors whose subordinates' conduct occurred outside the United States.[62]

Interestingly, these applications are not to be confused with the *respondeat superior* doctrine, according to whose case law the defendant is an employer within a corporate context.[63] It is also important to note that these accountability fora employed by domestic regimes do not align with the understanding of the criminal nature of superior responsibilities explored in this book. The current accountability fora for holding superiors liable for the human rights violations committed by their subordinates, at least within the US context, are civil in nature. As previously noted regarding the (un)promising development of the doctrine of superior responsibility across the three regimes in ICL, its application fails to encompass the broader scope of human rights violations. Accordingly, the United States' reliance on monetary penalties to address this gap remains, at best, a limited and remedial measure.

Against this conclusion, in terms of proportionate redress, civil remedies are insufficient and indeed inefficient as accountability fora with respect to international criminal justice and the aggravated nature of the criminal offenses handled by domestic regimes. In this regard, in a case regarding the rape of a sixteen-year-old girl with learning disabilities, the *European Court of Human Rights* once decided that these monetary-based accountability fora do not redress wrongdoing where "fundamental values and essential aspects of private life" are at stake. The Court also held that

[58] Walsh and Berry 2016, n. 2.

[59] Presidential Proclamation 8697. (Suspension of Entry as Immigrants and Nonimmigrants of Persons Who Participate in Serious Human Rights and Humanitarian Law Violations and Other Abuses) (4 August 2011).

[60] Ibid., § 2(a).

[61] Ibid.

[62] Walsh and Berry 2016, n. 2.

[63] Van der Vyver 2021, p. 601.

"[e]ffective deterrence is indispensable in this case and can be achieved only by criminal law-provisions".[64]

Despite the suggestion in this section that the domestic prosecutions of superiors can serve as an original tool to administer criminal justice, it is not always optimal to rely on such regimes to this end, particularly when applying the doctrine of superior responsibility. For instance, domestic prosecutions of a superior for human rights violations, much like those for international crimes, could face problematic impunity challenges, such as self-amnesty laws, as well as theoretical flaws. For example, given that superiors typically enjoy either *ratione personae* and/or *ratione materiae* statuses, domestic trials could prove worthless if they were to stand. In terms of theoretical flaws, even those domestic systems that have implemented superior responsibility, as I shall discuss in the concluding section, do not address this doctrine in line with its international criminal character, according to which a superior must be charged with human rights violations committed by their subordinates, rather than merely for their omission *per se*. As discussed in this book, an omission offense is not a fitting punishment for a superior's criminal responsibility. Indeed, if such an approach were taken, it would often result in a mitigated sentence. Therefore, at this stage, the shift to international law accountability fora has proven to be highly effective for prosecuting superiors by overcoming impunity and ineffective domestic accountability fora.

In terms of the ICC's forum, the Rome Statute is a powerful instrument for overcoming the impunity of superiors. However, it must be noted that prosecutions by this institution must align with its subject-matter jurisdiction and cannot extend to offenses outside the context of its law. As noted in Chap. 4, in addition to ending such impunity, the pedigree of this institution emphasizes the importance of prosecuting human rights offenses as part of its universal goal. Before the formal establishment of the ICC, a proposal was made that "there is a price to pay for the commission of serious international offenses".[65] Given its central goal of prosecuting human rights offenses, the only proxy for achieving this was to amend its statute, as with the inclusion of the recent crime of aggression and the starvation offense committed in a non-international armed conflict context.[66] Accordingly, the Rome Statute could—in the long run—be amended to include gross human rights violations other than those crimes already prosecuted.

[64] *ECtHR 1985, X and Y v The Netherlands, Series A no. 91, para 27.*

[65] Report by Lawyers Committee for Human Rights 1996, pp. 3–5.

[66] Van der Vyver 2021, p. 415. Starvation was recently added as a crime to the subject-matter jurisdiction of the Rome Statute, under crimes committed by perpetrators in a non-international armed conflict, based on a proposal made by Switzerland. *Resolution on amendments to article 8 of the Rome Statute of the International Criminal Court Resolution ICC-ASP/18/Res.5*, ICC-ASP/18/Res.5, Article 8-2-e-(xix), 6 December 2019.

It is also worth noting that, in 2020, an *Independent Expert Panel for the Legal Definition* put forward a proposal to include an environmental crime—Ecocide[67]—in the subject-matter jurisdiction of the ICC. Belgium recently took steps to implement this in its domestic law.[68] There is growing interest in scholarly writings in its legality and admissibility, however, which may be outside the scope of this chapter.[69] However, for the present purpose, if the international community is taking concrete steps to prosecute superiors for violations committed against the environment, *a fortiori*, it should also be prioritizing the prosecution of superiors for moderate human rights violations. In my view, the failure to address this rapidly growing issue will undermine the international community's efforts to ensure peace and accountability.

To conclude, the criminal responsibility of superiors is a matter of international concern and addressing it could thus serve as a springboard for the international community to ensure justice by providing redress for human rights abuses—as well as treaty crimes—primarily arising from a superior's failure to properly control their subordinates. As has been illustrated, the doctrine of superior responsibility began as a military phenomenon targeted at military commanders for war crimes. Incorporating new elements, the international community extended the application of this phenomenon to include non-military superiors, for crimes other than war crimes and committed during peacetime. Given these developments, extending the doctrine of superior responsibility to encompass serious human rights violations at the international level may then be both necessary and appropriate. However, to achieve this objective effectively, the doctrine itself, as I shall note subsequently, may be further refined to ensure conceptual clarity, consistency, and fairness for both victims and accused superiors.

5.3 Concluding Remarks and Suggestions for Improvements

"[A]bsolute power corrupts [or prevents] absolutely."[70] We, then, can deduce that international law imposes quiet an apt presumption of responsibility on superiors. As such, the superior's power to prevent the commission of crimes through their effective also renders them responsible for such crimes. At the outset, the doctrine

[67] *Independent Expert Panel for the Legal Definition of Ecocide*, COMMENTARY AND CORE TEXT, STOP ECOCIDE FOUNDATION (June 2021), available at: https://static1.squarespace.com/static/5ca2608ab914493c64ef1f6d/t/60d1e6e604fae2201d03407f/1624368879048/SE+Foundation+Commentary+and+core+text+rev+6.pdf.

[68] *Chambre des représentants de Belgique*, Res. No. DOC 55 1429/000, 4 December 2021.

[69] See, for example, Fischels 2021; Robinson 2021, Your Guide to Ecocide: Part 1, available at: http://opiniojuris.org/2021/07/16/your-guide-to-ecocide-part-1/; Alberro and Daniele 2021; Chiarini 2021.

[70] In a letter to Bishop Creighton (1887), Lord Acton wrote that the same moral standards should be applied to all men, political and religious leaders included, especially because "Power tends to corrupt and absolute power corrupts absolutely."

of command responsibility was inherently geared toward the prosecution of military commanders for war crimes committed by their subordinates during armed conflict. Over time, however, further developments of this military phenomenon extended these responsibilities to also include political superior as well as crimes other than war crimes and those committed outside wartime.

However, these developments have led to issues regarding both the conceptual characterization and procedural application of this phenomenon. For example, they have given rise to interpretations that overlap with other existing theories that only partially capture the essence—at the domestical level—of the international criminal doctrine of superior responsibility. These theoretical and practical developments have also resulted in incoherent reasonings on the part of judges and scholars, which, indeed, have formed the basis of the critical analysis conducted in this book.

5.3.1 Concluding Remarks

In this subsection, I set out my concluding remarks on the holistic assimilation of the doctrine of superior responsibility with which this book concludes. The following subsection is devoted to suggestions for improvement.

First, in terms of the analytical approach adopted, superior responsibility is a product of ICL, which should not be seen to correspond to domestic criminal principles. To expand on this point, the doctrine of superior responsibility is a form of derivative criminal responsibility that imputes offenses committed by subordinates to their superior vicariously. ICL justifies this concept, which should not be equated with domestic criminal law, by focusing on the obligations entrusted to the superior. When these entrusted obligations are violated, potentially resulting in the commission of crimes by their subordinates, the superior is held accountable for such crimes. Thus, if a superior fail—either purposefully or negligently—to fulfill these obligations, they are held accountable for the resulting offenses, because the gravity, along with the foreseeable consequences, of the offenses is equated with the gravity, again along with the foreseeable consequences, of the violation of these entrusted obligations.

Accordingly, the nature of a superior's responsibility corresponds to the gravity of the crimes committed by the superior's subordinates and is best understood through a framework of culpability based on structural/consequentialist reasoning, which justifies liability in light of the superior's authoritative position and the systemic consequences of their failure to act. Michael Scharf further noted that the failure to punish superiors for their subordinates' crimes sends a long-lasting signal of impunity for such conduct.[71] If history teaches us anything about the doctrine of superior responsibility, it is the gravity of the responsibilities entrusted to a superior and their consequences. In cases of mass criminality, superior responsibility should then be

[71] Morris and Scharf 1995, pp. 100–101.

uncoupled from personal culpability and recognized as a principle in its own right—namely, superior responsibility based on structural/consequential culpability. That being said, because the "doctrine of command responsibility is ultimately predicated upon the power of the superior to control the acts of his subordinates",[72] as well as the superior's legal authority and practical ability to exert control over their troops,[73] the superior must keep in mind their entrusted obligations and the legal repercussion (prosecutable offenses) associated with them.

Second, superior responsibility must not be understood as a separate omission offense, because ICL is not in charge of prosecuting this particular form of omission. However, if this doctrine were to be interpreted as a *sui generis* crime of omission, such an understanding would raise several problematic issues that are incompatible with the international character of ICL. For example, as I have noted in this book, an omission offense is a standalone prosecutable offense whose legality derives from domestic criminal laws, as well as the disciplinary measures clause set out in Article 86 of the AP to the Geneva Conventions. The disciplinary measures clause concerns domestic prosecutions and should apply only to a superior (or their subordinates) in a military court at the domestic level. The criminal responsibility clause of the same provision, on the other hand, applies to (or conducted at) international criminal trials, where offenses committed by subordinates can be imputed to their superior as a result of the latter's grave dereliction of duties.

Misinterpreting superior responsibility as merely an omission-based offense at the international level risks distorting its proper application within domestic legal systems, for example, under the principle of complementarity.[74] Upon accession to the Rome Statute, States Parties are entitled to reconcile the Statute's subject-matter crimes with their domestic legal systems—including, in my view, the framework of Article 28—given its *sui generis* nature (*i.e.*, vicarious liability for international crimes) when compared to traditional domestic modes of liability.[75] To this end, the doctrine of superior responsibility must then also be reconciled with these to prosecute a superior for crimes committed by their subordinates vicariously within their domestic courts.[76] Against this conclusion, some states, such as the UK, Australia, and Canada, have incompatibly incorporated the international criminal doctrine of superior responsibility into the subject-matter of their Commonwealth Criminal Codes.[77] For example, these codes describe the *mens rea* for negligence

[72] *Prosecutor v. Delalic*, Case No. IT-96-21-T, Judgement of the Int'l Crim. Trib. Former Yugo., Tr. Chamber, para 377, 16 November 1998.

[73] *Ford v. Garcia*, Jury Instructions, p. 7, available at: http://www.lchr.org/archives/arc_ijp/lac/nuns/courtdocs/instructions.pdf.

[74] Meloni 2010, p. 205.

[75] Ibid.

[76] I would argue in favor of interpreting superior responsibility as a form of omission liability, as reflected in Articles 7(3) of the ICTY Statute and 6(3) of the ICTR Statute. These provisions are embedded within the broader framework of individual criminal responsibility, thereby supporting the argument that superior responsibility retains an element of individualized culpability, despite its indirect or non-participatory nature.

[77] Cryer et al. 2010, pp. 397–398.

as recklessness. As noted in Chap. 4, this reckless state of mind has been conceptualized as closer intent, whereas the negligent state of mind envisioned under the Rome Statute's military (or military-like) command responsibility provision refers to negligence in acquiring knowledge—*i.e.*, should have known.

Germany has also incompatibly incorporated Article 28 of the Rome Statute into its *Völkerstrafgesetzbuch* (its ICL Code).[78] This code characterizes superior responsibility as an omission offense, assigning a sentence of up to five years' imprisonment that does not align with the exclusive meaning of Article 28.[79] Moreover, like the Commonwealth Criminal Codes, the text on superior responsibility included in Germany's ICL Code excludes the superior's negligent state of mind.[80] This conclusion may have prompted Judge Chile Eboe-Osuji at the ICC in the *Bemba* case (along with other scholars) to conceptualize superior responsibility as a form of complicity-based liability, based on an interpretation of the intentional negligence in superior responsibility as evidence of participation in the crimes by means of complicity.[81]

Third, a Conceptual misapplication can be seen when it comes to whether or not superior responsibility can be applied as an alternative to other modes of liability at the international level. To this end, superior responsibility has been called on as an alternative mode of liability, which should not be the case.[82] This book has often indicated that judges and scholars address it as such.[83] For instance, in the *Gbagbo* case, the Pre-Trial Chamber referred to superior responsibility as an alternative mode of liability.[84] This, as noted in Chap. 4, also applies to the *Yekatom* case in the Pre-Trial Chamber's decision regarding this case. In principle, however, when the same conduct is prosecutable on the grounds of multiple modes of liability, it would be appropriate to refer to it only as alternative charge under superior responsibility.[85] In such cases, the conviction may pertain to other crimes that are committed within the overall scope of charges but that are attributed to the superior's failure to execute supervisory duties. However, when it comes to the various modes of liability involving superior responsibility, the approach to alternativity applies only when the charged crimes were committed through more than one mode of liability. Let us consider the following scenario, for example: if a superior ordered their subordinates to pillage a civilian dwelling, and during the act of pillaging, the subordinates committed rape against the inhabitants, the superior could stand trial for the crime of pillaging as a principal and for the crime of rape as a superior (assuming the requirements of

---

[78] *Code of Crimes Against International Law* (Völkerstrafgesetzbuch), § 4 VStGB, 26 June 2002.

[79] Ibid., § 14.

[80] Ibid., § 4.

[81] See Chap. 4, Sect. 4.2.

[82] ICTY – UNICRI 2009, *ICTY Manual on Developed Practices*, p. 13.

[83] See, for example, Meloni 2010, p. 245.

[84] *Prosecutor v. Simone Gbagbo*, Case No. ICC-02/11-01/12-75-Red (OA) Judgment on the appeal of Côte d'Ivoire against the decision of Pre-Trial Chamber I (Decision on Côte d'Ivoire's challenge to the admissibility of the case against Simone Gbagbo), para 73, 27 May 2015.

[85] *PROSECUTOR v. DOMINIC ONGWEN*, Case No. ICC-02/04-01/15, at 64, 23 March 2016. (The Pre-Trial Chamber correctly asserted that alternativity is a corollary to the charges, not the mode of liability.)

superior responsibility were met). This is a recurring theme at the international level, where subordinates exceed the execution of unlawful orders leading to unlawful conducts. A superior can be prosecuted on the grounds of superior responsibility as a principal for the pillaging and also as a superior for rape due to their failure to prevent and punish such a crime.

Fourth, regarding its applicable requirements, the elements of the doctrine of superior responsibility must be applied in full; lock, stock, and barrel. A single requirement does not trigger the superior's criminal responsibility alone. In other words, if the requirements of superior responsibility are not fully satisfied, the superior cannot be charged under superior responsibility. For example, if it were clearly established that an accused superior did not have effective command/authority and control over their subordinates, they cannot be held criminally responsible for the crimes committed by their *de jure* subordinates, even if they knew about them. Similarly, if the superior took all necessary and reasonable measures to prevent and repress the crimes and submitted the matter to the competent authorities, then they cannot be charged with the crimes.

Fifth, concerning the imputed liability of a superior, the *mens rea* of the superior must not be confused with the *mens rea* inherent in their subordinates' crimes. In this sense, the superior's intentional neglect of their duties, or mere negligence in discharging these duties, is the only fault element required to trigger superior responsibility in relation to their duties. Conversely, the prosecutor is not required to provide evidence of the subordinates' *mens rea* of the specific nature of the crimes committed or about to be committed by them to establish the superior's criminal responsibility.

Sixth, causality is an essential component of a crime, meaning that a crime must be attributed to the perpetrator's action or omission (*i.e.*, their participation) in committing it. That being said, superior responsibility is a construct of ICL, and thus does not inherently require participation. Thereby, the domestically oriented criminal principle of causality is not required, as long as the superior's failure to execute their duties results in the commission of crimes. In my view, a theoretical understanding of the nature of superior responsibility is necessary here, namely that a crime would not have been committed if the superior had properly discharged their duties.

Seventh, the doctrine of superior responsibility must not be confused with the domestic doctrine of *respondent superior*. Domestic systems apply this doctrine to remedy civil matters, such as torts and contracts, where the defendant is required to pay monetary damages. The doctrine of superior responsibility, on the other hand, deals with the criminal liability of superiors, where the superior is held indirectly liable for their subordinates' crimes (*e.g.*, war crimes, crimes against humanity, genocide). This attribution of crimes to superiors in ICL does not reflect the theoretical components of *respondent superior* in domestic laws but could, however, be analogized with the US Pinkerton Doctrine.[86]

---

[86] See Chap. 3, n. 182.

5.3.2 Suggestions for Improvements

To ensure both the conceptual and practical sustainability of the doctrine, the following appraisals may offer valuable clarifications and contribute to strengthening the foundational elements of superior responsibility, thereby helping to address the persistent challenges surrounding its application:

Starting with the Rome Statute, the requirements of superior responsibility are indeed heterogeneous when it comes to the status of the superior concerned, the fault element, and, to some extent, the element concerning *all necessary and reasonable measures*. Regarding the superior–subordinate relationship, the Rome Statute does not differentiate between the status of subordinates, whether they are military forces or civilian/political subordinates. This lack of distinction may filter out civilian/political subordinates who may commit crimes outside the context of their work, which may enable the superior to argue that they lacked effective authority and control.[87] In the conclusion of this book, referring to subordinates as military or civilian/political subordinates in the relevant provision/s concerning superior responsibility may help to eliminate the confusion surrounding this issue.

Regarding the fault element, another issue related to the *mens rea* of superior responsibility under the Rome Statute is its inconsistent requirement for political superiors compared with military and military-like superiors. Interestingly, from the early stages of the drafting process until its adoption and entry into force, the Rome Statute depended on attracting the most powerful states. The goal of the treaty was to put an end to the impunity of the most responsible perpetrators. From a diplomatic perspective, however, this goal was subject to compromises, especially at the outset. The arguably heterogeneous text concerning superior responsibility was affected by such compromises, allegedly in favor of powerful states such as the United States and France. For instance, in this context, the United States at first expressed some concerns regarding the *mens rea* requirements involved in prosecuting political superiors, which resulted in the exclusion of the higher-threshold negligence standard as the requisite mental element for political superiors. Consequently, the fault element required for political superiors raises the burden of proof required of the ICC Prosecutor, who is, under the current provision, tasked with proving a political superior's intentional failure to discharge their duties.

Oddly, the *mens rea* fault element of superior responsibility was clearly regulated in the United States' *Military Commissions Act of 2006*. Section 950q of this act takes a comprehensive approach to the fault element, which is attributed exclusively to the military commander's state of mind. It stipulates as follows:

> Any person punishable under this chapter who … is a superior commander who, with regard to acts punishable by this chapter, knew, had reason to know, or should have known, that a subordinate was about to commit such acts or had done so and who failed to take the necessary and reasonable measures to prevent such acts or to punish the perpetrators thereof, is a principal.[88]

---

[87] Sadat 2002, p. 207.

[88] Van Schaack 2021, p. 1584, quoting 189. 10 U.S.C. § 950q (2006).

With this in mind, although the act is intended to address military commanders, the emphasis on applying all forms of fault collectively—*i.e.*, knew, had reason to know, and the duty to acquire knowledge—is in line with the nature of the doctrine, irrespective of the superior's status, thus reflecting a strict mode of liability. That being said, a superior who is assigned a full range of duties and possesses the full capacity to exercise control must be prosecuted not only if they knew of or had reason to know about the commission of the crimes concerned but also when they negligently failed to acquire such knowledge. Even counterarguments suggesting that the mental element of political superiors cannot be equated with that of military commanders—due to the latter presumed higher operational capabilities—ultimately lead to an impasse. This is because, particularly in modern contexts, whether in times of peace or war, political superiors may in fact possess greater capacities and access to information than their military counterparts. In this particular instance, I find Robinson's advocacy for adhering to deontic constraints especially resonant.

With regard to the *all necessary and reasonable measures* requirement, one major issue with the text of superior responsibility under the Rome Statute is the absence of a clear and exhaustive definition of what constitutes such measures. Sandesh Sivakumaran has commendably attempted to articulate these measures in the context of irregular armed groups—a useful effort that could inform a broader, more comprehensive framework.[89] While this definitional *lacuna* may be seen as limiting—or even problematic—it also raises a legitimate question of justice: namely, whether superiors should be expected to determine, *in concreto*, the precise measures they are required to take, rather than relying solely on retrospective, case-by-case judicial determinations. Given the existing body of jurisprudence on superior responsibility, the ICC—or any competent institution responsible for shaping international criminal law—could begin to extract and codify these measures more concretely, thereby enhancing both legal clarity and fairness.

In any case, all of these appraisals of the thoroughly elaborated doctrine of superior responsibility, as envisioned in the Rome Statute, could also inform and strengthen future domestic or international legal instruments tasked with prosecuting superiors under this mode of liability.

In conclusion, the overarching aim of this book was to establish an apodictic guideline to provide a defined, refined, and unified understanding of the doctrine of superior responsibility, which is both theoretically intelligible and fit for practical application. As the doctrine of superior responsibility emerged and has developed through a somewhat unstable process, this book has sought to recalibrate the courts' incoherent interpretations of its conceptual components and practical applications. In doing so, I have analyzed these intertwining interpretations in relation to one another through a critical analysis of case law, customary international law, and relevant doctrinal writings toward examining the texts of courts' statutes, and more importantly, setting out strikingly relatable historical insights.

[89] See generally Sivakumaran 2012.

Together, these approaches have formed the basis of this book, leading to many conclusions, *e.g.*, superior responsibility is a distinct and exclusive international criminal mode of liability geared structurally at putting an end to the impunity of the most responsible superiors as well as boosting the protection of victims' rights. In elaborating this point, ICL, when addressing superior responsibility, is animated by the overarching imperative of combating impunity. Superiors who abdicate their duties are criminally responsible for the foreseeable crimes of their subordinates; such liability then is not only derivative construct but can be viewed as a direct expression ICL's objective of ending impunity. It follows that the recognition of vicarious liability within ICL—although anomalous when measured against domestic criminal law—coheres with teleological interpretations under the Vienna Convention on the Law of Treaties (as discussed in Chap. 4) and, to varying degrees, with the textual articulation of superior responsibility in Article 28 of the Rome Statute. To this end, the doctrine appears to have been fashioned, as a matter of contingency, to safeguard victims' rights in the face of mass criminality, yet its more profound justification lies, as a matter of principle, in the consequentialist rationale elaborated in Chap. 3.

Lastly, this study of the doctrine of superior responsibility is also intended to serve as a reference for both lawmakers and practitioners when considering potential amendments to existing laws, judicial decisions, and scholarly writings to overcome current issues associated with the practice of superior responsibility. As discussed in this chapter, and with a view to strengthening the administration of international criminal justice, this book further aims to support practitioners in embracing superior responsibility as a *sui generis* mode of liability—derivatively attributing responsibility to superiors for serious human rights violations, including treaty crimes—beyond its traditional omission-based interpretation. Whether applied domestically or under universal jurisdiction, such an expansion holds significant promise for closing persistent accountability gaps and promoting a more coherent and equitable framework, wishfully, in the short run.

References

Alberro H, Daniele L (2021) Ecocide: Why Establishing a New International Crime would be a Step towards Interspecies Justice. Available at: https://theconversation.com/ecocide-why-establishing-a-new-international-crime-would-be-a-step-towards-interspecies-justice-162059 (Accessed 16 June 2022)

Bassiouni M C (2011a) Phenomenological considerations. In: Bassiouni MC (author) Crimes against Humanity: Historical Evolution and Contemporary Application. Cambridge University Press, Cambridge, pp 121–146

Bassiouni M C (2011b) A Survey of National Legislation and Prosecutions for Crimes Against Humanity. In: Bassiouni MC (author) Crimes against Humanity: Historical Evolution and Contemporary Application. Cambridge University Press, Cambridge, pp 649–723

Bassiouni MC (2011c) Crimes against Humanity: Historical Evolution and Contemporary Application. Cambridge University Press, Cambridge

Bassiouni C (2013) Introduction to International Criminal Law, 2nd rev. edn. Martinus Nijhoff Publishers, Leiden/Boston

Chehtman A (2020) A Theory of International Crimes: Conceptual and Normative Issues. In: Heller KJ, Mégret F, Nouwen SMH, Ohlin JD, Robinson D (eds) The Oxford Handbook of International Criminal Law. Oxford University Press, pp 317–340

Chiarini G (2021) Ecocide and International Criminal Court Procedural Issues: Additional Amendments to the 'Stop Ecocide Foundation' Proposal. Legal Research Series, Centre for Criminal Justice & Human Rights, University College Cork, No. 15, pp 1–28. Available at https://www.ucc.ie/en/media/academic/law/CCJHRWPSNo15GiovanniChiariniEcocideandtheICCNov2021.pdf (accessed 16 June 2022)

Clapham A (2015) Human Rights: A Very Short Introduction, 2nd edn. Oxford University Press, Oxford

Clapham A (2016) Human Rights and International Criminal Law. In: Schabas WA (ed) The Cambridge Companion to International Criminal Law. Cambridge University Press, Cambridge, pp. 11–33

Cryer R et al. (2010) An Introduction to International Criminal Law and Procedure, 2nd edn. Cambridge University Press

Damrosch L, Henkin L, Murphy S, Smit H (2009) International Law: Cases and Materials. Thomson Reuters Publishers, St. Paul

Danner A M, Martinez J S (2005) Guilty Associations: Joint Criminal Enterprise, Command Responsibility, and the Development of International Criminal Law. 93 California Law Review 75, pp 75–169

Fischels J (2021) How 165 Words Could Make Mass Environmental Destruction an International Crime. https://www.npr.org/2021/06/27/1010402568/ecocide-environment-destruction-international-crime-criminal-court (accessed 16 June 2022)

Gomez V (2001) Inter-American Commission on Human Rights and the Inter-American Court of Human Rights: New Rules and Recent Cases. Human Rights Law Review 1, pp. 111–126

Independent Expert Panel for the Legal Definition of Ecocide (2021) Commentary and Core Text, STOP ECOCIDE FOUNDATION. https://static1.squarespace.com/static/5ca2608ab914493c64ef1f6d/t/60d1e6e604fae2201d03407f/1624368879048/SE+Foundation+Commentary+and+core+text+rev+6.pdf (accessed 16 June 2022)

Jerončič A, Moreno M (2016) Command Responsibility (2nd ed.). Case Matrix Network, Belgium

Lawyers Committee for Human Rights (1996) Establishing an International Criminal Court: Major Unresolved Issues in the Draft Statute. See https://www.iccnow.org/documents/2PrepCmtEstablishICCLCHR.pdf Accessed August 2021

Letsas L (2006) Two Concepts of the Margin of Appreciation. Oxford Journal of Legal Studies 26, pp. 705–732

Locke J (1690/1988) Two Treatises of Government. In: Laslett P (ed). Cambridge University Press, Cambridge

Meloni C (2010) Command Responsibility in International Criminal Law. TMC Asser Press, The Hague

Meron T (2003) International law in the age of human rights – general course on public international law. Recueil des cours de l'Académie de droit international de La Haye (Collected Courses of the Hague Academy of International Law), vol 301. Martinus Nijhoff Publishers, Leiden/Boston

Meron T (2021) Standing Up for Justice: The Challenges of Trying Atrocity Crimes. Oxford University Press, Oxford

Milanovic M (2020) The Murder of Jamal Khashoggi: Immunities, Inviolability and the Human Right to Life. Human Rights Law Review 20(1), pp. 1–49

Morris V, Scharf M (1995) An Insider's Guide to the International Criminal Tribunal for the Former Yugoslavia. Brill, Leiden

Office of the United Nations High Commissioner for Human Rights (2015) Who's responsible? Attributing individual responsibility for violations of international human rights and humanitarian law in United Nations commissions of inquiry, fact-finding missions and other investigations. United Nations, Geneva, pp 30–31. Available at: https://www.ohchr.org/sites/default/files/Documents/Publications/Who_is_Responsible.pdf Accessed August 2021

Parker B S (2012) Applying the Doctrine of Superior Responsibility to Corporate Officers: A Theory of Individual Liability for International Human Rights Violations. Hastings International and Comparative Law Review 31(1), pp. 1–27

Pérez-León Acevedo J P (2017) The Close Relationship Between Serious Human Rights Violations and Crimes Against Humanity: International Criminalization of Serious Abuses. Anuario Mexicano de Derecho Internacional, Mexico City, pp. 387–420

Powderly J (2010) The Trials of Eichmann, Barbie and Finta. In: Routledge Handbook of International Criminal Law. Routledge, UK, pp. 143–154

Reinisch A (2001) Developing Human Rights and Humanitarian Law Accountability of the Security Council for the Imposition of Economic Sanctions. American Journal of International Law 95(4), pp. 851–872

Robinson D (2021) Your Guide to Ecocide: Part 1. http://opiniojuris.org/2021/07/16/your-guide-to-ecocide-part-1/ (accessed 16 June 2022)

Sadat LN (2002) The International Criminal Court and the transformation of international law. Transnational Publishers, Ardsley, NY

Sadat LN (2017) Putting Peacetime First: Crimes Against Humanity and the Civilian Population Requirement. Emory International Law Review 31, pp. 199–242

Seibert-Fohr A (2010) Prosecuting Serious Human Rights Violations. Oxford University Press, Oxford

Sivakumaran S (2012) Command Responsibility in Irregular Groups. Journal of International Criminal Justice, Volume 10, Issue 5, December, pp. 1129–1150

Stahn C (2018) A Critical Introduction to International Criminal Law. Cambridge University Press, Cambridge

Van der Vyver J (2021) International Criminal Law: Crimes within the Jurisdiction of the International Criminal Court, vol. II. LAP Lambert Publishing, Germany

Van Schaack B (1997) The Crime of Political Genocide: Repairing the Genocide Convention's Blind Spot. Yale Law Journal 106, pp. 2259–2291

Van Schaack B (2019) House Foreign Affairs Committee, Tom Lantos Human Rights Commission Hearing on Ending Genocide: Accountability for Perpetrators [Testimony]. U.S. House of Representatives, Washington, DC

Van Schaack B (2021) Animating the U.S. War Crimes Act. International Law Studies 97. Stockton Center for International Law, Newport, Rhode Island, pp. 1–61

Walsh P, Berry J F (2016) Expanding Command Responsibility beyond War: The Application of the Doctrine of Command Responsibility to Human Rights Law. Liberty University Law Review 11, pp. 641–676

Yun J (2010) Special Tribunal for Lebanon: A Tribunal of an International Character Devoid of International Law. Santa Clara Journal of International Law 7, pp. 447–4

Case Law

Ford v. Garcia, Jury Instructions, available at: http://www.lchr.org/archives/arc_ijp/lac/nuns/courtdocs/instructions.pdf. (accessed 16 June 2022)

Hilao v. Estate of Marcos, 103 F.3d 767, 777 (9th Cir. 1996)

Prosecutor v. Delalic, Case No. IT-96-21-T, Judgement of the Int'l Crim. Trib. Former Yugo., Tr. Chamber, 16 November 1998

Prosecutor v. Dominic Ongwen, Case No. ICC-02/04-01/15, 23 March 2016

Prosecutor v. Simone Gbagbo, Case No. ICC-02/11-01/12-75-Red (OA) Judgment on the appeal of Côte d'Ivoire against the decision of Pre-Trial Chamber I (Decision on Côte d'Ivoire's challenge to the admissibility of the case against Simone Gbagbo), 27 May 2015

SITUATION IN THE PEOPLE'S REPUBLIC OF BANGLADESH/REPUBLIC OF THE UNION OF MYANMAR, Case No. ICC-01/19 (Decision Pursuant to Article 15 of the Rome Statute on

the Authorisation of an Investigation into the Situation in the People's Republic of Bangladesh/ Republic of the Union of Myanmar), 19 November 2019

The Prosecutor v. Georges Anderson Nderubumwe Rutaganda, Case No. ICTR-96-3-A (Dissenting Opinion of Judge Pocar), 26 May 2003

X AND Y v. THE NETHERLANDS, EUR. CT. HUM. RTS., Series A, vol. 91, a, (at 13), 26 March 1985

Other Documents

Code of Offenses Against the Peace and Security of Mankind (1954) U.N. GAOR, 9th Sess., U.N. Doc. A/2693

Convention against Torture and Other Cruel, Inhuman or Degrading Treatment or Punishment (1984) December 10

G.A. Res. 39/46, U.N. GAOR, 39th Sess., Supp. No. 51, U.N. Doc. A/39/57 (1984), entered into force 26 June 1987, draft reprinted in 23 ILM 1027 (1985), with final changes in 24 ILM 1027

Statute of the International Criminal Tribunal for Rwanda (1994) S.C. Res. 955, Annex. 33 ILM 1602

Statute of the International Criminal Tribunal for the Former Yugoslavia (1993) U.N. Doc. S/25704, Annex. 32 ILM 1192

United Nations (2006) International Convention for the Protection of All Persons from Enforced Disappearance. UN Doc A/RES/61/177, adopted 20 Dec 2006, entered into force 23 Dec 2010

Bibliography

Abou El Fadl K (2017) Islamic Law, Jihad and Violence. UCLA Journal of Islamic and Near Eastern Law 16(1), pp. 1–27

Abu al-Tayyib bin Hasan bin 'Ali al-Hayyinia al-Qanuji al-Bukhari (1985) al-'Ibra mimma Ja'a fi al-Ghazw wa al-Shahada wa al-Hijra. Dar al-Kutub al-'Ilmiyya, Beirut

Adachi S (1988) The Asian Concept. International Dimensions of Humanitarian Law. UNESCO, / Martinus Nijhoff Publishers, The Netherlands, pp. 13–19

Afifi A (2018) Jus in Bello and General Principles Related to Warfare According to Islamic Law. In: Gray T (ed.) Islam and International Criminal Law and Justice. Torkel Opsahl Academic EPublisher, Brussels, pp. 101–120

Ajijola AD (1978) The Essence of Faith in Islam. University of Virginia Press, Charlottesville

Akande D (2009) Sources of International Criminal Law. In: Cassese A, Akande D, Acquaviva G (eds) The Oxford Companion to International Criminal Justice. Oxford University Press, Oxford, pp 41–53

Al Sallabi A (2019) Reasons behind the isolation of Khalid Ibn Al waleed. https://www.aljazeera.net/blogs/2019/12/12/. Accessed May 2021

al-Badr AR (1425 AH) al-Qutuf al-Jiyad min Hikam wa Ahkam al-Jihad. Dar al-Mughni, Riyadh

al-Biqa'iyyi IBUH (2002) al-Istisshhad bi Ayat al-Jihad. Cairo: Dar al-Risala, Cairo

Al-bukhari M. Sahih Bukhari, Vol. 5, Book 59, Number 375. https://www.sahihbukhari.com/Pages/Bukhari_5_59.php. Accessed 22 May 2021

Al-Dawoody A (2011) The Islamic Law of War: Justifications and Regulations. Palgrave Macmillan

Al-Dawoody A (2017) Islam and International Humanitarian Law: An Overview. Humanitarian Law & Policy. medium.com/law-and-policy/islam-and-international-humanitarian-law-an-overview-78d2df80712f. Accessed May 2021

Al-Dawoody A, Murphy V (2019) International humanitarian law: Islamic law and the protection of children in armed conflict. International Review of the Red Cross 101(911), pp. 551–573

Al-Fadhli H (2025) From Nuremberg to the Hague and beyond: Reincorporating "taking a consenting part" into international criminal modes of liability. Netherlands International Law Review, 72(2) (forthcoming)

Al-Rashidi K, Al-Fadhli H (2025) Corruption in the MENA: Between State Crime and International Criminal Law. In: Carrington K, Dixon R, Zajdow A, Marotta S (eds) The Palgrave Handbook of Criminology and the Global South, 2nd edn. Palgrave Macmillan (forthcoming)

Alberro H, Daniele L (2021) Ecocide: Why Establishing a New International Crime would be a Step towards Interspecies Justice. Available at: https://theconversation.com/ecocide-why-establishing-a-new-international-crime-would-be-a-step-towards-interspecies-justice-162059 (Accessed 16 June 2022)

Alien Tort Claims Act (28 U.S.C. § 1350). https://crsreports.congress.gov/product/pdf/R/R44947

H. Y. Al-Fadhli, *Prosecuting Superior Responsibility in International Criminal Law*,
https://doi.org/10.1007/978-94-6265-735-9

Allo A K (2018) The ICC's Problem Is Not Overt Racism, It Is Eurocentrism. Al Jazeera, 28 July 2018. https://www.aljazeera.com/indepth/opinion/iccproblem-simple-racism-eurocentricism-180725111213623.html (accessed 16 June 2022)

Alverez J E (1996) Nuremberg Revisited: The Tadić Case. European Journal of International Law 7, pp. 245–264

Amann, D. M. 2018. In Bemba and beyond, crimes adjudged to commit themselves. EJIL: Talk! https://www.ejiltalk.org/in-bemba-and-beyond-crimes-adjudged-to-commit-themselves/ (accessed 16 June 2025)

Ambos K (1999a) General Principles of Criminal Law in the Rome Statute. Criminal Law Forum 10, Kluwer, Dordrecht, pp,1–32

Ambos K (1999b) General Principles of Criminal Law. In: Triffterer O (ed.) Commentary on the Rome Statute of the International Criminal Court. Nomos Verlagsgesellschaft, Baden-Baden, pp. 475–492

Ambos K (2002) Superior Responsibility. In: Cassese A, Gaeta P, Jones JRWD (eds.) The Rome Statute Of The International Criminal Court: A Commentary. Oxford University Press, Oxford, pp. 823–872

Ambos K (2003), Current Issues in International Criminal Law, Criminal Law Forum, vol. 14, Springer, pp. 225–260

Ambos K (2009a) Command responsibility and Organisationsherrschaft: Ways of attributing international crimes to the 'most responsible'. In: Nollkaemper A, Van der Wilt H (eds) System Criminality in International Law. Cambridge University Press, Cambridge, pp 127–157

Ambos K (2009b) Critical Issues in the Bemba Confirmation Decision. Leiden Journal of International Law 22, pp. 715–726

Armour (1922) Customs of Warfare in Ancient India. 8 Transactions of the Grotius Society. Grotius Society, London, pp. 71–88

Arnold R, Triffterer O (2008) Article 28: Responsibility of Commanders and Other Superiors. In: Triffterer O (ed) Commentary on the Rome Statute of the International Criminal Court: Observers' Notes, Article by Article, 2nd edn. Beck, Munich, pp. 795–843

Askin KD (2002) Reflections on Some of the Most Significant Achievements of the ICTY. New England Law Review 37(903), pp. 903–933

Badar M E, Porro S (2017) Article 30 Mental Element. In: Klamberg M (ed.) Commentary on the Law of the International Criminal Court, FICHL Publ. Series No. 29, pp. 314–322

Bantekas I (2002) Principles of Direct and Superior Responsibility in International Humanitarian Law. Manchester University Press, Manchester

Bantekas I (2006) Reflections on some sources and methods of international criminal and humanitarian law. International Criminal Law Review 6, Brill, pp. 121–135

Baragwanath D (2014) The Interpretative Challenges of International Adjudication across the Common Law/Civil Law Divide. Cambridge Journal of International and Comparative Law 3, pp. 472–494

Bassiouni M C (1992) The United Nations' Commission of Experts Established Pursuant to Security Council Resolution 780. American Journal of International Law 88, pp. 784–805

Bassiouni M C (2002) World War I: "The War to End All Wars," and the Birth of A Handicapped International Criminal Justice System. Denver Journal of International Law and Policy 30, pp. 244–291

Bassiouni M C (2011a) A Survey of National Legislation and Prosecutions for Crimes Against Humanity. In: Crimes against Humanity: Historical Evolution and Contemporary Application. Cambridge University Press, Cambridge, pp 649–723

Bassiouni M C (2011b) Crimes against Humanity Historical Evolution and Contemporary Application. Cambridge University Press, Cambridge

Bassiouni M C (2011c) Phenomenological considerations. In: Crimes against Humanity: Historical Evolution and Contemporary Application. Cambridge University Press, Cambridge, pp 121–146

Bassiouni M C (2011d) The Theories and Elements of Criminal Responsibility. In: Crimes against Humanity: Historical Evolution and Contemporary Application, . Cambridge University Press, Cambridge, pp. 472–580

Bassiouni M C (2013a) Introduction to International Criminal Law: Second Revised Edition Leiden/ Boston: Martinus Nijhoff Publishers

Bassiouni M C (2013b) The Shari'ah and Islamic Criminal Justice in Time of War and Peace. Cambridge University Press, Cambridge

BBC News (2018) Profile: Jean-Pierre Bemba, DR Congo's ex-rebel and vice-president. BBC News, 8 June 2018. Available at: https://www.bbc.com/news/world-africa-35845556/. Accessed 1 December 2019

Bellot HHL (1922). In: International Law Association, Report of the Thirty-First Conference, pp. 451–456

Bishai C (2013) Superior responsibility, inferior sentencing: Sentencing practice at the international criminal tribunals. Northwestern Journal of International Human Rights 11, pp. 83–108

Blank L, Noone G (2013) International Law and Armed Conflict Fundamental Principles and Contemporary Challenges in the Law of War. Kluwer Press, Dordrecht

Blank LR (2021) The Use of Force to Prevent Recurrence of Conflict: Where Are the Limits of Self-Defense? Brooklyn Law Review 83, pp. 1–41

Boisard M (1987) Humanism in Islam. American Trust Publications, Indianapolis, IN

Boister N (2009) Treaty Crimes, International Criminal Court? New Criminal Law Review: An International and Interdisciplinary Journal 12(3), pp. 341–385

Bonaparte N (2001) Napoleon on the Art of War. In: Lavaas H (transl) Slip-Cased A (ed) Free Press

Bonney R (2004) Jihad From Qur'an to Bin Laden. Palgrave Macmillan, New York

Bradfield P (2020) Alternative charges and modes of liability in the latest CAR case at the ICC – Trouble ahead? EJIL: Talk! https://www.ejiltalk.org/alternative-charges-and-modes-of-liability-in-the-latest-car-case-at-the-icc-trouble-ahead/. Accessed 16 June 2025

Brand CE (1968) Roman Military Law. University of Texas Press, Austin, TX

Bruce M (2014) International humanitarian law and criminal justice: An introductory handbook. Commonwealth Secretariat. Available at: https://production-new-commonwealth-files.s3.eu-west-2.amazonaws.com/migrated/inline/Law%2BIntroductory%2BHandbook%2BEB.pdf (accessed 21 August 2021)

Bugnion F (2003), The International Committee of the Red Cross and the Protection of War Victims Macmillan Education, Geneva

Burnett WD (1985) Command Responsibility and a Case Study of the Criminal Responsibility of Israeli Military Commanders for the Pogrom at Shatila and Sabra. 107 Military Law Review, pp. 71–122

Cassese A (2002) Crimes Against Humanity. In: Cassese A, Gaeta P, Jones JRWD (eds) The Rome Statute of the International Criminal Court: A Commentary, vol. 1, pp. 1–20

Cassese A (2004) The ICTY: A living and vital reality. Journal of International Criminal Justice 2: pp. 585–597

Cassese A et al. (2013a) Cassese's International Criminal Law. Oxford University Press, Oxford

Cassese A et al. (2013b) Cassese's International Criminal Law, 3rd edn. Oxford University Press, Oxford

Chehtman A (2020) A Theory of International Crimes: Conceptual and Normative Issues. In: Heller KJ, Mégret F, Nouwen SMH, Ohlin JD, Robinson D (eds) The Oxford Handbook of International Criminal Law. Oxford University Press, pp 317–340

Chiarini G (2021) Ecocide and International Criminal Court Procedural Issues: Additional Amendments to the 'Stop Ecocide Foundation' Proposal. Legal Research Series, Centre for Criminal Justice & Human Rights, University College Cork, No. 15, pp 1–28. Available at https://www.ucc.ie/en/media/academic/law/CCJHRWPSNo15GiovanniChiariniEcocideandtheICCNov2021.pdf (accessed 16 June 2022)

Childress JF (1976) Francis Lieber's Interpretation of the Laws of War: General Orders No 100 in the Context of His Life and Thought. American Journal of Jurisprudence 21, pp. 34–55

Clapham A (2015) Human Rights: A Very Short Introduction (2nd ed.). Oxford University Press, Oxford

Clapham A (2016) Human Rights and International Criminal Law. In: Schabas WA (ed.) The Cambridge Companion to International Criminal Law. Cambridge University Press, Cambridge, pp. 11–33

Clark R S (2001) The Mental Element in International Criminal Law: The Rome Statute of the International Criminal Court and the Elements of Offences. Criminal Law Forum: American International Journal 23, pp. 291–334

Code of Offenses Against the Peace and Security of Mankind (1954) U.N. GAOR, 9th Sess., U.N. Doc. A/2693

Convention (No. IV) Respecting the Laws and Customs of War on Land, with Annex of Regulations, 1907, Article 25, 36 Stat. 2277, U.S.Y. 539, reprinted in 1 BEVANS 631 and 2 AM J. INT'L L. (Supp.) 90 (1908)

Convention against Torture and Other Cruel, Inhuman or Degrading Treatment or Punishment (1984) December 10

Crawford J (1997) An International Criminal Court? Connecticut Journal of International Law 12, pp. 255–278

Cryer R (2004) General principles of liability in international criminal law. In McGoldrick D, Rowe P, Donnelly E (eds.), The Permanent International Criminal Court: Legal and policy issues. Hart Publishing, Oxford/Portland, pp 233–254

Cryer R (2014) An Introduction to International Criminal Law and Procedure. Cambridge University Press, Cambridge

Cryer R (2015) International Criminal Law: General Principles of Liability in International Criminal Law, vol. II. Routledge, London

Cryer R et al. (2010) An Introduction to International Criminal Law and Procedure, 2nd ed. Cambridge University Press, Cambridge

Cryer R, Friman H, Robinson D, Wilmshurst E (2019) An Introduction to International Criminal Law and Procedure, 4th edn. Cambridge University Press, Cambridge

Damaška M (2001) The shadow side of command responsibility. American Journal of Comparative Law 49, pp. 455–496

Damrosch L, Henkin L, Murphy S, Smit H (2009) International Law: Cases and Materials. Thomson Reuters Publishers, St. Paul

Danner A M, Martinez J S (2005) Guilty Associations: Joint Criminal Enterprise, Command Responsibility, and the Development of International Criminal Law. 93 California Law Review 75, pp 75–169

Davanzo J (1999) An Absence of Accountability for the My Lai Massacre. Hofstra Law & Policy Symposium 3, pp. 287–288

Davis GB (1918) A Treatise on the Military Law of the United States, 3rd rev. edn. John Wiley & Sons, New York

Dawod F (2014) How Samarkand Was Conquered. http://islam.ru/en/content/story/how-samarkand-was-conquered. Accessed 22 May 2021

De Hart WC (1846) Observations on Military Law, and the Constitution, and Practice of Courts Martial. Wiley and Putnam, New York

De Pizan C (2003) The Book of Deeds of Arms and of Chivalry, 2nd edn. Trans. In: ed. Willard C. (ed) (Willard S (transl.)). Penn State University Press. https://books.google.fr/books?id=epXQh7B1w20C&lpg=PP1&dq=book%20of%20deeds%20of%20arms&hl=fr&pg=PP1#v=onepage&q&f=false. Accessed 22 May 2021

De Preux (1977) The Affirmative Duties Established by Article 87 Additional Protocol I of 1977 and its Commentary. In: Pilloud C et al. (eds) Commentary on the Additional Protocols of 8 June 1977 to the Geneva Conventions of 12 August 1949, pp. 1017–1023

Donner F (1991) The Sources of Islamic Conceptions of War. In: Kelsay J, Johnson JT (eds) Just War and Jihad: Historical and Theoretical perspectives on War and Peace in Western and Islamic Traditions. Greenwood Press, New York, pp 31–70

Doty G (1982) The United States and the Development of the Laws of Land Warfare. Military Law Review 156, pp. pp. 224–255

Dressler J (1985) Reassessing the Theoretical Underpinnings of Accomplice Liability: New Solutions to an Old Problem. Hastings Law Journal 37(91), pp. 91–138

Drumbl M (2009) The Push to Criminalize Aggression: Something Lost Amid the Gains? Case Western Reserve Journal of International Law 41, pp. 291–316

Dungel J, Ghadiri S (2010) The Temporal Scope of Command Responsibility Revisited: Why Commanders Have a Duty to Prevent Crimes Committed After the Cessation of Effective Control. U.C. DAVIS Journal of International Law & Policy 17(1), pp. 3–61

Ellis M S (1999) Non-Negotiable; War Criminals Belong in the Dock, Not at the Table. *Washington Post*. Available at https://www.congress.gov/106/crec/1999/05/10/145/66/CREC-1999-05-10.pdf (accessed 16 June 2022)

Falk R, Kolko G, Lifton R (eds) (1971) Crimes of War. Random House, New York

Fenrick W (1999a) Commentary on the Rome Statute of the International Criminal Court: Article by article. In: Triffterer O (ed) Commentary on the Rome Statute of the International Criminal Court. C.H. Beck, Munich, 108–180

Fenrick W J (1999b) Responsibility of Commanders and Other Superiors. In: Triffterer O (ed) Commentary on the Rome Statute of the International Criminal Court. Nomos Verlagsgesellschaft, Baden-Baden, pp. 515–522

Fenrick W J (1999c) The Rome Statute of the International Criminal Court: Article 8 – War Crimes. In: Triffterer O (ed) Commentary on the Rome Statute of the International Criminal Court: Observers' Notes. Baden-Baden: Nomos Verlagsgesellschaft, Baden-Baden, pp 555–603

Firestone R (1999) Jihād: The Origin of Holy War in Islam. Oxford University Press, Oxford

Firuzabadi M (1933) Al-Qamus al-Muhit, Cairo, vol. 1

Fischels J (2021) How 165 Words Could Make Mass Environmental Destruction an International Crime. https://www.npr.org/2021/06/27/1010402568/ecocide-environment-destruction-international-crime-criminal-court (accessed 16 June 2022)

Ford S (2014) Complexity and Efficiency at International Criminal Courts, Emory International Law Review 29(1), pp. 1–94

Friedman L (ed) (1972) The Law of War: A Documentary History (Vol. II). Random House, New York, NY

Fritz F (2018) The ICC: A Common Cause Between John Bolton and Africa? Al Jazeera, 16 September 2018. https://www.aljazeera.com/indepth/opinion/icc-common-johnbolton-africa-180915095755954.html (accessed 16 June 2022)

G.A. Res. 39/46, U.N. GAOR, 39th Sess., Supp. No. 51, U.N. Doc. A/39/57 (1984), entered into force June 26, 1987, draft reprinted in 23 ILM 1027 (1985), with final changes in 24 ILM 1027

Galand A S (2020) Bemba and the Individualisation of War: Reconciling Command Responsibility under Article 28 Rome Statute with Individual Criminal Responsibility. International Criminal Law Review 20, pp. 688–725

Galand A S, Hunter E, Utmelidze I, Bekou O (2016) International Criminal Law Guidelines: Command Responsibility, 2nd edn. Centre for International Law Research and Policy (CILRAP), Florence

Gasser H P et al. (1987a) Commentary on the Additional Protocols of 8 June 1977 to the Geneva Conventions of 12 August 1949. ICRC/Martinus Nijhoff Publishers

Gasser H P et al. (1987b) In: Sandoz Y, Swinarski C, Zimmermann B (eds) Commentary on the Additional Protocols to the Geneva Conventions, ICRC, pp. 1013–1014. https://www.loc.gov/rr/frd/Military_Law/pdf/Commentary_GC_Protocols.pdf. Accessed 22 May 2021

Giles L (transl) (1910) trans. Sun Tzu on the Art of War: The Oldest Military Treatise in the World. London: Luzac & Co., London

Goldstone R (1997) Conference Luncheon Address, Transnational Law & Contemporary Problems 7, pp. 1–4

Goldstone R J (2018) The International Criminal Tribunals for the Former Yugoslavia and Rwanda. In Crane D N, Sadat L N, Scharf M P (eds) The Founders: Four Pioneering Individuals Who Launched the First Modern-Era International Criminal Tribunals, pp 57–84

Gomez V (2001) Inter-American Commission on Human Rights and the Inter-American Court of Human Rights: New Rules and Recent Cases. Human Rights Law Review 1, pp. 111–126

Green L (2008) The Contemporary Law of Armed Conflict, 3rd edn. Manchester University Press, Manchester

Green LC (1995) Command Responsibility in International Humanitarian Law. Transnational Law & Contemporary Problems 5, pp. 319–342

Green LC (1999) War Crimes, Crimes against Humanity and Command Responsibility. In: Essays on the Modern Law of War, 2nd edn. Transnational Publisher, New York, pp. 77–117

Gross L (1955) The Punishment of War Criminals: The Nuremberg Trial. Netherlands International Law Review 11, pp. 356–370

Grotius H (1964a) De Jure Belli ac Pacis Libri Tres (Kelsey FW (transl.)). Oceana, New York, Bk. II, Ch. 1(ii)

Grotius H (1964b) On the Laws of War and Peace. In: Kelsey FW (transl.). Wildy Wiley & Sons, London

Grover L (2010) A call to arms: Fundamental dilemmas confronting the interpretation of crimes in the Rome Statute of the International Criminal Court. European Journal of International Law, 21(3), pp. 543–583

Grover L (2014) Interpreting Crimes in the Rome Statute of the International Criminal Court. Cambridge University Press, Cambridge

Guénaël M (2009) The Law of Command Responsibility. Oxford University Press, Oxford

Guerra Medici MT (1999) The Mother of International Law: Christine de Pisan, Parliaments, Estates and Representation 19(1), pp.15–22

Guilfoyle D (2011) Responsibility for Collective Atrocities: Fair Labelling and Approaches to Commission in International Criminal Law. Current Legal Problems 64, pp. 255–286

Guilfoyle D (2016) International Criminal Law. Oxford University Press, Oxford

Guilfoyle D (2019) Lacking Conviction: Is the International Criminal Court Broken? An Organisational Failure Analysis. Melbourne Journal of International Law 20, pp. 401–429

Hargreaves J (1970) The Rule Book of Warfare. U.S. Marine Corps Gazette, vol. 54

Harmon M B, Gaynor F (2007) The Sentencing Practice of International Criminal Tribunals: Ordinary Sentences for Extraordinary Crimes. Journal of International Criminal Justice 5(683), pp. 683–71

Heller KJ (2011) The Nuremberg Military Tribunals and the Origins of International Criminal Law. Oxford University Press, Oxford

Heller K J (2016–17) Taking a Consenting Part: The Lost Mode of Participation. Loyola University of Los Angeles International & Comparative Law Review 39, pp. 247–257

Henkin L (1997) Conceptualizing Violence: Present and Future Developments in International Law, Albany Law Review 60, pp. 569–581

Henkin L, Pugh R C, Schachter O, Smit H (1987) International Law: Cases and Materials. 2nd ed. West Publishing, St. Paul, MN

Hibbert S (2019) The Bemba Acquittal: A Blow to the ICC's Legitimacy in a Time of Crisis. Temple International & Comparative Law Journal 34, pp. pp. 95–121

His Majesty's Stationery Office (1948) History of the United Nations War Crimes Commission and the Development of the Laws of War. http://www.unwcc.org/wpcontent/uploads/2017/04/UNWCC-history.pdf. Accessed 22 May 2021

Howard K (1972) Command Responsibility for War Crimes. Journal of Public Law 21, pp. 20–44

Hudson M O (1931) The Ninth Year of the Permanent Court of International Justice. The American Journal Of ICRC (1949) Remarks and Proposals submitted by the International Committee of the Red Cross: Documents for the Consideration of Governments Invited by the Swiss Federal Council to Attend the Diplomatic Conference at Geneva (21 April 1949). https://www.loc.gov/rr/frd/Military_Law/pdf/RC_Remarks-proposals.pdf

Ibn al-Nahhas (2002) Mashari' al-Ashwaq, vol. 2

ICC (2018) Statement of ICC Prosecutor, Fatou Bensouda, on the recent judgment of the ICC AC acquitting Mr Jean-Pierre Bemba Gombo. https://www.icc-cpi.int/Pages/item.aspx?name=180613-OTP-stat (accessed 16 June 2022)

ICRC (1971) Introduction. Report submitted to the Conference of Government Experts on the Reaffirmation and Development of International Humanitarian Law Applicable in Armed Conflicts, Geneva

ICRC (1987) Commentary on the Additional Protocol (I) to the Geneva Conventions of 12 August 1949, International Law 25(1)

ICRC (2009) Analysis of the Punishments Applicable to International Crimes (War Crimes, Crimes Against Humanity and Genocide) in Domestic Law and Practice. International Review of the Red Cross 90

ICRC (2017) Ad hoc tribunals. Available at: https://www.icrc.org/en/document/ad-hoc-tribunals/. Accessed 1 December 2019

Independent Expert Panel for the Legal Definition of Ecocide (2021) Commentary and Core Text, STOP ECOCIDE FOUNDATION. https://static1.squarespace.com/static/5ca2608ab914493c64ef1f6d/t/60d1e6e604fae2201d03407f/1624368879048/SE+Foundation+Commentary+and+core+text+rev+6.pdf (accessed 16 June 2022)

International Criminal Court (2019) Decision on the confirmation of charges against Alfred Yekatom and Patrice-Edouard Ngaïssona (ICC-01/14-01/18-403-Conf-Corr). Pre-Trial Chamber II (11 December 2019)

International Military Tribunal (Nuremberg) (1947) Judgment and Sentences. American Journal of International Law 41, pp. 172–221

J. Locke, Two Treatises of Government, ed. P. Laslett (Cambridge: Cambridge University Press, 1988 [1690])

Jackson M (2019) Command Responsibility. In: de Hemptinne J, Roth R, van Sliedregt E (eds) Modes of liability in international criminal law. Cambridge University Press, Cambridge, pp. 409–431

Jackson, M., Causation and the Legal Character of Command Responsibility after Bemba at the International Criminal Court (2022) Journal of International Criminal Justice 20(2), pp. 437–458

Jackson R (1946) Closing Address before the International Military Tribunal (26 July 1946), Nuremberg Trial Proceedings, Vol. 19. U.S. Chief of Counsel, International Military Tribunal

Jerončič A, Moreno M (2016) Command Responsibility (2nd ed.). Case Matrix Network, Belgium

Jia B B (2000) The Doctrine of Command Responsibility. Yearbook of International Humanitarian Law 3(131), pp. 131–165

Joyner C C (1994) Enforcing Human Rights Standards in the Former Yugoslavia: The Case for an International War Crimes Tribunal. Denver Journal of International Law & Policy 22, pp. 231–276

Kadduri M (1984) The Islamic Conception of Justice. Johns Hopkins University Press, Baltimore

Khalid H (1971) al-Shahid fi al-Islam. Dar al-'ilm li-al-Malayin, Beirut

Klamberg M (ed) (2017) Commentary on the Law of the International Criminal Court. TOAEP, Brussels

Knoll E, McFadden J (eds) (1970) War Crimes and the American Conscience. Holt, Rinehart and Winston, New York

Kortfält L (2017a) Individual criminal responsibility. In: Klamberg M (ed) Commentary on the Law of the International Criminal Court. TOAEP, Brussels, pp. 781–844

Kortfält L (2017b) Individual Criminal Responsibility. In: Klamberg M (ed) Commentary on the Law of the International Criminal Court. Torkel Opsahl Academic EPublisher, Brussels, pp. 279–304

Kortfält L (2017c) Responsibility of commanders and other superiors. In: Klamberg M (ed.), Commentary on the Law of the International Criminal Court, FICHL Publ. Series No. 29, pp. 279–304

Lael R (1982a) The Yamashita Precedent: War Crimes and Command Responsibility. Rowman & Littlefield, Lanham

Lael RL (1982b) The Yamashita Precedent: War Crimes and Command Responsibility. Scholarly Resources Inc., Delaware

Landrum B D (1995) The Yamashita War Crimes Trial: Command Responsibility Then and Now. Military Law Review 149, pp. 293–322

Lanni A (2008) The Laws of War in Ancient Greece. Law and History Review 26(3), pp. 469–489

Latty F (2019) Founding "Fathers" of International Law: Recognizing Christine de Pizan. https://www.ejiltalk.org/founding-fathers-of-international-law-recognizing-christine-de-pizan/. Accessed 22 May 2021

Lauterpacht H (1944) The Law of Nations and the Punishment of War Crimes. British Yearbook of International Law 21, pp. 58–95

Letsas L (2006) Two Concepts of the Margin of Appreciation. Oxford Journal of Legal Studies 26, pp. 705–732

Levie S (1997/1998) Command Responsibility. Journal of Legal Studies 8(1), pp. 1–19

Lieber F (1863) Instructions for the Government of Armies of the United States in the Field (24 April 1863) [The Lieber Code]

Linder DO (1999) An Introduction to the My Lai Courts-Martial. In My Lai: An Account Famous Trials, University of Missouri-Kansas City. http://law2.umkc.edu/faculty/projects/ftrials/mylai/Myl_intro.html. Accessed 22 May 2021

Lippman M (1993) War Crimes: The My Lai Massacre and The Vietnam War. San Diego Justice Journal, 1, pp. 360–397

Mälksoo L (2019) The Treaties of Brest-Litovsk, Versailles and Moscow: Contesting Sovereignty and Hegemony in Eastern Europe in 1918–1939. German Yearbook of International Law, pp. 189–209

Manu (Lawgiver), The Laws of Manu: Translated with Extracts from Seven Commentaries, ed and trans by Georg Bühler (Sacred Books of the East, vol 25, Clarendon Press 1886)

Mao Z (1965) Problems of Strategy in China's Revolutionary War. In: Selected Works, vol. 1. For (for the original version, see Mao Zedong xuanji. Foreign Languages Press, Beijing)

Maridakis GS(1952) Un precedent du Procès de Nuremberg tire de l'histoire de la Grèce ancienne. Revue Hellénique De Droit International 5

May L, Fyfe S (2018) International Criminal Tribunals: A Normative Defense, Cambridge University Press, Cambridge

McCormack, Timothy T LH (1997) From Sun Tzu to the Sixth Committee: The Evolution of an International Criminal Law Regime. In: McCormack T L H, Simpson G J (eds) The Law of War Crimes: National and International Approaches. Kluwer Law International, The Hague, pp 31–63

Mégret F (2011) The Legacy of the ICTY as Seen Through Some of its Actors and Observers. Goettingen Journal of International Law 3, pp. 1011–1052

Meloni C (2007) Command Responsibility: Mode of Liability for the Crimes of Subordinates or Separate Offence of the Superior? Journal of International Criminal Justice 5(3), pp. 619–637

Meloni C (2010) Command Responsibility in International Criminal Law. TMC Asser Press, The Hague

Meloni C (2015) The Evolution of Command Responsibility in International Criminal Law. FICHL Publication Series No. 22

Memorandum of Reservations Presented by the Representatives of the United States to the Report of the Commission on Responsibilities, Annex II (1920) April 1919, 14. American Journal of International Law

Meron T (1993) Henry's Wars and Shakespeare's Laws: Perspectives on the Law of War in the Later Middle Ages, Oxford University Press, Oxford

Meron T (2000) The Humanization of Humanitarian Law. 94 American Journal of International Law, pp. 239–278

Meron T (2003) International law in the age of human rights – general course on public international law. Recueil des cours de l'Académie de droit international de La Haye (Collected Courses of the Hague Academy of International Law), vol 301. Martinus Nijhoff Publishers, Leiden/Boston

Meron T (2004) Procedural Evolution in the ICTY, Journal of International Criminal Justice 2, pp. 521–539
Meron T (2021) Standing Up for Justice: The Challenges of Trying Atrocity Crimes. Oxford University Press, Oxford
Mettraux G (2009) The Law of Command Responsibility, Oxford University Press, Oxford
Mettraux G (2009) The Law of Command Responsibility. Oxford University Press, Oxford
Milanovic M (2020) The Murder of Jamal Khashoggi: Immunities, Inviolability and the Human Right to Life. Human Rights Law Review 20(1), pp. 1–49
Miller RH (1971) The Convention of the Non-Applicability of Statutory Limitations to War Crimes and Crimes against Humanity. American Journal of International Law 65, pp. 494–508
Minkova L (2023) Responsibility on Trial: Liability Standards in International Criminal Law. Cambridge University Press, Cambridge
Morris V, Scharf M (1995a) An Insider's Guide to the International Criminal Tribunal for the Former Yugoslavia. Transnational Publishers, New York
Morris V, Scharf M (1995b) An Insider's Guide to the International Criminal Tribunal for the Former Yugoslavia. Brill, Leiden
Mundis D A (2001) The Legal Character and Status of the Rules of Procedure and Evidence of the Ad Hoc International Tribunals, International Criminal Law Review 1, Brill, pp. 191–214
Murphy R (2019) Command responsibility after Bemba. Yearbook of New Zealand Jurisprudence, Brill, Leiden, The Netherlands, pp. 94–118
Murphy S D (2012a) Principles of International Law, 2nd edn. Reuters, London
Murphy S D (2012b) The International Court of Justice. In: Giorgetti C (ed.) The Rules, Practice, and Jurisprudence of International Courts and Tribunals. Brill, Leiden, pp 11–35
Nafziger GF, Walton MW (2003) Islam at War A History. Praeger Publishers, Westport
Naqvi AR (1974) Laws of War in Islam. Islamic Studies, 13(1), pp. 25–48
Neff SC (2012) Hugo Grotius on The Law of War and Peace. Cambridge University Press, Cambridge
Nerlich V (2007) Superior Responsibility under Article 28 ICC Statute - For What Exactly Is the Superior Held Responsible? Journal of International Criminal Justice 5(3), pp. pp. 665–682
Nsereko D D (1994) Rules of Procedure and Evidence of the International Tribunal for the Former Yugoslavia, Criminal Law Forum 5, pp. 507–552
Nuremberg Trial Proceedings (1945) Trial of the Major War Criminals before the International Military Tribunal, vol. 2, 23 Nov 1945
O'Brien TM, Diefendorf O (1864) General Orders of the War Department Embracing the Years 1861, 1862 & 1863, vol. 2, . Derby & Miller
O'Malley JM (1964) Justice in Shakespeare: The English Kings in the Light of Thomistic Thought. Pageant Press, New York
Ögren K (1996) Humanitarian Law in the Articles of War Decreed in 1621 by King Gustavus II Adolphus of Sweden. International Review of the Red Cross
Osiel M (2005) The Banality of the Good: Aligning Incentives against Mass Atrocity, Columbia Law Review 105, pp. 1751–1862
Parker B S (2012) Applying the Doctrine of Superior Responsibility to Corporate Officers: A Theory of Individual Liability for International Human Rights Violations. Hastings International and Comparative Law Review 31(1), pp. 1–27
Parks, W (1973) Command Responsibility for War Crimes. Military Law Review 62, pp.1–104
Peniguet M (2018) CPI: Jean-Pierre Bemba, chronique d'un acquittement surprise. Dalloz, Actualité. Available at https://www.dalloz-actualite.fr/flash/cpi-jean-pierre-bemba-chronique-d-un-acquittement-surprise (accessed 16 June 2022)
Pérez-León Acevedo J P (2017) The Close Relationship Between Serious Human Rights Violations and Crimes Against Humanity: International Criminalization of Serious Abuses. Anuario Mexicano de Derecho Internacional, Mexico City, pp. 387–420
Philipson C (1911) The International Law and Custom of Ancient Greece and Rome. Macmillan and Co., London

Pictet J (1960) Geneva Convention for the Amelioration of the Condition of Wounded, Sick and Shipwrecked Members of Armed Forces at Sea. ICRC, Geneva

Pigeau R, McCann C (2002) Re-conceptualizing Command and Control. Canadian Military Journal 3(1), pp. 53–63

Pjic J (1997) The Tribunal and the ICC: Do Precedents Matter? Albany Law Review 60, pp. 861–872

Powderly J (2010a) Judicial Interpretation at the Ad Hoc Tribunals: Method from Chaos. In: Darcy S, Powderly J (eds) Judicial Creativity at the International Criminal Tribunals, Pages 17–44

Powderly J (2010b) The Trials of Eichmann, Barbie and Finta. In: Routledge Handbook of International Criminal Law, Routledge, UK, pp. 143–154

Powderly, J (2018) Introductory Note to Prosecutor v. Jean Pierre Bemba Gombo. International Legal Materials 57(6), pp. 1031–1035

Prosecutor v. Ratko Mladić, Case No. IT-09-92-A, Appeals Judgment, 8 June 2021, International Residual Mechanism for Criminal Tribunals

Prosecutor v. Zdravko Mucić aka "Pavo", Hazim Delić, Esad Landžo aka "Zenga", and Zejnil Delalić, Case No. IT-96-21-A, Appeal Judgment, 20 February 2001, (ICTY)

Protocol Additional to the Geneva Conventions of 12 August 1949 and relating to the Protection of Victims of International Armed Conflicts (Protocol I), 1125 UNTS 3, adopted 8 June 1977, entered into force 7 December 1978

Provisional Congress of Massachusetts Bay (1775) Articles of War, April 5, 1775

Pruitt K (2014) Destroying the Legacy of the ICTY: Analysis of the Acquittals of Jovica Stanisic and Franko Simatovic, 15 San Diego International Law Journal 15, pp. 15–47

Reinisch A (2001) Developing Human Rights and Humanitarian Law Accountability of the Security Council for the Imposition of Economic Sanctions. American Journal of International Law 95(4), pp. 851–872

Report of the Ad Hoc Committee on the Establishment of an International Criminal Court, UN GAOR, 50th Sess., Supp. No. 22 (UN Doc. A/50/22, 1995)

Roberts A (2019) Foundational Myths in the Laws of War: The 1863 Lieber Code, and the 1864 Geneva Convention. Melbourne Journal of International Law 20(158), pp. 165–192

Robinson D (2008) The Identity Crisis of International Criminal Law. Leiden Journal of International Law 21, pp. 925–963

Robinson D (2012) How command responsibility got so complicated: A culpability contradiction, its obfuscation, and a simple solution. Melbourne Journal of International Law 13, pp.1–58

Robinson D (2020) Justice in Extreme Cases: Criminal Law Theory Meets International Criminal Law. Cambridge University Press, Cambridge

Robinson D (2021) Your Guide to Ecocide: Part 1. http://opiniojuris.org/2021/07/16/your-guide-to-ecocide-part-1/ (accessed 16 June 2022)

Rome Statute of the International Criminal Court (1998) 2187 U.N.T.S. 3 (entered into force 1 July 2002). http://untreaty.un.org/cod/icc/statute/romefra.htm, Article 28. Accessed May 2021

Rome Statute of the International Criminal Court (1998) 2187 UNTS 90

Rosenberg C (2020) He waterboarded a detainee. Then he had to get the C.I.A. to let him stop. The New York Times. https://www.nytimes.com/2020/01/22/us/politics/cia-torture-interrogation-guantanamo.html. Accessed 21 August 2021

SáCouto S, Sellers PV (2019) The Bemba Appeals Chamber judgment: Impunity for sexual and gender-based crimes? William & Mary Bill of Rights Journal 27, pp. 599–622

SáCouto S, Viseur Sellers P (2019) The Bemba Appeals Chamber Judgment: Impunity for Sexual and Gender-Based Crimes? William & Mary Bill of Rights Journal 27, pp. 1–52

Sadat L N (2002a) The International Criminal Court and The Transformation of International Law: Justice for The Millenium. Transnational Publishers, Ardsley, NY

Sadat L N (2002b) The Legacy of the ICTY: The International Criminal Court, New England Law Review, pp. 1073–1090

Sadat LN (2017) Putting Peacetime First: Crimes Against Humanity and the Civilian Population Requirement. Emory International Law Review 31, pp. 199–242

Sadat L N (2019) Prosecutor v. Jean-Pierre Bemba Gombo. American Journal of International Law 113, pp. 353–361

Sadat L, Dixon R (1997) Developing International Rules of Evidence for the Yugoslav and Rwanda Tribunals, Transnational Law and Contemporary Problems 7, pp. 81–120

Sadat L N, Jolly J M (2014) Seven Canons of ICC Treaty Interpretation: Making Sense of Article 25's Rorschach Blot. Leiden Journal of International Law 27, pp. 755–778

Saland P (1999) International Criminal Law Principles. In: Lee RS (ed) The International Criminal Court: The Making of the Rome Statute. Brill, Leiden, pp. 189–216

Sandburg C, Lincoln A (1961) The Prairie Years and the War Years. Harcourt, Brace & World, New York

Sandesh Sivakumaran (2012) Command Responsibility in Irregular Groups, Journal of International Criminal Justice, Volume 10, Issue 5, December, pp. 1129–1150

Schabas W A (1998) The General Principles of the Rome Statute. European Journal for Crime, Criminal Law, and Criminal Justice 6, pp. 417–440

Schabas W A (2003) Interpreting the Statutes of the Ad Hoc Tribunals. In: Vohrah LC et al. (eds) Man's Inhumanity to Man, Essays on International law in Honour of Antonio Cassese. Kluwer Law International, The Hague, 847–888

Schabas W A (2004) The right to a fair trial. In: Lattanzi F, Schabas WA (eds) Essays on the Rome Statute of the International Criminal Court, vol. 2. Il Sirente, Rome, pp. pp. 241–278

Schabas W A (2007) An Introduction to the International Criminal Court, 3rd ed. Cambridge University Press, Cambridge

Seibert-Fohr A (2010) Prosecuting Serious Human Rights Violations. Oxford University Press, Oxford

Sengheiser J (2007–8) Command responsibility for Omissions and Detainee Abuse in the "War on Terror". Thomas Jefferson Law Review, 30, pp. 1–44

Sereni A (2004). Individual Criminal Responsibility. In F. Lattanzi & W. A. Schabas (Eds.), Essays on the Rome Statute of the International Criminal Court (2nd ed.). Ripa di Fagnano Alto, Italy: Editrice il Sirente, pp 139–146

Shahabuddin M (2004) Does the Principle of Legality Stand in the Way of Progressive Development of Law? Journal of International Criminal Justice 2, pp. 1007–1028

Shelling F (1927) Shakespeare and 'Demi-Science'. University of Pennsylvania Press, Philadelphia

Sherman EF (1970) The Civilization of Military Law. Maine Law Review 22(1), pp. 3–40

Simonovic I (1999) The Role of the ICTY in the Development of International Criminal Adjudication. Fordham International Law Journal 23(2), pp. 440–474

Smidt ML (2000) Yamashita, Medina, and Beyond: Command Responsibility in Contemporary Military Operations. Military Law Review, pp. 155–175

Solf WA, Cummings ER (1977)) A Survey of Penal Sanctions under Protocol I to the Geneva Conventions of 12 August 1949. Case W. Res. J. Int'l L. 9, pp. 205–254. https://scholarlycommons.law.case.edu/jil/vol9/iss2/2. Accessed 23 April 2021 (citing Draper (1972) Implementation of International Law in Armed Conflict. INT'L AF 48, pp 46–58)

Sprik L (2020) Protection of Civilians and Individual Accountability: Obligations and Responsibilities of Military Commanders in United Nations Peacekeeping Operations. Routledge, UK

Stahn C (2018) A Critical Introduction to International Criminal Law. Cambridge University Press, Cambridge

Stahn C (2019) A Critical Introduction to International Criminal Law. Cambridge University Press, Cambridge

Statute of the International Criminal Tribunal for Rwanda (1994) S.C. Res. 955, Annex. 33 ILM 1602

Statute of the International Criminal Tribunal for the Former Yugoslavia (1993) U.N. Doc. S/25704, Annex. 32 ILM 1192

Stearns J K (2011) Dancing in the Glory of Monsters: The Collapse of the Congo and the Great War of Africa. Public Affairs, New York

Stewart D (2014) International Criminal Law in a Nutshell, 2nd edn. West Academic, St. Paul
Stone J (2011) Aggression and World Order: A Critique of United Nations Theories of Aggression. Law Book Exchange edition
Sun Tzu (1963) The Art of War, trans. by Griffith SB. Oxford University Press, Oxford
Sun Tzu and, Minford J (2002) The Art of War. New England Review 23(3):5
Swaak-Goldman O (2017) Prosecutor v. Delalic. No. IT-96-21-T, The American Journal Of International Law 93(2), pp. 514–519
Taulbee J L (2018) War Crimes and Trials: A Primary Source Guide, ABC-CLIO Publishing
The Qur'an, https://quran.com/search?query=not+fight+them+invite+them&language=0&translation=0. Accessed 22 May 2021
Triffterer O (2002) Causality, A Separate Element of the Doctrine of Superior Responsibility as Expressed in Article 28 of the Rome Statute? Leiden Journal of International Law 15, pp. pp. 179–205
Triffterer O, Arnold R (2016) Article 28 Responsibility of commanders and other superiors. In: Triffterer O, Ambos K (eds) The Rome Statute of the International Criminal Court: A Commentary, 3rd edn. C.H. Beck, Munich, pp. 1056–1106
U.S. Department of State (2019) Public Designation Due to Gross Violations of Human Rights of Burmese Military Officials. Available at: https://www.state.gov/on-public-designation-due-to-gross-violations-of-human-rights-of-burmese-military-officials/
U.S. Military Tribunals (1950) Trials of War Criminals before the Nuremberg Military Tribunals under Control Council Law No. 10, vol V. U.S. Government Printing Office, Washington, DC, (Pohl et al.)
U.S. Military Tribunals (1952) United States v. von Weizsäcker et al. (The Ministries Case), Trials of War Criminals before the Nuremberg Military Tribunals under Control Council Law No. 10, vol XII. U.S. Government Printing Office, Washington, DC, p 1127, (Powers, dissenting)
UN War Crimes Commission (1949) Law Reports of Trials of War Criminals, High Command Case, Vol. XII, p. 76. https://www.loc.gov/rr/frd/Military_Law/pdf/Law-Reports_Vol-12.pdf. Accessed May 2021
United Nations (2006) International Convention for the Protection of All Persons from Enforced Disappearance. UN Doc A/RES/61/177, adopted 20 Dec 2006, entered into force 23 Dec 2010
Universal Declaration of Human Rights (1948) G.A. Res. 217A, U.N. GAOR, 3d Sess., 1st plen. mtg., U.N. Doc. A/810
Urs P (2024) Gravity at the International Criminal Court: Admissibility and Prosecutorial Discretion. Oxford University Press, Oxford
Van Aarde TA (2018) The relation between religion and state in Islam and Christianity in the rise of ISIS. In Die Skriflig 52(1), pp. 1–8
Van der Vyver J (2005) The International Criminal Court and the Concept of Mens Rea in International Criminal Law. University of Miami International & Comparative Law Review 12, pp. 57–95
Van der Vyver J (2015) Acts of Aggression and Prosecuting the Crime of Aggression. LAMBERT Publ., Germany
Van der Vyver JD (2021a) International criminal law: Crimes within the jurisdiction of the International Criminal Court. LAP Lambert Academic Publishing, Saarbrücken
Van der Vyver J (2021b) International Criminal Law: Crimes within the Jurisdiction of the International Criminal Court, vol. II. LAP Lambert Publishing, Germany
Van Schaack B (1997) The Crime of Political Genocide: Repairing the Genocide Convention's Blind Spot. Yale Law Journal 106, pp. 2259–2291
Van Schaack, B (2008) Crimen sine lege: Judicial Lawmaking at the Intersection of Law and Morals. Georgetown Law Journal 97(1), pp. 119–192
Van Schaack, B. (2019). House Foreign Affairs Committee, Tom Lantos Human Rights Commission Hearing on Ending Genocide: Accountability for Perpetrators [Testimony]. U.S. House of Representatives, Washington, DC

Van Schaack B (2021) Animating the U.S. War Crimes Act. International Law Studies 97. Stockton Center for International Law, Newport, Rhode Island, pp. 1–61
Van Sliedregt E (2003) The Criminal Responsibility of Individuals for Violations of International Humanitarian Law. T.M.C. Asser Press, The Hague
Van Sliedregt E (2011) Command Responsibility at the ICTY—Three Generations of Case-law and Still Ambiguity. In: Swart B, Zahar A, Sluiter G (eds) The Legacy of the International Criminal Tribunal for the Former Yugoslavia. Oxford University Press, pp 367–390
Van Sliedregt E (2012a) Individual Criminal Responsibility in International Law. Oxford University Press, Oxford
Van Sliedregt E (2012b) The curious case of international criminal liability. Journal of International Criminal Justice 10(5), pp. 1171–1188
Van Sliedregt E (2018) Criminalization of Crimes Against Humanity under National Law. Journal of International Criminal Justice 16(4), pp. 717–743
Van Sliedregt E et al. (2019) Co-perpetration Based on Joint Control over the Crime. In: Cupido M, Ventura MJ, Yanev L (eds) Modes of Liability in International Criminal Law. Cambridge University Press, Cambridge, pp 85–120
Vark K (2016) Superior Responsibility and Indirect Liability. Occasional Paper No. 2/06, Eur. Network of Diplomatic & Sec. Stud.
Vetter G R (2000a) Command responsibility of non-military superiors in the International Criminal Court (ICC). Yale Journal of International Law 25, pp. 92–123
Vetter G R (2000b) Command Responsibility of Non-military Superiors in the International Criminal Court (ICC). Yale Journal of International Law 25(90), pp. 89–149
Vetter G R (2000c) Command Responsibility of Non-Military Superiors in the International Criminal Court (ICC). Yale Journal of International Law 25(89), pp. 89–149
Vetter, G. R. (2000d) Command Responsibility of Non-Military Superiors in the International Criminal Court (ICC), Yale Journal of International Law 25, pp. 89–143
Walsh P, Berry J F (2016) Expanding Command Responsibility beyond War: The Application of the Doctrine of Command Responsibility to Human Rights Law. Liberty University Law Review 11, pp. 641–676
War Department (1917) Rules of Land Warfare, Doc. No. 467, Office of the Chief of Staff, approved Apr. 25, 1914 (G.P.O. 1917)
Watson G R (2002) The Changing Jurisprudence of the International Criminal Tribunal for the Former Yugoslavia, New England Law Review 37, pp. pp. 871–878
Watt M (2018) In: Partridge C, Dowley T (eds) A Historical Overview. A Brief Introduction to Islam, vol. 4,1517 Media, Minneapolis
Weeramantry CG (1988) Islamic Jurisprudence: An International Perspective. Palgrave Macmillan Press, Basingstoke
Werle G, Jessberger F (2005) Unless Otherwise Provided: Article 30 of the ICC Statute and the Mental Element of Crimes under International Criminal Law. Journal of International Criminal Justice, Vol. 3, Issue 1, pp. 35–55
Williamson J A (2008) Some Considerations on Command Responsibility and Criminal Liability. International Review of the Red Cross 90(870), pp. 303–326
Wilson P (2017) The Myth of International Humanitarian Law. 93 International Affairs 563, pp 563–579
Winthrop W (18951920) Military Law And Precedents, 2nd edn. Government Printing Office (G.P.O.), Washington, D.C. Available at https://archive.org/details/cu31924020024570/page/n3/mode/2up Accessed 22 May 2021
Wise E M, Podgor E S (2014) International Criminal Law: Cases and Materials, 3rd edn. LexisNexis Matthew Bender, New Providence, NJ, pp 496–515
Witt JF (2012), Lincoln's Code: The Laws of War in American History. Free Press, New York
Wood D A R (2010) Punishment: consequentialism, Philosophy Compass 5(6), pp. 455–469

Wu T, King Y S (1997) Criminal liability for the actions of subordinates: The doctrine of command responsibility and its analogues in United States law. Harvard International Law Journal, 38(1), pp. 272–294

Yacoubian M (2018) A New U.S. Strategy Will Keep American Troops in Syria. U.S. Institute of Peace. https://www.usip.org/publications/2018/01/new-usstrategy-will-keep-american-troops-syria [https://perma.cc/6NSJ-W3NF]. Accessed 22 May 2021

Young S (2001) Surrendering the Accused to the International Criminal Court. The British Yearbook of International Law, Oxford 71(1), pp. 319–392

Yun J (2010) Special Tribunal for Lebanon: A Tribunal of an International Character Devoid of International Law. Santa Clara Journal of International Law 7, pp. 447–4

Zacklin R (1994), Bosnia and Beyond. Virginia Journal of International Law, 34, pp. 277–286

Zavis A, Dixon R (2018) Only Africans Have Been Tried at the Court for the Worst Crimes on Earth. Los Angeles Times. Available at https://www.latimes.com/world/africa/la-fg-icc-africa-snap-story.html (accessed 16 June 2022)

Other Documents

Convention on the Non-applicability of Statutory Limitations to War Crimes and Crimes Against Humanity, Article 2. https://www.un.org/en/genocideprevention/documents/atrocitycrimes/Doc.27_convention%20statutory%20limitations%20warcrimes.pdf. Accessed May 2021

Instruction for the Government of the United States in the Field by Order of the Secretary of War, in Washington D.C., Apr. 24 1863, NO. 100 and approved by President Lincoln, Schindler, and Toman, 3

Memorandum of Reservations Presented by the Representatives of the United States to the Report of the Commission on Responsibilities, Annex II (1920) April 1919, 14. American Journal of International Law

Protocol Additional to the Geneva Conventions of 12 August 1949, and Relating to the Protection of Victims of International Armed Conflicts (Protocol I) (1977) Article 86(2), U.N. Doc. A/32/144, 1125 U.N.T.S. 3, reprinted in 16 I.L.M. 1391

Protocol Additional to the Geneva Conventions of 12 August 1949, and Relating to the Protection of Victims of International Armed Conflicts (Protocol I) (1977). Article 86(2), U.N. Doc. A/32/144, 1125 U.N.T.S. 3, reprinted in 16 I.L.M. 1391

Report of the International Commission of Inquiry on Darfur to the United Nations Secretary-General, paras 558, 561 (Jan. 25, 2005) Report of the Secretary-General on the Establishment of a Special Court for Sierra Leone, U.N. Doc. S/2000/915, Annex (Oct. 4, 2000), the Special Court for Sierra Leone Statute, Article 6(3)

Treaty of Peace with Germany (Treaty of Versailles), 28 June 1919. https://www.loc.gov/law/help/us-treaties/bevans/m-ust000002-0043.pdf. Accessed 22 May 2021

Legislation

Allied Control Council Law No. 10: Punishment of Persons Guilty of War Crimes, Crimes Against Peace, and Crimes Against Humanity (1945), 20 December 1945, Official Gaz. of the Control Council of Germany, 3(50)

Law on the Establishment of Extraordinary Chambers in the Courts of Cambodia for the Prosecution of Crimes Committed During the Period of Democratic Kampuchea (2004) NS/RKM/1004/006

Statute of the International Criminal Tribunal for Rwanda (1994) S.C. Res. 955, Annex, 33 ILM 1602, Article 6(3) (1994)

Statute of the International Criminal Tribunal for the Former Yugoslavia (1993) U.N. Doc. S/25704, Annex, 32 ILM 1192

The Convention on the Non-Applicability of Statutory Limitations to War Crimes and Crimes Against Humanity (1968) 754 U.N.T.S. 7, Article II. The Lieber and the US's Military Commissions Act of 2006 (2006) 189. 10 U.S.C. § 950q

Case Law

Aloys Ntabakuze v. The Prosecutor, Case No. ICTR-98-41A-0012/1, 8 May 2012

Aloys Simba v. The Prosecutor, Case No. ICTR-01-76-A

Ferdinand Nahimana, Jean-Bosco Barayagwiza & Hassan Ngeze v. The Prosecutor, Case No. ICTR-99-52-A, 28 November 2007

Ford v. Garcia, Jury Instructions, available at: http://www.lchr.org/archives/arc_ijp/lac/nuns/courtdocs/instructions.pdf. Accessed 16 June 2022

Hilao v. Estate of Marcos, 103 F.3d 767, 777 (9th Cir. 1996)

Prosecutor v. Alfred Yekatom & Patrice-Edouard Ngaïssona, Case No. ICC-01/14-01/18, 11 December 2019

Prosecutor v. Ali Muhammas Ali Abd-Alrahman ("Ali Kushayb"), Case No. ICC-02/05-01/20 OA8, para 91, 1 November 2021

Prosecutor v. ANTO FURUNDZIYA, Case No. IT-95-T, 10 December 1998

Prosecutor v. AUGUSTIN NDINDILIYIMANA, Case No. ICTR-00-56-T, 17 May 2011

Prosecutor v. Bosco Ntaganda, Case No. ICC-01/04-02/06, 9 June 2014

Prosecutor v. Dario Kordić & Mario Čerkez, Case No. IT-95-1A-A, para 46, 26 February 2001

Prosecutor v. Delalic, Case No. IT-96-21-T, Judgement of the Int'l Crim. Trib. Former Yugo., Tr. Chamber, 16 November 1998

Prosecutor v. Dominic Ongwen, Case No. ICC-02/04-01/15, 23 March 2016

Prosecutor v. Dražen Erdemovic, Case No. IT-96-22-A (Joint Separate Opinion of Judge McDonald and Judge Vohrah), para 40, 29 November 1996

Prosecutor v. Enver Hadžihasanović et al., Decision on Interlocutory Appeal Challenging Jurisdiction in Relation to Command Responsibility, Case No. IT-01-47-AR72, 16 July 2003

Prosecutor v. Germain Katanga & Mathieu Ngudjolo Chui, Case No. ICC-01/04-01/07-572 (OA4) (Judgment in the Appeal by Mathieu Ngudjolo Chui of 27 March 2008 against the Decision of Pre-Trial Chamber I on the Application of the Appellant for Interim Release), para 25, 9 June 2008

Prosecutor v. Jean-Pierre Bemba Gombo, Appeals Chamber, Case No. ICC-01/05-01/08 A, 8 June 2018

Prosecutor v. Jean-Pierre Bemba Gombo, Case No. ICC-01/05-01/08 A, Judgment, 8 June 2018

Prosecutor v. Jean-Pierre Bemba Gombo, Judgment, Case No. ICC-01/05-01/08 A, 8 June 2018

Prosecutor v. Jean-Pierre Bemba Gombo, PTC II, Decision on the Confirmation of Charges, Case No. ICC-01/05-01/08-424, 15 June 2009

Prosecutor v. Jean-Pierre Bemba Gombo, Request for Leave to Appeal, Case No. ICC-01/05-01/08, 13 April 2018

Prosecutor v. Jean-Pierre Bemba Gombo (Decision Pursuant to Article 61(7)(a) and (b) of the Rome Statute on the Charges against Jean-Pierre Bemba Gombo), Case No. ICC-01/05-01/08-424, para 274, 15 June 2009

Prosecutor v. Joseph Kanyabasid, Case No. ICTR-96-15-A, (Dissenting Opinion of Judge Shahabuddeen) para 21, 3 June 1999

Prosecutor v. Laurent Gbagbo & Charles Blé Goudé, Case No. ICC-02/11-01/15-1263-AnxC-Red, 16 July 2019

Prosecutor v. Mathieu Ngudjolo Chui, Case No. ICC-01/04-02/12-271 (A), (Judgment pursuant to Article 74 of the Statute", para 22, 27 February 2015

Prosecutor v. Milan Milutinovic el., Case No. IT -99-37-AR72, para 3, May 21, 2003
Prosecutor v. Milorad Krnojelac, Appeals Chamber, Case No. IT-97-25-A, 17 September 2003
Prosecutor v. Radoslav Brdjanin, Judgment, Case No. IT-99-36-T, 1 September 2004
Prosecutor v. Rasim Delić (Decision on Interlocutory Appeal Challenging the Jurisdiction of the Tribunal), Case No. IT-04-83-AR72
Prosecutor v. Simone Gbagbo, Case No. ICC-02/11-01/12-75-Red, 27 May 2015
Prosecutor v. Simone Gbagbo, Case No. ICC-02/11-01/12-75-Red (OA) Judgment on the appeal of Côte d'Ivoire against the decision of Pre-Trial Chamber I (Decision on Côte d'Ivoire's challenge to the admissibility of the case against Simone Gbagbo), 27 May 2015
Prosecutor v. Tihomir Blaškić, Case No. IT-95-14-AR108bis, Judgment on the Request of the Republic of Croatia for Review of the Decision of Trial Chamber II of 18 July 1997
Prosecutor v. Tihomir Blaškić, Judgment, Case No. IT-95-14-T, 3 March 2000
Prosecutor v. THOMAS LUBANGA DYILO (Decision on Confirmation of Charges), Case No. ICC-01/04-01/06-803-tEN, para 318, 29 January 2007
Prosecutor v. Zdravko Mucić aka "Pavo", Hazim Delić, Esad Landžo aka "Zenga", and Zejnil Delalić, Case No. IT-96-21-A, Appeal Judgment, 20 February 2001, para 239 (ICTY)
Prosecutor v. Zejnil Delalić et al., Appeals Chamber, Case No. IT-96-21-A, 20 February 2001
Prosecutor v. Zejnil Delalić et al., Judgment, Case No. IT-96-21-T, 16 November 1998
Prosecutor v. Zlatko Aleksovski, Case No. IT-95-14/1-A, Appeal Judgment, 24 March 2000
Prosecutor v. Zlatko Aleksovski, Case No. IT-95-14/1-A, Judgment, para 127, 24 March 2000
S.S. Lotus (France v. Turkey), Judgment, 1927, Permanent Court of International Justice (PCIJ), Series A No. 10
SITUATION IN THE PEOPLE'S REPUBLIC OF BANGLADESH/REPUBLIC OF THE UNION OF MYANMAR, Case No. ICC-01/19 (Decision Pursuant to Article 15 of the Rome Statute on the Authorisation of an Investigation into the Situation in the People's Republic of Bangladesh/ Republic of the Union of Myanmar), 19 November 2019
SYLVESTRE GACUMBITSI v. THE PROSECUTOR (Separate Opinion of Judge Schomberg on the Criminal Responsibility of the Appellant for Committing Genocide), Case No. ICTR-2001-64-A, para 143, 7 July 2006
Statute of the International Court of Justice, June 26, 1945, 59 Stat. 1055, 33 U.N.T.S. 933, Article 38
The Prosecutor v. Georges Anderson Nderubumwe Rutaganda, Case No. ICTR-96-3-A (Dissenting Opinion of Judge Pocar), 26 May 2003
United States of America v. Karl Brandt et el., 2 Trials of War Criminals Before the Nuremberg Military Tribunals Under Control Council Law No. 19 (October 1946–April 1949) (Judgment) 171, p 207. Washington D.C.: U.S. Gov. Printers (1950–1953)
Vienna Convention on the Law of Treaties, Article 31–33, U.N. Doc. A./CONF.39/27, 22 May 1969, 1155 U.N.T.S. 331, 8I.L.M. 679 (1969)
X AND Y v. THE NETHERLANDS, EUR. CT. HUM. RTS., Series A, vol. 91, a, (at 13), 26 March 1985

Index

H. Y. Al-Fadhli, *Prosecuting Superior Responsibility in International Criminal Law*,
https://doi.org/10.1007/978-94-6265-735-9

F

G

H

I

MIX
Papier aus verantwortungsvollen Quellen
Paper from responsible sources
FSC® C105338

If you have any concerns about our products,
you can contact us on
ProductSafety@springernature.com

In case Publisher is established outside the EU,
the EU authorized representative is:
Springer Nature Customer Service Center GmbH
Europaplatz 3, 69115 Heidelberg, Germany

Printed by Libri Plureos GmbH
in Hamburg, Germany